HEAVEN and HELL

HEAVEN and HELL
MY LIFE IN THE EAGLES (1974–2001)

DON FELDER
with Wendy Holden

John Wiley & Sons, Inc.

To
my mother and father
and
*all those who dream of making it
in the music business.*

ACKNOWLEDGMENTS

I am indebted to so many people who have helped me over the years, and I fear that my memory might fail me. Frankly, the exact details of some events in the seventies have long since left my consciousness. If I've made any mistakes, misquoted or overlooked anyone, then please forgive me.

My thanks go to Susan Felder for sticking it out through all those years; my children, Jesse, Rebecca, Cody, and Leah; Jerry and Marnie Felder; Buster Lipham for allowing me to charge my instruments and for supporting me in the beginning; the members of the Continentals and Flow; Stephen Stills; Bernie Leadon; the Allman Brothers; Creed Taylor; Paul Hillis for teaching me music theory; Fred Walecki; David Geffen; David Blue; Graham Nash; David Crosby; Randy Meisner; Joe Walsh; Timothy B. Schmit; Bill Szymczyk; J.D. Souther; Larry "Scoop" Solters; the late Isa Bohn; and all the road crews during the entire trip. Also to

John Belushi, Joel Jacobson, Linda Staab, Skip Miller, Barry Tyerman (for supporting me through it all), Jackson Browne (for standing in for me when my son was born), Cheech and Chong, Jack Pritchett, and Jimmy Pankow and the Bass Patrol, not to mention B.B. King.

Alan Nevins, my literary agent, and Calvin Warzecha (for the best fried oysters I've had since my dad passed away), the people at Hyperion, and all those I have left out who should be included here.

Wendy Holden for wrapping herself in my life while hers was in such pain.

Kathrin Nicholson for loving me through it all.

Don Felder

Without **Alan Nevins** this book would never have happened. Without Calvin Warzecha, there would be no Alan Nevins. I am indebted to them both for their professionalism, generous hospitality, and cherished friendship. My husband, Chris, has held my hand through this and so much more; I'd have drowned without him. My friend Robin Richardson has been a source of great comfort and strength, as have my siblings. I shall miss my wonderful parents, Ted and Dorothy Holden, more than words can say.

Don and Kathrin welcomed me into their lives and their home with open arms and made one of the worst years of my life somehow bearable. Thank you.

On a professional front, I am grateful to Ronin Ro for the work he did in the beginning and Marc Eliot for his brave book *To the Limit: The Untold Story of the Eagles*. Where Don's memory had failed him, Marc's text was able to prompt some answers. I also need to thank Marc Shapiro for *The Long Run*, Ben Fong-Torres for *Not Fade Away*, Cameron Crowe for the inimitable *Almost Famous*, John Einarson for *Desperados: The Roots of Country Rock*, Dave Zimmer for *Crosby, Stills & Nash*, Anthony Fawcett for *California Rock, California Sound*, William Knoedelseder for *Stiffed: A True Story of MCA, the Music Business, and the Mafia*, and John Swenson for *Headliners*. Also thanks to Randy Meisner for lunch, Karima Ridgley and Mindy Stone for their infinite patience and efficiency, and to Stephen S. Power and all at Wiley for their vision.

Wendy Holden

HEAVEN and HELL

ONE

We could hear the rumble of the crowd in the dressing room. It sounded like a thunderstorm brewing somewhere far above us. As we emerged one by one from the bowels of the stadium, our lips wet with beer, white powder rings around my nostrils, the rumble grew louder and louder.

The stage was dark as we fumbled across to our respective instruments with well-practiced skill, the cool wind ruffling our hair. The murmur suddenly swelled. Those at the front of the crowd spotted our shadowy figures moving around in the red glow of the amplifiers. They lit candles or cigarette lighters and held them above their heads, hoping for an early glimpse of their rock idols. Others followed in sequence until all we could see was a vast, shimmering sea of light. The anticipation was so heady we could almost taste it.

We stood in the half-light for a few seconds, catching our breath, trying to focus our minds on who we were and how we came to be there. Me, a poor boy from small-town Florida, almost crippled by polio as a child, whose dream was to play like B.B. King, stepping out to the front of the stage. The other four members of the band behind me, from all over the country, in bell-bottom jeans, each of us the living embodiment of the American dream.

There we stood, peering out at the tens of thousands of expectant fans who'd paid top dollar to be here, people who knew each note, every word of our music and who'd come from miles around just to hear us play. The cocaine and the thrill and the adrenaline made my heart pound hard against my ribcage.

Suddenly a spotlight flicked on. Shining straight down on me, standing alone in a beam of brilliant light, holding a white, double-necked Gibson guitar. The rest of the band silhouetted against a giant reproduction of the distinctive cover photograph of *Hotel California,* an image of the Beverly Hills Hotel flanked by palm trees in the L.A. sunset. My fingers tingling, I opened with the first distinctive bars of the title track, a song I'd cowritten a few months before, sitting cross-legged on the floor of my beach house with my son playing nearby.

A roar went up. Nobody expected this to be the first number. They thought we'd close with it. The audience exploded. For those first few seconds, there was no sound but that of the crowd—a deafening cacophony of screaming, cheering, bellowing, whistling, and tumultuous applause. Swaying in the spotlight, soaking up the intense, electrically charged atmosphere, I wiped the sweat from my forehead and closed my eyes. As my fingers moved automatically up and down the frets, I allowed myself a small smile. This was it. All that I'd ever dreamed of in the depths of the night—to hear those voices calling from far away—the exhilarating sound of success.

TWO

Gainesville, Florida, probably wasn't the ideal place to grow up—or at least not the poorer quarter, where we lived. When I was a child, it was an unassuming Deep South community once called Hogtown Creek, where the only means of escape was through dreaming, something I became especially good at.

Its chief attraction was its location, slap bang in the middle of the Sunshine State, three hours from the capital, Tallahassee. It was a ninety-minute drive from Daytona Beach to the east and from the Gulf of Mexico to the west, and about two hours from Orlando, which was nothing until Mr. Disney decided to move there in the seventies. Gainesville's saving grace was the University of Florida, which for some reason chose to base itself there in 1905, bringing in thousands of people. Hogtown Creek was never the same.

The climate was hot and swampy, the air thick with mosquitoes. In the winter, it was dispiritingly cold and wet. But it was the kind of place where homeowners never had to lock their doors; crime was virtually nonexistent. Held in a sort of rose-tinted time warp, it was populated by good, wholesome folks who bred decent kids with strong moral values, helped along by a little healthy Bible-thumping. *The Yearling*, with Gregory Peck and Jane Wyman, always reminds me of my hometown, with its sugary, apple-pie sweetness. It came as no surprise that Marjorie Kinnan Rawlings, the author of *The Yearling* and other novels, grew up just outside Gainesville.

My parents, Charles "Nolan" Felder and Doris Brigman, first met on a blind date in 1933, when they were in their twenties. They stepped out for five years—literally walking during their courting because there was no gasoline for Dad's old Chevrolet during the Depression. Their weekly routine was to stroll downtown to Louie's Diner, still there today, for a twenty-five-cent hamburger and a strawberry milkshake before heading off to the Lyric Theater to watch one of the new "talking" movies starring the likes of Fred Astaire and Ginger Rogers.

My mother's family were so poor that she and my grandmother actually shared a pair of shoes—Mom borrowing them once a week to wear to Bible school on Sunday. Such poverty often breeds ill health, and Grandma Caroline died of heart failure when Mom was just nine years old, forcing her to drop out of school to care for her father, her older brother, "Buddy," and her two-year-old sister, Kate.

Dad was of German origin. His ancestors settled in America after riding the trail to Hogtown Creek from North Carolina. They look like something out of an old Western—bearded, with hats and rifles, and with coon dogs lying lazily at their feet. Dad was the eldest of four children abandoned by their mother after she became a chronic epileptic. He was raised by his devout father, who used discipline and the Bible to browbeat his children into submission.

After several years of dating, my father decided, on New Year's Day, 1938, to take Doris as his wife. They were in Daytona Beach, and to celebrate he bought a bottle of sparkling wine—a rare moment of frivolity. He was twenty-eight years old, and she was five years his junior. With his two best friends, Jim Spell and Sam Dunn, and their girlfriends, they drove to the town of Trenton at ten o'clock that night and woke up the Justice of the Peace. "We wanna get married," they told the bleary-eyed magistrate. He kindly obliged. They spent their wedding night at the Central Hotel in Gainesville, before going back to their respective homes until they could find a place of their own.

That fall, Dad started work on a building plot he'd acquired at 217 Northwest Nineteenth Lane, Gainesville, right next to the house he grew up in, using his meager savings to pay for the lumber and supplies he needed. The house was built on concrete blocks, with wood framing, designed to circulate cool air underneath and stop snakes and alligators from crawling in. Standing on the edge of a dirt road, surrounded by Florida scrub known as palm meadows, it was flanked at the back by a swampy lake with Spanish moss hanging from the trees. Grandpa Felder helped him with the construction, as did Mom, and so did Jim Spell, who lived next door. My parents moved into a white clapboard shell with a tin roof, identical to Grandpa's house. They added to it over the years, installing some inside walls to make two bedrooms, a kitchen, and a bathroom. Dad was always so proud of the fact that he'd built his home with his own hands.

For his entire life, he toiled as a mechanic at Koppers, a factory four blocks away at Northwest Twenty-third Avenue, which pressure-treated wood for telephone poles and the railroads. Recently felled trees were brought in by the trainload, and huge machines lifted them onto conveyor belts leading to a giant lathe that peeled off the bark and spat out skinned poles. Another machine loaded them onto rail cars, from which a diesel train backed the poles into a long metal tube. The tube was three hundred feet long and completely enclosed with a giant door. The bolts closed down, and blackened creosote was pumped in under pressure. When the process was finished, the machine depressurized, opened up, and released the sticky black poles onto a rail spur, where another train came in and carted them off to Oklahoma or wherever they were destined for. It was an incredibly slick operation.

Apart from a few years when he was laid off during the Depression,

Dad had worked at Koppers since he was twelve years old, long before they had child-labor laws, servicing much of the complicated machinery. Like his father before him, who'd also been a mechanic at the plant, he endured hideous work conditions and unbelievable hours. It was a twenty-four-hour operation, and if there were any problems, night or day, he'd be summoned. I'd hear the telephone ring at two or three in the morning and listen to him stumble from his bed, then come back at dawn for an hour's sleep before beginning his regular shift. He inhaled creosote and diesel fumes all day long and would arrive home black from head to toe. "Take off them coveralls, Nolan," my mom would yell at him as he stood out back, before he even set foot in the house. He'd dutifully peel them off and pull open the screen door in his shorts and socks. Taking a long hot shower, he'd try to wash the worst of it away, but the dirt was permanently ingrained under his fingernails and around his cuticles. There was always a lingering smell.

I was born in Alachua County Hospital on September 21, 1947, five years after my brother, Jerry. Dad had missed the fighting because of the importance of his work to the war effort, although I think he might have benefited by escaping from Gainesville for a few years and seeing something of the world. His experience of the Depression had hardened him into a stern workaholic who broke his back for very little pay. Even during brief periods when he was laid off, he'd found employment—laying bricks in the town square outside the courthouse for ten cents a day—and he was always extremely cautious with money. He never owned a credit card, took a mortgage, or bought a car on credit. His frequently repaired '42 Chevy was our only transport, and he hid cash in his dresser drawer in case the banks ever closed again. Abject poverty can break a man's trust.

Living as we did on the equivalent of Tobacco Road, I mostly ran barefoot in cutoff jeans and a T-shirt, my faithful cocker spaniel, Sandy, zigzagging enthusiastically at my side. With Jerry and my best friend, Leonard Gideon, I'd play in the palm meadows, where we'd make little forts by bending a sapling to the ground with a rope, tying it down, and weaving the loose fronds into a thatch.

Irene Cooter, a matronly sort who lived right behind us, acted as unofficial babysitter to most of the neighborhood kids. Leonard and I would go there for a couple of hours each day after school. In her garden was a huge chinaberry tree, whose roots burled and bubbled up from the ground. "Don't you go climbing that tree, son," she'd warn me as I stared longingly into its twisted branches. By the time I was four, the temptation became too much. Needless to say, a branch broke and I fell to the ground with an almighty thud, shattering my left elbow on one of the gnarled roots. Screaming, I ran into the house with the bone sticking through the skin.

The doctors at Alachua County Hospital said I'd end up with very restricted movement and would never be able to do much with my left arm. My mother believed otherwise. As soon as the plaster cast came off, she filled a little pail with sand and made me carry it around morning and night to try to straighten my arm out. I'd cry with the pain and she'd hold my hand and walk around with me, crying too. Thanks to her determination and an agonizing couple of months, I have pretty much full range of motion—very important for a future guitar player.

A year after that accident, I became very ill. I complained to my mother about headaches and feeling tired all the time. It was unusual behavior for any five-year-old, but for a little firecracker like me, it was unheard of. She whisked me off to a doctor, who diagnosed the early symptoms of polio. An epidemic was sweeping the country, leaving thousands of children paralyzed and hundreds dead. I was lucky. They gave me the new Salk vaccine, not yet widely available, and through some miracle, I never developed the full symptoms. But I still spent four interminably long months in the children's polio ward, frightened and alone. I wondered what I had done to be abandoned by my parents in such a place. Was it because I'd been naughty and climbed that tree? My only salvation was a little radio next to my bed. It had a detachable plastic speaker, and at night I'd slide it under my pillow and lie there, drumming my fingers in time to the music for hours.

The sounds of Al Martino and Frankie Laine comforted me and drowned out the wheezing rise and fall of the iron lungs that did the breathing for those less fortunate than me. "Here in my heart," Al Martino would sing to me as I lay in my bed, staring at a fan slowly whirring on the ceiling, "I'm alone, I'm so lonely." I like to think it was the soothing music and lilting voices of those fifties crooners, and not the vaccine, that pulled me through.

My mother worked full time, Monday through Saturday, at the first one-hour dry cleaner in Gainesville, which opened at a new shopping center in the middle of town. She'd come home each night with the scent of the solvent and the clothes on her skin. One of the few shouting matches I can ever remember her having with Dad was over her wish to work. "I want my own money, Nolan," she complained. "I don't like having to come to you each time I wanna buy something for the boys." In truth, he'd usually refuse her anyway. My father was indignant. Most wives stayed at home, and he was worried how it would look at the plant. But he gave in to her in the end, as he usually did.

With Mom and Dad both at work, there was hardly ever anyone around the house. Grandpa Brigman, my mother's father, lived on the far side of town, and we only visited him Sundays after church. Grandpa Felder lived next door, chewing tobacco and spitting great globules of stinking brown saliva into an old coffee can by his feet, but he always took a nap in the afternoons, and I could usually slip away. Without supervision, I'd get into all sorts of trouble—mostly playing music too loud or fighting. I spent a lot of time riding around the neighborhood, filling up the basket of my rickety second-hand bicycle with empty two-cents Coke bottles. If I collected enough empties, I could afford to go to the drug store— MoonPie and RC Cola were the dietary staples of my misspent youth.

I wasn't the naughtiest pupil at the Sydney Kinnear Elementary School by any means. I was more of a daydreamer, really. I'd spend the hours looking out of the window, thinking about everything from ways to impress Sharon Pringle, a girl I had a crush on, to what scam I could come up with next to raise a few extra cents. School just didn't interest me. I did the minimum I needed to scrape by and no more.

My parents were forever grabbing me by the ear and ticking me off. My father was determined that his sons should rise above the class we'd been born into and away from the life sentence of menial work he and Mom had been allotted. I think his greatest fear was that I'd end up working at Koppers like him and Grandpa Felder. A dozen times a week, he'd tell me, "Cotton, why can't you be more like your brother and do something with your life?" (My nickname was "Cotton" because my hair was so white. Later, my nickname became "Doc," after the famous Bugs Bunny question, "What's up, Doc?")

Brother Jerry and I couldn't have been more different. Bigger physically, diligent, polite, and extremely focused, he seemed to realize early on that the only way to escape the destiny our parents' limited education had allowed them was to do well academically. A straight-A student who loved to read, he also happened to be a great athlete. A pitcher for the baseball team, he went on to win a scholarship to college and law school. He even married his homecoming sweetheart. In other words, he was an impossible act to follow. I looked up to him in admiration, awe, and envy. Every class I attended, every Little League game I played, the teacher or coach would tell me, "Oh, Felder, we hope you're half as good as your brother." Before long, I came to resent the comparison. I soon realized I didn't have a hope of competing, so I didn't even try. It was too tall a shadow to walk in, and I'd just slide by instead with D and E grades.

Jerry and I shared a bedroom, with two single beds and a desk between. Most nights he'd sit up late studying, his artist's lamp shining right into my eyes while I was trying to read *Mad* magazine, which I could only afford every now and again. One minute, it seemed, we'd been playing together, and then, almost overnight, he was older and more sophisticated, with friends who weren't remotely interested in his kid brother hanging around. The five-year age gap seemed a chasm between us, and the only time we spent together after that was on vacation or in some sort of competitive sport, at which I'd always lose. He even beat me at Monopoly and chess, having taught me just enough so he could trounce me. Man, I'd be really pissed that he owned all these hotels and houses, and yet he'd make me hold onto one little pink property until he killed me.

I'm sure I was a constant source of exasperation to my father. The memory of his leather strap across my butt and the backs of my legs can still make me wince. It was far worse than the wooden paddle we received at school, and it left angry red weals. I regularly endured his beatings throughout my childhood. It was just part of the deal.

Whenever I think of my mother, on the other hand, I can't help but smile. It was she who insisted we get Sandy. My father didn't want pets, but Mom told him firmly, "Every boy needs a dog." Sandy was my greatest friend, far more so than our cat, Blackie, who seemed to have a litter every other week, usually in the bottom of my closet. Sandy devotedly followed me to school every day and waited patiently outside the classroom until the bell rang. The principal called my parents several times to have him brought home, but if they came to get him, he'd just run straight back, so they finally gave up.

One day, when he was about four years old, I took him to the mom-and-pop drugstore to buy some Pepsi and peanuts. While I was distracted, chatting with the owner about the latest baseball scores, Sandy ducked behind the counter before I could stop him and gobbled up some rat poison. To my horror, he began convulsing almost immediately. Scattering my purchases across the floor, I scooped him up and ran him straight across the street to the vet.

"Please, help my dog," I said, cradling him as my tears splashed his fur. "He ate some poison and he's very sick. Don't let him die."

Sandy's eyes were rolling back in his head and he was frothing at the mouth between fits. The vet lifted him from my arms and hurried him into a back room, shutting the door behind him. I sat in that waiting room for over an hour, sobbing piteously, until the vet eventually emerged, somber-faced.

"I'm sorry, son, there was nothing we could do," he told me as I stood expectantly before him.

I never thought anything could hurt so bad, and I howled all the way home on my bike, ignoring the curious stares of passersby. Fortunately, Mom had received a call at work and was waiting to console me. It was weeks before I was able to go into the drugstore again.

• • •

Every Sunday, no matter how tired she was after six straight days working, Mom cooked fried chicken with mashed potatoes and cornbread. I still can't smell cornbread without thinking of her. For rare treats, Dad would take us to Morrison's Cafeteria for its Sunday special—ninety-nine cents each for all we could eat. We'd line up with trays piled high with Salisbury steak, chicken, and potatoes, cramming as much as we could into our hungry little mouths until our stomachs were stretched and tight. If they'd have let us, we'd have taken a wheelbarrow.

Regardless of how little money we had, Mom made sure we never starved and were always clean. "Wash your face, hands and feet, behind your ears, and brush your teeth," Mom would say every night like a mantra. "And don't forget to say your prayers." She was a strong Southern Baptist and firmly believed in the Lord. We had to say grace before every meal, even though Dad was often impatient to get on with the important business of eating.

Mom dragged Jerry and me to Sunday school from the time we could walk. Dad never came. "I've heard all they have to say," he'd state flatly, and set about cooking his favorite weekend treat—fried oysters—while we were marched off to the North Central Baptist Church.

Enrolled into Bible-study groups, Jerry and I were being groomed for baptism, which took place in a clear glass tank of water like a giant fishbowl that the preacher and his "victim" would step into. One day, the preacher immersed this big fat lady from the congregation. He placed his handkerchief over her mouth and recited prayers while he held her under the water. Well, that old dame started kicking and thrashing and trying to get some air, but he wouldn't let her up. I sat watching, horrified, as she finally burst through the water, gasping.

"Did you see that?" I cried, aghast. "The preacher almost drowned her!" After the service, I walked right across to the Methodist church on the opposite side of the road and signed up there and then. "Methodists," I told my mother firmly, "only sprinkle."

The best thing about church for me was the music, not in ours so much, but in the colored churches. Most Sundays, when our service had long finished, I'd walk the mile and a half to one of the "holy roller" churches and sit on the grass outside, swaying softly in time to the powerful sounds and amazing voices that used to pour out of those open windows. Man, those souls knew how to sing a tune.

My parents didn't have many friends. Neither of them was very outgoing, and both were painfully aware of their shortcomings, having left school at such early ages. The only thing I ever saw my father read was the newspaper, or "mullet wrapper," as he called it each night when he told me to bring it in for him from the front yard. Even if they had been sociable, which they weren't, Mom and Dad simply didn't have the money or the space to entertain. The kitchen was only eight by eight, with a sink and a stove run on bottled gas. You could just about get two people in it if they circled each other. Our tiny living room didn't allow for parties either.

My mother rarely complained about her lot, but one summer she decided that she simply had to have something—a dining room. Her younger sister Kate had married well, and she and her husband Ursell were the richest people we knew. He'd joined up in the war and stayed on in the military, serving at Wright-Patterson Air Force Base in Dayton, Ohio. Each time they came to visit, with their kids, Jean and Frank, they'd arrive in the latest Cadillac or Oldsmobile. They lived in a house with a landscaped yard and a garage, and Frank had a motor scooter he'd let me hop a ride on. But most impressive of all, as far as my mother was concerned, they had a separate room for dining.

Each summer vacation, Dad and Jerry and I would spend a week or so working on the house—cleaning or repainting the clapboard, repairing the screens, and making general improvements. There was so much heat and humidity in Florida that the paint constantly cracked and peeled and needed to be scraped off and redone. But this particular year, there were bigger fish to fry: We had to build a dining room. We worked all summer long, every evening and most weekends, sawing boards by hand, hammering, fixing, and painting. When Mom came home from work each night, she carefully scrutinized what we'd done. It was just a box stuck on the back of this old shack, but she'd built it up in her mind to something grander.

Once the dining room was finished, we sat around a table to eat for the first time, instead of from our laps in front of the television. It felt kinda strange having to look at each other over our supper plates. Very rarely was anyone else invited over to enjoy the experience. She even had jalousie windows fitted, louver windows consisting of several horizontal slats of glass, opened and closed by a crank. Lord, she was proud of those windows. So much so, that when Jerry and I accidentally broke them for the first time—fooling around in the yard, I think—she must have taken some small measure of enjoyment from the beating Dad subsequently gave us.

My father was a creature of habit, whose working life revolved around shifts and rosters, everything happening in an endlessly repeating cycle. He made sure his personal life was just as well ordered. For him, there was no stepping outside the box. Every Sunday afternoon, almost without fail, we'd drive somewhere in his old Chevy. My father loved that car. It was an ugly thing, with running boards, but you could stand on the back seat holding onto a rope instead of seat belts. Unattractive as it may have been, it never once broke down. It was such a simple design that Dad could easily repair it. I'd spend a lot of time watching him with his head under the hood, the radio blaring big band music, handing him tools and learning about car maintenance almost by accident.

Undoubtedly, the best times I had with Dad were out in his garage on weekends, fixing something. He'd always secretly wanted to be an electrical repairman, and his workshop was filled with parts of radios, soldering irons, cables, and old stereos. It was his way of relaxing, and he'd never flop down in front of the television with a whiskey like many fathers I knew, chiefly because he couldn't afford it.

Soon after Sunday lunch, he'd fire up that Chevy and we'd head off to Jacksonville or Palatka or Daytona Beach. For our annual summer vacation, we'd go much farther afield, maybe even to visit Uncle Buck. Dad's kid brother, whose real name was Jesse, was his jovial opposite. On the rare occasions Dad smiled—and it was usually only when Buck was around—he looked like a different man, his face transformed by lines around his eyes and mouth that were completely unfamiliar to us.

Bored with the seemingly endless journeys Dad took us on, Jerry and I would spend much of the time fighting, nagging, or teasing each other. Conversation was kept to a minimum by the loud music Dad insisted on playing, and we'd stop only for meals or to sleep at nine-dollar motels when he was too tired to drive anymore. The tedium was relieved by the Burma-Shave ads that lined the old two-lane highways. The famous rhyming slogans for shaving cream would be spaced out every five miles, a line at a time, and we'd watch for the next one and wait for the punch line.

Dad smoked Lucky Strike cigarettes, and he'd flick them out of the window when he'd finished, showering us in the back with hot, stinking ash. "Hey, Dad, stop that!" we'd yell indignantly, brushing ourselves off. In my mind's eye, I can still see his left arm, permanently tanned, hanging out of the window.

Summers in Gainesville were excruciating. Each day dawned with the early promise of heat. By noon, the tin roof was cooking the house. At night, we lay in pools of sweat, barely able to breathe. It was as hot outside as in, and you couldn't step beyond the screen door for the bugs that would eat you alive.

The winters were cold and damp. The only source of warmth we had in our house was an old kerosene heater, which sat in the open fireplace of the living room. "Doc, go and light the heater," Mom would call, when it was still dark outside. Reluctantly, I'd jump out of bed, grab some clothes, and rush as fast as I could in the freezing cold. The others would hear the heater fire up and wait ten minutes before daring to peek a toe out of bed. I still bear scars on my butt from where I bent over in front of the heater one morning to pull on my pants and accidentally backed into the metal grate, branding me for life.

My cousin Frank had planted the seed of desire in me for a motor scooter, and I wanted one so bad, but I knew from overhearing Jerry's battles with Dad on the subject that it would never happen. At fourteen, he could qualify for a motorcycle license and he wanted one even more than I did. Dad thought differently. "You just wait until you're sixteen, son, and we're going to put a big piece of metal around your butt. A car's what you need, not them two-wheel hell on wheels."

Never one to pay much attention to my dad, I used to sneak around and take rides on the back of other people's bikes whenever I could, even though I'd almost always end up getting my butt chewed up. I'd come limping home with grazes and bruises all over my legs and arms and try to pretend I'd done it climbing trees.

"Haven't I warned you about that?" Mom would say, frowning. One day, an older boy with a scooter visited my neighbor across the street. "Please, can I have a ride?" I begged. "Just down to the market?" Under incessant pressure, he finally relented and laughingly rode me downtown and back. On our way home, just a few yards from my house, my neighbor reversed his car out of his long dirt-and-gravel driveway and straight into the side of us. I took the brunt of the impact and was thrown over the top of the car, landing head first on the road before tumbling, unconscious, into a drainage ditch right outside my house. My mother was sitting on the front porch and watched the whole thing in open-mouthed horror.

I woke up in Alachua County Hospital an hour later, bloodied and bowed, with a concussion but without a single broken bone. A year later, my cousin Frank was killed riding his motorbike. I never sat astride one again.

My mother was very happy with my father but not with her station in life. I think, secretly, she always wanted something better, especially with Aunt Kate doing so well. One particular source of embarrassment to Mom was the family car, which she often complained was old-fashioned and rusty.

Unbeknownst to us all, one day she drove herself to the car dealer and traded in Dad's beloved Chevy on a clean, used, green two-tone '56 Pontiac with power windows. He came home from work that night and nearly dropped dead.

Jerry and I waited just inside the house, holding our breath.

"Where's my Chevy?" Dad exploded, staring in disbelief at the gleaming Pontiac.

"Probably in the junkyard where it belongs," Mom replied, hands on her hips defiantly. Then, more sheepishly, she added, "I traded it."

"You take that damn car back to where it came from and you bring me my Chevy," Dad shouted, a vein pulsing in the side of his neck.

"If you don't want this car, then I'm gonna pay for it," she yelled back. "I've been working and I've been saving. Me and the boys deserve a better car."

The screaming match went on until Dad stormed into the house, slamming the screen door so hard I thought it would fly clean off its hinges, and Mom drove off in the Pontiac. An hour later, she returned with Dad's old car, parking it haphazardly in the drive before stalking into the house by the back door. Jerry and I watched this power struggle in stunned silence.

Within a week, the Pontiac was back. I don't know what she did or said, but Dad just rolled over like a lazy dog after a meal and let her get her way. Man, we loved that car. It was a four-door hardtop. Suddenly, I felt like I could travel for weeks without wanting to stop. With our "new" car parked in the drive, we could hold our heads up in the neighborhood at last. I'd never realized how poor we were until suddenly we didn't feel quite so poor anymore. It was a good feeling.

THREE

The radio in the polio ward first introduced me to the pleasures of music, but my father latched onto my early interest and used it as common ground. He'd always had some sort of stereo, no matter how poor we were, that played 33- and 45-rpm vinyls. By the time I was old enough to appreciate it, our home entertainment center—cobbled together from parts—was the biggest feature of our living room. After a hard day at work, Dad would come home, clean himself up, and kick back by listening to tapes. It was his only real escape from the life he'd been born to. That and television, although I think we must have been the last family in Gainesville to buy a set. It was so big and tall, it looked like a wooden washing machine with a twelve-inch screen.

He'd borrow albums from friends, play them on his turntable, and record them on his secondhand Voice of Music tape recorder. He knew it was illegal duplication, but it was all he could afford. When he got tired of hearing something, he'd erase it, borrow a record from someone else, and tape that instead. Soon, he had an extensive collection by the likes of Tommy Dorsey, Lawrence Welk, Benny Goodman, and Glenn Miller. I still can't hear "Moonlight Serenade" without thinking of my dad.

Thanks to him, I had my first introduction to jazz and country music. Well, him and the *Grand Ole Opry*. We'd listen to that on WSM Radio from the Ryman Auditorium until we acquired a television and could watch it live from Nashville on Friday and Saturday nights. Despite the poor quality of the set, we had the best reception in the neighborhood, because Dad rigged up a sophisticated rotating antenna so that, when the channel changed, a motor pointed it in the right direction. I thought that was pretty cool.

I remember seeing Elvis Presley on the *Ed Sullivan Show* one Sunday night in 1957 and going wild. He sang "Hound Dog," "Heartbreak Hotel," and "Love Me Tender," and I was completely blown away. Even though he was only shown from the waist up because of complaints about the sexual nature of the way "Elvis the Pelvis" danced, I'd never seen anybody move like that before. Soon afterward, there came a flood of music called rock and roll, and I knew right away that this was for me. Something about it really made the hairs stand up on the back of my neck.

My first introduction to the technical side of music also came through my father. One day, he called me over to his tape recorder, which consisted of two boxes, one with a reel-to-reel and a tiny six-by-nine speaker, the other with a small amplifier and a second speaker. Without explaining anything, he set up a microphone, put it in front of me, and instructed, "Okay now, Doc, I want you to count every odd number aloud."

I duly counted, one, three, five, seven, and so on. After rewinding the tape, he played it back and said, "Now, when you hear one, start counting even numbers."

Within minutes, he played the finished result back to me. Via the stereo's sound-on-sound capability, I heard my voice on the left channel saying "one," then on the right channel saying "two." It was the first stereo overdub I'd ever heard, and I thought, "My God, this is incredible!" I was hooked.

First and foremost, I needed a guitar. The Elvis explosion had hit America, and a guitar was suddenly the coolest instrument to play. I'd been raised on a diet of Nashville guitar and banjo music, and there was no other instrument I was remotely interested in. By the time I was eleven years old, everybody on the block seemed to be playing guitar but me. Trouble was, I didn't have the money to buy one. Utterly despondent, I suddenly realized I might have something valuable to trade—cherry bombs. Jerry and I would buy them when we visited Uncle W. L. in Carolina, then bring them home to Florida, where they were illegal. If you threw one into the concrete culvert in the ditch outside our home, it would make such a bang that all the kids in the street would come running, long before the cordite had dispersed.

The boy directly across the street from us owned an acoustic guitar I badly wanted, so one day Jerry and I got going with the firecrackers. As planned, the kid came right out. "Hey, can I have some of those?" he asked, his eyes bright.

"Sure," I said, with youthful cunning, "but it'll cost you that old guitar on the top of your closet." It was a horrible instrument with three strings missing and full of holes, but it was my first true love. I took it to the drugstore and bought new strings with the last of my savings. A neighbor across the street taught me how to tune my new toy and work my way through those agonizing first D and G chords. I'd monopolize the sliding glider seat on my parents' front porch, strumming away for hours. I nearly wore it out.

Later, with a little extra from Dad, I saved up what seemed like a fortune and sent twenty-eight dollars off to Sears, Roebuck for a Silvertone archtop, which seemed to me like the height of musical sophistication. Every morning for a week, I was late for school, waiting for the mailman to deliver it. I can still remember the pungent whiff of fresh varnish when I first opened the case. I'd never had anything so glossy and shiny and new. I took unbelievably good care of that guitar. Everything else had been a hand-me-down from Jerry; his clothes, his shoes, even his old bike. This was the first possession I had that was mine and mine alone.

Music was the only thing I was better at than Jerry. He could just about manage a couple of chords on the piano. It was also the only activity my father positively encouraged me in. The double incentive of pleasing Dad and being better at something than my brother was enough to make me want to do it real bad.

Dad seemed to be genuinely excited by my enthusiasm for something other than daydreaming. Ever the innovator, he took the back off the television and found that it had a little jack at the back where I could plug in my guitar and play out of the set's speakers. Every Saturday morning, when my brother was playing baseball and my parents were at work, I'd plug in and watch cartoons like *Mighty Mouse* and *Winky Dink and You* and make up musical soundtracks to go with them.

Dad would boast about me to people at the plant. "My youngest boy has a great ear," he'd say proudly. "I think he could be a natural."

One day he overheard one of his buddies complain that he'd bought his daughter an electric guitar that she never played. "The damn thing just sits in her closet, gathering dust," he moaned.

"Oh, yeah?" Dad commented, knowing that I'd already outgrown the Silvertone. He came home later that night and told me about the electric guitar, but warned, "When we go over to take a look at it, act like you don't really care."

The minute I set eyes on that guitar—a cream and gold Fender Musicmaker in a little tweed case—our cover was blown. Dad knew from the expression on my face that he'd never get a good deal now. It was probably the cheapest Fender money could buy and with its gold pick guard, it looked like a girl's guitar, but I was in love. I wanted it so bad, especially when I saw it came with a little amplifier not much bigger than a shelf radio. I proudly took it home and played it so much my fingers bled. Dad helped me upgrade the amp to a Fender Deluxe, which was really something. Now all I had to do was improve my performance.

I practiced and practiced, and as soon as I thought I was good enough, I took myself off to the State Theater movie house, where, on Saturday mornings, most of the kids in Gainesville could be found watching a twenty-five-cent movie like *Creature from the Black Lagoon* or *King Kong*. Most weeks, the theater also put on a live talent show immediately after the film. Many of the kids would go early and pay their quarter and get more for their money—a movie and a bit of amateur talent.

I was just eleven years old, my white blond hair slicked to one side, wearing my best Sunday shirt and pants, when I stood up on that stage for my first public performance. A chill fear gripped my heart. I was so nervous that I had a sheen of sweat on my as yet hairless upper lip. My shirt was sticking to the skin on my back, and my face turned bright pink. Placing my fingers in the correct positions with the utmost concentration, I played the opening bars of "Red River Valley," a seminal American country song I'd heard played by Porter Wagoner a dozen times on the *Grand Ole Opry*. It wasn't exactly Elvis, but I didn't yet have the courage to publicly perform the moves I'd practiced for hours alone in my bedroom.

There were only a few people in the crowd I knew. The rest were complete strangers, and, in some ways, that made it easier. They sat hunched in their seats, talking and laughing, drinking sodas, and throwing popcorn at each other while I played.

I didn't sing or anything. I couldn't. I had little or no confidence in my voice back then, and, in any event, I could never have generated enough saliva to lubricate my vocal cords. Nor could I stop my mouth from moving strangely while I was playing the most difficult parts on the frets. I just hoped that anyone sitting near the front would think I was mouthing the words to myself.

The reception to my standing there stiffly playing guitar was less than enthusiastic, but after a while, a small silence fell, and I noticed that some of the kids were actually listening. Allowing myself a little smile, I relaxed into it and began to play with more confidence. I even strayed slightly from the song, injecting a touch of personal improvisation. There was hardly a standing ovation as I went into the last chorus, but I wasn't being booed and they weren't throwing paper cups at me, which I knew was a good sign.

As I heard the final chord echo away, I focused on a couple of pretty young girls in the second row who were, for some unknown reason, beaming back at me with a look of adulation. I knew that this was what I had to do. Stumbling off the stage in a daze, as if I had just woken from a long sleep, it wasn't as if I had a choice. From that day on, my life would never be the same.

Puberty was, for me, an agony of teenage confusion. Hairs sprouted, bones grew, skin erupted, my voice broke, and all manner of alarming thoughts stole into my head. Ripples of heat would pass through my body at the very thought of a girl. A close encounter with the likes of Sharon Pringle probably would have killed me.

Along with the physical changes came unforeseen psychological ones—like not appreciating how impoverished my family was until my first day at F. W. Buchholz High School. Almost overnight, I discovered completely new areas of embarrassment. Just by looking around at other people's clothes, bikes, and even cars, and comparing them with my own painfully visible lack of assets, I came to understand what I was: dirt poor. And with that realization came a searing, scorching shame.

Friends like Kenny Gibbs, whose father owned the furniture store in town, lived in new cinder-block houses with air-conditioning, something I could only dream about. I found myself spending more and more time over at his place, enjoying the permanently cool air along with unimagined luxuries like a color television and a refrigerator full of candy bars and Coca-Colas we could help ourselves to. I'd readily accept an offer from his mother to sleep over, just for the novelty of not lying in a pool of sweat.

I rarely, if ever, invited Kenny back to my house in return. Or anyone else, for that matter. I usually made the excuse that Mom was home or my brother was studying. Everything about my parents suddenly seemed excruciating to my teenage mind. Their English seemed very broken; they weren't articulate like other people's parents, and I felt that the minute anyone met them, they'd know I came from limited means.

Every now and again, my family background would rear up and threaten to expose me, if someone asked me a personal question like, "Isn't your dad a mechanic at Koppers?" or "Didn't I see your mom in the thrift shop?" But I usually managed to quash it before it was too late. Music, ever my escape route, continued to be my salvation.

I couldn't afford my own records to keep up with the latest sounds, so I listened to the radio endlessly. I had an old wooden one in my room, which quickly usurped any attention I might otherwise have given to homework. In Gainesville, most of the white-owned stations stopped broadcasting at sundown. If the weather was good and there wasn't a big storm between Florida and Tennessee, I could wiggle the antenna around until I picked up WLAC in Nashville, at 1510 on the AM dial, the only station playing black music. Through its crackly broadcasts hosted by Gene Nobles, I was introduced to legends like B.B. King, Bo Diddley, Chuck Berry, and Muddy Waters. Tired of Pat Boone's mind-numbing version of "Tutti Frutti" all day on the regular channels, I'd listen at night, open-mouthed, to Little Richard strutting his stuff.

With my hair greased to one side and my jeans pegged in on my mother's pedal Singer sewing machine, I started getting into the North Florida music scene in a serious way. I took a lead from Dad and began to borrow other people's records—Elvis, Buddy Holly, Bill Haley and His Comets—in fact, just about everything from the dawn of rock and roll. Using Dad's Voice of Music machine, I'd record them on one channel while I played guitar on the other, trying to mimic the rock-and-roll greats. Once my dad upgraded to a better stereo, I requisitioned his old one and carried it carefully to my bedroom, giving up all thoughts of academic study, to spend my nights devoted to music.

My second public performance came when I was fourteen. I entered a talent contest at junior high school and walked onto the stage alone with a guitar and an amp. "OK now, boys and girls, let's hear a rousing round of applause for our next contestant—Donald Felder," the host announced, feedback screaming through his mike. I was far more nervous than my last gig, chiefly because I now knew everyone in the audience, but I somehow managed to play "Walk Don't Run," by the Ventures, well enough to be recognizable. There was a crowd of about five hundred, and the reaction was surprising. They seemed to like me, and by the end of the gig, I'd acquired newfound status. My peers were at the age when, like me, they were identifying with their rock-and-roll heroes, and I suddenly found that, as the nearest Gainesville equivalent, I had fans. Best of all, some of them were girls. With my fair complexion and lean looks, I was apparently considered a catch, now that I had proven musical talent. Needless to say, I reveled in my new cool.

Three weeks after that performance, one of my teachers suggested I contact the local radio station, WGGG, which regularly aired Gainesville's best amateurs. He came with me and, because he knew one of the DJs, fixed it for me to play live. Standing in a tiny recording studio, in front of a microphone, I hammered out two instrumental songs, "Apache," written by Jerry Lordan and popularized by the Shadows, and my old standby, "Walk Don't Run." A few of my friends heard the broadcast. "You done good, Don," they told me. "It was real neato." They made me feel like someone, like Elvis even. I was amazed even then how just stepping up to the microphone affected the way people viewed me. The DJ, a guy called Jim, whose full-time job was as a driver for the local Williams-Thomas funeral home, offered to help me make up some tapes. He and I became good friends and used to hang out in the viewing room of the funeral parlor at night, playing Frisbee beside the plinth where the open caskets stood.

I put together a small band at school with Kenny Gibbs and his brother, and we practiced regularly in their garage. His mother wanted us to call ourselves the Moonbeams, but we thought that name sucked. I can't remember what we decided on in the end, but we eventually evolved into the Continentals. It was sort of my band. I put it together and had cards made up with my telephone number on it for bookings. As was the nature of teenage bands in a college town, players came and went as they dropped in and out of Gainesville for their studies. Kenny played bass for a while, not because he was particularly talented; he just looked good and pulled in the girls. He also had the money to buy equipment, which was vital. There were two other bass players who were much better, Barry Scurran, a college student from Miami, and a guy named Stan Stannell.

I'd go over to Stan's house for a rehearsal, and he'd be sitting on his bed in his underwear for hours, foot propped up on a little stool, reading sheet music for classical guitar. He was a phenomenal player, but if you put an electric guitar in his hand, it sounded awful. The only thing that worked for him was bass, because of the similarities with classical technique. He played with us for about a year and then moved on, ending up as head of the guitar department of the Boston Conservatory of Music. I had probably one of the best classical guitar players in the country playing bass in my teenage rock-and-roll band, and I didn't even know it.

The other players in the band's various incarnations included a drummer named Jeff Williams, a freshman at the university who fixed us some great bookings for fraternity parties (we lied about our age); Lee Chipley, a sax player; and a guitarist and singer called Joe Maestro. The most itinerant of all was a young man who arrived in Gainesville out of the blue. He met Jeff at a gig and asked if he could recommend somewhere to stay.

"I ran into this kid at a frat party, and he sings and plays real good rhythm guitar. I think he should be in our band," Jeff told us one day.

"Great! What's his name?" I asked.

"Stephen," Jeff replied, "Stephen Stills."

Jeff was right. Stephen had one of the most distinctive voices I'd ever heard. He was fifteen, with short, blond hair, incredibly funny, outgoing, and confident—the type who'd sit with a guitar and play and sing by himself without any qualms. He had a rebellious, independent streak in him, but he wasn't off the tracks. I don't think he'd been especially bad to warrant being sent to a military academy; he was just caught more often than the rest of us. He lived at Jeff's house for a while, and we wound up doing some shows together, with him as the newest member of the Continentals.

One night we did a gig at the Palatka prom and stayed overnight in a hotel room with two double beds. I think we got a lift to the gig in the back of someone's pickup truck. Somehow, even though we were underage, we managed to get hold of a bottle of Jack Daniel's. Stephen and Kenny and Jeff and I ended up jumping up and down on those double beds, screaming at the tops of our voices, like kids who'd been left alone in the house by themselves. We were laughing and bouncing around, breaking bedsprings, and having a gas. It was probably one of my fondest memories of that whole time.

Next thing I knew, Stephen was gone. He just disappeared, without an explanation or a good-bye. I always assumed his trail had started getting hot, but I heard later that he took off for Tampa and then Latin America when his family moved there. Whatever the reason, he just evaporated. I didn't think I'd ever see or hear from him again.

In the summer of '61, Dad drove me to Daytona Beach to see "Mister Guitar," Chet Atkins, in concert, a legend of Nashville and later a guitar designer for Gibson and Gretsch. Dad and I went alone, on a rare outing together. The gig was amazing. I sat open-mouthed as Chet captivated an audience of two or three thousand fans, just him and his guitar. Not only did he use an incredible syncopated thumb and finger technique, but he'd developed a routine of playing different tunes with his left and right hand simultaneously. On the lower strings he'd play "Yankee Doodle" and, on the upper, "Dixie." It was like the North and the South finally reunited. I was dazzled and started borrowing his records from friends, copying them religiously. I learned by ear, listening where each note was, guessing the fingering. I couldn't afford sheet music.

I figured that if I recorded stuff on Dad's tape machine at seven and a half inches per second and played it back at three and three quarters, it would be an octave down but the same key and the same tonality, just half as fast. That way I could listen string by string, pick by pick, finger by finger. I tried to get my speed up to where I could actually play it in unison with Chet. I must have struggled with that "Yankee Doodle"/"Dixie" piece for over a year, working on it for a couple of hours every day, but I still couldn't figure it out. One night I'd had enough and threw my guitar down on the bed in disgust. I went off to sleep, and somehow, during the night, my brain ran the sequences and came up with the solution. In the morning, I picked up the guitar and, to my complete amazement, I had it, note-perfect.

Not that my entire life revolved around music. There were plenty of other distractions for a boy teetering on the brink of manhood. First, I had to earn some money to pay for tapes and guitar strings. Along with paid chores for the neighbors, I took a Saturday position working for Sharon Pringle's father in his shoe store, on the corner of Main Street, right opposite the five-and-dime. It was an absolutely miserable job for a horny young guy to be in—kneeling at the feet of all these pretty young girls, inhaling their scent as they tried on shoes, my face coloring scarlet every time they spoke to me. I didn't last long. The pain was too much to bear.

My next job was working at the new music store in town. Lipham Music opened in the shopping center just down from the old drugstore, the only place I could buy guitar strings previously. Run by old man Lipham and his son Buster, the new store was revolutionary for Gainesville and its big-band fans. There wasn't a saxophone, trombone, or piano in sight—just guitars and sheet music. It was truly a symbol of the new rock-and-roll era.

Walking past one day, I stopped in my tracks and stared hard into the window. There, almost as if it were waiting for me, was a Fender Stratocaster, just like the one Buddy Holly played. Right in front of my eyes. In Gainesville. It was pretty beat up, and could do with some work, but it was for sale and I simply had to have it. Pushing open the door, I hovered around the edges of the shop until Mr. Lipham finally approached.

"Can I help you, son?" he asked, a bemused smile on his face.

"I'd like to buy the Fender Stratocaster in the window," I said, all in a rush. "I have a Fender Musicmaker to trade, in its original case, and I don't have any money right now, but I could pay you something every week."

Mr. Lipham rubbed his chin with his hand and looked me up and down. "Can you play?" he asked, suspiciously.

"Yes, sir," I volunteered, confidently.

"Show me," he replied, reaching for a used guitar from the rack. I slung the strap around my neck and duly gave him a sample of my rapidly expanding repertoire.

"Hmmm. How about paying me off at the rate of ten dollars a month?" he asked, when I'd finished. Seeing me falter, he added, "You can work here when you can, tuning and cleaning the guitars, clearing up, and showing people how to play. I'll pay you a dollar fifty an hour."

"Sure," I beamed, and within an hour I was back home in my room banging the life out of that old Stratocaster.

My job in the store soon extended to that of music teacher. Mr. Lipham recommended me to some of his customers, and before I knew it, I was teaching ten-year-old snot-nosed kids who whined all the time because their fingers hurt and they thought they'd be able to play like Elvis the minute they picked up the guitar their parents had just bought them. My salary doubled, and I'd soon paid off the Stratocaster, even if the price—working with children—often seemed too high.

One of my students, however, showed real promise. His name was Tommy Petty, and he was my star pupil. Tommy was three years younger than me, skinny, with buckteeth and an awful guitar. I went over to his house to give him lessons, and he had a microphone set up and was belting it out, standing in his living room, singing and playing for all he was worth. I was impressed.

Tommy wasn't an outstanding guitar player, but he had a voice somewhere between Mick Jagger and Bob Dylan, and a whole lot of nerve. Not long afterward, he became the lead singer with a band called the Rucker Brothers. I remember telling Tommy that one day he might even make it.

I advised his band on improving their guitar techniques and helped put together some of their arrangements. Sometimes I'd even travel out with them on a gig, standing in the audience to hear them play. Tommy was very good looking, with long silky hair he used to flip, which attracted the girls. While I was standing watching him perform in a Moose lodge one night, a really cute chick came up and started talking to me. She'd seen me help unload the band's equipment and knew I was with them. To my surprise and delight, she invited me to go for a ride in her car during the break, and of course, I agreed. She drove down the road a little bit and pulled over, and we started kissing. But before anything serious happened, a car pulled up beside hers and a young man, as drunk as he could be, started yelling at us.

"Oh, Lord, it's my boyfriend!" she screamed, pushing me away from her.

Ashen-faced, I watched as this linebacker pulled up in front of us, stepped out, and walked back along the asphalt road in the middle of nowhere, a murderous expression on his face. Happily for me, he was so drunk, he suddenly tripped and collapsed facedown in the road.

"Quick! Start the car!" I yelled at the girl. "Let's get the hell out of here."

"We can't just leave him there," she whined. "He's lying right in the middle of the road. Someone's gonna hit him. We've gotta pull him to the side."

With severe doubts about my sanity, I climbed out of the car and helped her get her boyfriend to his feet. As we pulled him up, he belched foul beer breath. Reluctantly, I placed one of his arms around my shoulders and one around hers, and we started dragging him back toward his car. We were only a few feet from safety when he came to.

"Get your filthy hands off me," he said, throwing back his arms with a violent jerk, completely dislocating my left shoulder. Letting out a primal scream, I grabbed my arm and jammed it back into its socket.

"Take me back to the gig," I gasped at the girl. She took one look at her boyfriend, now slumped over the hood of his car, and another look at me, doubled up in pain, and agreed.

I staggered back into the Moose lodge, halfway through the second set, holding my shoulder, which hurt real bad, and tried to make my way up to the stage to ask one of the guys to take me to a hospital. A few steps behind me was the drunken boyfriend, who'd regained consciousness and followed me back. "Hey, you little jerk!" he yelled, shoving me hard in the back. "What the hell are you doing with my girl?" I couldn't defend myself. My shoulder was all swollen, and I was in so much pain, I could have cried. The Rucker brothers, though, were big, bad, mean, tough-ass Florida rednecks whose father owned a garage. They saw me being harassed, threw down their instruments, jumped down off the stage, grabbed this guy, and dragged him outside, where they gave him a good whupping. That was probably one of the most memorable Tom Petty gigs I can recall. Even today, if I pull my shoulder back a little too far, I get a painful reminder of that night.

My schoolwork undoubtedly suffered from all the extracurricular activities I was involved in. In addition to my weekend jobs selling shoes, tuning guitars, and trying to teach tearful little kids how to play "King Creole," I also started doing solo gigs, just me, my Fender, and my little amp, playing in town and at venues farther afield, which I rode to on a Greyhound bus.

"Don Felder, Guitarist," I billed myself, taking lowly paid jobs at women's social clubs and kids' parties, playing anything from movie themes to Elvis. I also played drums at a bar called Gatorland, which was right across the street from the University of Florida, and lead guitar in a band at Dubs Steer Room, a smoke-filled steakhouse that served meat and beer. You could shoot pool, dance the "Gator," or just watch the wet T-shirt contest every Friday and Saturday night. Man, I thought I'd died and gone to heaven.

Jerry didn't like me playing in such places, and when he found out, he threatened to tell our folks. "It ain't right," he'd tell me. "You're underage and shouldn't even be in those dives. Besides, it's embarrassing having my kid brother on the stage." But I didn't care. I was happy playing music and having fun. Ever since I'd stepped on the stage of the State Theater, this was what I'd wanted.

I still loved black music, after my early contact with the church soul singers and my love affair with late-night radio stations, but during the late fifties and early sixties, there weren't any concert halls for black artists. Racism was rife in the Deep South, and that's just how it was. I didn't like it, and I didn't understand it. My father worked with "coloreds" and got on well with them. One of Dad's friends, known to all as "Pig," had a sugarcane farm outside town. We'd sometimes go there on weekends and work alongside his men cutting the cane. Pig's mule would pull the grindstone, and the coloreds would cook up some of the sugarcane to make syrup for our pancakes. Dad lent money to one man in particular, who was a regular visitor at our home. I was always mystified as to why, when he came to call, he had to use the back door instead of the front.

There was a part of Gainesville that everybody called Colored Town. Whites didn't go there, but I did. I'd sneak out as a young teenager and run down to the bars to jam with the musicians. My parents would have had a fit if ever they knew. My father was still taking his belt to me, and I dread to think what he'd have done if he'd ever found out I wasn't sleeping over at a friend's house, after all, but hanging out with the coloreds.

One of the musicians I played with down there, a drummer called John, told me that B.B. King was coming to town as part of what was known as the "Chitlin Circuit" for black performers. He'd be playing in an illegal bar in a barn out on somebody's farm. Back then, promoters would find a building in the middle of cow pastures and simply move the haystacks out of the way for the gig. They'd set up tables and chairs made out of crates and put down a few kegs, sell beer, and charge five dollars admission. Five bucks to see B.B. King. It was a small fortune.

I was completely starstruck about B.B., whom I'd heard on WLAC a hundred times, and I badgered John to take me with him. "Please can I go, please, please, please?" He eventually agreed, much to my delight, and so, one night I sneaked out of my house, ran to his Jeep, and drove off with him to the barn.

The place was steaming. I was the only white person for miles. I couldn't afford to go in, so I stood outside, peering through the window. B.B. absolutely blew me away. Men were hollering and women were crying, just listening to him play. I watched him, wide-eyed, and knew that I wanted to be like him more than anything else in the world—standing at the front of the stage, eyes pressed shut, making women weep with my guitar.

When he was done, he set down his guitar in a horse stall and took a seat on a hay bale, along with everyone else, to drink some of the illegal booze. My heart pounding, I burst in through the door and rushed across the crowded barn to where he was sitting.

"Mr. King," I said breathlessly, "I just wanna shake your hand."

His face lit up like a candle, and he flashed me a mouth filled with dazzlingly white teeth. "Well, OK, boy," he replied, his eyes bright, "here it is." He extended his huge hand and I took it in mine. His fingers were the size of sausages, and his breath smelled faintly of whiskey. Unable to say another word, dumbstruck as his gaze cut straight through me, I backed away and walked home that night in a daze. I don't think I washed for a week.

For the next few months, I saved every penny until, finally, I could afford what I wanted. The first album I ever bought was *Live at the Regal*, by B.B. King. I bought it mail-order from Randy's Record Shop in Gallatin, Tennessee, advertised on WLAC in Nashville as "the world's largest phonographic record shop." The album cost $2.98, which I painstakingly saved and sent off in the mail. It was one of the greatest blues recordings ever made. I learned every note.

World events largely seemed to pass Gainesville by, but some, like the Cuban Missile Crisis and the assassination of President Kennedy, were unavoidable. I was in high school when JFK and Russian premier Nikita Khrushchev faced off over nuclear warheads being located in Cuba in the fall of 1962. The name Castro became as synonymous with evil as Osama bin Laden is today. There was a small speaker on the wall in the corner of each classroom, through which we'd hear the latest news reports on the radio. During daily air raid drills, we'd hide under our desks when a siren went off. The announcement would say, "This is a test. This is just a test. In case of a real emergency, go to your designated area," and it would be followed by a series of loud blasts on a horn.

The teacher would say, "OK now, children, remember the procedure. Hats on, heads down, eyes shut." As if our plywood desks and tin hats would have saved us from a nuclear holocaust. I remember wondering how long it would take me to run home if a missile hit Florida. It was a time of national fear, and the first casualty was logic. Some people in our neighborhood tried to build bomb shelters, but with the water table just three feet under the soil, they quickly realized they'd drown before they'd be nuked. The threat of war seemed unreal and almost fun, as though we were being involved in something fantastical, not about to disappear under a giant mushroom cloud.

The following year, JFK was shot. That felt entirely different. The news was so unbelievable and earth-shattering, I remember our teacher broke down as she told us in the schoolyard. Everyone seemed suddenly afraid, paranoid even. Adults cried openly on the street, something I'd never seen before. It was as if the whole of Gainesville had suddenly been jerked awake from its rose-tinted dream by the firing of that bullet. Nothing felt safe or sure any more. The apple-pie sweetness had gone sour.

We were given the day off from school to watch the funeral on television with our families, and I remember sitting on the floor in front of our black-and-white set and watching little John John standing silently by his mother's side at Arlington National Cemetery, while my own mother sat sniffling on the couch. Even my father looked wild-eyed. Man, that was strange.

Everyone remembers where he was when he heard that JFK was shot. I know I always will. Nineteen sixty-three is indelibly marked in the American psyche. But it was momentous for another reason for me. It was the year I met the man who was to become one of the most pivotal to my whole life. His name was Bernie Leadon.

FOUR

Bernie was kinda different. He came from the West Coast—San Diego, California, to be precise—and had this cool-dude air about him. With impossibly curly sandy blond hair, and bell-bottom jeans covered in patches, he looked as if he'd just stepped off a surfboard. The first time I met him, I'd just stepped off a Greyhound bus from Palatka in a button-down shirt, my straight hair slicked to one side, after playing some small gig at a women's club in the swampy flats of eastern Florida. I wasn't yet sixteen years old.

"Are you Don?" he asked, strolling toward me. "Don Felder?"

"Yeah," I replied, a little warily, holding my guitar case to my chest. I'd been expecting my mother to pick me up from the bus station.

"I'm Bernie Leadon," he said with a smile that lit up his whole face. "Your mom said I'd find you here. Do you need a ride?"

He pointed over to a '63 Ford Falcon, brand-new, in light baby blue. Open-mouthed, I nodded.

"I'm new in town," he explained as we pulled away. Looking around, I noticed an acoustic flattop Martin on the back seat. "I went into the music store and asked them for the name of the best guitarist in Gainesville. Someone named Buster gave me yours. I went to your house, but your mom said you were on your way back from a gig. So here I am." Again that grin.

"Oh, OK," I said.

"I'm hoping to put together a band and thought maybe you and I could jam together for a bit," he went on, as I sat silently next to him. "What do you play?"

"Fender Stratocaster," I replied, proudly.

"Anything else?" he asked.

My face fell. "No . . . , not really. Drums, a little. How 'bout you?"

"Acoustic, banjo, mandolin, flattop bluegrass, that sort of thing."

Back at my parents' house, all thoughts of embarrassment temporarily forgotten, I led Bernie up to my room and watched as he pulled out his guitar. I didn't even own an acoustic guitar; I felt I'd sort of graduated past that. If I couldn't plug it in and turn it up, I didn't want it. You didn't see B.B. King playing acoustic, after all. But Bernie just blew me away that afternoon with his amazing flat-picking music. I was dazzled that someone so young could be so unbelievably well versed.

Almost shyly, I pulled out my Fender and played the best I could for him. I think I cobbled together a medley of Chet Atkins, Elvis, and Ventures hits.

"Wow, man, that's great," he said, grinning from ear to ear in open appreciation. "Buster was right. You're good, real good."

Within a week, we'd walked into Lipham Music together and ordered two new guitars—an electric Gretsch for him and an acoustic for me— determined to teach each other everything we knew. Over the next few months, he taught me the finer nuances of country-and-western music, and I taught him rock and roll. Before long, we started putting some songs together, and I felt I'd found a completely new level to rise to. Meeting Bernie was one of the best things that ever happened to me.

Bernie's father was a nuclear physicist who'd been relocated from San Diego. He was to put together one of the largest of all nuclear development research centers, at the University of Florida. Bernie was the oldest of ten children, one of whom was a young guitarist called Tom, who ended up playing with Tommy Petty's new band, Mudcrutch, which was right behind us on the fraternity circuit. Every time I went over to see Bernie, there seemed to be another new baby brother or one on the way, but it didn't seem to matter, because their house was four times the size of mine, with air-conditioning and every modern convenience.

Bernie had already played in several different bluegrass bands in San Diego, including one called the Scottsville Squirrel Barkers with a singer/songwriter and mandolin player named Chris Hillman, who later helped form the Byrds and the Flying Burrito Brothers. The Squirrel Barkers had even had an album released. As well as the talents I already knew about, Bernie was an amazing five-string banjo player—the best I've ever heard. He'd have given Earl Scruggs a run for his money. He'd been playing since he was a kid and was proficient since the age of thirteen. He knew all the best Smoky Mountain songs, and before I knew it, we wound up forming a bluegrass band together, in which I played acoustic guitar and he played banjo, while a friend who worked for the Florida Fish and Game Commission played mandolin.

Inspired, we pieced together another band called the Maundy Quintet, to play the sort of music I was into. We found a singer named Tom Laughon, whose father was a local minister, and a drummer named Wayne "Boomer" Hough. We came up with the name Maundy Quintet because it sounded so English at a time when there was a passion for all things British, especially the Beatles. Boomer's mother bought him an old van to travel to gigs in, on the side of which was painted: PLAYS FOR QUILTING BEES, FUNERALS, AND WILD PARTIES, the same motto as on our business card. We thought we were so cool.

As the Maundy Quintet increased in stature, so the bookings became more and more frequent. I could make us two hundred dollars for a Friday or Saturday night fraternity party or a high school prom, which was probably more than my dad was making in a week. He'd have been really hurt if he'd known, or put it down as a flash in the pan. At least I was keeping busy—and what else was I going to do? Get a job working at Koppers? That wasn't going to happen.

Those frat parties were wild. It was just like *Animal House*, with everyone drunk out of their minds. Near-lethal cocktails of hard liquor were guzzled in alarming quantities and ever more outrageous dares dreamed up. My brother had been in a fraternity briefly, but had stepped out because it was too crazy for him. These boys knew how to party, and we were more than happy to provide the soundtrack to their madness.

Personally, I never had much taste for alcohol. If I did drink, my poison of choice was pop-top beer. I went to a party once where everyone was drinking gin and I tried it, but it tasted like aftershave lotion. I excused myself and went outside to retch violently.

My first attempt at smoking pot was similar. I didn't know anything about marijuana, but someone took me to see a guy who grew his own. In those days, you could buy a quarter of an ounce for five dollars—hence the term "nickel bag."

"What is that?" I asked, looking at the mound of green grass on his kitchen table.

"Try some," my friend said, smiling, and handed me my first joint. I'd never laughed so long or so loud in my life. When the laughter finally subsided, leaving my ribs aching, I was suddenly incredibly hungry. The dealer fetched a jar of peanut butter, and we took a spoonful each, but when it stuck to the roofs of our mouths, we laughed even harder, spitting globules of it all over his kitchen. After that, we listened to some music, and everything sounded really great. I thought, "Oh my God, these guys are geniuses, absolutely brilliant," and it was someone perfectly ordinary, like the Kingston Trio.

Once the fun was over and I was by myself, though, I became paranoid. There was a great deal of propaganda in those days about drug abuse, especially in a university town full of kids. The ads said that marijuana automatically led to heroin and that you'd grow hair on the palms of your hands, go blind, and die. My father would have killed me if he'd known what I was up to, and if he hadn't, my brother—the law student—would have gladly prosecuted me. I didn't get overly involved in drugs for fear of their wrath and of turning my brain to mush.

That summer we managed to book some gigs in Daytona Beach and Fort Lauderdale, which seemed real grown-up. There were dozens of openings for musicians in Daytona during the high season, and we were prepared to do anything for cash, in or out of the Maundy Quintet. I played solo with house bands for people like Tommy Roe and the Romans, and in a band on the Pier for a visiting black singer called Rufus Thomas, who dubbed himself the "world's oldest teenager" and had a big hit at the time called "Walking the Dog."

Nineteen sixty-four was the height of the Beatles' success with "I Want to Hold Your Hand" at the top of the charts. The Fab Four arrived to a hysterical reception in New York and, after appearing on the *Ed Sullivan Show*, took America by storm. The look and sound of the Maundy Quintet remained very English. We mainly performed covers of pop songs like "Louie Louie," by the Kingsmen, the old soul instrumental "Green Onions," or the latest from John, Paul, George, and Ringo. During each set, we'd play at least one of our original numbers, which the audience had to suffer through.

We made many new friends, mostly other musicians also working the Strip in bands like the Nightcrawlers or the Houserockers. Among our new buddies were two brothers named Duane and Gregg Allman, who were about the same age as us and who'd moved to Daytona with their mother from Nashville. Duane was an unbelievably gifted lead guitarist and Gregg had a great soulful voice and played keyboards. They had a killer band, including a bass player and a drummer named Maynard, who was missing two front teeth. They wore their hair really long, all the way down their backs, and Duane had big sideburns, which was a very modern look for the time. They were true hippies, heavily into pot, as was Bernie, although I still didn't care for it much. Their band was initially called the Spotlights and then later the Allman Joys, after the candy.

Bernie and I would play a gig at a teenage bar called the Wedge, where they didn't serve booze, and when we'd finished, we'd go over to the bar on the Pier or to the Martinique on Main Street, where the Allman brothers were playing until 2 A.M., to sink a few beers. On afternoons off, we'd hang out at their mother's house and smoke pot, because our only alternative was to stay in our fleabag hotel on our own. She never seemed to mind her house being filled with her sons' friends and would often cook us all breakfast.

Duane was the first guy I ever saw play slide guitar. I remember watching him placing the smoothed-off neck of a bottle of Budweiser on his finger and sliding it up and down the frets in his mom's living room and being as amazed by what he could do as I had been with Bernie's flattop and banjo. It was yet another level opening up to me. Until then, Bernie had been the most talented musician I knew. Now Duane was surpassing even his high standards. He inspired me to play slide and that summer showed me my first couple of tunings. "Close your eyes and listen to the music, man," Duane told me, as I slid my own longneck Bud top along the strings. "Feel it in your heart, and when your spine tingles, you'll know it's right." I felt like I was getting the best tutorial anyone could have, because he was quite simply a phenomenon.

With my musical maturity came a newfound desire for better and better instruments. I knew that I'd outgrown my Fender by then, and I really wanted a Gibson. When a second-hand Les Paul Custom came into Lipham's, I knew I had to have it. The finish was cracked and the gold was fading, but it was a beautiful guitar. Even Mr. Lipham could see that.

"I'm gonna send this back to Gibson and have them refinish it," he told me, "and when it comes back, I'll sell it for a good price."

"Well, when that guitar comes back, I wanna buy it," I told him. "I'll trade in my Stratocaster, so just put it on my account and I'll pay it off." It was going to cost in the region of $250, which was a huge upgrade.

That summer I worked over at Daytona Beach real hard to earn the money, and when I returned, I asked Mr. Lipham if the Les Paul had come back yet.

"Yes, son," he said, sadly, "it did, and it looked mighty fine. I took it out of its case and put it on the wall and some guy from New York walked right in and offered me a wad of cash. I'm sorry, Don."

I was really upset, especially as I'd waited so long. Mr. Lipham took the charge off my account, but then I ordered a new, red Gibson 355 that looked just like the guitar that Chuck Berry played.

Chuck was totally cool. He'd had a string of hits in 1964 with songs like "Nadine," "You Never Can Tell," and "No Particular Place to Go," and he had already made music industry history by being the first black man singing to a white audience and achieving mainstream success, with songs like "Maybelline" and "Johnny B. Goode." Every red-blooded guitar player in the country wanted to be like Chuck.

That thin-line, hollow-body Gibson took over a year to be built in the factory. I loved it from the moment it arrived. It was the best three hundred dollars I ever spent. You know you've got yourself a good guitar when you pick it up, tune it, and after you've played it for a while, it's still in tune. No matter how good the sound and the action are, if the intonation isn't good, the guitar isn't good. I'd only had it a couple of months when the Maundy Quintet was invited to Miami for an audition at a huge new club called the World, which had two stages. With our matching red guitars, we drove all the way down there from Gainesville in our van. The gig went really well and we thought the World was the best club we'd ever played in. However, when we arrived home and unloaded our stuff, my guitar was missing. Someone must have stolen it from the back of the van while we were loading up. I hadn't even paid for it yet and I didn't have any insurance. I was heartbroken. Worse than that, I was guitarless. Needless to say I had to go back to Lipham's and buy another guitar, a Les Paul off the wall, so I wasn't only paying for the one that was stolen but the new one too.

My life took an upturn when my parents finally bought me a car. Up until then, my friends were all driving around in hot rods, while I still had my bicycle. Dad presented me with a baby blue Simca Aronde P60 as the perfect vehicle for me. It was an old French car, a make I'd never even heard of before. He must have done a deal with someone at work and bought it cheap. It was tremendously ugly and turned heads for all the wrong reasons, but it had four wheels and a running engine, and I was in no position to complain.

Better even than the car, I had a new girlfriend, Sue McVeigh, my first true love. She was sixteen, a freshman in high school, and I was her first real boyfriend. My relationship with Sue came to an abrupt end after a road accident we had on our way to Georgia to get married. Her parents discovered that we were planning to elope and banned her from seeing me again. Either way, I always thought it was divine intervention: I wasn't ready to be married at seventeen. Someone was telling me they had other plans for me, and, with hindsight, I guess they were right.

Teenage entertainment in Florida revolved around music, girls, and the spectacular scenery all around us, which we'd pretty much taken for granted during our blinkered youth. In the summers of the mid-sixties, however, there was more fun to be had than ever before, taking advantage of all three.

Bernie and I were making reasonable money with our bands, almost enough for me to replace the Simca with a '62 Volkswagen Beetle. Dad helped me pay for it, something he felt he ought to do. He was still after me to concentrate on my schoolwork and get a real job, but I felt I was doing all right. I was working, and I had a car and a couple of girlfriends. Life was sweet.

I spent most of my time hanging out with Bernie, Barry Scurran, Tom Laughon, or the Rucker brothers, and I often stayed over with them when Dad and I had one of our frequent fights. Gainesville had its limitations, though, so whenever we could spare the time, we'd drive out to the lake for a change of scene where several of our wealthier friends' families owned second homes. Tom's father had a boat and a house there, and the father of a boy in my class at school owned the local Mercury dealership. Their family house was on the edge of Blue Run, one of the underground springs that feed the river systems in that part of the state. Beautiful fresh water bubbles up and runs off into crystal clear rivers thirty feet deep. They were far too tempting for teenage boys to ignore.

We'd spend whole days swimming or just lying on the dock in the sun. Tom taught me how to water-ski with the added incentive that the lake waters were infested with snakes, alligators, and snapping turtles. If I lost my footing, I had to tread water as calmly as possible and hope the boat would turn around soon to pick me up. The best fun of all, though, was hydroplaning. We'd cram into a low, small boat with a seven-and-a-half-horsepower engine on it and a ski rope attached to the back. Onto that we'd hook up a little wooden board, about two and a half feet long and twelve inches wide. One of us would get into the water and float along behind the boat, wearing a face mask while holding onto the board.

As the boat gathered speed and towed you along with the board, you could put pressure on it to take you down under the water. If you tilted it to one side, you'd literally soar through the water like a bird. When you couldn't hold your breath anymore, you'd aim the board upward and emerge spluttering and gasping for air before going back down again. The water was full of wildlife and you could see as clear as day. There were even manatees down in that part of the Blue Run, gentle seal-like creatures that sailors once mistook for mermaids. The risk with hydroplaning was that at any time you could have been slammed up against a hidden tree root or some other underwater obstacle, but we were young and idiotic and we didn't care.

At night, we'd go frog-gigging in the swamps. With one of us carrying a flashlight, we'd row out on a pole boat to where the frogs were floating on top of the water, croaking their affection to each other for all they were worth. When we shone the high-powered light across the surface of the swamp, all we could see were yellow and red eyes—yellow for frogs, red for alligators. Creeping up on the floating, half-blinded frogs, one of us would yell, "Gig!" and we'd "gig" (spear) the creature with a long pole at the end of which was fixed a three-pronged barb, lifting it, still wriggling, into a basket. Once our basket was full, we'd head back to the shore, pick off the legs and dip them in batter before frying them up on a campfire.

They tasted kinda like fried chicken and were mighty good washed down with a couple of cold beers.

Bernie was dating a girl named Judy Lee, whose family owned a house out at Micanopy, which was on one of our favorite lakes. Bernie and Judy were getting quite serious at a time when I was between girlfriends and was more than a little jealous. One night, after a teen dance gig we played at a local Holiday Inn, Bernie arranged to meet Judy outside the Howard Johnson motel in Gainesville, and she brought her best friend along.

"Hi," she said, waving at me shyly, "I'm Susan Pickersgill. I've heard a lot about you." She smelled of almonds.

"Hi," was all I could manage in reply. I took one look at this sweet little baby-faced angel with straight blonde hair, and I was smitten. Fortunately, she looked at me, with my greased-back hair and cigarettes tucked into the sleeve of my T-shirt, and felt the same way.

Susan came from the right side of the tracks. She was from a long line of Pickersgills, far superior to the Teutonic Felders who rode down the tracks on mules. She was a direct descendant of Mary Pickersgill, who made the original Star-Spangled Banner for Fort McHenry in 1813, which now hangs in the Smithsonian. Best of all, her mother liked me. I was clean-cut and my parents had taught me manners. I was courteous and showed a lot of respect, with my "Yes, ma'am's" and "Thank you, sir's." They were pleased that Susan had found someone like that. If they only knew how few courtesies I showed their daughter in their absence.

Mr. Pickersgill was a well-regarded civil engineer from the Northeast, on a short-term contract to build a veterans' hospital in Gainesville. The project was six months from completion, after which Susan would be returning home to Boston with him and the rest of her family. The clock was ticking against us, but we fell madly, crazily in love.

Susan was a student at P. K. Young, a private high school for the children of the professors and other professionals involved with the university. She and Judy were in the same class. Before long, we became a regular foursome, two couples who went to gigs and hung out together. Bernie and I would drop the girls off and then go smoke pot together in the back of his car in the high school parking lot. I was always terrified one of my teachers would come out and catch us inside his smoke-billowing Ford Falcon. Worse, I feared my father might drive by.

Dad and I were not getting along at all well. We argued at almost every encounter, usually about where my life was heading.

"How long are you gonna go on bumming around, playing guitar, and getting high with your friends?" he'd ask.

"As long as I damn well choose," I'd reply, slamming the screen door behind me in anger. Music had once been the glue that bonded us together, and now it was tearing us apart.

Whenever the atmosphere became too intense, I'd slip away for a couple of days and stay with friends—especially Jim, the DJ at the local radio station, who still lived above the funeral home.

I'd come home after a couple of days and spend my time avoiding Dad. It wasn't any better when Jerry left. He and Marnie married when he turned twenty-one and graduated from law school. I helped him pack his few belongings in the room we'd shared for so many years, and drove them over to the second-story apartment they'd rented in an old house in the next neighborhood.

"Thanks, Don," Jerry said, patting me on the back as I finished unloading the last of his stuff. "Maybe you could try to get along a bit better with Dad now that I'm gone. OK?"

I shook his hand and nodded silently, still in awe of him, even more so now that that he was married and leaving home. I drove straight back to our house, rearranged the bedroom to my liking, and moved in Dad's Voice of Music machine. Standing on a chair, I removed the hundred-watt light bulb from the overhead lamp. Reaching into my pocket, I replaced it with a low-wattage red one I'd bought specially. This was my room now, and I could play my guitar when I liked, as loud as I liked, in a scarlet spotlight just like Jimi Hendrix.

With my brother sorely missed at home as both a steadying influence and a companion, Dad became increasingly frustrated with me. Jerry was respectable. He'd been the model son, and his morals and lifestyle only highlighted my shortcomings ever more sharply. By contrast, I'd taken part in several anti–Vietnam War demonstrations and political rallies, I'd let my hair grow even longer to fit in with the rest of the guys, and my father quite rightly suspected me of being involved with drugs.

My final bust-up with Dad was a long time coming. It had been such an adversarial relationship for so long, something had to give. One day, I was supposed to come home and do some mundane task, like wash the dishes or mow the lawn or take the laundry out and hang it on the line. For some stupid reason, probably because I was too busy playing guitar or smoking dope, I didn't do it. When I eventually came home, my mother gave me flak about it and, peeved, I gave her a bunch of sass right back.

"I don't have to do your damn dishes," I told her. "I'm not your slave."

She stopped and looked at me for a moment, her eyes narrowing. "You just wait till your father comes home," she said, through thin lips.

I went up to my room to sulk and heard Dad arrive home a few hours later. Within minutes, he was at my bedroom door.

"You'll never speak to your mother like that again, you lazy, no-good, long-haired hippie," he yelled as he pulled off his belt. "Why can't you be more like your brother?"

I remember sitting on the bed, trying to protect myself with my hands while he started beating me on the back with the strap of his belt. I'd put up with that goddamn belt my whole life, but for some reason, I suddenly decided I wasn't going to take it anymore.

Jumping up, I clenched my fist and struck Dad as hard as I could across the chin. He staggered back with the force of the blow, hands and belt flailing, and crashed to the floor, landing awkwardly against a bookshelf and a pile of long-playing records. I'll never forget the look on his face. I think he was more stunned than anything. I literally ran out of the bedroom, jumped into my car, and took off before he could grab me. I could hear him all the way through the house as I fled, but I don't know if he was yelling at me or screaming for Mom to help him get to his feet. I left home, vowing never to speak to him again. It was six years before I did.

I moved in with Barry Scurran, the bass player with the Maundy Quintet, who was a sophomore at the university with an apartment in an off-campus housing area. He put me up on his couch for a few days but eventually gave me his spare bedroom, for which I began paying rent. I went back to my parents' house a couple of times when they were at work to retrieve some clothes and some LPs I simply couldn't live without. I didn't leave a note and they had no idea where I was staying.

I finally picked up the phone and called Mom to let her know I was all right.

"Please come home, Don," she pleaded. "I'm . . . , we're . . . , worried about you."

"No, Mom," I replied, flatly. "I'm just not going to come back and do that anymore."

My father made no direct contact but told me, through my mother, that if I wasn't going to live in his house, I was to bring back the car he'd helped me buy. Furious, I drove the Volkswagen home and parked it outside, leaving the keys in the ignition. He knew how much being without a car would cramp my lifestyle. Even more gallingly, he took to driving it himself. I'd see it around town and curse him under my breath.

At least I still had Susan, and the Maundy Quintet was doing well. Bernie, Tom, and I continued to write songs together, although our repertoire mainly featured covers of popular numbers to keep the kids happy. There was never any conflict between us. We got along fine and were guided by what Tom was able to sing. Bernie and Tom were pretty much the driving force, musically, and they wrote the bulk of our original numbers, although I have to admit now that they weren't very good. We thought they were at the time, but they weren't classics. Still, you have to start somewhere.

What I'd always most admired about Bernie was his single-minded determination. If he decided that he was going to learn pedal steel guitar, he'd go and buy one, sit down and learn it so that, within a month or so, he could play it to his satisfaction. He taught me such flexibility and adaptability, to rise to the musical challenge of taking on a completely new instrument and genre. I never mastered pedal steel or mandolin like he did, but I was OK, and without him I'd never even have tried.

Bernie was seriously into the Beatles and English music. George Harrison was his hero. He even wore a Beatles wig at one time and adopted a kind of English accent. He dressed "English" and tried straightening his impossibly curly hair. Then he bought a brown Gretsch Tennessean guitar, the same model Harrison played. Man, he loved that instrument. I admired the Beatles enormously and appreciated how gifted they were, but for me, rhythm and blues had so much more soul. There was a big difference between women crying over B.B. King and girls screaming hysterically at the Beatles at Shea Stadium. I was also smart enough to realize that what the Beatles lacked in emotional drive, they made up for in cool.

When the Hollies came to Gainesville and played a gig at the university, I jumped at the chance to go see them. Distinctive and well respected, the group from Manchester, England, had enjoyed a string of chart hits with songs like "Searchin'," "Just One Look," and "I'm Alive." I pushed my way to the front of the crowd and watched Allan Clarke and Graham Nash singing their latest hit, "Bus Stop," and I was mightily impressed. They looked so different. I took mental notes on their clothes and how they wore their hair. And there was something about Graham Nash's voice that really appealed to me. He not only played well; he looked like he was having fun. When he smiled down at me in the front row, while singing, I couldn't help but smile back.

While Bernie struggled to straighten his hair, I favored the classic pageboy cut, long but curled under at the sides. Still white-blond, I looked more like Brian Jones from the Rolling Stones. As a band, we fully embraced the "flower power" era with its big, blousy sleeves and flared pants. We had some publicity photographs taken of the Maundy Quintet in which we look risible now, especially Boomer Hough, the drummer, with his perfect hair and English-gent double-breasted jacket, his arms folded across his chest. Lord knows what people made of us.

We cut two singles and began a regular circuit tour of Daytona, Tallahassee, Atlanta, New York, Miami, and Lauderdale, often with Susan and Judy in tow, acting as our personal groupies. Susan ferried me everywhere in her MG TD, which her father had bought her. It was a stick shift, and once she got it into fourth gear, she'd put her left foot up on the walnut dash and cruise us around Florida, tired of using the clutch.

That spring, her parents returned to Boston, leaving Susan and her brother Bill behind. Bill was staying on in Gainesville for a few years as a student, and his presence gave Susan and me a few months' respite, until the end of the summer. The family had sold their house, so Susan moved out to Judy Lee's house at Micanopy, about ten miles south of Gainesville. To get there, I had to cross part of Paynes Prairie, a vast area of marsh, wet prairie, and open water, which is now a state reserve and national park. Back in the sixties it was just another unmarked bog.

There was a road called Savannah Boulevard running right through the middle of the bog, with deep culverts on either side. The smart reptiles—the frogs, lizards, snakes, and alligators—climbed up onto the asphalt each night to soak up the warmth from the heat of the day. Every time I visited Susan, on Barry's motorcycle, I'd have to ride for about three miles with my feet up on the handlebars, in case I ran over a snake and it hit the wheel and rode up my leg. It felt like a medieval test—"Make it through this, young knight, and you can win the fair damsel."

That summer, we opened for a band called the Cyrkle, who had a number-two hit by Paul Simon called "Red Rubber Ball." They even gained a coveted spot on the Beatles' final U.S. tour. Their manager liked us and took us to New York to play a few club gigs, but a couple of the guys grew homesick and nothing more came of it, so Bernie and I went back to Daytona Beach, gigging around. Susan and Judy joined us when they could. One night, I had a big fight with Susan over something stupid and she stormed off. I think she wanted me to pay more attention to her and I was far too busy having fun and getting high. When we finished our gig, Bernie and I went over and watched The Allman Joys as usual, and afterward we smoked some pot.

"Hey, I'm starving, man," I told Duane and Gregg, with a sudden pang of the munchies. "Let's go get something to eat." We found a diner that was open at 4 A.M., and the four of us sat in a booth by the window, drinking coffee, eating doughnuts, smoking cigarettes, and feeling pretty mellow with the sun coming up on the horizon.

Unbeknownst to me, Susan had been hunting for me all over Daytona Beach with Judy, hoping to patch things up. The two of them finally walked into this diner and saw us sitting there. All they could see of Duane and Gregg was the back of their heads, each with beautiful, long, silky hair. Assuming the worst, Susan ran out, crying.

Judy, furious, marched up to confront us. "Hey," she yelled at Bernie, "what the hell do you think you're doing with these two girls?"

Gregg and Duane looked up at her in surprise. As soon as she saw their beards and moustaches, she realized their mistake. Man, we laughed till we cried.

Just when things seemed to be going so well with the band, my personal life, and my musical ambitions, Bernie dropped a bombshell. He'd been dissatisfied for a while, wishing for greater success, and still wasn't getting along with his family. Like my parents, they were often nagging him about what he was planning to do with his life, and wanted him to pursue an academic career. Bernie was upset that they weren't more supportive.

"There's nothing here, musically, man," he'd complain. "New York or California's where it's at, and I'm never gonna live in New York. I hate it. One of these days I'm gonna blow, and just go back to California and make some real music."

He'd been saying it for so long, I'd almost come to ignore it. Then, one day, he announced that he was leaving.

"Come with me, Don," he urged, his eyes bright. "California has great weather, great women, and everything's really happening there. It's where my roots are. We could start up a band together and get something good going."

I shook my head. "Gainesville might have little to offer, but it's all I've ever known," I told him. Truth was, I was scared to leave. I'd hated New York too. By contrast, California seemed faraway, alien, and frightening, like moving to the other side of the world. All the magazine articles and television program I'd seen implied it was a sin state, where people "turned on, tuned in, and dropped out." Drug abuse was rife, and not just pot. LSD and other hallucinogens were all the rage, and anything went, sexually. I was still a naïve young teenager with a rather old-fashioned set of moral values, despite what my father thought. I knew the West Coast wasn't for me. Not yet, anyway.

Coming from poverty had also made me inherently cautious. I needed certainty, a surefire scheme to make money and pay the rent. It felt so scary to head off somewhere unknown with no offers of work and no solid opportunities identified. Bernie didn't really know anyone in Los Angeles and had few music contacts there anymore. In my worst night-mares, I imagined him falling in with drug dealers and pimps and never playing banjo again. However, he was determined to make a go of it, and there was nothing I could say to make him change his mind.

The day he left, I went over to his parents' house and helped him load up his car.

"I wish you were coming with me, buddy," he said, giving me a hug.

"I know," I said, feeling unnervingly close to tears.

He flashed me that huge grin of his and patted me warmly on the back. "I'll call you just as soon as I'm settled. If things work out, then maybe you could come out and join me?"

"Sure," I lied. "As soon as you're settled."

He climbed into the driver's seat of his Ford Falcon and turned the key in the ignition. The engine fired up into life with a big blue cloud of smoke from the exhaust. The car was loaded to the roof with instruments and clothes and equipment. Only the front passenger seat was empty. Bernie was leaving. He was driving to California to follow his musical dream. As I waved him off and watched his car disappear down the dusty trail west, it took all my nerve not to chase after him and jump into that empty seat.

FIVE

Summer ended, and with it my dream—Susan had to return to Boston. We were still madly in love, but part of her desperately wanted to go home. She missed the northern weather, the myriad colors of fall, and the long, cold winters. She'd also enrolled at a respected girls' college and was looking forward to starting her next academic phase. In that respect, we couldn't have been more different.

When she left town, in the front seat of her brother Bill's car, I thought I'd die, it hurt so bad. In the space of a couple of months, I'd lost my first true love and my best friend, and I had cut off all communication with my parents. I was barely able to grasp that so much bad stuff was happening to me at once.

I'd rarely been out of Florida—only a few childhood car trips to Oklahoma and Washington and to a couple of gigs in New York—but now I traveled to Boston whenever I could, catching a bus or hitching a ride with Bill whenever he was going home. Once, I even scraped together enough money to fly there. It was my first time in an airplane, a DC-3 tail-dragger, and it seemed like a miracle to be flying over America instead of driving. Susan and I had a great time in Massachusetts, picking up where we'd left off, until I had to fly home again. This time, the parting seemed even harder.

Alone again in Gainesville, everything changed. I was eighteen years old and I felt bereft. The Maundy Quintet disbanded when Tom Long went off to college, leaving me with a drummer and Barry, the bass player. For the first time in many years, I had no band and was, for a while, completely without direction.

My relationship with Susan was under incredible strain because of the distance between us, and—after several months of commuting back and forth, trying to keep it going—I realized it was impossible.

"This isn't going to work," I told her, long distance. "Not unless one of us is prepared to move to where the other one lives, and that ain't gonna happen." I think I broke her heart and mine too, but I knew it couldn't last. When I hung up the phone, I didn't think I'd ever see or hear from her again.

I was still teaching kids how to play guitar, and I had a couple of other jobs, but I couldn't decide if I should go back to school or not. My parents and Jerry were pushing me to go to college and learn a profession, but I felt that would be a betrayal of all I'd tried to achieve. Whatever I decided, I knew I desperately needed to play music, which was the only thing I felt remotely good at.

A guy named Paul Hillis, who'd also worked at Lipham's as a music teacher, had just returned from two years in Boston at the Berklee College of Music. He was six years older than me, an excellent guitar player fluent in jazz techniques. When he came back, I couldn't wait to hear him play, and see what he'd learned, but, to my surprise, he'd switched instruments. "Guitar is so limiting," he told me, dismissively. He claimed it was easier to compose, harmonize, and understand theory on a piano.

He opened up the Paul Hillis School of Music in Gainesville, and I signed up to learn jazz theory and composition from him, in exchange for teaching his incoming guitar students. For each hour I'd do for him, he'd give me an hour of his time. In less than six months I learned what Berklee College of Music had taught him in two and a half years. I soaked up every scrap of information.

Through the fraternity circuit and friends in the music business, a young band called Flow, based in Ocala, approached me. "Join us," they said. "We've heard the Maundy Quintet and we know your work. We need a strong lead guitarist." There were three in the band—Mike Barnett, the drummer, John Winter, who played keyboards and soprano sax, and Chuck Newcomb, who sang and played bass.

Flow was, without doubt, what my father would have called a hippie band. They specialized in free-form jazz-rock and were heavily into pot. I had to travel down to Ocala to practice with them, and at two in the afternoon they'd still be in bed, stoned, or recovering from the night before. Their rental house was filthy, with a sink full of dirty dishes that no one ever seemed to wash. They were complete stoners, but they were good musicians, too, and when we were together, we played really well. They had a genuine commitment to music, not to great songwriting or marketing like the Beatles, but a dedication to writing songs in a pop-rock genre using the framework of improvisation that jazz players use—a free flow of creative energy, they called it.

We'd start off singing a couple of verses and a chorus and then have a free-form solo section in the middle that could be anywhere from a minute to five minutes long, depending on how well it was going. Winding down, we'd sing a verse and a chorus, and that would be that. It was perfect tripping music but with a more modern sound than a jazz band. It was really quite innovative for its time, and the best part was that every time you played, you were thrown naked out onto the floor, figuratively speaking.

Two of their friends were the road managers for a successful band called the Young Rascals, who had a big hit with a song called "Good Lovin'" and had appeared on the *Ed Sullivan Show*. They'd promised to come down from New York and listen to Flow play once we felt we were ready. I was brought in to help sharpen up their act. In return, I got to latch on to this incredible spark of creativity: Every night, every time I played, I was given a chance to improvise. Using all that Paul Hillis had been teaching me about melodic phrasing, I learned how to play spontaneously and think freely, without inhibitions or fear. At first it was very scary, but when I'd been thrown out there often enough, I began to become comfortable with the tools I had. Somebody would play a groove and I'd just start playing stuff, some of which would be OK and some of which would be great. There was a constant creative stream. The freer I became, the more confidence I gained. It helped me amazingly in my ability to write and come up with parts for songs later in life.

With Susan and Bernie gone and nobody else to take their place, I could easily have gone off the rails, especially with the band smoking so much pot. Fortunately, for some reason I never fully understood, I didn't have an addictive personality. I enjoyed the occasional joint, of course, but I'd always stop myself at the point where I felt like I was losing control. I'd had a couple of paranoid experiences, and I'd seen heroin addicts lying on the streets in New York. As far as I could see, pot smoking just made my fellow band members unmotivated and lethargic. I don't think any of them ever held a steady job. Worse than that, the whole drug thing still scared the shit out of me. Some rock and roller I was cut out to be!

I spent a lot of time moping around, missing Susan and feeling sorry for myself. I dated a couple of girls, but nothing ever sparked like Susan and me. One girl, who went by the unusual name of Season Hubley, came from New York to Gainesville to visit friends on the campus. She was the first girl since Susan that I really liked, and I thought we might have had something going, but she didn't seem very interested in me. She was just passing through. Then Susan's brother Bill introduced me to Jan Booty, his girlfriend's roommate. Jan, the daughter of a diplomat, was more permanent, studying art in Gainesville. She was very creative, and I liked that about her. We ended up living together for a while, sharing a house with a couple, Barry and Patti, and Jan's two pet dogs, Rhythm and Blues.

It was while I was living with Jan that my brother, Jerry, came to call.

I'd had little contact with him since he'd gotten married. He was working in a small law firm in Gainesville, and we didn't have much in common. Now that I was living immorally, however, he felt obliged to come and tell me what he thought of me. I always suspected that Dad put him up to it.

"What the hell are you doing with your life, Don?" he asked me, his face pinched. In his suit and tie, he seemed far older than his twenty-five years. "Because it looks to me like you're just wasting it." Before I could respond, he let rip about how everything I was doing was wrong: My views on the Vietnam War were unpatriotic; my associations with protestors, musicians, and drug users were questionable; my morals and values were all screwed up; and I was headed for disaster. He thought I was a lost cause, and he let me know it.

We got into an intense argument, and I said many things I knew I was going to regret. "You're worse than Dad," I berated him. "You've been toe-ing the line for so long, you have no idea what real life's all about. What are you gonna do next, Jerry, take your belt off and whip me?"

He eventually walked away in disgust, but not before we'd both said our piece. As I watched him go, I doubted if we'd ever speak again. Everyone I loved, it seemed, eventually walked away from me.

Music lifted me from the sadness that was my life. With the dual influences of Flow and Barry, the husband of the couple Jan and I shared a house with, I became interested in jazz for the first time. Barry came from New York and was addicted to jazz, which he seemed to play endlessly. Because of him, I began listening to it more closely, studying jazz guitar, learning specific solos and acquiring a taste for people like Sonny Rollins and Django Reinhardt. I soon began to view the guitar differently. Country, rock and roll, and bluegrass sounded pretty archaic compared with something much more sophisticated and intellectual. Having been exposed to so much theory with Paul, jazz suddenly made sense.

One Friday morning, I was listening to Mel Bay while Barry read aloud from the *Village Voice*, which he got by mail from New York, as it was next to impossible to buy in Gainesville.

"Oh, my God," Barry said, sitting up suddenly. "Miles Davis is playing at the Village Gate tomorrow night."

I'd heard of Miles Davis, but I'd never heard anyone play live jazz except at the Holiday Inn cocktail lounge, and then just movie themes. "Miles Davis?" I asked, innocently.

"Only one of the best jazz musicians in the world!" Barry cried incredulously. Staring at me in silence for a moment, he added authoritatively: "Pack a bag. We're going."

There was no arguing with him, so we grabbed some clean T-shirts and a toothbrush each, filled up his VW with gas, and took off. We drove nonstop, taking turns sleeping. The journey took more than sixteen hours. We arrived in Manhattan, found some seedy little nineteen-dollar-a-night hotel, took a shower, put on clean T-shirts, and hopped a cab to Greenwich Village. We walked into the Village Gate and sat down near the front. About twenty minutes later, the band we'd been reading about the morning before in Gainesville was standing right in front of us on the stage.

Those musicians proceeded to shred me. The finesse and the improvisation and the freedom in their art was unbelievable, with numbers like "Bitches Brew." It was one of the most incredible lineups Miles Davis ever had—him on horn, seventeen-year-old Tony Williams on drums, Herbie Hancock on piano, Wayne Shorter on tenor sax, and Ron Carter on bass.

Halfway through their second set, Miles Davis took a break and sat down at a table by the restrooms to have a beer. There were no dressing rooms and nowhere else for him to escape to. Determined to go over and tell him how much I liked the way he played, I started walking toward him with that intention. When I was just a few paces away, he looked up at me with these intense eyes, as if to say, "Come near me, boy, and I'll eat you alive," so I just kept walking right past him and into the men's room.

Inside, I stared at myself in the cracked mirror and whipped up my courage. "I gotta go say it, I gotta go say it," I repeated like a mantra, and out I came, determined to shake his hand like I had with B.B. King, but of course, by then, he was gone.

That gig was probably one of the most formative experiences of my life. B.B. King had blown me away with his rhythm and blues, but this was undoubtedly my strongest jazz influence, an event that showed me what real musicians could do. The dexterity, ability, and dynamics were from another, altogether more sophisticated, genre. This was yet another level for me, a challenge to confront at a time when I was already into jazz in a big way and playing it with Flow. I hardly slept a wink that night in the hotel for replaying the gig over and over in my head, and Barry and I drove home in reverential silence the following morning.

Not long afterward, I was lying in bed with Jan one sunny summer afternoon, watching the curtains billowing in the breeze, when a song came on the radio. Sitting up, straining to listen, I recognized the voice instantly. The presenter announced the number as "For What It's Worth," by Buffalo Springfield, but I knew better. The voice I'd heard belonged to Stephen Stills, the runaway kid with the military haircut who'd played in the Continentals.

"Wow!" I thought, lying back on the pillow with a smile. "He struck oil after all! That's really cool. Maybe I could do something like that one day."

Every time I heard that song, which became an anthem for the country's most turbulent decade of young people railing against the establishment, I thought of Stephen and smiled. However, unlike him and Bernie, I wasn't yet driven enough about my music to pursue it at the expense of everything else.

By the fall of 1968, Flow was ready for its showcase concert in New York. John Calagna and Andy Leo, the road managers, had come down to Florida to hear us and liked what they heard. They felt they'd "discovered" the band, through their friendship with Mike and John, and could promote us through their relationship with the Young Rascals. They were right, and they were certainly the best access we'd had since the Cyrkle to someone famous.

The gig was to be at a small club in Manhattan called the Fillmore East. The Allman brothers had played there just before us. They were steaming ahead of us in terms of success. Duane had been doing some impressive session work, they'd recorded an album in L.A., abandoning the name the Allman Joys in favor of the Hourglass, but they still kept in contact through friends in Daytona and Gainesville and we wished each other well.

We drove up from Florida in a van, with borrowed equipment from the Young Rascals, and set up on the stage. The road managers had invited some record company executives along to hear us play. Among them was Creed Taylor, a legend in the business, who'd worked with Stan Getz and had just produced the Quincy Jones album *Walking in Space*, a phenomenal creation. He was the man.

We were one of three bands playing to around five hundred people that night, in a club that was relatively new and unheard of. I knew Hendrix had once played there, and I'd seen Paul Butterfield and a monster blues-guitar player named Buzzy Feiten in the past, so I was impressed enough to know this was for real. Fortunately, we played really well that night, and when the gig was over, Creed Taylor came backstage to see us.

Creed was middle-aged, wore a suede jacket with patches on the sleeves, and exuded calm. "Okay, guys, I liked what I heard tonight. You were great," he told us. "I'm prepared to offer you a recording contract worth five thousand dollars. What do you say?"

It was the most money we'd ever made. We couldn't believe our luck. After a hasty band meeting with the road managers, we accepted immediately and signed on the line the next day. Despite all my reservations about leaving Gainesville, here I was, a few months later, in the Big Apple with a record deal. New York was somehow less scary than California. I'd been here a couple of times before. I could drive home in less than twenty-four hours if I wanted to, and anyway, I was too excited about the future to be frightened anymore.

Our five-thousand-dollar advance lasted less than a month. We put a deposit on a Dodge delivery van—I was the only one with a good enough credit rating to take on the payments—a warm coat each, and a couple of microphones for our PA system. The rest went on grass, food, rolled cigarettes, and Jack Daniel's.

Signed up with Creed Taylor Incorporated (CTI), we found a small apartment on Horatio Street on the Lower West Side. It was in the meat-packing district and not a particularly good place to be in those days. I was nearly mugged at knifepoint, and a friend who came to stay was hit in the back of the head with a wooden plank by another robber.

The road managers helped us with our writing and rehearsing, and they organized a few gigs around town to keep us working. The Young Rascals became our sponsors. They'd had another couple of hits after "Groovin'" and "A Girl Like You," and they gave us some of their old in-struments and loaned us a PA so we could play clubs. There was a set of drums from Dino Danelli and a Hammond B3 keyboard from Felix Cava-liere, and Gene Cornish gave me one of his guitars, a big Gibson electric.

Living in New York as part of a band with a record deal was all very well, but my excitement was tempered by the fact that my fellow musi-cians were lethargic and excessively drug-oriented.

I'd always been the motivator before, booking the gigs and making the contacts; I was as much a manager as a player. But this band's contact was through Mike and John, not me, and the rest of the guys had the idea that they didn't have to do very much, because the road managers were going to make them stars. I felt kind of helpless, unable to do anything about the situation. We were living in a crappy apartment with no money, and none of them ever did anything except play music. Jan and I had split up, because of the distance, and I felt increasingly lonely and miserable.

My frustration was only highlighted whenever Bernie came to town. He and I had stayed in touch, and he was doing very well for himself. When he'd first moved back to California, he'd joined a folk-rock band called Hearts & Flowers as a banjo and guitar player and performed on their second album. Through his old friend Chris Hillman, he met Gene Clark from the Byrds and the legendary banjo player Doug Dillard. Bernie also had helped found the band Dillard & Clark, until he joined the Corvettes, Linda Ronstadt's backup band for the tour to promote her debut solo album after leaving the Stone Poneys, *Hand Sown . . . Home Grown.*

"You gotta come back west with me. That's where it's all happening, man," Bernie would say every time I saw him. We'd meet backstage at whichever gig he was playing, jam a little, and have a few beers. "I've made some great contacts, and I'm sure I can get you work."

"Thanks, Bernie," I'd say stoically, "but I'm gonna hang around here first and see what happens with Flow. We have a record deal now, and I'd be crazy not to see it through. Besides, I don't have any money, or even a car. How am I supposed to get around in L.A. without wheels?"

When it finally came time for Flow to go into the recording studio and cut its first album, we were all pretty scared. Creed Taylor used a studio over in Englewood Cliffs, New Jersey. The room we used was round and was supposed to have a natural ambience. It was owned and run by Rudy Van Gelder, a German optometrist by trade, who'd become a recording engineer with impeccable credentials. He'd worked with Miles Davis, John Coltrane, and Thelonious Monk, and was said to be responsible for the Blue Note sound. He had top-notch Neumann microphones and state-of-the-art eight-track recording equipment with mixing consoles and equalizers. He sat in his recording booth manning the controls like some mad scientist. He literally wore white gloves to make his very antiseptic, high-fidelity recordings.

One day, Andy and John took us into Atlantic Studios and allowed us to listen in while the Young Rascals were cutting their latest single. We knew them well, and the atmosphere was relaxed. They were on the last take by the time we arrived, and we stood at the edges of the studio and listened to them record "It's a Beautiful Morning." I liked it immediately. It had bongos and sounded really cool. I wondered if it would be a hit.

When it was our turn to set up, in the Englewood Cliffs studio, we were very edgy. It was our first real recording, and we felt under immense pressure in this clinical environment with a man in a white lab coat and the latest high-tech equipment all around us. Creed came in, sat down in the control room, looking for all the world as though he were going to pull out a pipe and smoke it, but he didn't say a word. There was no musical direction, nothing.

I realized suddenly, and with considerable discomfort, that it wasn't Creed Taylor or Rudy Van Gelder who made all those legendary recordings, it was the artists themselves. I wasn't the only one with butterflies in my stomach. We began to play, but you could hear and feel that it was a very forced performance. In fact, it was a train wreck, and there was nothing any of us could do to pull it back from the abyss.

The album was called *Flow* and the cover featured a stencil of the band's name with soapsuds dripping from it. We hated it. We thought it looked like an ad for laundry detergent. I was proud of the album because it was my first, but I was also hugely disappointed. I'd expected to take it out of the sleeve, put it on the turntable, and be blown away like I was with Quincy Jones's record. I'd used the same recording techniques, engineer, and producer. I just couldn't understand why my record didn't affect me in the same spine-tingling way. There was further disappointment. We had a fair amount of airplay around New York, but we weren't "AM-oriented," and a lot of radio stations wouldn't play us because of our long jazz solos. Word came back that we were all right, but we weren't the Young Rascals. We might have looked and sounded a bit like them, but we were a marketing nightmare because there was no obvious slot for us. We picked up an eclectic following of jazz buffs instead of the mainstream fans that were going to the clubs and buying records.

There was no talk of a follow-up album, and suddenly there were longer and longer periods without work. Even though we'd had some success, drugs, not music, had motivated it. Our managers were frustrated. They'd pretty much explored all the limited avenues they had access to. When we did get some gigs, we wound up having to do mostly cover versions of other people's songs to pay the bills. We tried to slip a few of our original numbers into the set, hoping that people would understand what we were about, and some seemed to like it, but most just wanted to dance.

I realized we had to get out of New York and into an environment that would be more conducive to songwriting and taking the band to the next level. Mike had driven to Poughkeepsie to see a friend the week before and had spotted a For Rent sign at the side of the road in a little town called Dover Plains. He scrawled down the telephone number. After speaking to the owner and realizing that we could afford the rental, we piled onto packing quilts in the back of our Dodge van and drove north. Bob Dylan's backup group, the Band, had relocated to a modern pink house in West Saugerties in the Catskills and recorded their first album, *Music from the Big Pink*. The house we found wasn't pink. It was white, stood on three hundred fifty acres, and looked like something out of *Gone with the Wind*. It cost us $150 a month—far less than the price of our crummy New York apartment.

The house was huge. It had four white-painted Doric columns at the door, which opened onto an impressive hallway and grand staircase. There were a library, five fireplaces, and a butler's pantry. The attic had been converted into a ballroom, complete with bandstand, for parties. Much of the land had been left wild, although some must have been used to grow market produce at one time, because all that grew on it now, in great abundance, was zucchini. Impoverished and permanently hungry, we had scrambled zucchini for breakfast, zucchini sandwiches for lunch, and baked zucchini with cheese for supper.

We lived in that house for eighteen months, becoming poorer and poorer by the month. Our gigs in New York declined sharply, and half the time the rest of the band couldn't be bothered to make the three-hour round trip to the city for a lousy hundred bucks. We were often without transportation. If someone took the van to go and score some drugs or see a girlfriend, the rest of us would be stranded.

One day, Chuck Newcomb and I were in the house when the van was gone, and we ran out of tobacco. Both heavy smokers, we had no choice but to walk into town to buy some. We set off for Dover Plains, not even bothering to hitchhike, because we knew from experience that few people in the neighborhood would pick up a couple of long-haired hippies with beards. The local sheriff drove past Chuck and me as we strolled into town, stopped his patrol car, reversed, and picked us up. We were arrested and charged with walking on the wrong side of the road. The fine was twenty-five dollars.

The sheriff eventually drove us back to the house, where our surprised fellow band members saw the patrol car pull up in the driveway and quickly ran round and hid all the drugs. John Winter came wandering out of the house with a flute in his hand. "What's going on?" he asked.

The sheriff gave little explanation before he and his officers undertook a painstaking search of the house. It took some time, and when he emerged, his face was a picture of disappointment that he hadn't found bathtubs full of LSD. Trying to defuse the situation, which was now uncomfortably tense, I turned to John and said, "Hey, why don't you play something for the officer to send him on his way."

"Huh?" John asked, looking decidedly nonplussed.

"Your flute," I said, pointing to the instrument in his hand. "Why don't you play something to show there are no hard feelings?"

John shook his head. "No, not now. My lips don't feel right, man. I can't play a thing."

"Oh, come on," I urged, sensing his reluctance and the sheriff's unhappiness. "Just a few notes."

"Yeah, come on," the sheriff encouraged him. "You claim you're musicians. Let's hear you play."

John stood his ground. "No," he said, firmly. "I'm sorry. I'm not in the mood."

By the time the sheriff and his men left, Chuck and I were exhausted and upset from our day's exertions. All we had to look forward to was a zucchini omelet and a miserable night emptying the ashtrays for butts. Irritable, I bumped into John in the hallway and turned on him. "If you'd played your damn flute for the sheriff, none of this might have happened," I said.

John shrugged his shoulders. "I couldn't, man," he explained, pointing to a wad of something in the end of it. "That's where we shoved all the dope."

SIX

n **August 1969,** we heard through the hippie network that a big music festival was being held on a six-hundred-acre dairy farm not far from Dover Plains. Billed as "Three days of peace and love," it was to be held at a place called Bethel, near Woodstock.

"Hey, we should go to this," I suggested to my roommates one morning, after reading about it in a pamphlet someone had stuck under the windshield wiper of the van. "Just about everyone we know will be there. There's bound to be some guys coming up from New York and maybe even Florida. The lineup's incredible—Janis Joplin, the Band, the Who, Jefferson Airplane, Joe Cocker, the Grateful Dead. Even Hendrix is playing."

"Awesome," replied Mike. "OK. You organize it."

Buried in the list of bands, I spotted Crosby, Stills & Nash, whose debut album, *Suite: Judy Blue Eyes*, was fast climbing the charts. Something told me that the life path of young Stephen Stills was going to keep cross-ing mine.

I was right about everybody coming to Bethel—half a million people, actually. When we arrived, in an old Chevy Suburban with a gang of friends from New York, it seemed like everyone was trying to get through the same six-foot-wide gate we were aiming for. Among those in our con-voy was Season Hubley, the cute girl I'd fallen for when she came to Gainesville two years earlier. Sadly for me, she was with someone else, and wanting her to be with me instead of him marred my entire experi-ence of the three-day festival.

I do remember that it rained a lot. There was an incredible storm, which came rolling in from the east in great billowing clouds. The high winds nearly blew down the precarious speaker towers. We slept in sleep-ing bags in the Chevy, listening to the torrential rain drumming on the roof. Apart from when the storm was at its height, and all the electronics onstage had to be covered in plastic to keep them from shorting out, the music was nonstop. We'd lie in the back of the car, stoned out of our heads, waiting for the announcements for who was on next.

"Oh, man, I gotta see this," I'd say and drag myself up, out of the car, into the rain. Sliding down the slippery hill toward the stage, I'd listen to Santana, Hendrix, or Alvin Lee playing until my ears felt like they were bleeding.

It was a mudfest, absolutely horrible, cold and wet. The sticky clay squelched up between your toes and found its way into every pore and crevice, but nobody seemed to care. Along with thousands of other peo-ple, I'd stand in the driving rain, swaying in time to the music, before com-ing back to towel myself off and steam up the car windows until the caked mud finally dried. Woodstock was certainly an experience.

Back in Dover Plains after the festival, life seemed somehow harder to bear. I'd known Stephen Stills as a kid, and there he'd been at four in the morning, on the same stage as some of the rock-and-roll greats, bang-ing it out with the likes of Graham Nash, who I'd been so in awe of when he came to Gainesville with the Hollies. It was only the second time

Crosby, Stills & Nash had played live together, and they were steaming. Stephen sat up on a stool in a blue-and-white poncho and sang with that distinctively gravelly voice of his. It was so groovy. I wanted to be up there alongside him more than anything in the world.

Instead, I was bumming around some big old house in the sticks with a bunch of potheads, trying to salvage a situation I knew was fast becoming untenable. I felt completely isolated, physically and musically. We were miles from anywhere and there were no girls or friends outside the band. Winter was coming and we were broke. Nobody seemed to understand that we were going to freeze to death in that huge, heatless house unless we did something about it.

Winter came and, with it, the snow. It was like nothing I'd ever seen in my life. We'd had sprinklings in Boston and New York, but this was so deep it banked up against the front door, soft and fine like powder. It smelled of steel. To begin with, it was fun, having snowball fights and fooling around. Once the novelty had worn off, however, the snow brought further isolation to an already strained situation. Unable to escape, we were trapped inside together, day in, day out, and the tensions between us became less easy to hide. Those bitter few months reminded me of my final year in my parents' home, and I was sorry for the bad feeling I'd created. One day that winter I sat down at a desk I'd built out of old lumber that was lying around in the yard. Taking a pen and paper, I wrote my mother a letter, telling her where I was and that I was OK. "Thank you for all the years you raised me under harsh conditions," I said, "and for all you taught me. Only now am I beginning to appreciate what a good mother you were." I even thanked her for dragging me to church by my ear. I sent the letter off, with my address on the envelope. It was my first contact with my parents in two years, and a letter came back by return mail.

"Dear Don," she wrote. "How wonderful to hear from you. I've been worried sick. . . ." Thus began a correspondence that continued with her for many years. My father never wrote a word.

•　　•　　•

I began to realize that my dreams of musical stardom were probably pie in the sky. It was the post-Vietnam "Me Decade," but things certainly weren't happening for me.

Our only regular gig was at Goddard College in Plainfield, Vermont, a progressive liberal arts place, a few hundred miles north. We saw Carlos Santana playing "Black Magic Woman" there, a big hit at the time. Arlo Guthrie was a music student at the college and they had a gamelan band, an Indonesian percussion orchestra. Driving up to Goddard one day on the way to another gig, I succumbed to a sudden compelling urge. Pulling the van over at a pay phone, I fumbled for some change and dialed the number of Susan's family home in Boston, memorized for all time.

"Hey, Mrs. Pickersgill, it's Don, Don Felder from Gainesville. Is Susan there?"

"Hello, Don. My, it's been a while. No, dear, she doesn't live here anymore. She's found a place of her own. Would you like her number?"

Susan was very surprised to hear from me. It had been eighteen months since we'd last seen each other. She'd just broken up with her latest boyfriend, a singer/guitarist, and was working as a secretary at the Harvard History Research Center. We chatted until my money ran out, and I told her I'd call again. A week later, I did, then again the week after that. It felt good to talk to someone who wasn't stoned out of their mind all the time. She had a good job and her own apartment, something I couldn't possibly have afforded. I was impressed.

A couple of weeks later, Susan told me she'd be staying at her sister's house in Scituate, on Cape Cod, babysitting. "Do you wanna come out?" she asked. "We could get to know each other again." Looking around me at the mess of a life I was living in, I jumped at the chance. By the end of the weekend on that beautiful Atlantic shore, she and I realized how much we still loved each other. It felt like coming home.

For the next couple of months, Susan and I commuted back and forth between Boston and Dover Plains every weekend, making up for lost time. To begin with, she was enamored of the bohemian life I was leading, living in this old colonial mansion with a band that had just cut a record, existing on a diet of zucchini sandwiches. But after a while, the veneer wore off, and she could see all the ugliness underneath, especially with the drug abuse. When Jimi Hendrix and Janis Joplin died separate drug-related deaths that fall, I felt as I had when JFK had been killed—shocked and a little afraid. I'd seen both of them perform at Woodstock less than a year earlier. Now they were gone, cold in their graves, and their future promise had died with them. Through Susan's eyes, I came to have a new and even unhappier appreciation of where my life was heading unless I broke away from these influences. I knew it was only a matter of time before Flow and I parted company.

"Come to Boston," Susan urged. "You can move into my apartment and look for a job. There's bound to be some session work or a band that needs a guitarist."

I knew she was right, but it took me a couple of weeks to get up the courage. After all, wasn't I leaving our Woodstock dream behind? Hadn't I told Bernie this was probably the best chance we had at success? Where had it all gone wrong? When the dirt, apathy, and lethargy finally became too much, I called up Creed Taylor.

"Hey, Creed, it's Don Felder, of Flow," I said. "I just want to tell you that I've decided to quit the band. It's not really working for me, and I need to leave."

Creed didn't seem at all surprised and said he understood. "Where are you headed?" he asked.

"Boston," I said. "My girlfriend works at Harvard."

"Great," he replied. "Well, listen, I know some people in Boston. In fact, I'm on the board at the Berklee College of Music. If you want, I'll call them and see if I can get you in."

I was both surprised by and grateful for his kindness. "Oh, OK," I said. "Only I hadn't thought about going back to studying right now. I really need to make some money."

Creed laughed. "I didn't mean as a student, Don. I meant as a teacher. You have a great deal you could offer, you know."

Despite his apparent confidence in me, I wasn't quite ready to shave off my beard, cut my hair, and become part of the Boston teaching establishment. "Thanks anyway," I said, smiling inwardly at the thought of wearing corduroy and tweeds and telling kids how to play guitar. "I'll keep your offer in mind, but first I think I want to try and find another band."

My fellow musicians were not at all happy with my decision to leave. They saw it as a sellout. "What do you mean, you're leaving?" Mike gasped, when I told him. "We're just about to make it to the big time."

"You think so?" I asked, scathingly, looking around at the mess of a house we shared. Nobody had done any serious playing or songwriting in months. "Or are we just on the brink of almost getting ready to start thinking about maybe writing some songs for possibly another album? Get real, Mike, this ain't gonna happen."

The band's unhappiness quickly became focused around their only means of transport. "If you go, you're leaving that damn van here," John told me. "We're not going to be stuck out here without any wheels."

"Yeah," said Chuck, turning on me in the kitchen, "and you can leave that guitar Gene gave you as well."

"I'm not leaving the van if it's still registered in my name," I told him adamantly, backing away. "If you guys default on the payments, I'll have a bad credit rating for the rest of my life."

To my horror, Chuck lunged at me, but Mike pulled him off. "Hey, man, let's not get crazy here," he yelled. "We can work this out."

With far more rancor than was necessary, the paperwork for the van was eventually signed over to Andy Leo, and I was permitted to leave. I packed my things and walked out of that house, past the rest of the band standing silently on the front porch watching me. They'd agreed I could drive the van as far as Boston to offload my stuff, but Chuck, accompanying me as insurance, would drive it home. I looked back as we pulled out of the sweeping gravel drive and wished the ending could have been happier.

"Where did all the peace, love, and happiness go?" I asked Chuck.

He was too high and angry to answer.

•　•　•

Boston was another world. Susan and I were very happy living in her little basement apartment on Commonwealth Avenue, but at first I found it hard being back in a city, without a band to play in. It was 1970—the year the Beatles broke up—and no matter how relieved I was to be away from Flow, I couldn't help but feel as if I, too, had lost my way. I took on any musical job to make ends meet, even playing movie themes on a nylon-string guitar during the six-to-nine dinner gig at the Holiday Inn in Harvard Square. Mostly, I didn't even know the songs I was asked to play.

Some guy would come up and say, "Hey, it's our anniversary. Can you play my wife's favorite song? It's 'The Shadow of Your Smile.' She just loves it."

"Sure," I'd reply, grinning inanely. "After my next break."

My "break" would then be spent in my "dressing room" (a grubby corner of the hotel kitchen, right next to where they peeled potatoes), poring over a fakebook of songs and movie themes, learning the chords and practicing them so that when I emerged, twenty minutes later, I'd be able to play it as if I knew it perfectly—and earn my five-dollar tip.

Painfully aware that this was not what I'd planned as a career, I tried to get in touch with as many other musicians as I could, but Boston was hardly the hub of the musical universe, and there wasn't much work around. I did meet up with some interesting people, though. One was an eccentric Englishman named Peter Green, who'd recently given away most of his money and left the band that had made him famous— Fleetwood Mac. I met him while jamming at a free concert in the park. We got to chatting, and I discovered that he'd just arrived in town and had nowhere to stay.

"You can stay at my place for a while, if you like," I told him. There was something about his eyes that made me trust him. He came home and slept on our couch for a few days. We jammed together quite a bit—he was a great blues guitarist. He had a broad Cockney accent and a wicked sense of humor. We even discovered that we shared a passion for B.B. King, but he took far too many mind-altering substances for my liking, and then, one day, he just disappeared, so nothing ever came of our collaboration. I heard later that he'd got religion in a big way and given the rest of his money to charity.

I found a job for fifty dollars a week at a cut-rate recording studio called Triple A. My job was to hire the session musicians for recordings, many of them students at the Berklee College of Music. One was Abraham "Abe" Laboriel, who has since become one of the most noted session bass players in jazz and pop. As soon as he started playing, everyone perked up. His feel for rhythm was unbelievable. Abe and I became friends, and I hired him as often as I could.

Joe, the owner of the studio, ran it like clockwork. He was a master at persuading people they could have a singing career, even though he knew a dog might sing better. He placed ads in the newspaper looking for new singers, and anyone would respond, from bored housewives to the man who drove the downtown bus. He'd convince every one of them that they were the new Streisand or Sinatra and that their best chance of success was to make a solo album with him. They'd walk out of there floating on the dream that he was going to make them a star.

I had two other jobs, on evenings and weekends, in separate studios, writing jingles for car dealers and clothing outlets. I'd play guitar and a little bit of piano or drums, and a jingle singer would make up a lyric for my track. One of the studios was called Ace, and the owner's son, a kid named Shelly Yakus, used to come in and sweep up, roll the cables, and watch what I did. Now he's one of the premier engineers in the business, making Bruce Springsteen and U2 records, no less. I bumped into him years later and we recognized each other right away.

I worked day and night but made practically no money. I did session work all day and played rhythm and blues in a club from nine till two. It wasn't much of a life, not least because I was never home with Susan. I was seriously beginning to wonder about resurrecting my first job as a music teacher or even doing something completely different. I don't know where the idea came from, maybe from my difficult relationship with my father, but I started taking night classes in child psychology at Boston University. It wasn't easy going back to school, but my brother, Jerry—with

whom I'd had little or no contact—heard from my mother what I was doing and, out of the blue, sent me a check for five hundred dollars.

"Thought you might need this to help you through the next few
months," he wrote. "I know how tough it can be as a student." I will never
forget this loving gesture. I called and thanked him with all the grace I
could muster, and promised I would repay him one day. (I did, many years
later, having worked out the interest he'd have earned on the money he
lent me, but he sent the check back with a note saying he was proud to
have invested in my career.)

Bernie came into town every now and again, and I was always pleased
to see him. He'd been in Linda Ronstadt's backup band for a while, but his
biggest break was joining a group called the Flying Burrito Brothers,
headed by Gram Parsons. They had already recorded one successful album and were on the East Coast as part of a nationwide tour. Susan and I
went to see them in concert and they were great.

"You gotta get out of here, man," Bernie told me, when we went back
to his hotel after the show. "You can do better than writing car jingles.
You're a great guitar player, Don. You gotta come west." Susan's face told
me all I needed to know. She was from Boston, she loved being near her
family, and if I wanted to stay with her, then Boston was where I'd have to
remain.

"I found this great little duplex in a house in Hingham, honey," she
told me one wintry night in January 1971. "It's right near where I grew up."

"I dunno," I said. "I'm not sure how much longer I can keep on working at this pace, and I don't really want to move away from central Boston
and take on any extra rent."

She looked up at me with those big blue eyes of hers, and I couldn't
resist. "OK," I agreed. "If that's what you want."

Susan's mother, who'd always liked me and had been nothing but
friendly, suddenly decided that this was a step too far. Hingham was a
smart suburb of Boston, fifteen miles south on the coast, and—more
important—she still lived there.

"You're not moving back to your hometown to live in sin!" she told Susan in horror when we gave her the news. "Either you get married and live respectably, or you can find somewhere else to live."

We'd already seen the duplex and agreed to take it. We'd also given notice on our old apartment. It was bitterly cold and snowing outside, and I knew it was unlikely that we'd find anywhere as nice for the money at that time of year.

Saying nothing, I borrowed five dollars from Susan and went to a jewelry store near Harvard. When she came home from work later that night, I pulled a small engagement ring from my pocket and blurted out, "Will you marry me?"

"Yes, of course I will, you dope," was her laughing reply. It was very unromantic, not at all what she, or I, had expected. It felt like we were just pleasing her mother. To this day, I'm not sure if Susan and Mrs. Pickersgill cooked up the whole thing as part of a double conspiracy to get me to do the decent thing. Either way, it worked, and I never regretted it.

The wedding was planned for April 23, 1971. My parents, whom I hadn't seen since I'd left home, were going to drive up from Gainesville with my brother, Jerry, whom I'd invited to be my best man. They would be just about the only people on my side of the church—Bernie couldn't make it, because he was on tour, and I'd lost touch with most of my old friends from Gainesville—whereas Susan would have almost a hundred guests.

My father pulled up outside our old apartment in a white four-door Oldsmobile, for which he'd traded the green Pontiac. I stood there, with shoulder-length hair, muttonchops, and a moustache, feeling like a bashful kid, as he came around to the sidewalk to greet me. At that exact moment, two of the most overt homosexuals I'd ever seen—one in red hot pants and high heels, with his arm around the other's waist—walked between the two of us. I'd never seen them before in my life, and I thought my father's jaw was going to hit the curb.

I started to say, "Welcome to Boston, Dad. . . . Dad?" I could see his mind was reeling. All his worst nightmares were coming true. To his credit, he chose not to comment, although I noted that he didn't take my outstretched hand.

We ushered them into our studio apartment, with the bed in the corner, a rickety table and two chairs in the little bay window, a shabby couch, a small kitchenette, and a tiny bathroom. Susan put on a pot of coffee. Mom made all the right noises and was very excited about the wedding and helping Susan and her mother prepare for it. Dad wasn't hostile, just indifferent, and we certainly never discussed what had happened the last time we'd seen each other.

"You making enough?" he asked, looking around our home as if he had an unpleasant smell under his nose.

"Yup," I replied, uneasily.

"Good."

He seemed happy for me in his own way, but I could sense that, while he wholeheartedly approved of Susan and this marriage, he still thoroughly disapproved of me.

The wedding was to be in a historic church north of Boston that Susan's mother wanted us to get married in. My parents stayed in a cheap hotel somewhere nearby. Susan was going to wear her grandmother's wedding gown, which was a hundred years old and which her mother had worn. Her ensemble was to be topped by a large, white, lacy hat. Since I didn't own a suit, and jeans and T-shirts were apparently not permitted, I was dragged off by Jerry and Susan's brother Bill to a discount store to buy a double-breasted gray pinstripe suit and some decent shoes. I never wore either again.

At the ceremony itself, I was far less nervous. We even managed to recite our own vows; we thought that was pretty cool. The reception was in a nearby country club, with a half-decent high school band banging away in the corner. "Just don't play 'Louie Louie,' " I'd told them. Hearing the song I'd played a hundred times on Daytona Beach would have been too depressing. The women of the Pickersgill family made all the food and the wedding cake, which we ceremonially cut before fleeing in our car, a rusty white 1965 Volvo with 120,000 miles on the odometer. Susan's brother-in-law, Bobby, had decorated it with shaving cream and tied cans and streams of paper to the rear bumper.

Dad shook my hand just before I left. "Well, you've got responsibilities now, Don," he told me sternly. "Make sure you live up to them." Mom cried as we hugged good-bye, and she made me promise to come visit. Jerry wished me all the best, and I thanked them for coming.

We went back to our new home in Hingham, and I carried Susan over the threshold. "Where's the wedding certificate?" I asked her, once we were inside.

"Why?" she asked, handing it to me from her purse.

Before she could say anything, I pulled a hammer and a nail from my toolbox and pinned that damn certificate to the bedroom door so that nobody could question us further.

"It's official," I told her. "We're respectable enough to live here."

At the age of twenty-three, I was somebody's husband. The responsibility seemed awesome.

We didn't have very much money, but we were young, in love, and living in half a house next to a graveyard. Life suddenly seemed sweet. From the local dog pound, we rescued a white German shepherd mix, with huge, floppy ears. We called him Kilo, after a kilo of weed. He guarded the apartment while we went out to work each day, and he kept Susan company when I played the clubs at night.

Susan never minded having to be the main breadwinner, bringing home a steady wage while I bummed around town, doing session work and running in and out of studios looking for more employment. With Bernie's amazing versatility in mind, I was constantly trying to improve my musical skills to increase my commercial worth. Using the equipment available to me, I taught myself rudimentary drums, keyboards, and bass guitar, and I learned how to mix tracks and overdub them. I couldn't give up my day job to play any of my new instruments, but I could get by. I just wished I could find something worthwhile to do with my new skills.

"You're a musician, Don," Susan would tell me matter-of-factly, making me coffee when I got in late and tired from a club. "What else can you do?"

Despite my intense personal happiness, I couldn't help but feel that I'd somehow missed the boat. That feeling was compounded when John Winter, the former keyboard player and saxophonist from Flow, called up and asked if he could come and stay. He'd just been released from a mental institution in New York State after suffering some drug-related emotional problems, and he needed a place to crash until his mother and sister could take care of him. I was shocked by his appearance. He seemed like a shell of the gifted young man he'd once been. I called up his family to let them know he was safe, and we looked after him and gave him some money.

"Do you hear anything of the other guys?" I asked.

"Not much," he said, glumly. "All I know is that Mike Burnett moved to Woodstock and spends his time drawing and taking drugs. Andy Leo's living in a hippie commune in Hawaii." *There but for the grace of God,* I thought.

Bernie, meanwhile, was going from strength to strength with the Flying Burrito Brothers; Stephen Stills was an established rock star, with a million-selling solo album featuring Eric Clapton, Jimi Hendrix, and Ringo Starr; and the Allman brothers were flying incredibly high. Then, that fall, Duane Allman was killed in a motorcycle accident in Georgia. The band had just recorded its classic album *At Fillmore East* and was halfway through the next, *Eat a Peach*.

The news came as a terrible blow to those of us who'd known and loved Duane. Ripples of shock passed through the music community. Eric Clapton announced that, like me, he'd been inspired to play slide guitar after listening to Duane Allman play. Duane had been a huge part of *Layla and Other Assorted Love Songs* by Derek and the Dominoes and was on fire during that whole album. He played slide live with every note in tune, which is really hard to do. When I first heard it, I thought, "Oh, my Lord, Clapton is God, but Duane is the second God, and this is too much!" Every time I hear that distinctive guitar sound, I still think of him.

Duane was the same age as me. I felt like we'd grown up together.

He'd taught me so much. "Close your eyes and listen to the music, man," he'd once told me. "Feel it in your heart, and when your spine tingles, you'll know it's right." It hurt like a physical pain to think I'd never hear him play again.

The following summer, Stephen Stills came to Boston. Crosby, Stills, Nash & Young had split for a while as part of their ongoing development, and Stephen had set up a new band called Manassas, with a great pedal steel guitarist named Al Perkins, and Bernie's friend Chris Hillman from the Flying Burrito Brothers. I was very excited at the prospect of seeing Stephen again and went along to the gig to hear him play. He was great. He still had that distinctive voice and the ability to bang it out with great gusto. The band was really tight and the show impressive.

High on adrenaline and music, I wandered backstage. There was so much we had to catch up on. I wondered if he'd remember our mad night in Palatka, drinking Jack Daniel's and bouncing on the bed, or whether he was still in touch with Jeff, the drummer from the Continentals.

A gorilla in a security jacket stopped me in my tracks. "What do you want?" he growled.

"Oh, I need to speak with Stephen Stills."

"Why?"

"I'm an old friend of his." I grinned.

He looked highly skeptical.

"We were in a band together in Florida." Still no sign of movement. "Listen, just go tell him Don Felder would like to see him, OK?"

After much persuasion, the guard did as I asked. I stood waiting by the door along with a few other hopefuls, confident that at any minute my messenger would return with an apology and a backstage pass.

Finally, he came shuffling back to his post, his face as blank as it had been before. He didn't say a word.

"Well?" I asked, impatient now.

"Well nothing," the ape said. "Mr. Stills is too busy to see you right now."

•   •   •

I sank to an all-time low over the next few months and began to wonder if my father was right. I was married, nearly twenty-five, and if I hadn't made it by now, I probably never would. Maybe there was no future for me in music, and maybe I should have gone to college as Dad had always wanted. At least I'd have had something to fall back on. Then a friend of mine I'd met in New York, a great electric bass player, called me up one day.

"Hey, Don, I'm in Boston," he told me on the telephone. "I'm opening for Delaney & Bonnie, you know, that husband-and-wife band who worked with Clapton and George Harrison. Why not come and hear us? We're playing at the college campus."

I was impressed. Delaney Bramlett and his wife, Bonnie, had been linked with some pretty legendary names in the music business, and although they hadn't done so well since Clapton left the fold, I was still interested to hear their unique mix of vocals, brass, and percussion. At my friend's request, I arrived a little early and went backstage to jam with him first. I found him sitting with the bass player from the band, who was softly strumming to himself on an old Gibson. At the same time, I spotted an electric guitar leaning up against a wall.

"Mind if I join in?" I asked.

"Not at all."

I was so used to sitting and jamming with musicians in the studios, I thought nothing of picking that guitar up and starting to play with this man I'd never met before. I was fearless like that; there was really nothing anyone could throw at me that I couldn't deal with. I figured I had nothing to lose, other than someone grabbing me by the seat of the pants and throwing me out the door.

The bass player could play very well, and we had a good time. One by one, the other band members drifted into the dressing room, drawn by the music. After a while, somebody lit a joint, someone else opened a few beers, and we kept on having fun.

"Hey," Delaney finally said when we came to a natural conclusion and everyone broke into spontaneous applause, "why don't you come out and sit in with us onstage tonight?"

"What?" I said, amazed.

"Yeah, come on, it'll be fun," his wife added. She was a pretty pixie of a woman with short blonde hair.

"Oh, OK. I mean, sure," I said, smiling and shrugging my shoulders. Later that night I was introduced as Delaney & Bonnie's "new discovery" and brought out to play blues with them. It was a great gig, really spontaneous and fun, like the best days of Flow, and it did a lot to lift my spirits. Music was what I was good at, I reminded myself. From my earliest days playing Chet Atkins in my bedroom, I'd never been happier than when I was playing my guitar, and it was never better than this. After the show, the band surprised me by inviting me to go on the road with them.

"When?" I asked, suddenly excited by the prospect. If touring with them for a couple of weeks was half as enjoyable as that gig, then I couldn't see why not. I was sure Susan wouldn't mind my being gone for a while, and I could probably get some time off from the studios.

"Tomorrow morning," they replied brightly. "We're leaving on the bus at four A.M. for a three-month nationwide tour."

My heart sank. I knew I couldn't leave on such short notice, and three months was much longer than I could bear to be apart from Susan.

"Sorry, guys," I said, shaking my head sadly. "I'm married. I have responsibilities. I just can't do it."

Clearly dismayed, they told me they understood, and for the second time in my life, I watched a great opportunity slip through my guitar-playing fingers.

SEVEN

Bernie and I kept in touch as our lives and careers followed very different paths. By 1971, he'd split from the Burritos and was working with a series of bands, including one gig he did with Linda Ronstadt. He liked Linda and her producer John Boylan, and he was glad for the work. For this one gig, at Disneyland in Anaheim, his fellow musicians were three young men he'd met at various locations including the Troubadour in L.A. Bernie had the best track record of them all, after his experiences with the Scotsville Squirrel Barkers and the Burritos; the others were relative unknowns—Randy Meisner, Don Henley, and Glenn Frey—Henley and Frey being the driving force and the ones who were later to recognize what a rare combination of talent their group had.

Randy Meisner, known to all as "Meis," was a shy young singer and bass player from Scottsbluff, Nebraska, the son of sharecroppers. He'd married his childhood sweetheart at fifteen and had a son. In 1963, he kissed them good-bye and moved to L.A. with a band called the Soul Survivors, later renamed the Poor, because that is what they became. Randy joined up with Richie Furay and Jim Messina of the recently disbanded Buffalo Springfield and formed Poco. Randy passed the audition that a young bassist called Timothy B. Schmit failed, but Schmit later replaced Randy when he quit Poco over musical differences.

Randy then joined his musical hero Ricky Nelson in the Stone Canyon Band and did some session work on James Taylor's *Sweet Baby James* album, before getting homesick and giving up music altogether to work at the John Deere tractor plant so he could be with his wife and family. In 1971, Rick Nelson invited him back to L.A., and he decided to give his career one last try.

Don Henley moved to L.A. from Texas with his band Shiloh, bankrolled by country singer Kenny Rogers. After a false start with Amos Records, the band broke up. The fuzzy-haired Henley, with his sandpaper voice, soon became part of the furniture at the Troubadour, a former folk club on the corner of Santa Monica Boulevard and Doheny in Hollywood. It was a magnet for rock musicians, folksingers, and songwriters, where the likes of Neil Young and Linda Ronstadt would regularly hold court in the corner and plot their dreams.

Glenn Frey, a natural R&B guitarist and singer, whose idol was Bob Seger, had moved to L.A. from Detroit and teamed up with a talented musician and songwriter named John David (J.D.) Souther. They wrote songs together and in 1969 formed the duo Longbranch Pennywhistle. Their first album, put out on Amos Records, flopped. They shared an apartment complex with singer/songwriter Jackson Browne for a while, and by 1970, Frey decided he wanted a solo career. A huge Elvis fan, he dubbed himself the Teen King. David Geffen, an up-and-coming promoter and future record company executive with people like Joni Mitchell and Crosby, Stills, Nash & Young, urged him to stick with a group.

Recalling the Anaheim gig with Ronstadt and hoping to recapture the magic of that night, Frey and Henley approached Meisner and Bernie Leadon about forming their own group. The move was, one of them once said, born of a mix of "desperation, fear, and insecurity." They realized they played well together, but they only knew each other socially over a few beers and had no idea how they'd all get along. They signed up with David Geffen and his newly formed record label, Asylum, created as the antithesis of the cigar-smoking men in suits who'd previously run the record industry.

What they needed first and foremost was a name. The Doors, the Byrds, and the Beatles had all done well with something short and concise. Glenn Frey, the Detroit-born, would-be "James Dean" of the band, wanted something that sounded punchy, like a teen gang out of *West Side Story*. On a combination of peyote tea and tequila out in the Mojave Desert one night, Bernie recounted from a Carlos Castaneda book that the Hopi Indians revered the eagle above all other animals, because it flies closest to the sun and has a great moral spirit. The Eagles were born.

They may have barely known each other, but by the spring of 1972, just when I was at my lowest ebb in Boston, they were in England recording their debut album, *Eagles*, with Glyn Johns, the producer of classic works by the Rolling Stones, the Who, Traffic, Led Zeppelin, and Steve Miller. It was an uneasy relationship, made harder by Johns' perfectionism, his antidrug stance, and several differences of opinion as to how much of a country flavor the music should have. Despite the early tensions, within a few months, their special mix of country and rock gave them a record in the Top 10.

That summer, they toured with an odd assortment of British bands, including Yes, Jethro Tull, and Procol Harum, and they dominated the Top 40 with three hit singles: "Take it Easy," written by Jackson Browne and Glenn Frey, "Witchy Woman," written by Bernie and Don Henley, and "Peaceful Easy Feeling," by songwriter Jack Tempchin. Each number captured the laid-back, "anything is possible" culture of the time and found emotional resonance with every idealistic teenager who'd ever dreamt of a summer cruising chicks in a convertible. The Eagles' chart rivals, like Harry Nilsson, Don McLean, and Roberta Flack, didn't stand a chance.

I kept hearing "Take it Easy" on the car radio, in shops, diners, and gas stations, before anyone had ever really heard of the Eagles. Bernie's distinctive banjo playing filled the background, and every time I heard it, I smiled, I felt so proud. On "Witchy Woman," his eerie guitar chords sounded like something the Hopi Indians would have performed a ritual dance to. When the Eagles came to Boston in 1972, as an opening band for Yes, Bernie called me up.

"Hey, Don," he said. "I'm coming to town next week, playing at Boston University for one night only with this new band. Why don't you bring Susan over and come and meet the guys? We can have a bit of a jam. I'll put your names on the guest list."

"Sounds great," I said, delighted to hear Bernie's voice again and to know that my old buddy hadn't forgotten me. "See you there."

If Susan had any reservations about my going to see yet another old friend doing so much better than me, she didn't say a word. We traveled to the university campus in our trusty Volvo, and sure enough, Bernie had pulled it off so that we walked straight in past the security guards.

"Hey, man, good to see you!" he beamed, that same old grin lighting up his whole face as he patted me warmly on the back at the dressing room door. He hardly looked a day older than when he had met me off the Greyhound bus nearly ten years earlier.

Turning to Susan, he embraced her. "Hey, Mrs. Felder! Congratulations. You finally snared him, then?" Susan kissed Bernie almost shyly, and they talked for a while about old times and whether either of them still heard from Bernie's old flame, Judy Lee.

Stepping inside the dressing room the band shared, we came face to face with a bunch of young, fresh-looking guys, likeable, bright-eyed, with trademark long hair, jeans, football shirts, and cowboy boots. They were exactly like most of the musicians I hung out with every day in the studio.

"Hey, everyone," Bernie announced, "I'd like you to meet Don Felder, the man with the lightest fingers I know on a Stratocaster."

"Hey, Fingers," said a square-jawed man I was introduced to as Glenn Frey. He shook me firmly by the hand and introduced me to curly-haired Don Henley, who seemed a little uptight (I put it down to preshow nerves), and Randy Meisner, who looked like a shy, baby-faced boy. There didn't seem to be a clear leader, although I noticed that Glenn seemed the most confident and was the one who stepped up to make the introductions. They were just a young band, starting out, playing to crowds of one or two thousand, driving themselves around in rental cars between various indoor facilities like college campuses and small, old theaters.

They seemed to be having a lot of fun while they were doing it, too, from what Bernie had told me. All but Randy were single and were clearly enjoying the drink and the drugs and the girls that seemed to go with the territory. They played marathon poker games, knocked a basketball around on weekends, had pet nicknames for each other, and often socialized together. At the time, it felt to me, there was no special aura about them, no sense that they were going to do any better than any of the other bands we'd all tried our hand in. They were just a bunch of guys making music together. I felt completely at ease. As it turns out, later, they had three hits on their first album.

"Want to jam?" Bernie asked, passing me an electric guitar that was leaning against a table in the corner.

"Sure." I grinned, sitting astride a packing case next to him while Susan settled down on a cushion on the floor.

Bernie opened with a piece of bluegrass he and I had played in Gainesville together a hundred times before, and I fell right in. It felt good to be playing with him again. Up until that moment, I don't think I'd realized how much I'd missed his incredible musical gifts.

Pulling a worn bottleneck from my pocket and placing it over my left middle finger, I played some slide on the next number we did, and before long, everyone in the room was foot-tapping and clapping their hands in time. The room was filled with longneck Buds that were drained in quick succession. We were having a good time. Susan sat looking up at me with such love and admiration as Bernie and I went into a rousing finale. I felt truly blessed to have her for my wife and him for my best friend. This was what it was all about. The ability to sit down and create something out of nothing, to be surrounded by friends and people you love, and to fill the room with music. I never wanted to lose sight of that.

When we were through, the room went wild. Several people had wandered into the dressing room from down the corridor to listen to us

HEAVEN and HELL

Mom and Dad in early years

Me at six months and Jerry at six years

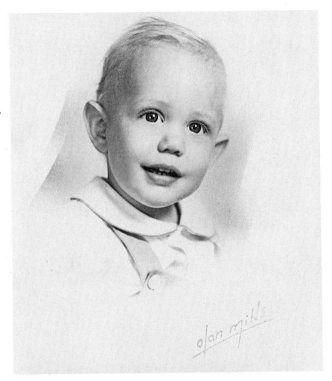

Me at one year

Me at three years with
banjo and cowboy boots

Me at seven years in
Sydney Lanier School

The old Felder house

Me with red Gibson
guitar at sixteen

The Continentals before Stephen Stills

The Continentals flyer

Me in the Kingsmen

My wedding to Susan, 1970

Kilo and me,
driving across the
country, 1973

Topanga house with rattlesnakes

Me on the road with Crosby-Nash

Bernie, Susan, and me at Topanga house

play, and the place was packed. Bernie threw his head back and laughed at the sheer pleasure of it, and I felt happier than I had in months. Glenn Frey came over and placed a hand on my shoulder. "Man, you're good," he said, clearly impressed. "You should come to L.A. We could use a few more players like you out there."

Bernie interjected, "You're onto a loser there. I've been trying to get Don to head west for ten years. I keep telling him that's where it's happening. But he won't listen, and he won't leave his lady."

I said nothing. I just shrugged my shoulders while Susan watched us pensively, a few feet away.

When it was the band's turn to go onstage, she and I stood in the wings, watching them play. They were very good, really tight together as a classic four-part harmony band, although maybe a little bit too static and country for me—no movement, no gimmicks, no political messages about Nixon's reelection or the latest atrocities in Vietnam or the quest for world peace. They just stood and played their music. If there was any talking to be done, and there wasn't much, then Glenn did it. He was up front, behind the mike, his long hair swaying, singing lead. Don sat way at the back, hidden behind the drums, singing at the same time as drumming, which is a phenomenally difficult double act to carry off in terms of physical coordination. Only Levon Helms from the Band had really done it well before. Just once, on "Witchy Woman," Don sang lead, and he was surprisingly good. He had a clean, clear rasp to his voice that cut through the air like a knife.

Overall, I decided that I liked them better personally than I did musically. Where I came from, country music was considered rather inferior, a backwoods sort of thing that the rednecks from the Deep South listened to with their rifles and shotguns in the back of their pickup trucks and the coon dogs on the front porch. Although I'd grown up on a diet of the *Grand Ole Opry*, I felt I'd moved beyond that, into a combination of free-form jazz, rhythm and blues, and good ol' rock and roll. I was still very interested in English music and was far more eager to hear Yes than I was the Eagles. I would never have rushed out and bought an Eagles album. Instead, I'd have spent my hard-earned cash on the latest by Fleetwood Mac, Hendrix, or Eric Clapton.

To give the Eagles their due, there was something spine-tinglingly magical about their sound. And I liked the fact that they all sang. Other than the Beach Boys and Crosby, Stills, Nash & Young, there were few other bands really doing that. Even in the Beatles, Ringo barely sang, and George was just sort of in the background. What these boys did in its simplicity and uniqueness was really cool. It was intelligible; you could understand the lyrics very easily, and each of them brought something to the party. Glenn was the lead singer, and Don sang great harmonies and played drums way behind the beat, giving an anticipatory tension to the music. I don't think it's something he did consciously or willingly, it was just where he felt the beat, and it became part of the Eagles groove.

Bernie played mean five-string banjo, mandolin, and pedal steel, while Randy played bass and contributed the most edgy high-pitched harmonies with his angelic voice. It was a combination that worked, although I'm not sure how truly appreciative the crowd that had come to see Yes was about an all-American, all-singing country-rock band. It seemed like a slightly odd pairing to me.

Yes were mind-blowing. We watched their progressive rock symphony from the wings and were mighty impressed. They had such a distinctive sound, and the crowd went wild. Jon Anderson's voice was crystal, Steve Howe was a fine guitarist, and Rick Wakeman was amazing on keyboards. I felt privileged to have been able to hear them play.

Susan and I went back to Bernie's hotel room after the gig and hung out with him for a couple of hours. The band was leaving early the next morning in their fleet of rental cars, heading for the next town. Their road manager, Richie Fernandez, would sit in the lead car with a map, navigating his little convoy across America. Bernie had to be up at dawn, and Susan and I were both working the next day, so we didn't stay late.

"I'll see you around, pal," I told Bernie, with some sadness, as I shook his hand.

"Yeah, sure. Maybe even in California, huh?" he joked, knowing how I stood on that particular issue. Giving Susan a squeeze, he mumbled into her hair, "You should let Don go to L.A., you know, just to prove to himself that he can do it. You'd never look back, either of you."

• • •

An idea can grow in your head like a seed. Planted by Bernie ten years earlier, nurtured over the years, and watered liberally by our latest encounter, the thought of moving to California and trying to make a go of it developed into a full-fledged organism in my brain. Bernie was living proof of what could happen—airplay on national radio, a tour with a famous country-rock band, musical success, and, with it, fulfillment and happiness. The whole music scene in Los Angeles had really blossomed from the Mamas and the Papas and the Beach Boys, evolving into something acknowledged by the world as unique. Before then, most American music came out of the East Coast, Detroit, or Atlanta.

The concept of moving west wasn't so scary anymore either. I'd left Gainesville, lived in New York, and seen a bit of the States. I'd encountered drugs on a daily basis and not been lured into heroin addiction, as all the teenage propaganda had warned me I would. My career in Boston was going nowhere. I could suddenly see that what Bernie said made sense, and I knew I had to go. The hard part would be convincing Susan.

"Honey, maybe Bernie's right," I ventured cautiously one morning over breakfast. "Maybe I should go out to L.A. for a while and take a look around. I could hop on a train and leave you here with your parents and your job and the apartment for a while, until I find some work, and then I could send for you."

Susan glared at me from across the table. I knew what was coming. She didn't want to leave Boston, and she didn't want to live in California. I braced myself for the outburst. "No way!" she said, firmly. "If you think I'm letting you loose on all those California girls on your own, you've smoked more weed than is good for you. If you go, I go."

Within two months of meeting the Eagles at Boston University, we'd made the decision. I called Bernie and told him, and he promised to make some inquiries about session or band work for me. "I can't believe you're finally coming, man," he laughed over the telephone line. "Get your ass out here, Don. You'll never regret it."

I handed in my notice at my various jobs, and Susan left Harvard. We held a yard sale and sold our furniture and most of our clothes. I decided to sell my beloved gold Les Paul I'd bought from a jazz session player in Boston; I took it to New York, where I hoped to get a better price for it. I went into several guitar shops, but the best I was offered was $150. Susan took me by the hand and led me outside the last shop we tried. "Don't sell it, Don," she said. "I know how much you love it. We don't need the money that bad." So I kept it, and now it's worth several hundred thousand dollars.

We went to U-Haul and rented the largest trailer they had, to attach to the back of our old six-cylinder Volvo. Whatever we couldn't fit in, we sold or gave away. We'd saved exactly one thousand dollars in cash, which we hid in the car, but we had no clue how we'd manage for money once that ran out. Undaunted, we packed our clothes, musical instruments, kitchen equipment—and, of course, Kilo, our dog—said an emotional good-bye to friends and family, and set off.

It was the summer of 1972, and we were headed three thousand miles across America for the City of Angels to what seemed like the Promised Land, chasing an impossible dream. I felt heady with excitement and fear. This was it—my last chance. If I didn't make in California, I was going to have to get myself a real job. My whole future lay before me like a rug. Tentatively, I prepared to cross it.

Driving across America with Susan toward the mystic landscape of California was all that I'd hoped it would be and more. The last time I'd taken the road west, I'd been nine years old, standing up and hanging onto a rope in the back of my dad's 1942 Chevy. Now I was twenty-five, with a guitar in the back of my car and a beautiful wife by my side, who was prepared to give up everything she knew and loved just to hold my hand on this big adventure. We were so crazy about each other, we felt indestructible.

On the long journey coast to coast across America, the cheap motels and diners we found along the way didn't eat into our savings too badly. Kilo sat in the back like a silent hitchhiker, hanging his head out the rear window for air, the wind lifting his big floppy ears. We headed southwest and traveled the nearly three thousand miles in marathon shifts, taking turns at the wheel. The Volvo dash was such that Susan couldn't rest her left foot up on it while cruising, so she did her share of the driving conventionally. Those endless highways, with little to distract or entertain, rekindled some nostalgic memories of Jerry and me and Mom and Dad driving across America in those rose-tinted days when we all got along.

Our journey felt symbolic. We were following the trail carved by thousands of prospectors before us, heading west for gold, through the Rockies, through deserts and prairies, under open skies and towering cacti, toward fertile valleys full of orange groves offering the chance of a better life. Jack Kerouac had defined the notion of crossing America in his 1957 book, *On the Road,* but for Susan and me, the passage was even more spiritual. It was the first real test of our marriage, and we'd come through it. In a lesser relationship, I could have gone off to L.A. alone and never sent for her, or she could have chosen never to come. My final stab for musical success might well end in disaster, but my wife believed in me enough to abandon her own hopes and wishes in support of mine.

We arrived in L.A. travel-weary, and Susan somehow navigated us through the maze of freeway spaghetti that surrounds the city, until we were on Highway 10, heading for Topanga Canyon, a remote area in the Santa Monica Mountains to the far northwest, where Bernie lived. His address at Skyline Drive turned out to be just what it said. It could only be reached by a series of dramatic snake turns on narrow mountain roads with no guardrails between us and oblivion. They were almost impossible to negotiate with an old Volvo pulling a trailer. I didn't even know if the brakes still worked; there hadn't been much call for them in Boston. We drove up and up until we could go no more, and finally we reached Bernie's little one-bedroom house, right on the peak of the canyon with the most amazing view across L.A., from downtown to Catalina.

"Hey, guys! How you doin'?" he greeted us with a grin as he opened the door. "You made it! Great! Come on in." In the hallway, right behind him, was a suitcase and a backpack, ready for loading into his car.

"Going somewhere?" I asked.

"Yeah. Oh, sorry, man, didn't I tell you?" he said, scratching his corkscrew curls. "I'm going on the road with the Eagles tomorrow."

"For how long?" I asked, anxious about finding work and being in L.A. without knowing a single solitary soul.

"Just a couple of weeks," he said, "but make yourselves at home. You and Susan can crash on the floor until you find a place of your own. If I were you, I'd start looking tomorrow. That floor's pretty unforgiving."

Trying to get comfortable on an assortment of lumpy cushions on a hardwood floor that night, I couldn't sleep for worrying what I'd brought Susan to. I'd made her give up her well-paid, rewarding job at Harvard and travel clear across the country to sleep on someone's floor with a guitar-playing loser who had no work and even fewer prospects.

I finally drifted off, exhausted by our long drive, only to be woken at dawn by Kilo whimpering piteously in the corner. Just as I was about to tell him to be quiet, there was the strangest of sensations. The glass in the window rattled in its frame, and then there was a sound like someone knocking violently on the front door. Within seconds, the entire house was shuddering in great spasms, from the roof shingles to the nails in the floorboards. Susan and I clung to each other for dear life, wondering what was happening. When it finally stopped, after what seemed like forever, Bernie came running out of his bedroom, wearing only his underpants. "Hey, did you feel that?" he asked, his eyes bright. "That was a big one!"

"What was it?" Susan asked, her face ashen, as Kilo scurried to her for comfort.

"It was an earthquake!" he exclaimed, laughing at our ignorance. "Welcome to California."

We found a crummy little second-floor apartment in a Hispanic section of Culver City, just off Washington Boulevard, at a cost of $110 a week. It was furnished but had no yard, and dogs weren't allowed. Once we'd unloaded the U-Haul and moved Kilo into a back bedroom where the landlord couldn't see him, we started trying to make it, like everyone else in L.A.

Susan found a job working as a secretary and bookkeeper for a wholesale food company. I cut off some of my hair and greased it back to try to look respectable. Wearing a jacket and tie, I went to the Manpower secretarial agency and told them I could type.

"How are you with the IBM Selectric?"

"Fluent," I heard myself lie. Well, how hard could it be when you could play a few musical instruments and had worked in studios?

I made up some companies I'd worked for in Boston, using part of the real names of the studios—Ace Trucking, Triple A Recruitment—and the agency eventually sent me to IBM. I lied on my employee information form and was given a job packing training manuals for their latest computer products. I also took a second job, running a photocopying machine for an accounting firm. The combined pay was just enough to pay the rent. In the evenings I toured the bars and clubs and picked up a few jobbing gigs.

Bernie came back from tour and started to make some inquiries for me about work. Through the grapevine, he heard that J.D. Souther, Glenn Frey's songwriting companion from Longbranch Pennywhistle, was look-ing for a guitarist to go on the road with him. J.D. had just put out a solo album called *John David Souther* on Elektra Records, on which Glenn had played guitar. He was also working closely with fellow Geffen pro-tégés Joni Mitchell, Crosby, Stills, Nash & Young, and Jackson Browne. I went along for the audition, nervous as hell, and it showed. My perfor-mance wasn't that great, and furthermore, I couldn't play pedal steel, and they needed someone who could. They hired a guy named Ed Black in-stead and went on the road without me.

Then Bernie told me that Terry Lee, an English singer and guitarist whom I'd heard play and who'd been likened to Clapton but with a better voice, was looking for someone for a new album. "Great!" I said. "Where do I find him?"

"They're rehearsing over at Studio Instrument Rentals in Holly-wood," Bernie told me. "Get your ass over there."

SIR was a rehearsal hall I already knew well. The Eagles often rehearsed there, and whenever they did, Bernie would call me up and invite me to drop by and jam with them. He, Glenn, and I would have a blast playing music and hanging out. In those days, studios had no security, and musicians would just open the door, walk in, and sit down. With my guitar and amp in hand, I did just that, once I found out exactly which studio Terry Lee was rehearsing in. Without introducing myself or saying a word, I walked in while his band was playing onstage, plugged my guitar and amp in, and was ready to play.

The band stopped playing. "Hey, man, what you doin'?" one of the sound engineers asked.

Terry Lee stared at me incredulously. "Who are you?" he said.

"My name's Don Felder," I said. "I've heard you play, and I think you're a great singer, and I want to play for you."

Terry Lee stared at me for a moment, and then smiled. "OK, Don Felder. Let's hear what you can do."

For the next hour, I played for them and jammed with them, and we got on really well musically. Finally, the session ended, and they told me, ever so politely, that they'd already found a lead guitarist and my services weren't required. As they watched in silence, I unplugged my amp, picked up my guitar, and walked out.

With my job at IBM, some session work, and Susan working at the food company, we were struggling—but I could sense there were prospects in L.A. and that I was in the right place for something to happen. I was far more inspired and positive than I had ever felt sitting in Boston making jingles.

Kilo was very unhappy, however. There was no yard, and he was left alone in the apartment all day long. We came home one day and found he'd shredded one of the cushions in the recliner seat the day before the landlord was coming to pick up his rent, which he did on the first of every month. We threw a big sheet over the couch so he wouldn't see the damage. When the landlord was on his way over, Susan would either hide Kilo in the back bedroom with the door closed or take him for a long walk.

We lived in that apartment for six months. Our only friends were our next-door neighbors, a French couple named Marina and Jacquie Luade. He was a mechanic with Citroën, and she was a housewife. The first time we met, Marina looked at me and smiled. "You're the one who walks with rhythm," she said.

"Pardon me?" I asked. Susan looked at her askance.

"When you walk up the stairs," Marina explained, "you walk with rhythm."

She fancied herself as a bit of a mystic and offered to read my tarot cards one afternoon. I agreed, more out of politeness than anything. "It can't hurt," I told Susan. "I mean, what can she tell me?"

I went to her apartment as arranged one afternoon and sat down opposite her at a small table. She shuffled the cards and spread them out in front of her.

"Oh my God!" she said, her accent as thick as butter, as her long fingers ran across the cards one by one.

"What?" I asked, concerned, looking helplessly at the table. "What is it?"

"You," she said, looking up at me, her green eyes huge.

"What about me?" I was getting a little edgy. Maybe I was wrong, maybe there was something terrible she could tell me.

Her face broke into an enormous smile. "You, my darling," she said, reaching across the table and squeezing my arm excitedly, "are going to be very famous and very, very wealthy."

"Really?" I asked, wondering if she'd had a little too much Pernod.

"Absolutely," she nodded firmly. "It's written in the cards."

EIGHT

David Geffen seemed to be the common denominator with many of the new West Coast bands having the most success. Aggressively ambitious, having worked his way up from the mailroom at the William Morris agency, Geffen was reaching for the stars, and whoever was hanging onto his coattails was undoubtedly in for a ride. Bernie knew Geffen was the key, and so he took me along to his cramped second-floor offices in a building at the Beverly Hills end of Sunset Boulevard one day and plugged me as a "hot new guitar player."

I have always been eternally grateful to Bernie for the introduction. L.A. was teeming with people who'd have killed for such an opening. Here I was, the new kid in town, being hooked right up with an incredible power base in the industry. David was not that much older than I, but he was like a light bulb, radiant with energy, ideas, and excitement. Along with his partner, Elliot Roberts, he was a dynamic driving force, creating avenues for the artists who would come to define the Southern California music scene. There was a tremendous buzz around him and his company, with its laid-back approach and talented young stars. David's office was a hotbed of creativity. He shrewdly took a unique combination of talented artists and combined them with great management skills. I don't think either one would have survived without the other element—each one propelled them to international level. Whatever he was doing, it was working, and with the Eagles he seemed to be trying to create the quintessential American band. It seemed that everything Geffen touched turned to gold, although I'm sure he crushed a few golden toes along the way.

No one wore a suit and tie. Most of his employees were in jeans with long hair, giving his office an atmosphere that was casual, yet up-to-the-minute. The hierarchy was clear. Elliot Roberts was in charge of the company's two biggest acts, Joni Mitchell and Crosby, Stills, Nash & Young, whom he'd personally managed from the start. Geffen ran the day-to-day side of the company and handled a few key players of his own. The man in charge of the new Eagles account—along with clients Dan Fogelberg and wild rocker Joe Walsh—was the management company's number three, a brash, diminutive twenty-something firecracker named Irving Azoff who'd joined Geffen's office the previous year.

Bernie introduced me to Irving, who was sitting at a desk in the middle of this large open-plan office, with dozens of telephones around him. He had long curly hair, enormous aviator glasses, and a beard. He was our age, from the Midwest, an obvious go-getter and, on first sight, less than impressive. David Geffen was of slight stature, but Irving was even smaller, around five feet. Bernie used to say "put them together and you get a pair of bookends."

Besides some of the more recognizable names in Geffen's stable of talent, there was also a young folk-rock artist named David Blue, who looked and sounded a bit like Bob Dylan. He was a friend of Dylan, and of Leonard Cohen and Joni Mitchell, and he'd just put out a solo album of original songs, *Nice Baby and the Angel,* on Asylum Records, starring and produced by Graham Nash and featuring Glenn Frey and Jennifer Warnes on backup vocals. The Eagles' second album, *Desperado,* based loosely on the story of the Dalton Gang—former marshals turned outlaws—had featured a song called "Outlaw Man," written by David Blue, which they'd released as a single. After that release, Geffen decided to promote David as the "West Coast Bob Dylan" and push him out on a tour of small clubs.

"So, Bernie tells me you can play guitar," Irving said, looking me up and down. I could tell instantly he wasn't the type to take prisoners. "Well, we'll see about that. You never know, we might have something for you."

New Yorker Elliot was far less dynamic, with red brown hair, but I liked him all the more for his common-sense, down-to-earth approach. "David Blue," he told me, "is looking for someone to go on the road with him. David Lindley played all the string instruments on his album, but he's on the road with Jackson Browne right now, so there might be an opening. Can you play lap slide and mandolin?"

"Sure," I lied, hardly daring to look across at Bernie, the mandolin king.

"OK," Elliot said, scribbling my number on a piece of paper. "I'll get David to give you a call."

The phone rang a couple of days later, one evening while Bernie was around having dinner with Susan and me. It was David Blue. "Come over and play for me tomorrow," he told me. "I'll give you the address. I'm living at Joni Mitchell's apartment right now."

Swallowing hard, I took my courage in both hands. "Mr. Blue?" I said.

"David," he corrected me.

"Could I possibly postpone the audition until Saturday? Only because I'm working full-time until then."

There was a pause on the phone and Bernie stared at me in astonishment. I think my old friend thought I was crazy.

"OK," David said, eventually, "Saturday it is. Three o'clock."

As I put down the telephone, Bernie said, "What are you doing? Postpone the audition to Saturday? Don't you know what a great chance this is? Surely you can skip out of work for an hour or two."

"I'm gonna have to take a lot more time off than that," I replied, scratching my head. "I've only got four days to learn how to play lap slide and mandolin."

Bernie took me to an amazing store on Westwood Boulevard called Westwood Music, run by one of the friendliest people I'd ever met in the music business, a man named Fred Walecki. He reminded me a little of a younger version of Buster Lipham. Fred was a wannabe musician, the same age as me, who could hardly play a note, but who inadvertently found himself at the heart of the rock and roll industry. What began as a store that sold rare harps, Stradivarius violins, and orchestral instruments soon became the hub of the West Coast music scene when nineteen-year-old Fred took over from his ailing father in 1966 and gradually phased out the classical instruments in favor of the new sounds of the sixties.

He particularly enjoyed helping struggling young musicians like me. It was vicarious enjoyment for him. He'd take personal calls at his home from anyone in desperate need of an instrument or a part and would turn up at rehearsal halls with some "new toys" for his friends to play with. He wasn't in it for the money; often he'd just lend instruments out, to his own financial detriment. He simply loved music but didn't have the skills or the dexterity himself. His friends included the Rolling Stones, Stephen Stills, Joni Mitchell, Emmylou Harris, Jackson Browne, David Lindley, and Linda Ronstadt. He lent me a C-quality mandolin and a lap slide guitar for three days, so that I could practice on them and take them along to the audition.

"Go ahead," he told me, "take them, if you have the chance for a job."

"You sure?"

"Yeah. And good luck," he added with a grin, as I walked out the door.

"Thanks," I replied, half to myself, "I'll need it."

Geffen-Roberts Management sent me a tape of David Blue's album, so I could listen to the parts I'd be required to play, and—in a throwback to my Voice of Music days in my parents' living room—I plucked away at those instruments religiously, note by note, until I had the whole album note perfect. Closing my eyes, I was transported back to the time of Chet Atkins and that annoying "Yankee Doodle"/"Dixieland" number I'd been so determined to learn. Once again, it was Bernie who'd given me the courage to even try.

Joni Mitchell lived in an old Spanish-style building off Highland and Sunset in Hollywood. It was a five-story block structure and her apartment was on the top floor. There was even an elevator straight to her door. Joni was a giant in my eyes—a pioneer in the folk music scene, a poet, and a true star. Sadly, she was on tour and wouldn't be walking in to say hello.

David Blue was quite a character. He'd been around the New York music scene for quite a while and felt it was his turn for success. Dylan and Joni were doing great, the other Geffen stars were in the ascendant, and now he wanted some of it. He had a considerable chip on his shoulder, but at the same time had commitment, a good sense of humor, and a willingness to lend a hand to a naïve newcomer like me.

I started out by playing some guitar for him, sitting cross-legged on the stripped wood floor of this huge, bright apartment. Then, we went through his album, number by number, and I played the mandolin and lap slide parts that multi-instrumentalist David Lindley had played. Between us, we worked out what I should play live to sound most like the record. There would only be the two of us onstage, so he'd have to decide which instruments he wanted for which parts, as I clearly couldn't play them simultaneously. At the end of the audition, he shook my hand and said, "Okay, Don, you're in. Let's get started right away."

I nearly collapsed with the shock. Someone actually thought that I had talent after all. Bernie was right all along, great opportunities were waiting for me in California, and now I was going to be on the road with someone who knew real stars in the business. Better still, they were going to pay me. The money on offer seemed like a lottery windfall compared with what I was getting at IBM and the accounting company. I quit both jobs without a second thought.

• • •

My first gig with David Blue was in September 1973 at the opening night of a brand-new club on the corner of Sunset Boulevard and Hammond Street, which was partly owned by Geffen-Roberts. It was called the Roxy Theater, and it featured state-of-the-art acoustics. Neil Young was the main act, halfway through his *Tonight's the Night* tour with the Santa Monica Flyers, and we were supporting him. David sat up at the front of the stage, playing guitar and singing in that half-speaking flat voice of his, and I sat beside him, playing guitar, mandolin, and slide, and singing harmonies. I was more nervous than I'd ever been in my life, even standing on the stage of the high school talent contest as a shy teenager.

David deliberately adopted a Western look for his Outlaw Man image, with tailored boot-cut jeans, cowboy boots, a Western belt, a shirt with pockets, and a cowboy hat. He smoked cigarettes all the time, even onstage, blue smoke spiralling permanently from the tip he held between his nicotine-stained fingers. I knew people wouldn't want to hear him play his original acoustic version of "Outlaw Man," since the Eagles version was being played so much on the radio, so I plugged him into a Stratocaster and a nasty amp and made him play an electric rendition, with me providing the background guitar and vocals. The combination worked, and we were well received. When Neil Young took the stage after us with his band, David and I sat in the wings and were completely blown away. That guy had such an incredible voice and such a laid-back approach to playing music, he was a pleasure to listen to.

One of our next gigs was at the Troubadour, the place where the Eagles had first met. There was an Italian restaurant next door called Dan Tana's, where we'd eat great platefuls of spaghetti before the show. The Troubadour remained a beacon for new talent. Everyone from Jim Morrison to Van Morrison hung out there, having a few drinks while listening to that night's turn, or getting up to join in. Don Henley and Glenn Frey still spent most of their evenings there, drinking single longneck Buds, playing music, and working the babes at the bar. Bernie and Randy were regulars too.

Joni Mitchell sometimes used to come in to hear David Blue play. I was childishly starstruck every time I met her, but I didn't hang around long enough to get to know the person beneath the megastar veneer. As

I kept reminding myself, I was only at the club for the gigs. My marriage wasn't going to work if I did anything else. I'd either go straight home to Susan and Kilo, or she'd come to the venue and wait for me. I wasn't cattin' around town. That was never the plan.

Joni asked me to play some guitar in a session for one of her records, which was like a dream come true. I went along to the studio and sat there with her and David and played my beloved sunburst Les Paul for them. Halfway through the session, I placed the guitar on a stand and took a short break. I was so nervous, I hadn't put it down carefully enough, and, to my horror, I watched it topple over and break at the neck. I fixed it myself with some wood glue and a clamp, but it never really played the same way after that. I don't know if Joni ever used what I laid down, but—despite busting my guitar—I was happy just to have been asked.

David and I traveled to places like Denver and Phoenix for a few weekend club gigs. Drugs were a frequent feature for everyone on the road and, for the first time, I came into contact with cocaine. It wasn't something I indulged in often, because I couldn't afford it—a hundred dollars for a gram of blow was way out of my league. Moreover, when your body isn't used to it, a little bit of that stuff goes a long way. One night, David gave me a bottle that had a quarter of a gram in the bottom of it, which was very generous. I snorted a little and flew to the ceiling. One of the truck drivers, who'd become a good friend, had a long night's drive ahead of him after the show, so when I'd taken what I wanted, I gave him the rest. "Hey, buddy, maybe this'll help," I told him. He was very happy to accept.

The next day, someone was chopping out some cocaine in a dressing room, and I took a snort. David watched me from the other side of the room. "Hey, Don," he said, "what happened to the blow you had yesterday?"

"I gave it to the truck driver."

David nearly fell off his chair. "You did what?" He never quite understood my camaraderie with the "hired help," as he called them.

The tour continued to go well, and Geffen-Roberts Management seemed pleased. They gave us the green light to expand and put a four-man band together, with bass and drums, using other songs that lent themselves to the same format. "You can open for the Eagles for a couple of local gigs," Elliot told us. "They're going on a nationwide tour for their new album, *Desperado*."

Within a few weeks, I was standing on the stage at the Santa Monica Civic Center with David Blue, playing accompaniment, with my old buddy Bernie Leadon standing in the wings watching me, ready to go on with his own band. It felt like a dream come true, Bernie and me on the road together at last, each one of us doing OK. Every night after the gig, we'd hang together like the old days, drinking a few beers. The more I saw of the Eagles, the more they seemed like a really nice bunch of guys. I was happy Bernie had found himself a good group.

Our next act was opening for Crosby & Nash. The legendary Graham Nash had stood on the stage in front of me in Gainesville and sung "Bus Stop" for the Hollies. Then he'd belted it out at Woodstock with Stephen Stills, the kid I'd played with in Florida. He'd even lived with Joni Mitchell for a while. Now I was going on tour with him and David Crosby. I could hardly believe my luck. Meeting Graham for the first time did nothing to disappoint. He was a true English gentleman, charming, genuine, and sincere. He personified the ideals of Woodstock. He'd always greet you with a smile, even if he was sometimes a little high on pot. He seemed to be delighted with me musically and with what I'd been able to add to David's act. He'd often sit in on our rehearsals and make useful suggestions about the house mix and how it was sounding, always in an extremely diplomatic and gentle way. I had the utmost respect for him musically and when I came to know him as a person, I added several tiers of admiration. He was a timeless, wise soul, whom I felt to be several thousand years ahead of me.

I was still very naïve when I started working on that nationwide tour in the fall of 1973. Our opening gig was at the Fillmore West in San Francisco. Susan had flown up with us to see the show and wave me off on tour. She was going back to L.A. and her secretarial job the following morning. We were both childishly excited.

"Wow, Don, you're really going on the road," she said, her eyes brighter than I'd seen them in years. "This is all you've ever wanted, isn't it?"

"Yes," I told her, my own stomach doing a somersault at the thought. I needn't have worried. We went onstage and performed very well. The fans really seemed to like our stuff. I played guitar and sang harmonies and stood in front of a club packed to the hilt with adoring fans, relishing every second. I felt so exhilarated, because I knew this was the start of something really big. Crosby & Nash came on after us and blew the crowd away with some of their best numbers, like "Woodstock," "Teach Your Children," "Love the One You're With" and "Marrakesh Express." They were awesome with their hypnotic harmonies, and the crowd loved their music.

We spent that night at the Miyako Hotel in San Francisco, a five-star Japanese fantasyland, with sushi, hot tubs, and shiatsu massage. Susan and I went back to our room after the gig, took a shower, made love, and lay side by side on the bed in the darkness, the glow of the city lights illuminating our room.

"I can't believe this is happening," I whispered. "It all seems so unreal."

"I know," Susan replied, her body pressed hard against mine. "It's really cool."

"I feel like we're on the brink of something here. Like this could really be the beginning, you know?" I reached down and kissed the top of her head.

"We *are* on the brink of something, Don," she told me, pulling herself up onto one elbow and staring at me in the half-light. There was a pause. "I'm going to have a baby."

I lay staring at her in stunned, unblinking silence for what seemed like an eternity. It was such unexpected news. Susan was the steady breadwinner, we were living in a crappy little rented apartment, and I was about to go on the road. I thought to myself: "I'm just a long-haired, rock-and-roll hippie, a guitar player, not someone's dad."

Susan sat up even more and stared down at me. "Don?" she said. "Are you all right? Did you hear me? We're having a baby."

I had a sudden stupid desire to cry. Grabbing her, I pulled her to me. "A baby? Are you sure?"

"Yes." She grinned. "Certain. Are you pleased?"

"Pleased? I'm thrilled! I feel like everything I touch at the moment turns to gold. I couldn't be happier, Susan. Really."

While I let the idea of being a father filter through, the tour continued, taking in most of the West Coast's hockey and sports arenas, theaters, university campuses, and college venues. Most nights, before the gig, we'd sit and jam with Crosby & Nash and their backup band in their dressing room. We had some good laughs, playing music together. Then, one night, guitarist David Lindley—whom I'd stepped in for with David Blue—took sick with the flu while the band was staying at the Watergate Hotel in Washington, D.C. He was so ill, he had to be flown back to L.A. Graham Nash came to my hotel room and asked me if I could play David's parts.

"W-w-what do you mean?" I stammered.

"You know all the songs, Don. You know us. It'd just be for a while, until David gets better."

I played with them that night at the Capitol Theater, and it worked really well. Graham liked my playing so much that he came to see me after the show. "You know, I don't think we're gonna have David back," he said. "We'd like you to stay with the tour. Do you think you can handle it?"

"Sure," I said, gulping down my excitement.

For a few short months, the band became Crosby, Nash & Felder. I'd play my set with David Blue, come offstage for the intermission, then return to play with Graham and David. They paid me double wages, once for each show, but saved a fortune by only having to pay expenses for one guitarist instead of two. Still, I wasn't complaining.

One night we were playing in Denver when, unbeknownst to me, they invited Stephen Stills—who was living in Colorado—to come and jam with us onstage during the show. It was a last-minute thing, arranged as a surprise for the audience. He was a successful solo artist now, but he sometimes missed the camaraderie of being in a band, and he jumped at the chance. We'd just finished "Marrakesh Express" when Graham suddenly introduced Stephen to uproarious applause, and he strolled onto the stage. We took one look at each other in mutual surprise. "Don!" he said, astonished, as the audience waited for us to begin, "What the hell are you doing here?"

"Being you," I replied with a smile. He took his place, and we all jammed together and blew the crowd away. It was the once-in-a-lifetime only performance of Crosby, Stills, Nash & Felder. After the show, Stephen told Graham that we'd been in a high school band together in Gainesville and had known each other since we were teenagers. I'd never mentioned our connection; it never seemed to come up, and in any event, when I'd tried to see Stephen backstage in Boston, I'd been given the brush-off, so I wasn't sure how I stood.

Graham was flabbergasted. "I can't believe you never said anything or tried to use your friendship with Stephen to your advantage," he told me. I think he took another view of me after that.

David Crosby was completely the opposite. He was the first person I'd ever met who used excessive amounts of cocaine, and the energy that came off him in consequence was paranoid, tense, and fearful. I remember walking down the hallway in a motel we were staying in one night and seeing David's door open, so I strolled in. We were working together, after all, and I had hoped we were friends.

"Hey, how you doing?" I said, thinking I could walk into his life the same way I could with Graham. On the bed, his suitcase was lying open, and inside was a bag of cocaine. David was really high, and the look on his face was one of paranoia. He'd been caught red-handed and there was no telling what he might do.

Stiffening, I said, "Oh, I forgot something, I've gotta go." I only worked with him for a few months, but there was always a distance between us, and I never stopped being slightly wary.

The tour ended and, with it, the fun. There were plans for a second leg early in 1974, and Graham and David asked me to go out again with them then. I agreed without hesitation. I returned home to Susan, who was happily pregnant and working full-time, and we set about looking for somewhere else to live until I went on the road again. Culver City was no place to bring up a child.

We found a place for $175 a month at Fernwood Drive in Topanga, near Bernie. We shared it with his younger brother Tom and Tom's girlfriend, Cathy. Topanga was so beautiful, with its mountains and woods, and it attracted an artistic community of singers, actors, writers, and instrumentalists, many of them known as "canyon musicians." Our neighbors, past and present, included Neil Young, Linda Ronstadt, Alice Cooper, the Mothers of Invention, and a singer named Taj Mahal, who had a big hit at the time called "Take a Giant Step," cowritten by Carole King. There was a bar called the Topanga Corral, where bands like Spanky and Our Gang, Canned Heat, and Spirit regularly honed their musical skills. We fit right in. Best of all, our cabin had a yard for Kilo, who rediscovered the pleasures of outdoor living.

The place we found was like a summer cabin, with screened windows and a hammock out back. There was one proper bedroom, which we had, and a little sewing room for Tom and Cathy. I installed a washer-dryer so Susan didn't have to go all the way to the coin-op in the Valley, and I made a dining table out of a giant wooden telephone cable spool I bought at a junkyard for fifteen bucks. Our bedroom was too small for a crib, so the baby would have to sleep with us for a while. Susan was getting further and further along, and blossoming with it. I loved watching our child grow inside her.

She was still driving the Volvo, which never once gave up the ghost, and I bought a faded blue '51 International Harvester pickup truck to run around in. It was truly horrible. You couldn't see your reflection in any part of the paint, and there was nothing left that resembled chrome either. It had six cylinders and you could hardly hear the clunk and grind of the engine over the clatter of the fenders and the noise the body made while in motion.

I fully expected to be home for a few months, barring any session work I was invited to do, and I planned to spend it getting the house ready for our new arrival. David Blue had been well received, and Graham Nash seemed to have no intention of taking his old guitarist back, but they both wanted a rest. If the timing worked right, I might even be home with Susan when our baby was born.

Bernie was back in town after the *Desperado* tour with the Eagles, who had started recording their third album, *On the Border*. It felt to me that the band was at something of a crisis point. *Desperado* hadn't done nearly as well as their first album, not even breaking into the top forty, despite great ballads like "Tequila Sunrise," written by Don Henley and Glenn Frey as one of their first collaborative efforts. The album was considered too country for rock aficionados and too rock for the country fans. Compared with current theatrical artists like David Bowie or Alice Cooper, who put as much into the spectacle of their shows as into the music, the Eagles were considered boring. The gigs they were playing were smaller than the venues I was playing with Crosby & Nash. They concentrated on theaters and college gigs, while we were playing clubs like the Fillmore West.

The band had just been in England for the third time, working with producer Glyn Johns, but things hadn't worked out. Johns was very hard on them with time, drug, and budget constraints, and there'd been further clashes over which musical direction they should be taking. Glenn wanted to do more R&B but Johns preferred Bernie's West Coast country sound.

After firing Johns and filling out the time with an eight-week tour of Europe and the States, they'd come back to L.A. to try to finish the album. They had just two usable tracks—"The Best of My Love," written by Don, Glenn, and J.D. Souther, and "You Never Cry Like a Lover," written by Don and J.D. This time they enlisted a young producer named Bill Szymczyk (pronounced "sim-zick"), who'd done some great work with Joe Walsh and had been largely responsible for the success of "The Thrill is Gone," a groundbreaking track by my hero B.B. King.

In a separate, unexpected move, David Geffen sold his new record label, Asylum, to the record and film giant Warner Communications for $7 million. Warner merged it with Elektra Records and put him in charge. Glenn was particularly unhappy that Geffen had "sold out" to the cigar-smoking men in suits he'd so railed against, without giving the Eagles any warning of the imminent merger or any credit for the part they might have played in the deal. Disillusioned, the band decided to leave what Geffen once described as his "benevolent protectionism" and switch to the ever-enthusiastic Irving Azoff, who'd left Geffen to set up his own management company called Front Line. Irving's other key clients were Joe Walsh, Dan Fogelberg—known to us as "Junior Bucks" until he made it big and became "Major Bucks"—and a relatively unknown band called REO Speedwagon. He soon added new artists Steely Dan and Boz Scaggs to the list.

Whenever I saw Bernie, he seemed increasingly unsettled. He'd been in several bands that had broken up after an initial flurry of success, and he thought he could see the writing on the wall with the Eagles. I knew from the past that he had a short fuse, and I felt he was brewing for something.

"Oh, man," he told me one night over supper at our spool table, "these guys never stop arguing."

"Who?" I asked, surprised.

"Glenn and Don. It's like being back at home again with eight siblings, always squabbling. Talk about creative tension! They think they're the new Lennon and McCartney. The whole concept of the band was equal partners with equal shares in writing, singing, playing, and royalties—we were no longer sidemen. Don and Glenn couldn't get along with this English guy, Glyn Johns, or decide which direction they wanted the band to go—rock or country.

"Nothing Randy or I wrote was ever good enough, and now we've left Geffen, Irving's in charge, and he and Don seem to be very thick. I'm seriously beginning to wonder what I've gotten myself into."

I sympathized and passed him another beer. At least I was free of all that in-band politics nonsense, I reminded myself, grateful once again for the benevolence of David Blue and Graham Nash. From what Bernie said, it certainly didn't sound like the Eagles were going to survive much longer, which was a shame, because I thought they really had something. I wondered what he'd do next.

A couple of days later, one morning in early January 1974, the telephone rang just as I was about to fix the squeaking screen door at our house out in Topanga.

"Don? It's Glenn, Glenn Frey of the Eagles," the husky Detroit voice announced on the other end of the line.

"Oh, hi Glenn. How you doin'?" I put down my tools and sat on the edge of the table.

"Good, thanks. Hey, listen, we were wondering if you could come into L.A. tomorrow, to the Record Plant, and help us out with a song we're recording for this new album. We need someone who can play some real dirty slide on it, and we obviously know you can play and thought you might be interested."

"Sure, Glenn," I said, happy for the extra session work, grabbing a pen. "Love to. What time do you want me?"

I scribbled down the details on the back of a supermarket bill and stuffed it in my back pocket without giving it a second thought. Putting on my tool belt, I got down to the more important business at hand.

NINE

was twenty-seven years old when I arrived at the Record Plant in West Los Angeles, on Third and La Cienega, with my newly mended Les Paul guitar, an amp, and a few foot pedals. "The Plant" was, at that time, one of the coolest places to record in L.A., with its psychedelic fabrics, raw wood surfaces, and living room environment. Jimi Hendrix, Frank Zappa, the Velvet Underground, and the *Woodstock* soundtrack had all been recorded there. Everybody was waiting for me in the studio as I walked in with my instruments and a tasselled leather shoulder bag full of my wah-wah pedals, cables, and other toys.

"Hey, guys, how you doin'?" I said, as I set my stuff down. "Nice to see you again."

The producer, Bill Szymczyk, introduced himself. He was a huge bear of a man, of Polish extraction, with a handshake that could crush cans. Later I heard it was he who'd decided that the band's attempts to play rock music needed stronger guitars, to compete with the big rock bands like the Rolling Stones, the Who, and Led Zeppelin. Critics had accused the Eagles of being too laid-back, even of "loitering" onstage. Fans simply couldn't rock to "Peaceful Easy Feeling," and commercial success was slipping through their fingers. Bill, whose nickname was "The Soul Pole," had asked the band if they knew any good incendiary guitar players.

The reply was apparently unanimous—Don Felder.

Joe Walsh had been considered briefly, but he had his own successful career as a solo artist and was considered a little too wild for the mellow Eagles.

I felt entirely comfortable that day. I wasn't thinking, "Oh my God, it's the Eagles." They were friends, the same age as me, and although they'd had considerable chart success early on, their bubble was in danger of bursting and I was very happy with the way my own career was going. This was just another session as far as I was concerned. I hoped it would buy a few extra things for the baby.

Everyone was as friendly as usual. Bernie seemed pleased to see me, although he was a little quiet. I put it down to some of the tensions he'd already told me about, and the constant jockeying for position among band members. I heard Don and Glenn ask each other, "Whose songs are we gonna work on next?" but there was nothing at that initial session that made me suspicious or uncomfortable.

Each of the guys had his own unique character. Glenn Frey was a rebel without a cause from the Motor City, with his reflector shades, flipping an unlit cigarette in his hand and catching it, offering quick one-liners while constantly flicking his hair back off his forehead. Later I heard that his mother once said he was so ambitious he reminded her of a rattlesnake. That made him witty and beguiling, if a little unpredictable.

Don Henley, the son of the manager of a Texas auto-parts store, was more of a soft-spoken, introspective songwriter. He was an English literature major and wrote wonderful prose. He could take little snapshots of life in just two or three lines. Whenever he read out something he'd written, it sounded profound, especially to someone like me, who'd barely made it through high school. He'd sit scratching away at his legal pad, constantly listening to the last track or editing what he'd just penned. He was always absorbed in literature of some sort and carried at least one book around in his shoulder bag. He was fair, rational, and levelheaded, if a little moody sometimes. I liked him from the outset.

Randy Meisner, of Nebraskan farming stock, was the nicest guy I ever played with in a band. No matter what went down, you could hang with "Meis" and have a laugh. Of German descent, he'd been turned on to music by his father, a classical violinist. Naturally shy and quiet, he hated it when the attention was focused on him or his playing, but there were few occasions when I saw him unhappy or not putting a bright face on a situation. He looked very young and continually attracted the ladies with his cute looks. Randy's sole purpose in life was to have a few drinks, roll a few joints, and make everybody laugh. He was a wonderful Midwestern guy with a great heart and a loving soul.

Bernie, meanwhile, was so brilliant musically that you could forgive him almost anything. The only original member of the Eagles to actually hail from California, he could play bluegrass, rock and roll, or country music on any acoustic instrument. He was also high-strung and extremely headstrong. Being the oldest of so many kids had left him with an ingrained belief that he always had to fight for what he wanted. With that many people around the dinner table, if you didn't fight, you didn't eat. His argumentative nature and lack of diplomacy sometimes made him unpopular with those who didn't understand or know how to handle him. In a group situation, it could be explosive.

Another person in the studio that day was J.D. Souther, probably the coolest person who wasn't in the Eagles, and one of the band's main ghostwriters. He should really have been the sixth member. He was a good singer, great to hang out with, warm, and funny, and he could fill a pad with great lyrics, right there on the spot. He started with the title "New Kid in Town," for example, and had a large part of that song written before Glenn and Don got involved. J.D.'s name appears in the credits, but he also co-wrote other stuff and helped refine many of the tracks. If J.D. was credited on a song, it was because it had originated with him or he had made a real contribution, and he always came through.

As for me, I was still Don "Fingers" Felder, the long-haired hippie in patchwork jeans with the Deep South accent and a laid-back attitude. My wife was expecting our first child, and I was primarily there to play some good music, take the money, and meet up with some old buddies. Music was my life. It was what had helped lift me from the grinding poverty of my childhood, and after years in the musical deserts of upstate New York and Massachusetts, I felt lucky to be doing what I loved and getting paid for it. I guess I was still trying to prove my father wrong.

I suppose we looked the part—young, fit, tanned, scruffily dressed, and adorned with fashionable turquoise jewelry in that endless Californian summer idyll. As one commentator put it later, we looked "like Jesus Christ after a month in Palm Springs." We had every reason to be friends, make great music together, and have a whole lotta fun doing it too. It all seemed so promising to a boy from Tobacco Road.

That first day, I was asked to play slide on a song called "Good Day in Hell," which Glenn and Don had written. Glenn, who was singing lead, liked what he heard of my guitar playing. He apparently told Bill Szymczyk afterward that I was Duane Allman reincarnate. It was the highest compliment anyone could ever have paid me.

We cut the record after just six takes, which seemed a good omen. The results seemed to impress the band so much that later they asked me to lay down a fiery guitar line on another song, a punchy rock-and-roll number called "Already Gone," playing toe-to-toe with Glenn in what became the first song on the album. At the end of the session, we played it back, laughing and having a good time. Someone cracked a few beers and we enjoyed listening to the playback of the day's work. It felt good. When it was over, I reluctantly packed my amp and guitar, placed them carefully in the back of my rusty old pickup, and drove home to Topanga.

The very next day, I was sitting having breakfast with Susan when the telephone rang. She watched as I took the call and tugged at my sleeve. "Who is it?"

"Glenn Frey," I mouthed.

"What's he saying?"

I gestured to her to come closer to the phone so she could listen in.

"We had a discussion last night after you left and decided that we all want you to join the band," Glenn was saying. "We never thought there'd be more than four Eagles, but we've had a band meeting and we've decided we'd like you to join us. You'd really fit in. Will you, Don? Will you join the Eagles?"

Susan and I looked at each other in silence. It was a lot to consider—giving up what I was doing with David Blue and Crosby & Nash—but this was a firm offer to be a member of an established band, not just a hired hand in somebody else's. It didn't take long to decide.

"Sure," I said, not letting on how excited I felt.

"Great. Well, will you come back to the studio at two o'clock tomorrow, so we can start working on recording the rest of the album?"

"No problem. I'll see you there," I replied, as calmly as I could.

Putting down the phone, I turned to Susan, her belly bulging, and said just one word—"Wow."

I thought joining the Eagles would mean less money than I was getting doubling for David Blue and Crosby & Nash, and it probably wouldn't come as a weekly paycheck, either. I'd also be playing smaller gigs. Nevertheless, I really liked the idea of being a full-time member of a band again, especially one that was to be an equal partnership, so I gladly relinquished all my other commitments. I even remember saying a prayer that night:

"Thank you, Lord, for your good timing. Here I am with this child on the way, and you've given me this great blessing, which is much appreciated."

My most difficult task would be telling Graham Nash and David Blue. They'd both been so kind to me, and I didn't relish having to break the news that I was leaving them just as they were about to go on tour. I knew they were flying into L.A. that very day, in preparation for rehearsals the following week, so I went to see them later that night at the rock stars' hotel, the Continental Hyatt House (known to all as the Riot House after Led Zeppelin rode their Harley-Davidsons down the corridor). Knocking on the door of Graham's room, I found him sitting cross-legged on the floor, hanging out and discussing the tour with a couple of other guys.

"Hey, Graham, can I have a word with you?" I asked, and he stood up in one fluid movement and led me out onto his balcony overlooking Sunset Boulevard.

"You're not coming on tour with us, are you?" He preempted me in his English accent, a thin smile on his lips.

"How did you know?" I asked, aghast. I hadn't told a soul about the Eagles yet.

"I heard something from Elliot," he replied, patting me on the arm. "What's come up?"

"The Eagles," I said, shrugging my shoulders. "They've asked me to join them, and, although I really appreciate all the help and the breaks you've given me, I've agreed."

"Smart move," he said, nodding his approval. "Better than being a sideman. I don't blame you. Anyway, we had some fun, didn't we?" Not once did he berate me for leaving him and David in the lurch.

His continuing kindness only made my unexpected desertion seem worse. I apologized profusely for letting him down on such short notice, came up with a couple of names of possible replacements, and fled, shamefaced, into the warm Californian night.

The next day I arrived at the Record Plant as agreed, feeling unusually nervous, and was greeted warmly by all the band members.

"Welcome aboard," Glenn said, patting me on the back.

"Good job," said Don, giving me a rare smile.

"Nice to have you with us," Randy, with that chipmunk grin of his, added. "We sure could do with some sanity around here."

"Hey, buddy," Bernie said, hugging me. In my ear, he whispered, "Don't say I didn't warn you." I wondered privately how truly comfortable my old friend was with my arrival, which surely represented a change in the band's chemistry and a decision to lean toward rock and roll instead of his beloved country.

The plan was for me to spend the day getting to know the guys better and to lay down some more solo guitar tracks on "Already Gone." Money hadn't even been mentioned, and I didn't yet have any clear idea of what my stake would be. I'd asked if Susan could come and sit in for the fun of it, and she turned up a few hours later, glowing in her cheesecloth maternity dress, and took a seat in the control room to remind me that I was doing this for her and our future together.

My nickname, Fingers, was soon added to the others—Baby Face or Chipmunk for Randy, Marty Martian for Bernie, because of his curly hair that looked like two antennas were sprouting from it, Roach for Glenn, because of his fondness for pot, and Guano or Sonic Bat for Don, because of his ability to hear an ever so slightly wrong note at five hundred paces. Despite the jocular terms, I soon came to realize that the first session at the Record Plant the previous day had been like a Thanksgiving dinner where everyone has been on their best behavior for the first few hours, until some little dispute gets blown all out of proportion and they lose it. In other words, it truly was a good day in hell.

Now I stood a few feet away from Susan, behind glass, holding my guitar and trying to play this heavy rock while Bernie bickered endlessly with Glenn, Bill tried to mediate, Don had his nose buried in his legal pad or sat with headphones on obsessively replaying the last track, and Randy sat strumming a guitar disconsolately in a corner. Turning to my wife, watching her confused expression, I prayed silently. "Oh Lord, what have I done? Please help me through this." Smart move indeed.

A reporter from *Rolling Stone* once quoted me as saying I felt I'd joined a band that was just breaking up. "Bernie was bouncing off the wall and Randy was threatening to quit," I told him. "It was like walking with a keg of dynamite on your back with the fuse lit, only you don't know how long the fuse is."

What I didn't say was that it felt like this *all the time.* Not a day passed during the recording of that album when someone didn't blow his top, throw something, or stalk out, slamming the door behind him. Each was fighting for control of the band and the musical direction it was taking. Glenn wanted to speed things up and Bernie wanted to slow them down.

As the Johnny-come-lately, and the one Bernie understandably viewed as edging him out, I stood on the periphery and wondered how long it would be before the fuse reached the keg.

Susan sensed it too. "Why don't you call up Graham Nash and see if there's any chance of going back on tour with him and David Blue?" she suggested, but I knew it was too late.

When the Eagles first formed, I was told, their goal was to divide the writing and singing equally. That way, they reasoned, nobody would become a star or feel like a sideman. That had happened in their previous bands, and they didn't create the Eagles to go through all that again. For whatever reason, the plan simply didn't work. Maybe the ego it takes for someone to step up on stage in the first place ends up destroying everything else. Maybe there was just too much talent, or the personalities and musical tastes clashed.

I often felt that if it hadn't been for the band, we wouldn't have had much in common. Glenn's hero was Bob Seger from industrial Detroit; Texas boy Don was from the Ray Charles R&B school; Bernie was pure West Coast country; and Randy, from Nebraska, idolized Ricky Nelson. I was from the Deep South, and my heart was somewhere between B.B. King and Clapton. Everyone brought something special to the group, be it guitar playing, singing, or songwriting, but the edgy creative tension that made the music sound so good when it was put together kept getting in the way of everything else.

Don and Glenn shared writing credits (sometimes with other writers) on no less than nine of the fourteen tracks of On the Border. Bernie had just two, and Randy one. J.D. Souther, who wasn't even in the band, had three. Don sang lead on five of the songs and Glenn on four, while Randy sang on two and Bernie on only one. None of this made Randy and Bernie—suddenly relegated to the George and Ringo positions in Bernie's Beatles analogy—very happy.

There was one explosive argument after another, usually while I sat silently in a corner, tuning my guitar and watching out of the corner of my eye. Never once did I feel, "Hey, I got it made. This thing's gonna last for years." I was committed but always kept an ear to the ground for other work. I watched Graham Nash and David Blue go out on the road with a new guy and hankered after the fun times we'd had together. I still did sessions for other people, just in case. I felt that the slightest bump in the road would cause the keg of dynamite to go off and blow us all sky high.

There were a few times when things went really well and the pressure lifted, especially if Don and Glenn were happy with the way a track was going. Bernie's pedal steel guitar and Don's singing on Bill's remix of "The Best of My Love" reminded us that this band could make great music. When the bickering stopped and they all got along, it was so great that it almost made the bad times recede in the memory. With that song in particular, there was no drum track, so for the first time, Don picked up an acoustic guitar and sang. Bill had always called him the Eagles' "secret weapon," and now I understood why. This new voice that emerged made the hairs on the back of my neck tingle.

The Record Plant was designed as a place for bands to have a good time in between takes, with three or four studios, Ping-Pong and pool tables, themed bedrooms for exhausted artists to crash in, a Jacuzzi, and plenty of places to sit and get stoned. The Jacuzzi was known as the "scum pond," because it always had this frothy sludge on the surface of the water. Nobody would ever go in it if they were sober, and the rumor was that if girls went in by themselves, they'd get pregnant.

I don't know how many nights I drove in all the way from Topanga to the Record Plant and home again in the small hours, my eyes red-rimmed. The rest of the band lived much closer. Sometimes they would pile back to Glenn's house in Coldwater Canyon, a place that used to be owned by James Cagney. Copious amounts of Acapulco Gold or lime-green Maui Wowee were smoked, and cocaine became the best way of pushing on through the night when every muscle in your body told you to lie down and get some sleep. It was no good if just one person took it and the others didn't; then one would be up all night, pressing on, while the rest of us would be lying around, yawning, resentful of the late hour.

I soon realized that it wasn't such a good idea for me to drive home so late at night, especially not after a few joints and some beers, so I started sleeping over at the studio. The first night I stayed, I can't even remember going to bed, but when I woke in the morning, I thought I'd died and gone to hell. The particular room I'd crashed in had an S&M theme, with a leather headboard, whips, chains, and a cage hanging from the ceiling. I stared up at it all, blinking hard. "What on earth did I take last night?" I asked myself.

During that sojourn at the Record Plant, I also came to understand, for the first time, that being in a band as successful as the Eagles brought with it a tremendous amount of prestige as far as beautiful young women were concerned. There was no shortage of them around the studio, waiting in the wings to alleviate the tensions for my musical colleagues. Bernie had told me some wild stories of life on the road during tours, which almost made my hair curl as much as his. From what he said, I realized I was a complete novice when it came to women, by comparison with these guys, and felt slightly embarrassed by the relatively small numbers of sexual encounters I had enjoyed.

"Irving came with us on the last one and said he thought he'd died and gone to heaven," Bernie laughed. "These girls just come crawling out of the woodwork and they'll do anything, I mean *anything*, to please you."

Amazed and more than a little jealous at witnessing some of it first-hand, I had to constantly remind myself that Susan was waiting for me at home, our baby growing inside her. "No thanks, honey," I'd say to girl after girl who threw herself at me, "I'm really flattered, but I'm a happily married man." It was a supreme test of my willpower.

Despite the continual infighting while we recorded it, *On the Border* became the Eagles' fastest-selling album, going gold two months after its release in March 1974. I was listed as a "late arrival" on the liner notes. The small contribution I made to the guitar section helped drive it up to number seventeen on the U.S. charts. It broke us internationally, and pushed the previous two albums, *Desperado* and *Eagles*, past the half-million sales mark. "Already Gone," on which I played lead with Glenn, reached number thirty-two on the singles charts. Even better, "The Best of My Love," as remixed by Bill Szymczyk, soared to number one and sold over a million copies.

The first band meeting we ever had with me as a member, shortly after the record had been cut, took place in Irving Azoff's office. "His Shortness has summoned us," Bernie told me. "We'd better not be late." I wandered in, bemused by and more than a little fearful of the idea of a regular meeting at which all could air their grievances. I stood silently at the back, waiting for the fuse to be lit.

Irving explained that we'd set up a corporation called Eagles Limited, and would each own a fifth of it. All monies from touring, merchandising, and recording royalties would come direct to Eagles Ltd. and be divided equally.

We looked at each other for a moment, and there were a few murmurs of discontent. Bernie, as usual the most vocal, was the first to speak.

"When I came into this band, it was meant to be a four-way split, and now that Don's arrived, the profits from this new album are gonna get split five ways. I don't think that's fair, when he only arrived at the last minute and didn't put in the hard time like the rest of us."

I agreed with him entirely, but was surprised and a little hurt that it was my old Gainesville friend who'd first raised the subject.

"There are no sidemen in this band," Glenn said firmly, with his gruff voice. "We've all been there and we know what that's like." I was pleased and relieved to hear it.

There were some general murmurs of discontent, and Irving made a suggestion. "Well, I think the way we can work this out is if Don only gets paid a fifth of the profits on the cuts he played on and a fifth of all other profits from here on. How does that sound?"

"Seems fair to me," I piped up, knowing what hell they'd all gone through in England with Glyn Johns and each other before I'd joined. The last thing I wanted at this stage was to rock the already unsteady boat still further. We all agreed to that arrangement and moved on to other business. Everything was done on a handshake and a promise. The common understanding was that the band, as a legal entity, was a joint, mutually owned, equally shared venture designed to make us more efficient in the industry. We appointed Glenn president and Don secretary. Later, at a lawyer's office, we all signed the piece of paper making Eagles Ltd. a reality.

I listened to the subsequent fine-tuning of the deal and marveled at Irving's mastery of all matters fiscal. I'd never been in a band at this level before, and I didn't yet have a business manager. Irving recommended a guy named Gerry Breslauer. In the past, the only official document I'd had was a gig contract drawn up for me by a Gainesville attorney in return for guitar lessons. It would specify which dates, how many hours we'd play, and for how much. I'd sign it and the organizer would sign it, so if there was a dispute, we had a written agreement to refer back to. I used that contract until I signed with Creed Taylor when I was in Flow, a document I never even properly examined.

It was the same with the Eagles. I can remember sitting in the office of the attorney Irving hired to draft the contracts for Eagles Ltd., and he kept watching me as everything was being explained. "I can see the wheels turning, son," he said. "You've got some questions, haven't you?"

I didn't even know what to ask, never mind being sophisticated enough to negotiate for myself. I think I inquired as to what publishing was and if he could explain record royalties, but I'm not sure I really understood his answers. I had no legal representation other than that which Irving had arranged, and I just had to trust that he and Irving were looking after my interests fairly. I was a musician, not a businessman, and I had no reason to doubt them. I couldn't have afforded a lawyer, even if I'd realized I needed one. I could have called my brother Jerry and asked his advice, but I didn't think it was necessary.

Come what may, Eagles Ltd. was born. I was an equal partner with Bernie, Randy, Don, and Glenn in a chart-topping band. There had been surprisingly little disagreement during the process, and the new album went on to be a big hit, so I kept my fingers crossed and hoped for the best.

However unstable the band was, I was suddenly a major player in one of America's up-and-coming rock bands. It had taken some pain to get here, but the hard times were finally over, for a while, anyway. Best of all, they were over just as my first child was expected. Once again, my prayers had been answered.

Susan and I bought our first little house together with the money we made in those early days. We found a small three-story property set on two acres in a remote part of Topanga Canyon, on a road called Everding Motorway, with spectacular views of the ocean. Marvin Gaye had rented it before we paid the princely sum of seventy thousand dollars, and it was ours.

We soon realized what a huge mistake we'd made. It was a hopeless house for a child, with its open-plan design and ladders to the loft, set on a steep hill at the end of a dirt road on top of a mountain, but we were new to this parenting thing. We'd fallen in love with the view and not realized that we were buying a place designed for a single guy, not a family. Its only plus was its location. I never tired of the view or watching the fog roll in from the ocean and creep up the valley beneath us and stop, so that we were above the clouds.

I'd hoped to be around to help in the final stages of Susan's pregnancy, but the *On the Border* tour began and, with it, the madness. The idea was that we'd start off in the States and follow with a world tour, but the album was selling so well that the pace quickly accelerated. Almost daily, we experienced an enervating and dizzying succession of airports, hotels, screaming crowds, and limousines speeding away from backstage doors behind the flashing blue lights of police escorts. With connecting flights, layovers, and long journeys by car, entire days were consumed by traveling. Irving and his team of managers suddenly accounted for every minute of our time. No one had any privacy. We hurtled from city to city at a breakneck clip. We'd arrive in town, sometimes by car, sometimes by plane, check into the hotel, hold some press interviews, do the sound check, perform the show, watch the others argue with each other or party with groupies all night, then fly on to the next town.

The backstage life was wild. Willing young women surrounded us constantly, virtually begging us to bed them. I quickly discovered there were large groups of bored young women in almost every town whose biggest kick was to sleep with a rock star. They even chalked them up, like plane spotters, bragging about how many they'd slept with and who. I kept urging myself to resist temptation. Like some of the other band members, I took full advantage of the uniquely carefree atmosphere with the weed and the blow yet did my best to ignore the girls, but the more the opportunity presented itself, the more normal it seemed. It was such an extreme, high-octane situation, and the girls were less than one-night stands to those who partook. There was something horribly clinical about it—fucking a groupie while stoned and then throwing her out. Every night, I'd go back to my hotel room alone, and whenever I could, I'd reach for the telephone and call Susan.

"Hey, honey, how you doing?"

"We're fine," she'd say, sleepily. "The baby's been kicking a lot today. I think he's going to be a quarterback."

"I wish I could be there to feel it."

"Me too."

Hanging around us a lot at that time was a quirky teenage boy named Cameron Crowe, working on assignment for *Rolling Stone*. He looked about thirteen but was probably older, and he seemed to be watching our every move, which was more than a little unnerving. He was a young kid in frumpy clothes, very shy and nervous, and he was witnessing all that was going on with the drugs, women, and booze. I wasn't the only one who was spooked by his presence. He was like a little doorstop, always in the corner, a weird-looking kind of gnome, nice but strange.

To his credit, he kept right up with us—although he did have youth on his side, while we had the Peruvian marching powder, youth in a bottle. Nobody had to wet-nurse him; he was very self-sufficient and self-aware. Most of the time he seemed harmless, like some innocent kid on a high school project following us around. He didn't seem like some big shot reporter, and none of us could understand why they'd sent a child and not a real writer, although Don and Glenn did keep a close eye on him. It was kind of interesting to see him witnessing all this stuff for the first time, watching him watching us.

If ever any of us stopped to talk to him, he'd whip out his notepad

HEAVEN and HELL • 123

and scribble down every word furiously, as if he was afraid he'd forget what we'd said and didn't want to lose a single gem. "You don't have to take it down verbatim, kid," I'd tell him, placing my hand over his notebook. "We're just chatting, right?"

"Sure," he'd say, swallowing and looking up at me with those baby eyes. "Whatever you say." I got the distinct impression that the minute my back was turned, he'd jot down every word anyway.

We never knew what might show up in print, and he made it difficult for us to completely relax when he was around, but he was a nice enough kid, and I knew if *Rolling Stone* had hired him so young, he was probably going to go far. He did, and years later he made the brilliant movie *Almost Famous*, based I believe, partially on our crazy life, but mostly on his experiences on the road with Led Zeppelin and my old friends the Allman Brothers.

One day blurred into the other, but the barnstorming did the trick. We were a huge success. More and more T-shirts, tickets, and albums sold. The touring went on and on. If a radio station played even one of our songs, Irving rushed us into that region as well. Soon, our opening acts, Dan Fogelberg and Jimmy Buffett—both Irving's clients—couldn't even finish their set without being drowned out to cries of, "We want the Eagles! We want the Eagles!"

We were thrilled to see the crowd accepting our new sound, some of which I was responsible for. To make the band a little tougher, I replaced its softer textures with much harder sounds. The first thing I did was to suggest that "Take It Easy" become a three-electric-guitar song with Bernie playing all the B-string bender stuff, me playing a Strat or something stronger, and Glenn also playing electric. The song was just too puny otherwise, and the larger venues we were now playing really didn't have good acoustic pickups. In those days, it was hard to stand onstage strumming an acoustic guitar and expect to fill a two- or three-thousand-seat auditorium.

Now, whenever I'd step into the spotlight to play my solos, even in the middle of a show, the cheers were overpowering. I realized with a mixture of humility and awe that the applause was in recognition of me and my guitar playing, not just the band. Life never felt as good as it did then.

It was surprising that we received so much airplay. Part of our success came from the openness of the AM band. Radio was truly diverse in the seventies. A station would play a rock track, then a country track, then something else. You didn't have to change the dial if you wanted to hear a certain kind of sound. We knew we had a good shot at getting on the radio with the original Eagles sound, but we also knew the best-selling hit songs were all rock-oriented, which was why everyone but Bernie wanted to head in this direction.

Despite the pressure and the ever-present threat of an argument simmering away somewhere in the background, we did have a lot of fun together on that tour. There are no words to describe the feeling of having made it to the big time and knowing that thousands of fans are waiting out there to listen to your music. Every night, just before we'd go onstage, we'd gather together for a voice rehearsal in the locker room of what was usually a sports arena. We chose the locker room for its privacy and the natural echo it provided. Huddling together, we'd open our mouths in unison and practice several ooohs and aaaahs from specific songs, like "Take It Easy." Once we'd opened our throats and warmed up, we'd all sing "Seven Bridges Road," a Crosby, Stills, Nash & Young–style a cappella song written by Steve Young. No matter what the mood between band members or how bad things were, we always had that private rehearsal together, and then when we went out onto the stage, the lights would come up and we'd be standing there at a single microphone to open the show with that same melodic, lilting song. It blew people away. It was always a vocally unifying moment, all five voices coming together in harmony.

I'd get goose bumps every night.

Cocaine abuse continued to be rife. In those years, nearly everyone was doing it, from members of the band to the crew to the record executives. People would wander around asking, "Hey, you holding? You got any?" At various times, they'd disappear off into the men's room and come back with white powder rings around their nostrils, a sure indication of what they'd been up to.

"Hey, buddy, you're showing," one of us would say, pointing to the other's nose. A quick wipe on the back of the hand would solve the problem.

Many of us still smoked a lot of pot and drank longneck Buds, but we'd rarely refuse some blow. We were generally well coked up before we even appeared on stage, but our roadies had instructions to leave lines of blow on our amps so that between songs we could go back and bend over as if we were adjusting the knobs, when actually we were snorting in front of an entire live audience. The drugs must have affected our performance, but at the time, I thought we sounded just great.

I doubt we could have continued at the pace we were being driven, unless we'd had some chemical help. Cocaine offered us the chance to keep going, pushing ourselves to the absolute limits, when all we wanted to do was stop for a while and catch our breath. Then, in April 1974, something happened that let me do so.

The tour was going full tilt, with five or sometimes six shows a week, but one of our final gigs of the first six-week stretch was in a theater in Phoenix, Arizona, an amazing venue with a revolving stage. You'd play to a different part of the audience every few minutes (and the other band members could closely inspect the girls who'd be invited backstage afterward).

I was quite literally in a spin after that gig and the backstage party that followed, where the usual amounts of drugs and tequila were consumed. We caught the last flight back to L.A. and landed around one thirty in the morning on April 6, almost too exhausted to leave the comfort of our seats. The plan was to jump in a fleet of rental cars and drive that night to Ontario Motor Speedway, about an hour east of the city. We were due to perform at one of the biggest gigs we'd ever played, the California Jam, in front of 300,000 people. The show was billed as "the Woodstock of the West Coast," and fellow artists included Deep Purple, Black Sabbath, Emerson, Lake & Palmer, Black Oak Arkansas, and Earth, Wind & Fire.

I was walking through LAX, feeling that bone-weary exhaustion that only a cocktail of drink, drugs, and sleep deprivation can bring, wishing I could just curl up and go to sleep in some quiet corner, when a message came over the paging system.

"Mr. Felder. Mr. Don Felder, please come to the information desk immediately, where there is an urgent call waiting for you."

My heart began pumping hard again, stirring up all the stuff I'd taken the previous night. Susan, could it be Susan? She wasn't due for a week or so, but as I ran over to the desk, I feared the worst. Grabbing the phone, I spoke into it breathlessly.

"Hello?"

"Don? It's Susan. The contractions have started and they're getting real bad. I need you to come home. *Now.*"

Without hesitating except for a quick word to the rest of the band, I grabbed my suitcase off the baggage carousel and ran to one of the waiting rental cars.

"Go for it, man!" I heard Bernie scream behind me.

"Tell Susan good luck from us," yelled Randy.

I drove out to Topanga at breakneck speed, my eyes smarting with tiredness, my body being kept awake on pure adrenaline. Susan was in bed, breathing hard. I helped her get up and drove her to the Santa Monica Hospital on Wilshire and Fourteenth Street. I didn't even have time to take my suede tassel-sleeved jacket off.

We'd agreed on natural childbirth, but it was a long and painful labor, and Susan really went through hell. There was a window right next to her bed, which looked out over the roof and the air-conditioning ducts. From where I stood, and in my hazy mental state, suffering as I was from chronic sleep deprivation, it seemed as if the building was in labor too, wheezing out steam in time with Susan's heavy breathing.

Back at the Ontario Motor Speedway, the band waited for word. They were due to go on at two o'clock that afternoon, and Irving had arranged for a helicopter at the Santa Monica heliport a few miles away, to fly me to the gig if the baby was born in the morning. My deadline was one o'clock, and I was watching the time and urging this child to hurry up, not wanting to miss such an amazing gig.

"Come on, Jesse," I'd urge the baby through Susan's convulsing tummy. I was convinced he was going to be a boy, and I'd already named him in honor of my kindly Uncle Buck. "Any time up to 12:45 would be fine. Just come out and meet us, son."

"Don!" Susan hissed through the pain. "Don't you think I want him out as soon as possible too?"

"Sorry, honey."

One o'clock came and went, and I called Irving up. "You'll have to go ahead without me," I told him. "This baby must be a Jackson Browne fan." Jackson, recently a father himself, had agreed to stand in and play for me. By the time Susan had dilated and was ready to go to the labor room for an assisted birth a few hours later, I was almost delirious with a combination of exhaustion, excitement, and nerves. I felt so faint, I could easily have blacked out, but when our baby was born and handed to my wife, bloody and bawling, I somehow found enough strength in my legs to stand up and kiss them both.

The physician let me cut the cord, and as I did so, I realized I was crying. Great droplets splashed down my face as I cradled our child in my arms. "Welcome to the world, Jesse Felder," I told him, wetting his face with my tears. Looking up at Susan, her own face wet, I'd never felt happier in my life.

TEN

I was only able to spend a couple of weeks settling Susan and Jesse in, while the rest of the band reacquainted themselves with the inside of the Troubadour club, before we went back on the road for what turned into a nine-month tour.

While I was home, I changed diapers, fed and washed Jesse, babysat when Susan needed a break, and enjoyed spending quality time with my new son. We had a Mexican matrimonial hammock in the backyard and I rigged up a clothesline from it to the house, so that I could sit on the couch watching baseball in the living room while rocking Jesse gently to sleep outside. As soon as I stopped, during a particularly engrossing part of the game, he'd exercise his lungs and yell just to remind me.

I'd maintained polite long-range contact with my parents ever since moving to L.A., sending them the odd card from on the road and calling them once in a while, but I hadn't seen them since my wedding, two years earlier, and they'd never seen Jesse. My brother, Jerry, who had two kids with Marnie and was living and working in Gainesville as a partner in a law firm he'd joined after college, called to tell me that Dad had finally quit working at Koppers, due to ill health. He'd never officially retired and was still being paid, but he had congestive heart failure and lung problems, probably exacerbated by years of smoking and inhaling toxic fumes.

"You might want to fly down and see him, Don," Jerry advised, long distance. "He's not doing very well."

Having a son had considerably mellowed my resentment toward Dad, making me realize how hard it was to be a parent. During a lull in the tour, when I had a week off to spend with my family before we went back on the road, I decided to fly to Florida and reacquaint myself with the old man.

We flew to Gainesville and rented a brand-new car, which I knew would impress Dad. The house looked just the same, although even smaller than I remembered it. Jesse was just a couple of months old, and when Mom opened the front door of that old clapboard house with the tin roof that Dad had built with his own hands, I felt so proud to hand her my son. She looked a little older, but she was very pleased to see us and to meet her new grandson.

"Hi, little Jesse," she said, cradling him in her arms and beaming down at him. "I've waited a long time for this." Jesse gurgled and wriggled on cue and gave her one of his winning smiles.

Dad was sitting in an armchair in the lounge, an oxygen tank by his side, a clear plastic tube from it hooked around his nose. He was thin and gaunt, with sunken eyes, and his whole body seemed to have shrunk and caved in as he slowly drowned in his own lungs. Gone was the granite mountain of a man who'd serviced the machinery at Koppers for fifty years, the Dad who'd driven us around America, his tanned muscular arm protruding from the driver's window. He was so diminished, he looked as if he could barely stand, let alone clamber onto a roof and fix the most high-tech television antenna in Gainesville.

His appearance shocked me to the core. He was only sixty-four, but he looked fifteen years older. Shakily, he got to his feet, clinging to the arm of his chair.

"Hey, Dad," I said, holding out Jesse. "Meet your grandson."

"I can't hold him, I've gotta sit down," he said, collapsing back into his chair. It was summer and the house was like an oven. I could hardly breathe myself.

Looking up at me weakly, he managed a half-smile as I lowered Jesse into his lap. He looked down at his grandson and then up at me, a shine in his watery eyes.

"Well, hello, Jesse," he said. "I'm your Grandpa Felder." Looking up at me again, studying my straggly beard, handlebar moustache, mutton-chops, and shoulder-length hair with a frown, he complained, "Don't you think it's time you went to the barber's, Doc, now you're a father?"

Within a year, he was dead. I'd spent some time with him on that initial visit, buying an air-conditioning unit to keep him cool and help him breathe (which he refused to switch on for fear of the electric bills). I offered him money, but he was too proud to accept. I'd taken some Eagles records and played them to him on his old music center and tried to explain to him how successful the band was, but I don't think he ever really understood. All he said about the music was, "There's no horns. I like horns."

His decline was quite rapid after my visit, and he was admitted to the North Central Florida Hospital, from where Jerry called me. I raced there from the West Coast, and when I arrived, Dad was hooked up to a special machine that sprayed mist to keep his airways clear. It reminded me of the iron lungs of my polio-scarred youth.

"Hey, Dad," I said, leaning over the bed to kiss him. "It's Don."

"When you gonna cut your hair and look like a man?" he growled through dry lips as my hair brushed his cheek. They were among the last words he ever spoke to me.

After a week of taking turns with Mom and Jerry in a bedside vigil, I had to go back to L.A. He died a few days later. My third flight to Gainesville in less than a year was for his funeral, but the finality of his passing didn't hit me until I walked into the Williams-Thomas funeral home, where my friend Jim and I had played Frisbee as kids, and stared down at my father's emaciated body lying in an open casket. He was dressed in his Sunday suit, a shirt and tie, his arms folded across his chest. I'd never seen his fingernails so clean.

A flood of sorrow overcame me. There was still so much unresolved. Jerry and I hugged each other and wept. He'd been there for my parents all these years while I was an absentee son, and I felt tremendous guilt about never having a proper, adult relationship with my father. Now it was too late. I was filled with remorse about this loss, not just of his life but so much else. When you lose a parent, the child in you dies. In the space of a year, I'd gained a son and lost a father, and it felt like such a huge transition. Everything had changed, and I was rushing through my life at a furious pace, not doing anything justice.

Sobbing in my brother's arms, I mourned the death of my father with an intensity I'd never expected. He was, I realized, the strongest single influence in my life. He'd taught me all he knew about music, bought me my first real guitar, and encouraged me to play. Everything I was, everything I'd achieved, was because of him.

"God bless you, Dad," I whispered and promised him silently that, one day, I'd cut my hair.

In late 1974, we went back to the Record Plant to make a new album. There had been a short lull after the *On the Border* tour, but then Asylum turned the screws for a follow-up record.

I wasn't looking forward to a return to the pressure-cooker atmosphere of the studio, especially not with the added burden of bettering the last gold-selling product. We knew the critics were waiting in the wings, knives sharpened, to cut us up and serve us in little pieces to the public. At least on the road, there had been enough space and time to get along reasonably well, but even out of the studio the differences that had been evident since I'd joined the previous year grew and grew. The band was becoming increasingly divided by the tensions within it, based on the type of music we played. In such a prickly environment, no new songs were immediately forthcoming. Bernie, meanwhile, became increasingly dis-satisfied with how the pair of them treated him and Randy. He didn't like them taking rough mixes back to their house to decide what tracks would stay or go, nor did he and Randy like what they described as Glenn's abil-ity to "change a word and gain a third"—coming to a song that was in their minds substantially done, with lyrics and music, making what to them seemed to be modest contributions, and suddenly becoming entitled to a third of the songwriting royalties.

I just wanted to keep my head down and do the best I could, even if the song credits were sometimes out of whack. The new album was provi-sionally called *One of These Nights*. The title track originally began life as an R&B song on acoustic piano, but it just didn't sound right to me when Glenn first played it to us. Randy was stuck in Nebraska, snowed in, and couldn't get to the studio, so I told Glenn, "Wait a minute, I'll play bass." I came up with an introduction and bass figure. We played a couple of demo passes with me playing the bass part over Glenn's piano, and I wound up writing the entire bass line for the title track. When the weather finally cleared and Randy was able to fly in, I taught him what I'd written, verbatim, and we recorded it for the album. As long as the track came out good, I didn't care.

I also wrote a song called "Visions," for which Don provided some of the lyrics, the only Eagles track I ever sang lead vocal on. I penned that song at my house in Topanga. It was the most up-tempo track of the whole album. I was still not confident about my singing voice, especially not when I had Don's to compare it with, but I tried really hard, and the fact that Don and Glenn deigned to let me sing it must have meant something, I reasoned, even if the track was sort of thrown onto the album at the last minute and I wasn't especially proud of the vocals. At one point in the lyrics, Don and Glenn sing, "Play on, El Chingadero, play on." I learned later that *chingadero* is Spanish and loosely translates to "motherfucker."

Someone once asked me which Eagles songs I wrote by myself. The answer is: not one. It would be interesting to hear what the answer would be if you asked Don Henley and Glenn Frey the same question. Those two would go hibernate somewhere and come up with the lyrics, or the melody, or the chords, or often all three, and only when they'd emerged with finished product would the rest of us help come up with ideas for how it should be performed. "After the Thrill Is Gone" was an idea Glenn had. He loved B.B. King's "The Thrill Is Gone," and while working to perfect a particular sound he wanted, he piped up, "Hey, how about calling it '*After* the Thrill is Gone'?" Our work together was almost always like that: a collaborative process, in which each one of us—while not exactly writing the songs—helped shape the final product.

I'd work tirelessly on pieces of music that came into my head, mixing and tinkering with them at home before excitedly going to Don or Glenn when I thought I might have something. "Hey, Glenn, I've been working on some licks, and I'd like to play them to you," I'd say, guitar in hand.

Glenn would look up from whatever he was doing and say something that became the catchphrase of that whole recording phase: "I'll tell you when." Then he'd go right back to his work.

"Maybe we could schedule some time for you to listen to them?" I'd push, ever hopeful.

"I'll tell you when," came the gruff reply.

When the Eagles first started, Bernie had been the proverbial fair-haired child. He was by far the best instrumentalist and played most of the great guitar, banjo, mandolin, and pedal steel parts. With *On The Border*, the band had deliberately shifted away from that direction. By *One of These Nights*, that shift had been graven in stone.

To Bernie, life was pretty much black and white. He didn't like rock and roll; he liked country. That's really where his soul was and what he did impeccably well. He could play anything with strings, but that sound wasn't what Don and Glenn wanted anymore. They did try to accommodate his tastes sometimes. For example, there's a definite attempt to maintain a country sound to "Lyin' Eyes," but for Bernie it was never enough. He and I would jam together all the time in hotel rooms and in between studio takes, just for fun, playing all those Smoky Mountain tunes he'd taught me back in Gainesville, but bluegrass didn't sell millions of albums. When Bernie repeatedly resisted the attempt to shift gears, personalities clashed and the arguments became even more explosive.

As much as we were friends, he didn't want the band to head in the direction Bill Szymczyk and the introduction of my guitar work was taking it. In fighting to win his point, he lost friendships, especially Glenn's. I felt Glenn was the type of person who felt you were either with him or against him. If you didn't agree with him one hundred percent, you were his enemy. Bernie had seemingly argued his way out of Glenn's camp.

Bernie was living with Patti Davis, the daughter of California Governor Ronald Reagan. He'd first met her over at Fred Walecki's Westwood Music. She'd even come on the European leg of our last tour, much to her father's disgust, especially as he was planning to run for president and the story made *People* magazine. Feeling left out now, Bernie insisted that Patti attend our studio sessions and be given a writing credit on the album for his song "I Wish You Peace," something the rest of the band weren't at all sure about. It was only much later that I realized that that song was Bernie's farewell to us all.

Tired of the constant bickering and madly in love with Patti, Bernie began to lose interest. One night, we gathered in the studio to hear what we'd recorded that day. For one track, we really wanted his input, but he stood up, threw his hands in the air, and said, "I'm going surfing." He didn't return for three days. It was at a crucial time in the recording process, and his absence caused serious problems for the rest of us.

There was so much strife and conflict during this time, it was wearing everyone down. Cocaine became my salve, and I went from being so disinterested that I'd given my coke to a truck driver, to being a man obsessed. It was Bernie who first took me to one side and warned me of the dangers. I'd asked him if he had any and he gave me his small vial, like the ones we all used to tap onto our thumbnails, but I tapped so hard that much more than the normal quantity came tumbling out. I couldn't put it back, so I just snorted it all up while Bernie stood watching.

"Hey, man," he said, alarm in his eyes. "You gotta be careful with this stuff! It'll run away with you, you know. Don't fry your brain." I stopped and stared at him, my eyes and nostrils still smarting, and realized that maybe he was right. I'd always managed to avoid being hooked on anything before, and now wasn't the time to start.

The arguments simmered on, while I did what I could to mediate. "The band's moved on from the early days," I told Bernie over and over. "We've evolved. Don and Glenn have formed the strongest songwriting team, and that's best for the band. They're entitled to have the final say." Despite all the promises of equal shares, I still felt like the hired hand, the session man who'd been invited in to hang around and take what crumbs I could get, but Bernie had been a founding member and refused to accept that.

"You weren't there in the beginning," he'd tell me, "when the Eagles were a *band* and everybody got two songs. That's all been forgotten, and it stinks."

He was headstrong and stubborn. He felt Glenn didn't have the authority to dictate what should or shouldn't be on an album—especially when he and Don decided that they didn't want Bernie to sing solo at all, that they didn't like his B-string bender guitar or the abstract, banjo-driven sound of his instrumental number, "Journey of the Sorcerer," and that they hated "I Wish You Peace."

Bernie and I had always been close, but I knew he had a short fuse. So did Glenn. If not about the songs, then they began to fight over everything, from where we should tour to what the merchandising should look like, until none of us knew where to put ourselves. I continued trying to play a diplomatic role between the two factions. I'd go to Bernie to support and encourage him and try to give him confidence in his writing and playing, and then I'd remind the guys what a key player he was in the band. I found myself constantly trying to help this thing stay together, but it seemed like Don and Glenn had already decided that Bernie wasn't suited to the band anymore, chiefly because they were so dissatisfied with the struggle he presented. It was always Bernie against the two of them. They unified against his writing, playing style, lyrics, voice, and guitar tone. No matter what he did, it was no longer good enough.

• • •

I only got through that difficult time because I had Susan and Jesse
waiting at home for me. I tried not to bring the bad stuff home and unload
it onto her, because I knew she was struggling with the demands of being
a new mother. She helped me sort it out anyway, and her common-sense
attitude always brought me down to earth. Better still, because of my new
responsibilities, I rarely if ever took drugs at home, which probably saved
my life.

I remember coming home one morning at about 5 A.M., when Jesse
was six months old, after another long session at the Record Plant. I was
still cranked out on coke, sniffing and grinding my teeth, and had somehow managed to drive my pickup all the way back to Topanga. Instead of
joining Susan in bed, I sat out on the balcony and watched the clouds roll
in from the ocean as the sun came up above them. I was soaring like an eagle, literally way above those clouds, zoned into another cosmos. I sat
there for almost an hour until I heard Jesse's first morning cry. I heard Susan get out of bed and tend to him, I listened to her moving around, and I
wanted to go in and say hello, but I couldn't pull myself together enough
to move from my chair.

When I finally managed to get my legs working and staggered inside,
I was met with the sobering reality of a wife and baby. The look on Susan's
face was not something I ever wanted to see again. "Look at the state
you're in!" she said. "Don't you ever come home this stoned again." She
drove the point home that this was not acceptable behavior for the father
of her child. I got the message. More and more, I didn't come home at all,
sleeping over in the S&M room at the Record Plant instead, a place that
suddenly seemed very appealing. In many ways, I think Susan was as
happy with the arrangement as I was. The little sleep she was getting
wouldn't be disturbed by my crashing in at 5 A.M., and she was relieved I
wasn't driving home alone, with coke in my pocket and paranoid delusions
that every set of headlights behind me was a cop car.

It was different when I went back on the road, though, and was away
all the time. Off we went that summer, and Susan was left by herself in

Topanga, feeling increasingly isolated. Her parents had retired to Florida; mine were there too; the friends she'd made in the Valley lived miles away; there were no other Eagles wives to be friendly with (Randy's was in Nebraska); I was on the road with Bernie, her nearest neighbor; and she had few friends locally to talk to or help her care for the baby.

One day, she took Jesse outside and laid a blanket on the grass so he could get a little sun while she cleaned the house. The area around the property was rough bush, full of coyote, and she was always cautious. Looking down, she was just about to lay him on the blanket when she spotted a small rattlesnake, coiled right beside him. It was one snake too much for a Boston girl.

I was out in the boonies somewhere, in a crummy hotel late at night, when she found my number from the itinerary. "We've gotta get out of Topanga," she said, crying. "There's far too many critters. I want to sell the house and find us somewhere else, Don. Somewhere with neighbors we can talk to."

"Oh, OK, honey," I said, half-asleep and more than a little bemused. It felt so strange having her telling me where we were going to be living, while I was thousands of miles away. She arranged everything and sold our house to the actor Will Geer, who played Grandpa in *The Waltons* television show. She found us a pretty 1950s Cape Cod–style house, painted pink inside and out, right on the sand at Broad Beach at the furthest point of Malibu, just before it becomes Ventura County. The first time she took me there, I inhaled the fresh, salty air and looked at the deep powdery sand, several hundred feet wide to the shore, and knew she'd made the right decision. Susan had erected a little swing set and an inflatable pool for Jesse in the front yard, which was like a giant sandbox. My only complaint about the house was the color. Some of the rooms were so shockingly pink you had to wear sunglasses to enter them. The actress Ali MacGraw, famous for the hit movie *Love Story*, had been the last tenant. Miss MacGraw moved three doors down with her boyfriend, Steve McQueen, next door to Keith Moon. Our other neighbors included Jack Lemmon, Joe Cocker, Goldie Hawn, Dick Martin, and Donald Sutherland.

I didn't suddenly feel incredibly rich, living alongside such people. On the contrary, I felt incredibly in debt. I was laboring under the delusion that being in a rock band would automatically make me fabulously wealthy. Without paying a great deal of concern to the dollars and cents, I just went along with what was offered. My new business manager, Gerry Breslauer, along with his partner, Joel Jacobson, both recommended by Irving, kept all the accounts and told me what I could or couldn't do. I was young and carefree, happy with the way my life was going. As long as there was cash in the bank, I didn't feel the need to doubt anyone. That was the way the rest of the band operated too, and probably most of our famous neighbors.

"Business managers take care of all that stuff," Keith Moon once reminded me. "Relax. That's what you're paying them for, man."

I was still driving the International pickup truck when I was in L.A., but I wanted Susan and Jesse to have something better than the old Volvo with a million miles on it, so I went to see my business manager.

"Can I afford to buy my wife a new car?" I asked Gerry.

"Sure," he replied, smiling. "What do you want?"

With the authority vested in my pen and a phone call from Gerry's company, I was approved for the purchase of a brand-new Chevy Vega family station wagon. Chevrolet out of loyalty to my father, but it turned out to be one of the worst automobiles I ever bought. The first thing it did was break down on the freeway with Jesse in the baby seat. Susan took it to the shop and had it fixed, but it broke down again. The Volvo had never once let us down, and as we hadn't yet sold it, she went back to driving that.

We talked to Gerry about replacing the Chevy, and he recommended a Mercedes. "I've been driving them for years, and they're really great," he told us confidently.

I didn't feel ready for a Mercedes. It seemed a step too far, but Susan was all for it. "Let's just go take a look," she pleaded, then drove me to the Beverly Hills Mercedes dealership, where she fell in love with a little four-door, chocolate brown 280. I was relieved she hadn't gone for one of the big Mercs for cigar-smoking rich men, so I arranged to buy the 280 on monthly payments. After that, I felt much better leaving her and Jesse to go on the road, even though I was heavily in debt with a car and a house.

My father, who'd never owed a penny to anyone, would have thrown up his hands.

One of These Nights became our first album to debut at number one, when it was released in June 1975, as Saigon fell, and it helped every other Eagles album skyrocket in sales. The title track, released as a single, with me playing the precise guitar solo I'd created for it, leaped into the Top 10. The underlying theme of Hollywood, with all its good and evil, struck a chord with critics and fans alike. The band had progressed from being dust-covered outlaws in the desert to living it up in the Hollywood hills. Songs like "Lyin' Eyes," with its incredibly evocative lyrics, enhanced our reputation for not only playing great music but for telling a story, too.

The idea for that particular track came one night in Dan Tana's restaurant, next to the Troubadour. We were sitting at a table when we noticed a pretty young blonde with a much older but clearly wealthy man. Glenn laughed and turned to the group and said, "Look at those lying eyes."

Don and Glenn received all the credit for writing five of the nine songs on the new album. The album marked another milestone: It moved Don to the front of the band. His days of singing as many songs as Glenn had ended.

We embarked on a sold-out world tour of fifty-nine stadiums. "Lyin' Eyes" was our second single, reaching number two on the pop charts and crossing over to the country charts. "Take It to the Limit," sung so soulfully by Randy, rose to number four, becoming our fourth consecutive top-five single. Bernie's songs, "I Wish You Peace," for which Patti Davis received joint credit, and "Journey of the Sorcerer," were never released as singles. Neither was the song that Randy and I wrote together, "Too Many Hands," a raucous rock-and-roll number with a rhythm guitar riff that Don and Glenn had really liked and with toe-to-toe guitar solos by Glenn and me.

That song actually made my hands bleed. The basic track was played on a twelve-string acoustic guitar, which you need the hands of a gorilla to play, because it just eats you up. During the recording at the Record Plant, I took a break and jumped into the "scum pond" to relax a little. The hot water softened the calluses on my hands, and when I went back in to finish laying down the track, the skin on my fingers opened up and bled.

Our new album, more than all the others, was composed of mainstream, AM-oriented cuts. Song structure, choruses, vocals, even the length—everything was written to be more commercial and achieve national and international airplay. AM radio used to play a set number of songs per hour with commercial slots in between. A five- or six-minute piece of music cost the station a commercial segue. Three minutes thirty seconds was the limit, they insisted, or they wouldn't play it. "Lyin' Eyes" was five minutes long and initially didn't get much airplay, but it bucked the trend and proved to us that, with the right track, anything was possible.

In September 1975, we were on the cover of *Rolling Stone*, a first for us. There was a front-page photograph of us all looking cool on a yacht in Chicago, wearing aviator sunglasses, and an article raving about how great we were. With typical media perversity, however, in the back of the same issue there was a formal record review panning our new album. For some critics, we were ballad-heavy and theatrically boring. We didn't have fireworks or wear makeup like Kiss, whose album *Alive* had sparked Kiss-mania. Fans could buy everything from Kiss makeup to Kiss-endorsed pinball machines. We didn't leap around on stage and smash guitars like the Who or dress up in outrageous costumes like Elton John.

The critics were missing the point. The Eagles were always about songwriting and song power, reaching people and touching their hearts with words and music that meant something. We wanted our songs to endure. Compare any Eagles verses to the repetitive, head-banging lyrics by some of these "rock opera" bands. We didn't need gimmicks, nor did we need to sell lunch boxes with our faces on them.

Don Henley was especially incensed about the *Rolling Stone* review and immediately fired off one of his poison-pen letters to the editor. To be fair to him, this time I think he was probably right. The magazine was using our celebrity to sell its product and at the same time telling the world we sucked. It was a perfect example of how the press sometimes exploits artists for its own benefit. For us, this was a stark realization. It sparked an ongoing feud with the media, and especially with *Rolling*

Stone, which has never really been resolved. Interviews were kept to a bare minimum after that, or strictly controlled by Irving, Don, and Glenn, and the Eagles consequently became one of the most intensely private bands in the world.

The same month as the prestigious cover article, we played to a crowd of fifty-five thousand people at Anaheim Stadium. It was the biggest gig we'd ever done in Southern California since the California Jam (which I'd missed)—an incredible, memorable night. It was the twentieth anniversary of James Dean's death, which meant a great deal to Glenn, who was a big fan. We followed Jackson Browne and Linda Ronstadt, and I can remember looking out on the sea of eager young fans camped out under the spotlights while the stage literally shook with the reverberation of their cheering and foot-stamping.

After the gig, we went backstage and bumped into my friend and Malibu neighbor Carole King, who at the time was married to a lovely guy called Rick Evers. I'd never seen Carole happier than she was with him. He was a songwriter and part-time leathersmith, and he presented each of us that night with beautiful handmade hide coats. I still have mine. I wore it in one of the Eagles photo shoots. It is sheepskin with tassels, Indian motifs, and elkhorn buttons. It's exquisite, and I cherish it both for the memory of that extraordinary night and in remembrance of Rick, who tragically died of a heroin overdose a few years later.

Time magazine named us the top U.S. rock band. The article described each of us in turn: I was a "recluse" because at my last house, "an eight-mile-long dirt road separates Felder's rustic ridgeline house from the Pacific Coast Highway far below." Don was called a "card-carrying intellectual," Glenn a "charming, harmless ladies man," Randy a "happily married family man," and Bernie a "loner who prowls music stores for new instruments." Right on, I'd say.

Far better than the incredible accolade of that article, though— which would have impressed even my father—was going back to my home state with the band. We had a gig playing on Florida Field in Gainesville, where the Gators play. I invited Jerry and Marnie and their kids, Mary and Brian, to come and see the show. Instead of staying in a hotel with the band, I rented a condominium in a golfing resort for four days, and Susan and Jesse joined us. I arranged for a stretch limousine to pick up my brother and his wife and the kids and gave them front-row seats at the side of the stage. It was one of the first times in all these years that Jerry had seen me play, and here I was, standing center stage in front of a crowd of tens of thousands, playing rock-and-roll guitar just like I used to in the bedroom we'd shared. I think he realized then the magnitude of what had happened with the Eagles and how successful we'd become.

Later that night, in the kitchen of our condo, we sat chatting about Mom and Dad and our childhood, when he suddenly got up, came over to where I was sitting, and hugged me. "I'm sorry I wasn't a very good big brother to you, Don," he said.

"What do you mean?" I asked, choked up.

"Well, I was pretty mean and beat you up and made you wash my car all the time. I think I should have been there for you more. I apologize."

I told him not to even think that, and we embraced as we had in the funeral parlor when Dad died. That night, I think we both recognized that our childhood hadn't always been easy.

With our continuing success and the simmering disagreements that lay behind it, life on the road became wilder and wilder as we toured North America, Canada, Japan, Australia, New Zealand, England, Germany, Holland, and France. Drugs and women featured heavily, and individual band members began to let their guard down.

Halfway through the American leg of the tour, during a rare break of seven days, we decided to fly to Nassau in the Bahamas and get some rest. We'd been flying around and dashing here and there in rental cars; we were exhausted. It made sense to stay out on the road, rather than fly home, unpack, and repack a few days later. So we chartered a Learjet out of North Carolina and slipped down to a place in the Caribbean called Paradise Island.

I recall when we arrived at Nassau's tiny airport, customs officials greeted us with some suspicion. Here we were, longhaired hippies with ripped jeans, in the rock business. I suppose we seemed like fair game. I had nothing to fear. I wasn't carrying any drugs, and as far as I knew, nobody else was either, because that's what we'd agreed. Keith Richards of the Rolling Stones had been caught bringing drugs through customs once, as Paul McCartney would be later in Japan. We didn't want to be tarred with the same brush.

Needless to say, the customs men pulled us over and started asking questions. Irving was running around, but I told him to chill. "It's OK, Irv," I whispered. "Nobody's carrying."

At that point, I saw Bernie stop, reach down, open his bag, and scatter handfuls of pills across the baggage-area floor. As people arrived from another flight, we could hear the pills being crunched underfoot. Glenn dragged Irving to one side for a quiet word. As the customs officers pulled each of us in and started searching through everything—the linings of our suitcases, our clothes—Glenn moved his way farther to the back of the line, so that he was the last one to be searched.

When Glenn was searched he was waved through. We grabbed our bags, headed out to the taxi stand, and piled into a series of cars. We'd only been off the airport complex a few minutes when Glenn pulled off one of his cowboy boots, retrieved some pot stuffed into the toe of it, and sat in the back rolling a big, fat joint.

The times grew still wilder. I remember coming offstage in Amsterdam once, sweating profusely, and a fan who had somehow managed to get backstage was standing there waiting for me, waving a huge brick of hashish.

"Give me your T-shirt and I'll give you this," he said. I looked down at my soggy, sweat-stained Eagles T-shirt, which I was about to throw away anyway, and nodded with a grin. Peeling it off, I made the best trade ever. Trouble was, we were leaving the country the next morning, and there was more hash in this softball-sized block than I could possibly smoke, so I handed it out to everyone I knew—the band, road crew, lighting guys, everyone. I was the most popular Eagle that day.

Touring was so much fun, especially when we did gigs that also featured the Rolling Stones or Tina Turner. The best part of the whole gig was when she came onstage. She'd light the place up, especially when she and Jagger sang "Proud Mary." The audience and even the band members seemed to crank it up a notch or two just because of her presence. We all knew she'd have a great solo career ahead of her if she wanted it.

The Stones were pretty wild boys, especially Keith Richards, who played real dirty, Neanderthal guitar and was a walking human chemistry set. I remember arriving at our first hotel, in Kansas City, a Holiday Inn or a Marriott, and being taken to "meet the boys." My tour guide was our ever-smiling, supremely likeable, and unflinchingly dedicated road manager, who'd been with the Eagles from the very beginning and who was good friends with many of the other road managers. The Stones kept to themselves usually, and we weren't allowed on the top two floors they occupied, which could only be reached by elevator and were patrolled by private security guards.

Richie got the OK on the telephone for us to go up, then escorted us. When the elevator doors opened, a wall of pot smoke hit us. We wandered into a room, and on the dressing table was a large mound of what looked like dirty cocaine. I didn't know what it was.

Someone in the room, asked, "Hey, do you want some H?" and I realized that I was looking at heroin for the first time. I passed. I'd seen what heroin did to young guys living rough in New York, and for me, that was a step too far. I drank a beer instead, and we sat chatting for a while until Richie said to the tour manager, "So, where are the guys? Don would sure like to meet Keith Richards."

"OK," the road manager said. "Come with me."

He led us down a corridor and into a large suite, its doors thrown open. From a distance it sounded like there was some enormous party going on, the music was so loud, but when we walked in, the room was empty except for a giant stereo system, about three feet tall and six feet wide, on casters. It could be wheeled into a room, opened up like a road case, and plugged in. There was a guitar amp built in, with two huge speakers, and it was cranking out some really heavy rock-and-roll track.

"Maybe he's in the bedroom," someone said, and we wandered into his bedroom and stared at the detritus of what had obviously already been a good night—Jack Daniel's bottles, beer bottles, clothes, and the residue of drugs.

"Nope, not here," Richie said, and we started to walk out.

Just then, out of the corner of my eye, I saw a man's foot sticking out of the open bathroom door. "Jesus!" I said. I ran around to find what nobody wants to discover—Keith Richards doing a very good impersonation of a corpse. His skin was gray, and he was completely motionless, facedown on the bathroom floor. I thought he was dead.

Barely batting an eye, the road manager grabbed the phone and called the tour doctors. Richie and I were unceremoniously ushered from the room and into the elevator. "I'm sure he's a goner, man," I told him, as we returned to our floor. "I've only ever seen one person look like that before, and he was in his coffin."

To my astonishment, there was no bulletin on the news that night, and the following evening, at the Kansas City Stadium, a very much alive Keith Richards, looking none the worse for his brush with death, pranced around the stage cranking out his raunchy rock-and-roll guitar for all he was worth. Now that's what I call stamina.

ELEVEN

There was considerable rivalry among the various rock-and-roll bands at that time over which of us were having the most fun on the road. Led Zeppelin were considered to be the world masters, with bands like the Rolling Stones and the Who a close second. Hotel rooms would be ceremonially trashed, industrial quantities of drugs and alcohol consumed, and excesses logged in folklore. By comparison, we were Little League, but the one area we did excel at was in attracting women. We were young, famous, good-looking, and rich. We'd made it to the big time and were right up there on the list of rock-star scalps the eager groupies wanted to add to their belts.

Glenn once publicly described our life on the road as "got crazy, got drunk, got high, had girls, played music, and made money." He challenged Led Zeppelin to the claim of supreme party animals, maintaining, "We threw the greatest traveling party of the seventies." He was right.

It wasn't just the regular groupies who were on offer. Adoring female fans of all ages, sizes, shapes, and colors threw themselves at us. Songs like "The Best of My Love," "Desperado," and "Witchy Woman" were heart-warming numbers that appealed predominantly to a female audience. They were, I soon realized, highly effective lures. Night after night, during *On the Border* and now on this tour, I witnessed the barrage of pussy that was offered up. It was a sleet storm of women; they were literally everywhere—in hotels, at shows, and on planes.

Before *One of These Nights,* the system of pairing up those who wanted to get laid and the women who were more than happy to oblige had been a bit haphazard. As a band, we had a policy of only ever doing two two-song encores, and that was now used to our advantage. While we were onstage, wooing the fans, trusted road crew would be asked to scout the audience for willing participants and offer them backstage passes for what became known as the Third Encore—the party after the show. Each was handed a laminated pass with the words 3E THE EAGLES printed on it in Gothic lettering. These passes became popular souvenirs. While the stadium was being cleared and the traffic was dying away, the band, crew, managers, promoters, local radio DJs, and just about anyone else associated with the business would remain backstage to meet the forty or so attractive young women who'd been handpicked. Some of the record company promoters would even bring Playboy girls or "special groupies" for the occasion, along with copious amounts of cocaine and champagne.

For the latest tour, however, Don and Glenn took the system to a higher level of sophistication. The laminated passes were dispensed with for being too indiscreet; in their place were specially made little buttons, small, round, beveled, like a campaign button, with a pin on the back, and "3E" written on them in yellow English Gothic on a black background. Very discreet. They were passed out to the road crew by the handful. They would hand them to the loveliest girls in the audience. Some crew members would even loiter by the ladies' bathrooms, eyeing the girls as they walked in and out. The message was that the Eagles were having a party and would like to invite these women back to their hotel suite. No boyfriends were ever invited.

When the show was over, no matter how much the crowd hollered for a third encore, threw beer cans, or lit all the lighters and matches they possessed, we were out of there. The house lights would be kept dimmed as we ran from the stage and bolted out the back door and into waiting limos before the audience even knew we'd left the building. Only after we were well ahead of all the traffic would the lights come up, and everyone would wander home clutching their T-shirts, programs, and memories. Back at our hotel, a suite would have been specially reserved for that night's Third Encore party, stocked with ice buckets full of beer, wine, and champagne, platters of hors d'oeuvres, and bowls of chips. By the time we'd all showered and changed in our rooms, the first of the fifty or so invitees would be arriving, desperate to meet us, their little buttons pinned proudly to their chests.

I can remember walking down the corridor toward the suite one night and bumping into a man we called the Party Doctor. He was carrying a huge prescription bottle, the size of a large mayonnaise jar, full of Quaaludes—then the recreational drug of choice—to distribute among our guests at the party if they wanted them. If one of the guys in the room wanted to select a girl to be taken back to a bedroom and laid, then it fulfilled the objectives of both parties. Seldom was a girl allowed to spend more than a couple of hours with the featured participant. Almost never could she stay overnight. A limo driver downstairs was entrusted to ferry them all home. On certain occasions in certain towns, specific women known to be group-sex girls would have a suite of their own. I never experienced any of that, but I heard a lot about it from others on the road. Little Rock Connie was a legend. Allegedly a schoolteacher by day, at night she transformed herself into a sexual animal par excellence, asking people to take Polaroids of her while they stood in line for a blowjob. To this day if you mention her name to anyone in this business from the seventies, it'll produce a smile.

To begin with, I watched in amazement all that was going on but tried to keep my hands clean. I felt totally out of my league. You could count on one hand the girls I'd had sex with. However, by the time the *One of These Nights* tour really got going, the 3E parties were organized to perfection and so entirely accepted as normal that I completely lost sight of who I was. I'd like to tell you I was a saint, and that's exactly what I'd have had to have been to resist the temptations thrust at me on a daily basis. Some of these women were goddesses, I mean really beautiful, sexy women. I had no interest in breaking up my marriage or spoiling what I had at home, but life on the road—especially in a band short on camaraderie—was extremely lonely.

I'd go from a real adrenaline rush onstage with all these women screaming and yelling and throwing themselves at me, reaching out to me with their hands while I stood in the spotlight, back to an empty hotel room, where I'd face about twenty-one hours of the day in which life was incredibly boring. I was left with an overwhelming sense of isolation, which really began to erode my sense of self. No matter how long I spent on the phone with Susan, I was still utterly alone. I don't think she really understood that, because she was at home, surrounded by children, friends, and neighbors, going out to dinner or to the movies or being involved with the family.

A big part of me wanted to be home with her and Jesse. By the summer of that year, she was pregnant again, expecting our second child, and I longed to share in every day of our baby's growth and be with her to help her through the morning sickness, the cramps, and the exhaustion. There wasn't an hour that passed when I didn't think of her. I'd imagine her sitting in her rocking chair knitting baby clothes and wonder what I'd missed of Jesse's development. Would he even recognize me when I got home?

Instead, I was thrown in with four crazy bachelors (Randy overlooked his marriage vows) who were doing drugs, drinking, and screwing everything that walked. Half the time I was so high I didn't know what I was doing anyway. It was such an extreme situation. I defy any man to resist temptation in such circumstances. After every single sexual transgression, I was wracked with guilt. I'd lie awake at night, wishing for some easy way out of this heaven-and-hell situation I found myself in—an angel waiting for me at home and demons taunting me when I was away.

The answer usually was to take a couple of Quaaludes, which acted as a rubber hammer to bring me down from the drink-and-drugs high and let me get some sleep before the early morning call. It was truly the rock-star life, and for better or worse, I was living it.

I make no excuses for my behavior. I was led along by the crowd in the circus of life on the road. The others would have been very suspicious of me if I hadn't joined in, but for what it's worth, I can say that all the women got what they wanted, and none of them meant a thing to me. I was being used and abused as much as I was using and abusing. I felt like two different people: the guy on the road being tempted by the carnal beast, and the loving homeboy who'd have gladly laid down his life for his wife and kid. When I was back in Malibu, I didn't drink, take illegal drugs, or fool around. I'd even given up smoking for a while when my son was born, so as not to be a bad example. I was a husband and a father, and I loved Susan and Jesse with all my heart. I just didn't know how to handle the perpetual struggle raging within me.

Despite the relief on offer, the tensions within the band continued to deepen. Everything from facial expressions to talking too much became an issue, and nerves were frayed. Don and Glenn became of the mindset that they were going to take control of every aspect of the Eagles, and a lot of emotion was vented in between drug-taking interludes. Bernie, who'd all but turned his back on the sex, drugs, and rock-and-roll aspect of the business and was now into surfing, fresh air, and healthy eating, was more often than not the one to vent it.

I tried my best to arbitrate and persuade him to chill, but I was frequently left straddling the fence. "If Don and Glenn want to control the situation, then let them," I'd tell Bernie. "It's gotta be easier than fighting all the time like this." My policy was to walk away, pretending not to care, rather than have a confrontation. I knew how fame and fortune could corrupt, and I didn't want to be a part of that. But Bernie was as stubborn as a mule. He'd disappear for days to go surfing and feel the sunshine on his face. He was the first of us to adopt a healthier lifestyle and turn his back on the drugs and late nights, which were making a difficult emotional situation worse. All of us but him had major stomach problems—ulcers, acid indigestion, and diverticulitis—and lived on a diet of Mylanta or Tums. Bernie's "Marty Martian" nickname no longer related so much to how curly his hair was but to how bright and clear his eyes were compared to ours.

One night about halfway through the tour, just before we were due to fly to Australia and New Zealand for the next leg, we were staying at the Holiday Inn in Cincinnati when Glenn called a band meeting in his room. We used to have a lot of band meetings in the early days and, although everybody dreaded them for what they might reveal, they were useful as a forum for discussion. The trouble was that, with everyone expressing their disparate views, there was usually conflict.

I don't recall exactly what started Bernie and Glenn arguing that December evening of 1975. Maybe Bernie was going on again about us having sold out and become too commercial. Maybe everyone else was pissed because Patti Davis was on the road with us again, which meant federal agents everywhere, to protect her because she was the governor's daughter. The feds were an unwelcome addition, cramping the band's lifestyle, especially when it came to drugs.

In any event, Glenn, sitting in the middle of the room in an aluminum chair, started in on Bernie, who was standing in the corner with a Budweiser in his hand, about how he screwed things up every time.

He said something like "You need to cool down, you fucking asshole," and emptied his entire beer over Glenn's head. All the while, he was staring him down, daring Glenn to stop him. Bernie was into karate and was super-fit. Few would have taken him on. Then he stormed out the open door and onto the balcony.

We sat there in amazement and watched what happened, including Glenn, who didn't move a muscle while the beer dripped down his face. I think I was the first to move. I followed my old buddy out onto the balcony, where he was gripping the railing so hard the whites of his knuckles were showing through his skin, and I asked him what was going on. I said, "This isn't good, man."

He told me he was prepared to quit.

Assuming it was just one of those moments where people say something in a fit of anger, I wandered back into the room, where Glenn was toweling himself down, and tried to mediate. I told him I knew the two hadn't been getting along, but if it continued like this, they'd come to blows.

I could see the muscles in Glenn's jaw twitching, and I realized what a good job he'd done of containing himself. Glenn said something like "That guy's a fucking liability," through clenched teeth.

Don agreed.

Randy and I looked at each other and then back at Glenn and Don. I knew, in that moment, that Bernie's days with the band were probably numbered.

The tour was cut short, and when we got back to L.A., Bernie packed up his guitar and surfboard and took off for Hawaii, where he bought a house. He decided to write his own songs and record a solo album of the type of music he liked. He'd been in and out of several bands in the past and had been through bust-ups before. I think he thought he'd just move on to his next project. When asked why he'd left, he told one reporter, "I kept asking, 'Are we gonna rest next month?' and we never did. I wanted to get in shape before the age of thirty, so I could have a chance at the rest of my life. I was afraid something inside me was dying. Leaving was an act of survival."

I felt really bad for him and was terribly torn. Bernie and I were good friends, and I hated to see him leave, especially under such a cloud. We'd had great times together in Gainesville, in Daytona Beach with the Allman brothers, and on the road with the Eagles. From the first time I ever met him, waiting at the Greyhound station in his '63 Ford Falcon, we'd hung out, chatted, gotten high together, and played good music. I'd known him since I was a teenager, and he was one of the closest friends I'd ever had.

With Bernie's departure and my inability to patch things up, I realized that my pacifist policy was going to be sorely tested. To my mind, Don and

Glenn were seizing full control with Irving's blessing; anybody who opposed them would be gone, and I felt powerless to stop it. I couldn't bring myself to leave with him so I suddenly found myself completely isolated.

A tremor of fear ran through the band and rippled down through the crew. With the new power dynamic, the Eagles began to function by maintaining insecurity. Would Randy be next? Or me? Neither of us knew. We all wondered about our long-term future. The loss of Bernie could so easily have been our downfall. Until that point, he was actually the musical foundation of the band, being such a gifted multi-instrumentalist. Would this new direction we'd been pushed into even work? Would radio stations accept new rock songs from an essentially country band? We were quietly confident but we didn't actually know. The doubt, fear, and worry caused even more upsets. The threat of further eruptions kept everyone walking on eggshells, feeling as if they should try to appease Don and Glenn. The original democratic band now seemed to me like a two-man dictatorship. Many wars were lost in silent combat. Opinions often went unsaid for fear that words would light the fuse that blew this band to hell.

On December 20, 1975, Irving Azoff issued a press release officially announcing Bernie's departure and the signing of his client Joe Walsh as the newest Eagle. The decision had been made in a matter of weeks, although Don had initially taken a great deal of convincing. He thought it was a colossal risk and worried that Joe's strident musical personality would not fit well within the Eagles. We were the most successful we'd ever been, having found the right combination of country and rock to appeal to all tastes, and yet Irving was suggesting we take on an out-and-out heavy rocker whose arrival would surely herald a radical transformation of our sound.

Joe had been a friend of the band for some time, coming around to the studio to hang out and play with us after sessions, and I would personally welcome a few duelling jams with him onstage, but for many he seemed a little too wild for the Eagles. Apart from his solid rock career

with the James Gang and songs like "Rocky Mountain Way," he had a reputation for being a maverick. Irving convinced us that Walsh wouldn't
overshadow the rest of us and wouldn't be allowed to play anything but
our music.

"Irving insisted that he didn't want people to think the Eagles were
finished." We had to replace Bernie right away and get back on the road.
There was still an image of cohesion on stage and in the media. Irving
tried to minimize the public damage by enforcing a news blackout, refus-
ing to let any of us talk to reporters for fear that they might see what we'd
become. He denied that there were personality conflicts and claimed that
Bernie genuinely wanted to pursue a solo career.

No other candidates were suggested, and Joe Walsh was given his
greatest Christmas present on a plate—membership in the Eagles. Bernie
had just walked away from the whole deal, leaving the remaining four of
us as Eagles Ltd.

The transition wasn't as easy as Irving had suggested. Joe's voice was
much more nasal than Bernie's, and the sound of the vocal harmonies
changed dramatically. Joe's performing style also couldn't have been more
different. He was a showman, accustomed to leaping around the stage,
jumping off risers, and playing spectacular solos. By now, Don and
Glenn's control had extended to our stage show. Except for Glenn announcing, "We're the Eagles from Los Angeles, California," the rest of us
rarely spoke to the audience, and we remained static and largely faceless.
Don sang more, but most of the audience couldn't even see him, sitting at
his drum kit, hidden behind the cymbals. After Joe joined, the show became pretty schizophrenic for a while, kicking off and ending with some
of our early numbers, like "Take It Easy," "Tequila Sunrise," "Lyin' Eyes"
and "Witchy Woman," with Joe Walsh sandwiched in the middle, offering
some comic relief and blowing everyone away with a raunchy James Gang
number.

He was soon put in his place. After an initial burst of activity onstage,
he started to toe the line, following Don and Glenn's strict instructions
that every note in every show on every night had to be played verbatim
like on the record, without variance. All the steps were choreographed,

including all the guitar moves and where we went on the stage in between songs. It was like a theatrical production. You could have written those charts out and had anybody play those pieces.

I feared that the precision playing and obsession with perfection made for a rather dull show. Yeah, sure, it's great to hear a live performance played exactly as you know and love it on the record, perfect if you want to sing along or clap or follow the lines. But wasn't the whole point of a live show that it was *live*, that you were seeing your idols for the first time and watching them actually *perform?* I wasn't the only one who felt that way. I know Randy and Joe were frustrated too. *Rolling Stone* magazine commented that by "eliminating spontaneity, particularly a Walsh-Felder guitar jam, the Eagles sacrifice any chance of creating anew onstage and reaching a higher peak."

Personally, I liked Joe a lot. What wasn't there to like? He's such an easy-to-love character, like a favorite drunken uncle with a bunch of crazy toys, a ready cache of funny stories, and a great sense of humor. Lord knows we needed to laugh. It was often mind-numbingly boring and lonely being on the road for weeks and months on end, and dealing with that was hard enough sober, much less when we were hung over, out of drugs, or feeling sick with sinus infections from bad blow out of Cuba. So we had to find ways to stay entertained.

Joe already had a reputation as a legendary hell-raiser and, given enough gin, that's exactly what he was—turning adjoining rooms into one giant suite with the help of a chain saw, cutting the legs off all the furniture in Irving's room to suit his diminutive height, and jamming coins into bedroom doors so they'd not open. In Chicago, I heard, he once pushed a grand piano out of a window onto the hotel manager's car after they refused to let him into the restaurant without a tie. He was also a great one for starting water fights. We wrecked one whole floor of a hotel in Evansville, Indiana, by knocking on people's doors, using Irving as a front man, and throwing ice buckets full of water at them when they opened up. He once painted the windows of a roadie's hotel room black so that he thought it was still night when he woke in the morning and went back to sleep.

Joe would get a key to your room, turn the spigot on in the bidet, and close the bathroom door so that by the time you arrived, the room would be flooded. With a glue gun, he'd glue hotel doors shut. He'd glue the handset to your telephone and then ring and ring your room at four in the morning, knowing you couldn't make it stop unless you ripped it from the wall, which, of course, you eventually did.

After Joe arrived, nobody ever returned a rental car in one piece or walked away from one in perfect condition. Joe's voice would come crackling over the walkie-talkies he'd bought us all at Radio Shack, just as we parked in the lot and walked away. "Hey, Fingers, what the hell do you think you're doing? It's only a rental, man!" So, we'd dump the cars on the curb right outside the airport, with the seat belts cut out, the alarm or ignition disabled.

Joe delighted in going to toy stores and buying just about every new gadget they had. He'd come back to the hotel with remote control cars or helium blimps that we could steer around in the grand lobby or the rest of the hotel. After the walkie-talkies arrived, he gave everyone a call sign, including himself. His was José, although we also called him Rubber Nose, because he had this great big rubbery nose up which alarming quantities of cocaine would disappear.

"Yeah, that's a big ten four, Whisky a-Go-Go."

My call sign for Irving was 411, because that's the number you dial for information. When someone claimed it was also his height, it stuck.

We spent huge amounts of money on batteries for the walkie-talkies to make sure we could reach each other day and night. The radio would crackle to life at 4 A.M. and a voice would say, "Hey, you still awake?"

"Yup. Am now."

"You got any left?"

"Yeah."

"OK, I'll be right down."

Joe was not at all confrontational and would acquiesce graciously to whatever Don and Glenn said, even if it meant he had to be virtually glued to the stage to stop him from moving about. However, his general stress of being on the road had to come out somewhere, and the rest of us encouraged him, because it allowed our own rage to be released by proxy.

The more frustrated he became, the more pride he took in his "work" offstage—especially playing bumper cars with rental vehicles or throwing televisions out of hotel windows.

Irving joined in the fun by buying Joe an electric chain saw. It had its own special carrying case and was much quieter than a conventional one. You wouldn't know what old Rubber Nose was up to until the blade started coming through your wall.

Joe and I had become friends long before he joined the Eagles. I'd played a couple of gigs with him, one at Dodger Stadium, and I'd helped him with a live record and a TV show he fronted called *Joe Walsh and Dr. John*. We played well together. The best lesson he taught me was how to adjust your phrasing so as to play behind someone without detracting from the solo. As a lead guitarist, it isn't always easy to allow someone to step forward into the spotlight and play while you're supporting them. Between us, we learned that little two-step, a sort of musical dance.

Joe's attitude was very laid-back. He'd been in the business long enough to know what was what. He probably thought this was the best gig he could get, and it beat being out there by himself. He'd often complained about being a solo artist, although from my experience, it seemed to me that it would be so much easier than being in a band. He set me straight: "No, man, it's a pain. You have to do everything yourself— approve all the photographs, set up all the touring dates, go to all the rehearsals, and oversee all the decisions. I'm sick and tired of it." Now he could be a well-paid sideman in a great rock band and wouldn't have to bother with that stuff anymore. He stayed out of the fights, only ever adding his five cents' worth if his opinion was invited.

My only concern with Joe was our transition from a pedal steel and banjo band to one that played stoned-out, blacked-out, chain-saw rock and roll. I really had a difficult time seeing Joe playing what the Eagles did. It was a little like asking Jimi Hendrix to sit in with the Boston Pops.

With all the upheaval going on in the band, plus touring and planning the next album, I didn't have very much time to spend with Susan, who was in the final stages of her second pregnancy. My visits home were all too short, and I missed her and Jesse more than I can say. I did manage to attend some Lamaze classes in Malibu with her, however, to remind us of the breathing techniques involved, and when I could be I was a totally hands-on husband.

One of the other fathers-to-be in the class was Adam West, who played Bruce Wayne, alias Batman, in the popular television series. He was in his mid-forties and into his second marriage, and I'll never forget sitting alongside him on the floor, each of us cradling our heavily pregnant wives while urging them on. His looks and voice were so distinctive that each time he said "Breathe!" or "Push now!" Susan and I half-expected the Penguin or the Joker to come flying through the window and attack him with an umbrella.

The band took a couple of weeks off for Christmas in 1975—our second with little Jesse and the first at our beach house in Malibu—so I was there for the crucial part. I remember, in the week between Christmas and New Year's, Susan was so pregnant she could barely walk, but she stripped, put on her bikini, and did a sexy model pose for a photograph, standing in our hallway. We were laughing so much, I thought she might go into labor there and then.

I was home with Susan on the morning of December 31, when her water broke and I drove her to the hospital in Encino. We chose one in the Valley, because we knew the roads would be clearer at holiday time and because they had the best facilities available. It was quite a hippie thing for husbands to be at the birth and involved in the breathing, but the nurses couldn't have been more accommodating. The labor was pretty straightforward this time. I remained at Susan's side throughout (without fainting), cut the cord, and welcomed our little girl to the world, before buying champagne for us and the nurses to help celebrate New Year's Eve. Much to her chagrin, Rebecca Felder will always be a true Valley girl.

My mother was still in mourning over the death of my father, but for Christmas that year, I presented her with a handmade card.

"Open it," I told her, smiling.

She did so and carefully read the words inside. I promised to buy her any house she wanted in Gainesville.

"I mean it, Mom. Any house you like. I can afford it now."

"What's wrong with the one I've got?" she asked, confused. I thought of that little shack with its tin roof and no air-conditioning, and winced.

By the time she returned home from her visit with us, I thought I'd won her over to the idea, but I never did. She went to look at a few properties at my insistence, but there was always something wrong. She'd tell me, "I don't know the neighborhood," or "It's too far from the church," or "All my friends live on the other side of town." Marnie, Jerry's wife, was extremely patient with her and drove her around to see house after house, but she never liked any of them. It was too much of an emotional wrench for her to leave the family home. It was paid for, and it was safe. For forty years, it was all she'd ever known. I had to content myself with redoing it and buying her a new car instead. She chose a Chrysler New Yorker to replace Dad's last car—a rusty Oldsmobile Rocket with over 200,000 miles on it.

The record label wanted another album, but a lawsuit made this difficult. In early 1976, David Geffen was in the process of selling his remaining financial interest in Asylum to Warner Communications. Believing that he was including Eagles' copyrights in the sale, Irving Azoff filed a $10 million suit against Warner for their return. Though later resolved, the action complicated the production of a new album.

Joe Smith, an executive at Elektra, once described Irving humorously at a roast as "a little bundle of hate." He was well aware that we were becoming Warner's biggest act and later he was right, when we were selling a million albums a month. Irving's suit meant Warner might have to wait longer for another album. Joe Smith tried to work things out, but negotiations dragged. We kept touring while the talks stalled.

In March 1976, Joe released a greatest hits album on Elektra/Asylum to buy more time. None of us had a say in the decision. We hadn't the slightest inkling how successful it would become. A week after its release,

Eagles—Their Greatest Hits 1971–1975 had sold one million copies. It became the very first album certified platinum by the Recording Industry Association of America. It remained on *Billboard*'s Top 200 for two and a half years and is still one of the best-selling albums of all time. The pressure was on. If our next album didn't sell more than our greatest hits, fans would think our new material was inferior to what we'd recorded in the past. It was an added pressure we could have done without.

The trappings of success were ours by now, especially when we went on the road again for a twenty-six-city tour that summer to introduce Joe to our American fans. We took Learjets the way other people took taxis. We drank champagne like water and snorted almost enough cocaine to finance a small Third World country. Fast cars were bought, mansions were purchased, and jewelry was bestowed. We'd rib each other about what luxuries we had in our hotel rooms, just to wind the others up. It was our way of coping with the absurdity of making all this money but still being able to walk down Sunset Boulevard without being recognized.

In the early days, the desk clerks at the hotels usually assigned rooms at random. They didn't know one player's name from another, and most hotels only had a couple of suites anyway. Sometimes I'd get the presidential suite, sometimes Don would. It was a lottery. One day we were all in an elevator in a Holiday Inn somewhere, en route to a gig, when I said, "I really like my room, but the Jacuzzi in my bathroom is noisy as hell."

The others all stopped and looked at me. "You got a Jacuzzi in your bath? I didn't get one!"

I grinned. "Well, mine has bubble bath, oil, and everything."

Glenn's face was like a thundercloud.

Somewhere else, a few weeks later, we stayed at this beautiful hotel, and my room had a grand piano in the living room. I thought it was fantastic. I sat and played it for a while. During the elevator ride down to the limos that were taking us to the gig, I said, "How's everybody's room?"

"Cool," they all said.

Without a hint of a smile, I said, "Mine's nice, but that grand piano's out of tune."

Everybody groaned, "Yeah, right."

"No, really, I have a grand piano in my living room."

"Sure, Felder," said Don, sniffily, "just like the Jacuzzi in the Holiday Inn." We all laughed.

After that, Glenn and Don somehow always had nicer suites and cars. I told myself, "You know what? I don't give a shit. All you do is sleep in the room for a night or two and then move on, anyway."

One of the earliest causes of disagreement was the number of hired hands Don and Glenn took on. Joe and Randy and I had virtually no one, apart from the odd guitar tech, to help with our stuff, but Don and Glenn hired lots of people, including a masseuse who traveled with Don for his bad back. Glenn's tennis coach was on the payroll (of which I was paying a fifth) to help handle luggage. He'd never been on the road before and was inexperienced. On one tour, he lost a fifteen-hundred-dollar leather suitcase of mine with about three thousand dollars' worth of Italian suits in it. Man, I was pissed. I was paying this guy, and yet he wasn't even looking after my interests properly.

My only assistant was my guitar tech, Jimmy Collins, who lived in Boston. When we came off the road, he'd go home to Boston and would receive a very small retainer to be on call. Don and Glenn's guys remained in L.A. and were given titles like transportation manager and ground transportation manager, in charge of rental cars and limos. They even had a van, paid for by the Eagles, with which Don Henley's guy ran errands for him and Glenn. I lived out in Malibu and had no help whatsoever. Once I got out of the airport and put my luggage in a rental car, that was it. I was on my own.

I once dared to complain about it to Irving. I was paying for all these lackeys, and I thought it only fair to confront Irving for my sake and for those in the band too afraid to say anything. I asked Irving, "When these guys are off the road and aren't actually working for the Eagles, just for Don and Glenn, shouldn't *they* pay for them, not the rest of us?"

Irving told me in no uncertain terms that this was the way it was going to be. "Stop complaining and stop being so cheap," he snapped.

Having come from such a dirt-poor background, I'd always been the least extravagant member of the band. Something inside my head warned me that I could lose my wealth as quickly as I'd made it. Even sending my kids to private school seemed excessive. The most I'd ever spend my money on was a guitar. I once paid $3,500 for a 1959 Les Paul, just like the one Mr. Lipham had sent to be remodeled and then sold out from under me to that customer from New York. One day, after flying home for a visit, I drove past a Porsche showroom in Beverly Hills and decided, on impulse, to stop. Strolling in, wearing jeans and sneakers, my long hair lank, I smiled at the clean-cut salesman and pointed to the 911 S in the window. "I'll take it," I said.

He looked up at me with a smile. "Sure," he said, disdainfully.

"No really," I said. "I'll take it. Can I drive it away?"

It took half an hour and a fax from my business manager before he believed me. I drove away that afternoon in the sixteen-thousand-dollar beauty, feeling almost ashamed. It was a far cry from my '59 Volkswagen Beetle in Gainesville. What would my father have said?

What would he have said, too, about my drinking? The man who only ever had the occasional beer wouldn't have approved of my new habit. I never really drank that much until I was in the Eagles and discovered tequila and peyote, a psychedelic cactus used by the Indians since ancient times for spiritual purposes. Made famous by the man who'd inspired the band's name—Carlos Castaneda—especially in his 1974 book *Journey to Ixtlan*, it generally produces nausea before its transcendental effects begin. One night, we played somewhere like God's Hole, Indiana, and we had a party after the show. I took some peyote and drank much more than usual before ending up back in my hotel room. I was so unbelievably drunk that I crawled into my bathroom on my hands and knees and threw up. It was about two thirty in the morning and the phone began to ring while I was leaning over the toilet bowl, my face pressed against the cold porcelain. I couldn't move. The phone stopped, rang again, stopped, and rang again. Eventually I crawled back to the bed and lay partly on it, with my knees on the floor, and picked up the receiver.

"Hello?" Susan said, waiting for me to say something.

All I could manage was "Aaaarrggh."

"Don? Don? Are you OK?"

"No." Slurring the words, I said, "I drank too much tequila. I'm really sick."

At that point, I passed out and collapsed onto the floor. I woke up, I don't know how much later, and heard her shouting, "Don are you OK? Don, speak to me."

I managed to reassure her before collapsing again, this time into sleep. When I woke the next morning, I had a hangover I could have sold to science. For three days, I felt poisoned. I've hardly touched tequila since.

Joe, whose nicknames included Meathead, was a legendary drinker before he went straight. He drank anything that didn't drink him first—mainly gin or Jack Daniel's but also Tullamore Dew whiskey and Courvoisier brandy. "Just a wee drop of the dew," he used to say in a phony Scots accent while pouring another three fingers. Courvoisier was like rocket fuel. It burned my throat every time, except after a few snorts of cocaine—then it slid down real smooth. It was so strong, though, that I'd start getting drunk and need more blow to even out the buzz. It soon became a constant juggling act between the two. With Joe's help, I discovered that midway between a coke high and a brandy high was a very happy place to be. This became my combo of choice.

Apart from the damage to my liver and my nose, the chief change that success brought to my life was that suddenly everybody wanted to be my friend. People came out from under every rock. They'd try to get to me through my brother, mother, or old high school friends in Gainesville. People I hadn't seen or heard from in years appeared on my radar.

Someone would call my mom and claim to be an old high school buddy of mine who needed my telephone number. Or Jerry would get a call at work from someone who claimed I'd asked them to keep in touch but they'd lost my address.

Each had "great investment ideas" for my money and kept trying to find unique ways to take advantage of my generosity, kindness, or naïveté. Even peripheral family members tried to get something from me. They had a newfound enthusiasm for our relationship. Before the fame and money, none of them paid much attention to what I was doing. I suspect they shared my father's view that I was a complete waste of time. Disillusioned and disenchanted by the shallowness of success, I tried to associate with those who knew me before I'd made it. I began to wonder about people's sincerity. Who was reliable? What were their motives? Who should I trust? Paranoia began to set in.

Between tours, in preparation for the next album, Don and Glenn rented a house together. It had once belonged to Dorothy Lamour and was located high in the Hollywood Hills, the whole of Los Angeles spread below it. They lived like the odd couple, one tidy, one a slob. The cloud had definitely lifted since Bernie left, and Don and Glenn became closer than ever. They were writing buddies and drinking buddies. On occasion, they'd even go out and try to get laid together. It was all about success and excess—too much too fast. Glenn spent a lot of time drinking longneck Buds or red wine. He prided himself on his appearance and preferred the mean, broody look, with his trademark Mexican moustache, to reel them in. Don, sporting an Afro haircut, a gold chain, and shirts wide open so you could see his chest hair, had dated just about every L.A. model or actress on the circuit. Decadence led to ruthlessness and ultimately a sense of paradise lost, a recurring lament in the songs they wrote together.

Groupies were a common feature of the wild early parties, but Don's discrimination and discretion increased with his wealth. He began dating high-class, high-profile women and would arrange to have them come out on the road one after another, because the quality of groupies for the 3E parties was very inconsistent from town to town. For what he considered the weakest part of the tour, he'd import girls from L.A. Glenn did this too. That really was a step too far.

After two serious relationships ended with the woman leaving him, Don began a two-year, on-off relationship with Stevie Nicks of Fleetwood

Reading *Rolling Stone*
in Topanga, first house

Jesse and me, 1973

Jesse and me in Topanga, 1974

Writing "Hotel California" in Malibu beach house

Me backstage during *Long Run* **tour**

Tim Schmit playing bass during the *Long Run* tour

Don Henley sneering
in a hotel room
(a familiar face)

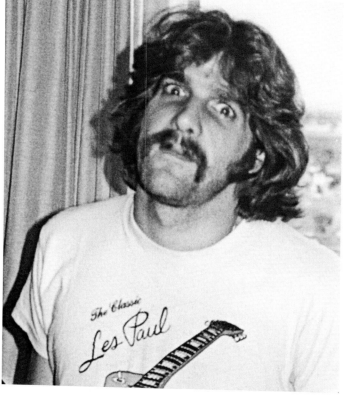

Glen Frey in a hotel room

Joe Walsh clowning with
Rebecca Felder

Buying vintage guitars
in Texas, 1975

Playing Gainesville stadium, 1977

On the Cover:

MUSIC

Don Felder:
Flying With
The Eagles
Has Rewards

SPOTLIGHT

When adults go to a circus they enter a world that still belongs to children.

Page 10

Manager of the Eagles, Irv Azoff also looked after other rock talents such as REO Speedwagon and Dan Fogelberg during the 1970s

MOVIES

Fan magazines are part of the tradition of Hollywood. And, the tradition is thriving.

Page 14

SCENE

Gainesville Sun
A Weekly Guide
To Entertainment
And the Arts
Week Of
September 9/16

The Eagles performing
live in the mid-1970s

Performing with the Eagles,
London 1977

Mac, the band that was our major rival in the charts, and who were on the road as much as we were. He began paying for her to be flown between Eagles and Fleetwood Mac gigs in a Learjet, engendering the band's new catchphrase, "Love 'em and Lear 'em." They eventually split up.

None of us ever really bothered to make friends with Don's women. There were so many, it wasn't possible. You'd just get friendly with one, and she'd dump him or he'd dump her and another would come along—the latest Bond girl or a newer model. He didn't poke his nose into my marriage, and I didn't interfere with his relationships. Stevie and I became friends later, and have remained friends to this day. I've done some work with her, but our friendship was always separate from her relationship with Don. Some of Don's best songs came out of his various heartbreaks. In fact, J.D. Souther and Glenn would almost root for him to break up so we could get some more good songs.

I didn't socialize with Don and Glenn very much—not that they ever asked me to. I went out with Randy and Joe occasionally, and the three of us often rehearsed over at Randy's, putting a few licks together, but the concept of us being best buddies never materialized. Apart from Randy and his long-distance marriage, I was the only one married with kids anyway, and I wasn't into hanging around the Troubadour night after night or attending their home-based 3E parties. Once I came off the road, I embraced the family life I had in Malibu and hung up my Eagles persona of a hard-drinking, drug-taking rock star, leaving it like a costume waiting for my return.

I often tried to break the ice with Don and Glenn, but it always felt like a professional relationship. When we first met, anyone could say or do anything, and there was a sense of all being in it together. As the fame and the stakes got bigger, the rest of us were less included in any of the decisions, until it got to the point where we became intimidated and didn't like to ask. It was like being at the office party when your boss is there, all the time. You just couldn't relax.

Among the crew, the word went out that Don and Glenn were in charge now. Nobody would do anything to challenge that, least of all the poorly paid crew members, only too happy to be affiliated with such a successful band. The band members became known as "the Gods." Larry "Scoop" Solters, our PR guy, was the first to use the expression. I started referring to just Don and Glenn as "The Gods" and even Irving picked up on it and called them that behind their backs. The lines were drawn, and Randy, Joe, and I were definitely mere mortals.

Drugs had always been a feature in our dissension, but by now we could buy as much as we liked whenever we liked. Cocaine was *the* drug, adored by many in the film and music industry.

It became increasingly difficult to be in the recording studio with four guys who were snorting so much cocaine. It would be late—one or two in the morning—and they were all still raring to go. To keep up, or in some instances lead them, I sort of fell into that level of use and abuse. Before I knew it, my consumption had spiraled, and I was doing half a gram a day. I'm not sure how many grams some of my fellow band members were up to, but I would guess nearly two.

I blame the drugs more than anything for what happened with the Eagles. It was fine when we were all just having a few beers or smoking weed, but hard drugs corrupt and distort and magnify paranoia and self-doubt. The great gifts we had had as a musical unit were being horribly abused. The spiraling use of cocaine caused us to waste incredible amounts of time obsessing over things we couldn't even really hear. It became hard to tell if a note was actually sharp *or* flat, but in the drug-induced fog, we'd decide this detail simply *had* to be resolved. We'd spend countless hours doing stupid stuff, overworking ourselves, and pushing already strained relationships still further.

There was this running joke: It would be three or four in the morning, and someone would say, "Well, I'm gonna do this last line, then I'll go right to bed." Which was ridiculous: One more line, and the last place you're headed is bed. Soon, it would be five in the morning, then six, and before we knew it, another day had dawned.

The next day, I'd feel real bad. I'd wake up with a headache and a hangover, especially if we'd mixed it with booze. I'd immediately want to make myself feel better by doing more blow. I'd do just enough to get a mild buzz, then drag my ass back to the submarine atmosphere of the studio, where everybody else felt equally burned and singed around the edges. In this way, we'd all try to cope with a stressful creative environment combined with all the physical and emotional problems that too much cocaine use can produce.

The music we made had always been the one good thing we did together. Now even that was in danger. We finally decided as a group to try to remain as close to clean and sober as possible while we were playing and tracking our songs. To maintain some continuity from take to take and day to day, we just had to.

While coke sometimes had a positive impact, inspiring lyrics and so on, it ultimately had a negative effect. Don and Glenn publicly projected unity, but privately they had a huge breakup. Both of them, meanwhile, began to fall out with Randy. The Eagles went from a bunch of young guys hanging out together, smoking weed and drinking a few beers, to five men who couldn't stand each other. Everything was reeling out of control.

Not that I was going to complain. I only had to look around, at my house, my wife and kids, my Mercedes and my Porsche, to know that I was onto a good thing. Regardless of the bad times, nothing I had yet experienced was going to make me blow this scene. I was gonna work as hard as I could, play my best, write as many songs as possible, be the first at rehearsals and the last to leave the studio, and be as diplomatic and easygoing as I possibly could—anything not to have the wrath of "The Gods" focused on me.

I honestly didn't know how much I had in the bank back then. As far as I was concerned, until I got a call to tell me I was broke, I didn't want to know. I'd made it. I was a rock-and-roll star, and the business managers could see to the cash flow.

TWELVE

The afternoon was perfect. It was July, and I was home for a few days, spending time with my family at our beach house in Malibu while Jesse splashed about in an inflatable wading pool nearby. I'd just been for a swim in my cutoff shorts and was still wet, sitting on a couch in the living room, looking out at the sun glittering on the water, and thinking how incredibly lucky I was.

Susan and I had produced two healthy, beautiful babies. We were rich beyond our wildest dreams and still very much in love. No matter what happened when I was on the road or in the studio, I never stopped wanting to come home to her and the children, and I fully intended to spend the rest of my life with her. She knew that, and whatever she may have suspected about what went on when I was away, she never once asked. Our wedding vows in Boston five years earlier had spoken of cherishing each other and nurturing what we had. Nothing had changed, including how

I felt inside. To me, she was still the pretty little blonde with the angel face I first met outside the Howard Johnson motel in Gainesville. I'd fallen for her then and had never quite picked myself up off the floor.

Now, here I was, sharing this beautiful life with her, playing music and being paid handsomely for it too. Regardless of the infighting, what we had achieved as a band was pure and bright and true. We'd created something far bigger than who we were or how we felt individually. The music we made really touched people. I promised myself never to lose sight of that and to try my hardest to make the others remember it too.

Feeling inspired and picking up an acoustic twelve-string guitar I had lying around, I started strumming absentmindedly while staring out at the ocean, inhaling the fresh salt air, and before I knew it, a few opening chords just kind of oozed out. I played with them, teased them, pushed them further than they'd ever intended to go, and suddenly had something that sounded pretty cool. It was about thirty-two bars long, with a verse and a chorus—a sparkling little gem that fell out of the spectacular view before me. When I had finished playing, the musical vibrations hung suspended in the air before fading into silence. The hairs on the back of my neck were standing on end. Duane Allman was right. If your spine tingles, it's working.

I had a little TEAC four-track studio set up in the spare bedroom, and I ran back there to put the idea down before I forgot it. I wanted a reggae-sounding backbeat, but the closest I had on my drum machine, an old Roland Rhythm Ace, was the cha-cha, so I played the twelve-string on top of that. It sounded OK, but I knew I needed to leave it for a while, so I went off to play with my kids and came back to it later. Over the next few hours, I kept tinkering around with it. The tempo was right, but it needed another section and a chorus, the payoff. I tried three or four different chord progressions and then finally I went back down and put a bass track with a reggae feel on it.

"If Joe and I had to do this," I thought, "how would we play it?" I was working to an exact cast, thinking of each band member's strengths and weaknesses, trying to find just the right arrangement. With Joe on board, it was a new challenge for me to come up with parts that would outdo him, against which he could retaliate and come back with something that was equal to or one up on me. I knew I couldn't write a complicated drum track for someone who was singing, too, but I could write a song that suited Don's voice, and one that Randy could provide a good bass backbeat to. Joe, Glenn, and I could take center stage and blow the audience away with some haunting guitar solos, I thought, so I wrote two guitar parts in descending harmony, a hornline sort of thing, until I got to the end, alternating them the way my dad had taught me when he had me count one, three, five, seven, then two, four, six, eight on my little Voice of Music tape recorder.

By the end of the afternoon, when I'd mixed the whole thing to mono, there was a little bit of everything that had ever happened to me in that song. There was some Maundy Quintet bass, some basic Paul Hillis classical phrasing, some free-form Flow-style solos with a bit of Miles Davis thrown in, and some good old Elvis Presley rock-and-roll guitar. I could imagine the harmonies that would go with it would be very Crosby, Stills & Nash and sounded positively sun-kissed. It was, I later realized, the soundtrack of my life.

The record company was pushing us to get going on the new album. We relocated to a ranch out near Calabasas, just outside Los Angeles, to listen to what new material everyone had and to rehearse. The actual recording was to be done and mixed later by Bill, the Soul Pole, at the Record Plant in L.A. and at Criteria Studios in Miami.

I'd put together a demo cassette with about ten or fifteen different tracks, including that glorious summer day's offering, fully expecting most of them to be dispatched to outtake heaven by "The Gods." Some had been milling around in my head that whole summer; some were even older. I was always tinkering around with sounds, singing into a Dictaphone in the car, laying down half-tracks, stray chords, or melodies that ran through my head, hoping that one of them might develop into something. More often than not, when I listened to them later, they were stillborns. The original concept had evaporated, the feeling had gone, and so had the glimpse of inspiration, so I'd erase them and start again. Some people work very methodically at creating music, putting in regular hours, but I can't work that way. I need to feel like it's a lover I haven't seen for a while and be excited and enthusiastic about our reunion. You can't force inspiration. If there's something in there to be released, it'll find its own way out.

We were at the Calabasas ranch, with old wagons in the yard. Photographer David Alexander was taking our photos for the new album sleeve, when Don, the Sonic Bat, put my demo tape onto a little blaster he had and started listening. Song after song came and went without much reaction from the bat cave, and I was beginning to feel a little dispirited.

When the one I wrote that fine day in Malibu came on, however, Don sat up, listened carefully, stopped the tape, rewound, and played it again. I'd pretty much worked out the entire arrangement. I'd added some harmony and electric guitar parts, and the whole thing was underscored by this reggae beat. At the very end, I had two guitar solos, trading between a Stratocaster and my favorite '59 Les Paul Starburst, as if Joe and I were going toe-to-toe. I could tell from Glenn's face that he liked that part the best.

"Hey, I love this track, Fingers," Don said, with a rare smile. "It sounds Spanish, like a matador or something. Very Latino."

Glenn nodded his approval. "Yeah."

"Oh, good," I said, feeling like a puppy that had just been patted for peeing outside.

"Let's call it 'Mexican Bolero,'" Don said.

"OK," I said, grinning. The fact that Don had granted it a name was a very good sign.

I originally recorded the track in E minor, which was great. The electric guitars were big and fat, and the twelve-string sounded nice and full. We continued playing it in that key right up until Don had to sing the lyrics and realized it was too high for him. "It's in the wrong key," he announced.

Disappointed, I replied, "Oh, OK, what do you need? D?"

"No," he replied, scratching his head. We sat down and eventually decided on B minor, although that's one of the worst possible keys for guitar. I struggled manfully with the new key, hating every second of it at first, because it sounded so thin and flat compared to the killer E-minor sound.

The only trouble was, the song was six minutes and change, with its unusual chromatic progression and its sudden shift from a minor key to the dominant major key for the chorus. Years of free-form jazz phrasing at jam sessions in Boston had made me slightly overindulgent when it came to track length.

Nobody seemed to notice. Best of all, Glenn had a germ of an idea while he was listening to it. He was great at conceptualizing and was listening to a lot of Steely Dan at the time. "This could be about the fantasy of California," he said. "I can see this guy driving down a desert highway at night in a convertible and seeing the lights of L.A. way off on the horizon."

We all knew that feeling; we'd all driven into LA from our respective homes and been overwhelmed by the awesome spectacle of the city, with its twinkling lights spread before us. Don snapped the image in his mind and took it from there, expanding it to the guy seeing a hotel in the distance and deciding to rest for the night. There, where he is served pink champagne under mirrored ceilings, a woman walks in. "It's such a lovely place," he muses with that uncanny gift of his, as he absentmindedly adds his smoldering cigarette butt to the dozen he already has lined up in front of him. "This could be heaven or this could be hell."

Don was very private about his lyrics. After he'd come up with a basic concept, he'd take it away and work on it secretly, and we wouldn't hear the finished product until we were ready to record it in the studio. No one had any problems with this. After all, he was the Lyric King, and we all knew it. The only time I can ever remember all of us daring to jump in and tell him something was wrong was when, in recording "One of These Nights," he sang that he'd been "searching for the daughter of God."

Bill Szymczyk suggested Don might want to change that.

Thinking of my mother's devout fellow churchgoers in the Deep South, I agreed he should change it unless he wanted every religious zealot in the States after him with a gun. The line was later changed to "I've been searching for an angel in white."

We finally figured my new song out, although it took weeks of demos and rehearsals, recording, dubbing, and overdubbing. I taught Randy how to play the complicated bass part, and Don picked up the reggae-style cha-cha beat on his drums. Joe worked out the other guitar solo that he'd play against mine at the end, and Glenn learned the rhythm part.

When Don first sang his lyrics for us all the way through at the Record Plant, we were completely stunned. I mean, that guy could sing the New York phone book and I'd buy it, but this was really something.

When the track was finally finished and laid down, and given its new name—"Hotel California"—Don said quietly, "I think this should be the single."

"Are you crazy?" I cried, as Glenn, Joe, and Randy looked up in mutual astonishment. "This thing's over six minutes long! We might have got away with "Lyin' Eyes," but AM radio won't play anything over three minutes thirty seconds, and never anything slow. They also won't play something that *stops* in the middle, then starts again, with a minute and a half of guitar solo. It ain't gonna happen."

I'd never been more wrong. When Elektra/Asylum asked us to shorten it, Don told them to release it as it was or not at all. He was right.

The final recording and editing of the *Hotel California* album took place at Criteria Studios, so we rented, among other houses, 461 Ocean Boulevard, Miami Beach, the white stucco beach house made famous by Eric Clapton and his comeback album, called *461 Ocean Boulevard*, released in 1974. We hoped that by renting the very same house, some of the magic would rub off on us, and we'd make a great record too.

We had some of our best times as a band in that place. It was right on the beach, and every Saturday and Sunday, we'd lie around the living room, watching football on the television, and then during halftime we'd go out and play touch football on the beach. We were all skinny, puny-looking, 150-pound guys, compared to the bulging musclemen of Miami, but we'd have a game until we got exhausted, then go back in and drink a bunch of beer and watch some more football. It felt, for once, as if we really liked each other.

Much to my delight, while we were there, Don and Glenn chose another of the songs I'd written at the beach house in Malibu. I'd called it "Iron Lung," reminiscent of my childhood illness, because it had a distinctive echo slap on it. They agreed that its rhythmic sound was just like someone wheezing away on a polio ward in the giant cylindrical machine that encased their body, doing their breathing for them. It was merely an idea, with no lyrics or melody, but with the help of "The Gods," it became one of our most recognized songs—"Victim of Love."

Glenn first came up with the concept. He and I, plus Don and J.D., were sitting up late over at Glenn's house one night, drinking and talking through various lyrical ideas about broken hearts, lost dreams, and power and anger in a relationship, all of which those three knew a great deal about. I often wondered if they sometimes deliberately broke off relationships with their various women, just to keep that emotional edge as songwriters.

"Having a broken heart is like being a victim of a car wreck," J.D. said broodily, still smarting from his latest split. "You wake up all battered and bruised in an emergency room."

"Victim's a good word," I pointed out.

They all nodded their approval.

"Victim of what, though?" I said, my brow furrowed. We all sat and pondered.

Glenn, sitting quietly in a corner, suddenly spoke: "Victim of luuuuuve."

He pretty much took over from there. My hesitant, wheezing "Iron Lung" was soon transformed into a hit. Easy as that.

Because I wrote the music for that song, and because of the original agreement to try to keep everything as equal as possible, I was supposed to sing the lead vocal. I was more than a little nervous. I can sing OK, but I'll never be in the same league as Don Henley. Still, I thought, I'll give it my best shot. We were in the studios in Miami, and I'd drunk some red wine when I went up to the mike and started to sing. I knew my performance wasn't great. Nothing was tingling. Don stepped up and sang, and it was immediately apparent to everyone, especially me, that he should sing it—even though, deep down, I wasn't thrilled at losing my slot. I just hoped there might be another opportunity later on, but there never was.

Joe had come up with a lick and he, Randy, and I jammed on the idea over at Randy's house one night. It eventually evolved into "Life in the Fast Lane." Randy had bought Ricky Nelson's old house, which overlooked Universal Studios and had a 360-degree view. He was a big fan of Rick, the singer of hits like "Hello, Mary Lou," especially since he had played in Rick's Stone Canyon Band. I believe the actress Helen Hunt bought the house from Randy afterward and tore it down to build a new one—a shame, because there was so much of Rick in that property, even his children's painted handprints on the bathroom tiles. Anyway, it was a great place to rehearse, and we were up there jamming and listening to a little cassette machine with Jage Jackson, a terrific roadie who also played drums.

"Hey, try this one," I said, playing a lick I'd first come up with in Boston. "I've had this one lying around for years, but I never did anything about it." It opened with a raunchy guitar riff and a fast-paced backbeat, but then it fizzled out.

Joe listened hard, his head hanging so low that his greasy hair flopped completely over his face, parting only to reveal his bulbous nose. "I have an idea what to do with that," he said suddenly, picking up a guitar. We all worked on it, with Jage adding some nifty drumbeats and me contributing a few licks that followed Joe's classic intro, but the song definitely became Joe's.

When the demo was done, Joe took it to Don and Glenn, who rushed away and came up with a concept. Glenn came up with the idea of driving in the fast lane, and he took that idea and expanded on it. I thought it was brilliant, sheer genius, to use the spaghetti-like L.A. freeways as an analogy of what it was like to be in the rock-and-roll business. Perfect. Don wrote some great lyrics that summed up how people destroy themselves with drugs in the "cold city"—lines of cocaine chopped out on a mirror creating lines on their faces. Pretty cool!

It was only when it was almost finished, when they set up the vocal track and Don started singing in that soulful Ray Charles voice of his, that we realized what he'd really achieved. We all thought, "Wow."

Many consider *Hotel California* to be our finest album, but it wasn't always an easy road to that elusive hotel. Just when we thought the departure of Bernie and the hiring of Joe had cleared the air, the pressure was *still* on to top the *Greatest Hits* album. How do you better your best? It was like raising the high jump bar another few inches, moments after you've won the gold medal. We worked many days and nights until the wee hours of the morning, squeezing the highest quality out of everyone involved. Whether it was engineering, writing, singing, playing, tracking, or editing, it was all done under the most intense scrutiny. Joe and I had calluses on our calluses. The ultimate goal was to produce the best possible record, but the process was extremely taxing and caused a lot of wear and tear on everyone's nerves. Everyone wanted to set an impeccable standard for Eagles records.

In trying to achieve this, however, we often wound up erasing performances that were fiery, motivated, and inspired. If a take had a tiny human glitch, one note out of tune, even if all the rest sounded fine, we'd junk it and do it again. This was before Pro Tools digital editing allowed someone to sit at a computer and insert sounds or fine-tune a few notes. None of that existed then, so we'd have to play the song over and over. Before we knew it, we'd squeezed the creativity out of it. We could strive for flawless music, but we couldn't force people to remain flawlessly inspired while delivering ten or twenty identical takes. The creative process was quickly robbed of its passion.

Fresh rifts began to open up, with Randy becoming the new focus of discontent. The sweetest-natured, gentlest of men, he was not someone to be easily riled, but every day in the studio, Don in particular seemed to find some reason for criticizing him. Maybe he'd stayed up too late the night before and was feeling a little the worse for wear (as we all so often did). Maybe he'd been a bit late arriving, or wasn't in the most talkative of moods.

What was ironic was that Don was the worst of all at being on time. We had this policy of arriving at the studio "two for three"—between two and three o'clock. I'd always be one of the first to arrive. I'd help Bill—who dubbed me J.E., for Junior Engineer—to tidy up a few tracks. Or I'd shoot a few hoops with him outside, or tinker with a guitar, or play pool with Randy or one of the engineers until the rest of the guys showed.

We'd play marathon poker games that lasted several days—"Eagle poker"—where thousands of dollars would be won and lost. One night, I lost eighteen hundred dollars in one hand to a roadie, and it hurt so much, I never really played again.

We had a saying, "Hurry up and wait," because you'd hurry to be in the studio on time, and then you'd wait and wait and wait. One by one, the others would arrive, bleary-eyed, disheveled, sniffing or coughing, suffering from the excesses of the previous night. Don would consistently show up at four o'clock or later, never with a reasonable excuse. It drove Glenn up the wall.

Worse than arriving late, when he did finally get to the studio, he was never in a good mood. One word best describes Don at that time: castigating. He had a constantly critical approach to everything. He'd always been a moody perfectionist, guarded with his lyrics and his personal feelings. We never really knew what he was thinking. Randy even slipped him a couple of Quaaludes once, to see what he'd be like when he was relaxed. They had a great night together, laughing and drinking and getting high, but the next morning Don was right back to his grumpy old self, the persona that had gained him the nickname Grandpa. In the words of Glenn Frey, "No one can suck the fun out of a room faster than Don Henley."

His perfectionism undoubtedly worked; look at the end result. Thanks to Don and his insistence on doing everything just so, we produced probably our most brilliant studio album, but the process was sometimes very difficult to live with. By comparison, Glenn was much more upbeat, now that Joe was on board. He was a high-energy person, and more often than not, in those days, he was a delight to work with. That was the fun Glenn, the one you wanted to stay up all night with, drinking beers and listening to his stories. When he was like that, he really personified all that we were and wanted to be—a bunch of young guys playing music, having fun, and getting high.

With Don's constant insistence on perfection, though, Glenn started to become edgy too. Glenn would do a first take, which sounded great to the rest of us, but Don wouldn't be happy. He'd do it again and again, taking the letter *c* from one rendition of the word *city*, as in "City girls just seem to find out early," then the *i* from another and the *t* from a third, and so on, until the final word *city* was made up of maybe five different takes. Bill Szymczyk was six three, and his new nickname became the Big Lopper, because he had to cut and paste so much tape together with a razor blade to make up a final take. There'd be what we called a pile of Big Lopper droppings all over the control room floor.

Don suddenly decided that we hadn't gotten the guitar parts right on "Hotel" and that he wanted it to be exactly as I'd had it when he first heard it on my demo cassette. He was a stickler for that, being just like the demo. The trouble was, we were way down in Miami, and the cassette was back at my beach house in Malibu.

"Is Susan home?" he asked, his expression blank.

"Of course," I replied.

"Then call her up and get her to play it for us over the phone."

Poor Susan, who was juggling two small children at the time, not only had to find the cassette among all my stuff, she had to get a small blaster, set it up, and play the tape over the phone to Don and Bill, who recorded it on another cassette in the studio.

With that sort of insistence that everything sound flawless, Glenn became more sensitive to exposure than photographic film. He started forbidding anyone from coming into the control room when he was singing, except occasionally Don. We wouldn't be able to hear what he'd done until the first comp was made. Only then would we be allowed in to listen and make suggestions and add our parts. It became an agonizingly slow process, taking five times as long to make the record as it should have, with tempers being lost along the way. These should have been the best times of our lives, and in many ways they were, but it could have been a hundred percent better.

In between takes, Don had become a prolific letter writer. Each letter took him a great deal of time, energy, and effort, but he seemed to feel it was worth it. It's a well-known trait of his, and Don's friend, Danny Goldberg, at one time, had copies of Don's letters hanging in his office. One of the best and most famous letters I clearly remember Don writing was one that he composed to the studio maid, insisting that the floral toilet paper be put on the roll the other way around so it rolled off the top, pointing out that if it was meant to come off the bottom, the little pink flowers would have been printed on the undersides of the sheets. Where you would see them.

Whenever I could, I escaped from the studio atmosphere through drugs or alcohol. Oblivion seemed preferable to the nightmare of working in such an intense situation. But heavy cocaine abuse left me and everyone else feeling burned out, which wasn't the best frame of mind for dealing with a highly stressful creative environment. I don't know how many nights I drove back to 461 Ocean Boulevard at five or six in the morning, with the sun coming up, my shades on, hardly able to stay on the road, having been up all night, before falling into bed, knowing I had to do it all again at two o'clock that afternoon.

Thank the Lord for Joe Walsh. He was the only source of humor. He and Randy and I used to have a blast. We'd take silly videos of each other in the studio, usually while waiting for Don to arrive. We also started playing "cutout man"—snipping pictures from nudie magazines and wrestling magazines, then sticking them together on the wall to make a sort of storyboard collage. Each day there'd be a new picture and a new storyline. Pretty puerile stuff, admittedly, but it whiled away the hours between takes and gave us some laughs.

Criteria consisted of five studios in a large complex, and anyone who was anyone recorded there. Clapton had just been in, the Bee Gees were in another studio, and you could walk down the hallway and bump into face after famous face. One day I went for a breather and ran into my old friend Stephen Stills in the corridor, coming out of an adjacent studio.

"Hey, Don!" Stephen cried, delightedly, when he saw me. "I heard you guys were in town. How you doin'?"

"Oh, OK," I said, reluctant to tell him the truth. "What's up?"

"Just laying down some tracks for a new album," he said. Smiling suddenly, he added, "Why don't you sit in and help me out with some guitar work? I could really do with your input."

Always happy to oblige, I went in and jammed with him for a few hours, adding some guitar parts to a couple of tracks. The last time we'd played together had been in that surprise gig in Colorado with Crosby & Nash. Before that, it would have been at some teen dance with the Continentals in Gainesville or Palatka, riding there on the Greyhound or in the back of someone's pickup. We had such fun together in Miami, I'd almost forgotten what it was like to work alongside someone who was just pleased to play music. We talked about the old days in Florida and wondered where friends like Jeff Williams were now.

"Do you remember that time we wrecked that bed in that motel?" Stephen laughed. "Man, we drank some Jack Daniel's that night!"

"Yeah, I remember."

It felt good to recall such happy memories with him. They almost made me homesick. Leaving him and wandering back to the Eagles studio, I had to stop and take several deep breaths before bracing myself to step inside.

We endured seven quarrelsome months in Miami, broken only by a concert tour sandwiched between studio sessions. We flew between Miami and our live gigs, sometimes working twenty-four hours straight. Bill would fly out to where we were playing, let us hear some mixes, get a couple more takes, and then fly back. After what seemed like an eternity, we finally delivered an album that continues to dominate the hearts and charts of America. The *Los Angeles Times* called it a "legitimate rock masterpiece." Besides the title track, it contains several other enduring classics, like "New Kid in Town," "Wasted Time," "Try and Love Again," and "The Last Resort." Don and Glenn once again dominated the songwriting credits, quite rightly, although I'd come up with "Hotel California" and "Victim of Love," and Randy wrote the words and music for the haunting ballad "Try and Love Again." Joe's chief contribution was a song called "Pretty Maids All in a Row" and, of course, the music for "Life in the Fast Lane."

Irving had negotiated the highest royalty rate in the history of the record business—a dollar fifty per album. Besides the distinctive opening shot of the Beverly Hills Hotel in silhouette, the sleeve featured wide-angle photographs of us with a group of disparate people posing as hookers, pimps, surfers, and weightlifters, all standing in the lobby of an old Hollywood hotel that once had been the epitome of sophistication but had become somewhat shabby and more than a little fake—a bit like California. The album sold five hundred thousand copies a week in the early days, and eventually topped fourteen million, remaining one of our best-selling records of all time.

On January 14, 1977, three weeks after the album's release, we kicked off a world tour in Cleveland, Ohio, with Jimmy Buffett as our opening act. We traveled everywhere by private jet, which became known as the "party plane," complete with a "party pilot" and "party stewardesses." Man, most of the time, we were several thousand feet above the atmosphere.

Because of the success of "Hotel California" as a single, we no longer opened with the lilting a cappella song "Seven Bridges Road." For some reason, we rarely even bothered to rehearse it in the shower of the dressing room any more. I sorely missed that moment of vocal and spiritual harmony. My song, the new album's title track, opened the show each night instead. Every evening, I stepped to the front of the stage in the spotlight to play those distinctive chords in front of a backdrop reproduction of the cover, the rest of the band in silhouette. Every night, there'd be thunderous applause and this incredible noise rising out the darkness, as the crowd reeled from the shock of that being the opening number. Don's voice would float out from behind the drum riser, strangely disembodied, leading the fans along that dark desert highway, and we'd join him for the chorus and those sun-drenched harmonies. The stadium would explode. I'll never forget that as long as I live.

We had a 16-mm film made of one of the gigs in D.C. In the movie, there's one part on the final cut where Joe and I are standing toe-to-toe playing the two main guitar parts in "Hotel California." Joe's wearing a bandana on his head because he hated to wash his hair. I say something to him, he looks at me, and we start laughing uncontrollably. Scores of people have asked me what it was I said to him that night.

Well, what I actually said was, "Hey, buddy, you're showing," pretending that he had a white powder ring around his nostrils, captured forever on film. He didn't, but he thought he did, so he said, "Oh, I am?" which set us off laughing. Now you know.

One of the other questions I'm asked more than any other is: What is "Hotel California" really about? For whatever reason, some of the fans have inexplicably read all sorts of hidden demonic messages into the lyrics, citing lines about heaven and hell, stabbing the beast with steely knives and hearing the mission bell. As far as I'm concerned, I just came up with a reggae-sounding music track that sprang from a glorious summer's day out in Malibu. Glenn and Don came up with the lyrics and the Mexican/Latino concept of an isolated hotel on a dark desert highway that attracts a weary, possibly drugged-out traveller. The elegance and the decadence are inexorably juxtaposed.

If Don Henley hadn't been a songwriter, he'd have written poems and sonnets. He is an English literature major, full of fine prose. I have always been in awe of his ability to take a concept and develop it so lyrically that when he sings a couple of lines, a whole movie starts rolling inside your head. The way he writes, he allows everyone to see their own version of the story. As they feel the textures of the music, they see images flicker on their own personal movie screens. With that gift in mind, my answer is always the same. It's like life. "Hotel California" is whatever you want it to be.

The tour continued, taking in more than a dozen countries. We were no longer playing as an opening act but headlining in our own right. This was a serious record. It had propelled us into another league, and we were delighted. In England, we played several sold-out gigs that ensured our future success there. For someone who'd started out admiring English bands and copying their style with the Maundy Quintet, that felt especially sweet.

In the dizzying round of press interviews in London during the tour, several of the music journalists asked me the same question.

"We just had another American band playing here," they said, "and their lead singer claims you first taught him how to play guitar. Did you?"

"Really?" I said, bemused. "What was his name?"

"Tom Petty," they replied. "He's on a world tour with his band, the Heartbreakers. They're going down very well."

Little Tommy Petty from Gainesville. I could hardly believe it.

Susan flew out and joined me in places like London, Paris, and Tokyo, to indulge in some serious retail therapy and to allow me to spend some precious time with Jesse and Rebecca. Aside from those snatched moments of happiness, however, the grueling nature of what we were doing began to take its toll.

Don had long suffered from stomach ulcers, as had Randy and Glenn to a lesser degree, but now he began to have serious back pain as well, after years of leaning over a drum kit. His on-tour masseuse realigned his spine nightly, but the pain didn't improve his mood. One of the things that bothered him was the addition of Joe Walsh's drummer to the tour. Joe Vitale could play better drums than Don Henley with an arm and a leg cut off. He also played keyboards and flute and was a welcome addition to our stage sound. With him providing the basic beat, Don could concentrate on his singing. Vitale also gave us a backup for the times when Don stepped off the drum riser to the front of the stage. For some reason, though, he saw Joe Vitale as a threat, a direct criticism of his competence as a drummer. He knew Joe Walsh wanted Vitale to be a permanent member of the band, and his simmering resentment, coupled with his health problems, caused him to flare up over the smallest issue.

In Montreal, when there was a screw-up on a hotel reservation, Don blamed our long-time road manager, Richie Fernandez, and ordered him fired. Irving duly obliged, claiming that Richie was a pothead, no longer doing his job properly. Poor Richie, who'd been a devoted member of the crew from day one, was given his papers. Ironically, he ended up working as Tom Petty's road manager instead. The firing led the remaining crew, already unhappy with the atmosphere, to dub the tour *Prison California*.

Glenn's power struggle with Don wasn't eased by the fact that Don's creative ability, with his writing and his singing, had just exploded in the previous couple of years. Having held himself back during the early albums, he suddenly became the driving force in lyrics and concepts and music, making everybody else's offerings pale by comparison. The consequence was that we suddenly had two presidents, vying for the same position. Don would usually back down in the end, knowing that to push Glenn too far would be unwise, but when they had one of their cocaine-induced arguments, the clouds descended. It affected everyone, even the road crew. Between gigs, Don would sit silently in his part of the Learjet and Glenn in his.

"Hotel California," the single, shot to number one in March 1977. It spent fifteen weeks in the charts and became our most successful single ever, outshining "The Best of My Love" and "One of These Nights." Its success pushed sales to an even higher level. Worldwide, at our peak, we were selling a million albums a month, but the growing tour was also taking me away from my family once more.

Susan understood that, whether it took ten days or ten months out of the year, I had to do whatever the band said. I had no control over scheduling. Furthermore, I was powerless to plead for more time off with my family. Susan never told me, "You gotta come home and help me raise these kids." She never made me feel I had to quit to be part of our home life, and I really appreciated that.

I rarely called her with problems. I didn't want to contaminate her life with any Eagles melodrama. When we'd finally stop touring, she'd always ask, "Well, how was it?" By then, three or four days would usually have passed and I'd have decompressed. I could just about describe the latest power struggle without raising my voice.

But this latest tour was going to take all my powers of decompression to get over, as the screws were tightened up a notch. Randy and Joe were both big Chuck Berry fans and started to do his famous "duck walk" onstage. Don berated them both. Joe let it slide, but Randy was furious that Don had addressed him in this manner. Randy hated any sort of confrontation, he lost many battles by attrition, but inside, he was festering. The gradual power shift bothered him enormously. He'd been in the band right from the start, just like Bernie, and he didn't think it was right that Don and Glenn should automatically assume the reins.

As I remember it, venting his own frustrations, Joe, decided to trash a hotel room in Chicago. He was clearly drunk and I helped him. Joe's fiancée was on tour with us at the time and had brought her parents along. The late Steve Wax, then executive vice president of Warner/Elektra/Asylum, mischievously introduced them to several groupies. Joe went crazy. He and I went up to Steve Wax's room while he was in bed with one of the groupies and tore that place apart. Joe smashed crystal decanters, then pulled some sort of knife or tool from his belt. I don't recall exactly what it was, but he stabbed at pictures and furniture and walls. He tore the drapes down and covered himself with them for protection while he smashed the chandelier with a leg he'd broken off the grand piano bench, which was collapsed in pieces on the floor. He was a one-man wrecking crew, destroying paintings and Persian carpets, even ripping the fabric wallpaper off the walls. I mostly stood watching and laughing, although I did take gleeful delight in hurling a table lamp into the fireplace. Steve Wax eventually ran in naked and stoned, the groupie holding a towel to cover herself behind him. There wasn't very much he could do. We were the biggest act on his label, and he knew he'd fucked up.

During the second leg of the domestic tour, in Knoxville, Tennessee, Randy's ulcers flared up, and he was sick with the flu. Don complained it was because he was having too many late nights. Maybe, maybe not. Either way, we'd been touring for eleven months straight, without much of a break, and everyone was starting to feel the strain. At this particular concert, the audience wanted to hear "Take It to the Limit" sung by Randy, but Randy told Glenn, "No way. Not tonight."

Randy had one of the best voices in the band. He made women scream when he sang that ballad in his tenor voice. Hitting the high note at the very end guaranteed an almost deafening round of applause, sometimes for several minutes. Glenn once called it "the ribbon on our package," and it was certainly one of the highlights of the show, but for whatever reason, Randy felt uncomfortable in the spotlight. Onstage, he'd always grab his microphone and pull it back by his bass amp. He'd stay by the piano, away from the front. When he was singing, he refused to have a spotlight on him; he'd only allow a blue light. He'd stand in profile by the piano and sing with his eyes pressed shut as if hiding from the audience.

"For me, it feels like standing on the railroad track in front of a freight train, the spotlight on the front of the train bearing down on me," he told me privately. "I can't stand it, man. I just can't. I get all nervous and sweaty, and I just want to run from it."

Glenn was furious. "I have to stand in the front of the stage and sing 'Take It Easy' in a white spotlight. Don does the same for 'Hotel California.' That's show business. You should just stand in the front of the stage and sing that song." Glenn was right. Everybody had to cope with the spotlight, and he was probably only trying to persuade Randy into doing it for his own good, but he didn't go about it the right way.

Man, he got into this big fight with Randy. The two of them started arguing constantly over exactly where Randy should stand, what color the spotlight should be, and how he should sing. Some nights, like when he was ill, Randy would refuse to sing the high note on the end; sometimes he wouldn't sing the song at all. He'd tell Glenn, "I don't feel like it. Not tonight."

Glenn would explode. "You got to! It's in the show! They wanna hear you sing. The fans expect it."

Randy was usually easygoing, but he'd reply, "I ain't doing it. My throat doesn't feel good tonight." He'd say to me afterwards, "Who the hell appointed Glenn Frey leader of the Eagles?"

There had been fewer and fewer band meetings of late and more closed door meetings between Irving, Glenn, and Don, leaving everyone else out of it. The band spent too much time fighting over stupid stuff: what publicity photographs would be used, whether somebody was doing something without clearance, or which hotels we should stay in. All of it served to inflame an already irritable situation.

For Irving, Glenn and Don were the chief singers and songwriters and, as far as he was concerned, they were running the show. They'd been natural allies from the start, and now that alliance was taking over. Since Irving paid a great deal of attention to their likes and dislikes, whatever they wanted usually happened. Whatever anyone else wanted was secondary. We were the country cousins. Irving made a show of trying to appease us, but we knew our opinions were irrelevant. After a series of closed-door meetings with Irving and Don, Glenn would emerge to hand decisions down and dictate what they expected. Randy was tired of it. He was also getting static from his wife.

He lived in L.A. because of work, but his wife and four kids were still back home in Scottsbluff, Nebraska, and the distance between them was getting harder for them both. Randy had married Jennifer right after high school, and, they had a lot of history together. Ultimately, Randy had to reach a difficult decision—the band or his family.

We were in Memphis in the summer of 1977 when he chose the latter. It began as a memorable night for another reason. We were supposed to be going over to Graceland to meet Elvis Presley. Someone had set it all up for us, and we were just waiting on a call. When it came, at almost midnight, it wasn't what we'd hoped for.

"The King isn't feeling so good tonight," one of his handlers told us. "He'd love to meet you next time you're in town, but he's not taking visitors today." Within a few weeks, Elvis was dead. His years of drug abuse were finally too much for his heart. He was forty-two years old.

After the news came through that we weren't going to Graceland after all, Joe, Randy, and I got high on Jack Daniel's and cocaine and stayed up all night, trying to convince Randy not to leave.

"You don't want to do this, man," I told him. "Not financially, musically, or careerwise. Imagine what it would be like having to start over."

"I've been out there on my own," Joe told him, glumly, "and it's no picnic."

We tried every which way to convince Randy not to quit, but he was adamant. By six in the morning, we'd exhausted every possibility. Randy had pretty much made up his mind. The crunch came two days later when Glenn and Randy got into another fight during the intermission about where Randy should stand onstage for the encore. It was the same old argument, and we expected the same outcome, but this time it was different.

"Stop being such a pussy," Glenn yelled.

Before we could stop him, Randy had Glenn up against a wall while security guards and the rest of us tried to pull him off. It surprised me beyond words. Glenn had somehow pushed Randy to the point that this gentle, easygoing guy, who wouldn't hurt a fly, flipped. He was probably the most difficult person in the world to drive to that point. It was scarily reminiscent of what had happened with Bernie.

As soon as the two brawling men had been separated, and while the guards continued to restrain a struggling Randy, Glenn grabbed a dirty towel, wiped the sweat off his face, walked right up to Randy, and threw it in his. That was the final straw. Randy decided there and then to retire back to Scottsbluff and raise his kids, tired of being dominated in a band that had started out being a lot of fun. He stayed only until the final date on the *Hotel California* tour.

"The Gods" were taking the reins, and those that opposed them were either expelled or driven out. In eighteen months, I'd lost my two best friends in the band—Bernie, that fiery streak of brilliance, and gentle Randy, the sweetest man in the music business. I was truly on my own now.

THIRTEEN

he *Hotel California* tour and the loss of Randy left us emotionally and physically drained. We returned to Los Angeles, where Irving's office issued a brief press release claiming Randy had left due to exhaustion. Irving initially promised to continue managing him, but little came of it after a first solo album, and they soon parted company.

There was never a suggestion we might disband because of Randy's departure, the assumption was always that we'd continue. Don and Glenn had indicated a band should not keep going on and on, way beyond the time it should, with only a few of the original members, but we were all in our late twenties or early thirties and still felt young and energetic enough to keep going. The only question was, who would replace Randy? We didn't have to look very far. The logical replacement was someone we knew and liked—Timothy B. Schmit, who'd taken Randy's place in Poco when Randy had joined the Eagles in 1972. Timothy sang high and played bass. He was perfect—everyone agreed he was the only choice.

Timothy, whose nickname became the Wanderer, because he was always wandering off somewhere, was married with kids, a soft-spoken, extremely likable vegetarian, heavily into yoga. He'd been a friend and ally from way back, when he was in Poco and I first joined the Eagles, and we used to sit backstage at gigs, jamming and talking about our kids like the proud dads we were. I never had that kind of camaraderie with Don and Glenn. Tim had spent a lot of time on the road and felt like one of the boys. I have nothing but praise for him as a musician and a human being. He is honest and straightforward, with a great amount of patience and humility. He was an undeniable asset to the band, and, since Bernie's departure, the only member of the Eagles who actually was born and raised in California.

There were now just three shareholders of Eagles Ltd. left—Don, Glenn, and me. Randy had blazed this incredible trail for Timothy, and he was able to step in and take over the extraordinary legacy that had been built up. He made no problems for anyone. Whatever anyone wanted was fine with Timothy.

Irving and his staff, lawyers, and business managers took care of everything, and there still seemed no reason to question them. The only time I really started to wonder was when my business manager, Gerry Breslauer, put together property partnerships involving eight or so of Irving's clients, including people like Boz Scaggs and Danny Fogelberg, along with the Eagles and others. As I looked at the percentages, I saw that Irving, Don, and Glenn owned twice as much as the rest of us.

"Hey, Irv," I said, "How come this isn't an equal split like everything else?"

Irving smiled and explained that those guys earned so much more money from writing and publishing that they had a much bigger cash fund to invest. Seeing that I wasn't quite convinced, he added, "Remember, Don, those boys are single, and they don't have kids."

I thought well, OK, that makes sense.

But then I began to think a bit more about percentages and income, wondering if it was all just as Irving said. How come he could afford such a big share? And was it normal for the on-tour accountant, employed to keep tabs on everything on the road, to be answerable first and foremost to Irving?

I never thought to speak to friends in other bands to see if they were getting the same deal or better. Everyone I knew was equally unsophisticated as far as even understanding how the royalty, merchandising, and tour-accounting side of the business worked, so nobody could have given me any straight answers. Still, I resolved that I'd keep asking questions if something came up that bothered me. After all, I had every right.

Hotel California **was nominated for several Grammy Awards,** including Record of the Year, which it won in March 1978. We had become the biggest selling U.S. band of the decade. We were holed up in my little studio out in Malibu, rehearsing and working on some demo tracks for the next album, sitting around drinking beer and watching television, when they announced the award, and Andy Williams stepped up to accept it for us.

"Why didn't we go accept it ourselves?" I asked someone.

"We don't want to be a part of this Hollywood jive business crap," came the reply.

Everyone looked at each other blankly.

The following day, there was a spate of heated press conferences, claiming and counterclaiming that Irving had, or had not, told the awards organizers we wouldn't go to the show to collect our prize unless we were guaranteed to win. I didn't know anything about it.

Later that summer, we challenged the editorial team of *Rolling Stone* to a softball game. If the reporters won, we'd give them a rare interview; if we won, we'd write an article describing how we trounced them. It would, we hoped, finally settle the score between us and Jann Wenner, the magazine's editor and driving force. The game took place on May 7, 1978, at the University of Southern California and was heavily attended by invited press. Pregame tactics included abusive notes left on Don and Glenn's doorsteps, calling them sissies and beach bums.

We all wore black-and-gold caps, and Irving wore a T-shirt that said, "Is Jann Wenner Tragically Hip?" Joe Smith, chairman of Elektra/Asylum, made the public announcements. The first was that Jimmy Buffett could no longer play on our side, because he'd broken his leg; the second was that we should stand for the "national anthem," a shortened version of "Life in the Fast Lane." Governor Jerry Brown was there rooting for us. We brought in a couple of ringers from our road crew, truck drivers and buddies from other bands who were good players, as an insurance policy, because Don and Glenn were pretty thin and puny in those days and not terribly athletic.

I always thought it strange that Don offered them a sports challenge and not a writing one, which he'd have won hands down. Fortunately for us, the journalists who turned up to play us were as out of condition as we were, and after a difficult game, we won. Everyone went to Dan Tana's afterward for a victory meal, and journalists and band members sat alongside each other, gobbling spaghetti, getting along fine. The feud was officially over.

To hear the songs I'd helped write or co-written being played on the radio all the time was a real treat for me, especially in the car. There was something about driving around L.A. in my Porsche, with "Hotel California" blasting out and the DJ saying, "Well, that was the classic song from the classic American band." Don always said the ultimate litmus test for a track was whether or not it sounded good on the car stereo. He'd spend a lot of time driving around, listening to demo tracks and giving them "the test." He thought up some of his best lyrics behind the wheel. Unlike him, I don't think I ever tired of listening to our songs being played after they'd been released, but our record company knew that the public soon would. They demanded a follow-up album.

I had something like fifteen or so tracks ready for what was originally planned as a double album, and Irving sent us back to Bill Szymczyk and his Bayshore Recording Studio in Coconut Grove, Florida, to record. Once settled in, our latest addition, Timothy, delivered the first usable song, "I Can't Tell You Why," which the band first rehearsed together in my little Malibu studio. It was a great ballad with Randy-style vocals and an opening for me to play some really sensual guitar.

"This is a killer track, Timmy," I told him. "I'm gonna have some fun working out my guitar parts for this."

Don and Glenn seemed burned out. They spent hours in stony silence facing each other, neither one able to suggest any new lyrics, each one staring at Don's trademark cigarette butts, which he left standing around on every available work surface. They appeared to resent our attempts to write more songs, and finally told the record label the album would be delayed until they had what they felt were "acceptable" songs. To speed them along, Joe Smith mailed them a rhyming dictionary.

It wasn't really surprising that there was a creative lull after *Hotel*, but the record company's expectations were unreasonably high. They expected us to deliver an album every year *and* go on the road. Irving would call or come down in person and tell us what they wanted.

We'd sit and listen to what he had to say, and Don would say quietly, "Don't rush us, Irving. They'll get it when it's done." He was often the one who stood up to the executives and put them in their place, I think maybe because it took the greatest toll on him. Naturally pensive, he became even more introverted, fretting inwardly about what we were doing and where we were heading musically. He was once reported as saying, "Every minute I'm awake, even when I'm asleep, I'm worried about the next album and what's going to be written on it and how it's going to do and how it's going to be accepted and how my peers are going to react and how we're going to make it better than the last one and how the record company is on our case about hurry-up-we-didn't-get-an-album-from-you-in-1978-and-it's-not-going-to-look-good-on-our-stock-report-and-what-about-the-profit-sharing-plan."

Months passed without any new songs. When it was clear the new album had definitely stalled, we spent the rest of that year on the road, not writing any new material at all. Instead of the moneymaking album they'd hoped for, the record company received one song, a cover of Charles Brown's "Please Come Home for Christmas." It reached number eighteen in the charts. On the flipside was a song called "Funky New Year," in which we all clinked glasses and made a lot of noise while Glenn played saxophone. He decided he wanted to play sax after hearing Dave Sanborn play, but he was nowhere near as good, and he never played sax on a record again, thank God.

It would have been really smart to take some time off, let everyone spend time at home and rest up after those blockbuster first five years, but instead we ran at a pace we couldn't possibly endure, especially not with the drugs and the pressure to produce new material. There was a lot of steam building up in the pressure cooker.

Worst, for me, were the long absences from my family. We'd be gone for six or seven weeks at a time, home for a couple of weeks, then back in the studio or on tour. We were working a good ten months out of every year, and it was a long, hard run without much time off. I had little kids who didn't travel well, and Susan was pregnant again with our third child, but my family needs weren't really considered by anyone in the band. I resorted to calling home several times a day to talk to Jesse and Rebecca on the phone. I'd send them gifts in the mail, or bring them toys and goodies whenever I came back, but it was no substitute for being a full-time dad. I was painfully aware that I was cheating them out of a normal family life because of my career.

When I did come home, I overcompensated massively. I'd take them to Bass Lake and teach them how to swim or up to Lake Tahoe to ski. I was great friends with Jimmy Pankow from the band Chicago, and we'd rent houses together, his family and mine, for camping weekends. All my kids learned basic survival skills from a very early age. I showed them how to fish, I told them about frog-gigging, and I made them their first aquaplane board so that they, too, could fly under the water as I had once done.

"Did you really see manatees under the water, Dad?" Jesse would ask, wide-eyed.

"Yes, son, and we had to avoid the snakes and the alligators in the water."

"Wow! Cool."

Our son Cody was born in October 1978 in a candlelit bedroom of our beach house in Malibu while I held Susan's hand and the moonlight danced on the waves outside. We called him Little Buddha or the Broad Beach Blubber, because he was so pudgy. Right from the start, he had a mind of his own and was a great kid. "This one's gonna be trouble," I told Susan, as he wriggled and kicked his way out of every diaper change.

I jumped at the chance to look after him and cuddle him when he cried at night—anything to make some sort of early connection with him. Susan and I were true "granola parents," never allowing the kids sugar or candy, red meat, or saturated fat. Instead they grew up on fruit, vegetables, yogurt, and lean white meat. When they went to friends' houses, I'm sure they ate entire boxes of Froot Loops. Susan didn't smoke, drink alcohol, or take other drugs. She was a yoga instructor and breast-fed all our children. Thanks to her, I was probably the healthiest drug addict in town. I was determined to be as diligent a parent as she and become a permanent figure in their lives, despite my long absences from home. I went from Rock God to Diaper God overnight. My so-called reclusiveness caused some frustration among the fans, because I was never out partying with Don and Glenn in L.A. or Colorado. I wasn't photographed as often as they were and seldom was able to sign autographs, so very few were able to collect a full set of Eagles autographs. I just wanted to immerse myself in the humbling, awe-inspiring business of being a father and a husband.

While the others were celebrating New Year's Eve in their various ways, I was pacing the floorboards, nursing a bawling Cody through colic.

Trouble was, most of the time, Susan and I were furiously treading water trying to keep our noses above the waves. Our lives constantly fluctuated between the times when I was there and the times when I wasn't. My career was the driving force behind our busy schedules, and there wasn't very much time for our relationship. We never argued, we just avoided confronting the issues that were eating away at both of us, like when we were going to be able to spend some quality time together. We would do anything rather than bring up difficult or delicate situations that might be explosive, because I'd just been dealing with that sort of conflict every day. When I came home, the last thing I wanted to do was be confrontational or demanding. Nor did I want to offload the turbulence of my relationship with the band onto my wife. I just wanted to relax and be caring and loving. Sadly, in the end, I think we avoided so much that our relationship itself became something of a void.

Glenn was facing other challenges. In the beginning, he'd written or sung most of the hits. He was the voice and face of the Eagles and he was still producing great songs like the number one hit "Heartache Tonight," but all that was changing. As Don's creative ability and individual successes surpassed his, Glenn's input seemed to be inferior. Everyone's was. Don kept the peace by stepping back as much as he could and letting Glenn believe he was still running the show. Glenn saw straight through that, though. He'd never liked sharing the driver's seat, but now he was being expected to shift into the back.

With Don ever more prominent, Glenn appeared to feel the need to focus his discontent on someone else. It didn't matter if it was a roadie or guitar player, Glenn often made someone the target of his abuse. We called them his "random victims." From one day to the next, he'd pick someone at random then humiliate them in order, I suppose, to make himself feel superior. He gave us all nicknames that seemed to be calculated to bring out our insecurities. David Sanborn, who had a withered hand, was called Flipper. When my hair started to thin slightly at the back, he started to call me Spot. One of the sound engineers was dubbed Larry, because Glenn decided, unfairly, that he looked like Larry from the Three Stooges. Tommy Nixon, Glenn's right-hand man, usually took the brunt, but when Glenn grew bored with baiting Tommy, he'd focus on someone else. Tommy was a nice guy, absolutely dedicated to Glenn after starting out as his guitar roadie in the seventies, and he was totally dependent on him for money and a job. I'm ashamed now that I stood by for all those years watching another human being so humiliated.

One of us should have stood up for Tommy, but taking on Glenn when he was in that kind of mood wasn't easy. Some of his victimization was done in the name of humor, but it was usually done at someone else's expense, allowing him to play his power card and keep everyone around him subservient. It was an emotional problem that should have been addressed with therapy of some kind, and maybe Prozac, not more cocaine. We were all finding it increasingly difficult to operate at our level of success with such heavy drug use, struggling through severe hangovers every day.

My turn to be a random victim would come whenever I asked awkward questions about management. Glenn saw this as an annoyance. "You shouldn't be bothered with all that, Fingers," he'd tell me, crossly. "Irving's in control."

For whatever reason, Glenn began to make me feel like I was the chief focus of his anger. I don't think I ever did anything directly to piss him off, except maybe not kowtow to him like some other people; it was just my turn. Besides the nicknames, Glenn seemed to delight in mimicking people in a humiliating way. He'd amplify something in your voice or character and act it out for an admiring, laughing audience. That's fair game, I guess, but then he found my Achilles' heel.

I'd never been overly confident singing onstage. If I stepped from the back of the line up to the microphone, I would never march up to it like him, the Teen King. I'd walk up, in step with the music, in a sort of stilted gait. My reticence was clear. I'm not a singer, I'm a guitar player, and I was always reluctant about singing, especially with Don glaring at the back of my head with eyes like lasers. I knew he was behind the drum riser, scrutinizing every note, which was very intimidating.

During one particular rehearsal, Glenn sarcastically announced, "And let's hear it now, gents, for Fingers Felder, singing his Number One hit, 'Hotel California.'" He then mimicked how I stepped to the microphone in my hesitant way. Everyone in the road crew and band, even the stagehands, was laughing. Normally I wouldn't have batted an eyelid, but for some reason, that day I lost it completely, instead of letting it wash over me. In fact, I was so angry that I followed him into the bathroom afterward, grabbed him, and threw him up against one of the metal partitions between the urinal and the toilet.

"You ever talk to me or humiliate me like that in public again, Roach, and I'm gonna break your fucking nose," I told him, holding him by his shirt collar, my fist balled. I was sick and tired of his abuse, not only of me but many others.

He seemed shocked. "Er, no, Fingers, I'm sorry. It was just a joke, man. Cool it," he said. I somehow managed to reel myself back in and walk away.

I didn't know it at the time, but this was a point of no return.

In the summer of 1979, we were back to the grindstone in Miami. Don's vocals on "The Long Run" made us think we might finally be able to finish the album and have our title track, but the days of Don and Glenn sitting down and happily writing songs together, and of us actually believing we could deliver a double album, had ended. Of ten songs, seven were collaborations with people like J.D. Souther or Bob Seger. One was Joe Walsh's solo work, "In the City." My contribution was two songs, "The Disco Strangler," and "Those Shoes," although there were at least three other tracks I'd brought to the album that Don had started to do something with but was never able to finish.

I remember sitting in the studio and playing one track that I'd written and was especially proud of, called "You're Really High, Aren't You?" We'd started to record it, and Don sat there and suddenly said, "I see it. I know what I gotta do with that track." Everybody thought, "Oh great, we've got another one," but sadly, he never followed through, and the track was consigned to the cutting room floor. It was very disheartening, and the frustration was immense. I put that track carefully to one side in the hope that maybe for the next album, Don's inspiration would return.

For "Those Shoes," which was accepted, I wrote most of the music—drum parts, bass, and guitar parts—except the solo, which was Joe's. I wrote it as a demo and gave it to Don and Glenn, and we added talk-box guitars and beefed it up a little. The concept behind the song was, I believe, how high heels turn a man on. Don took my basic track and ran with it. At the end, he sang, "Merci, Monsieur Jourdan," a tribute to the shoe designer Charles Jourdan.

"Disco Strangler" was designed as an antidote to the Bee Gees–discotheque craze that was going on at the time, after the success of the 1977 film *Saturday Night Fever*, with John Travolta. The one thing the Eagles agreed on was that we all hated disco music. It seemed so unmusical and repetitive to us ballad boys. There was no melody to it, just four-on-the-floor, straight quarter-note, bass drum beats, so I took that as a basis and played with it. Don sang the lyrics after coming up with the concept of a woman dancing in the spotlight, urging people to look at her and how beautiful she is. The disco strangler, who's been waiting in the wings all along, "the fiddler in your darkest night," is ready to slide his hands around her pretty throat. I had a good time recording that one cut.

One of the pieces I'm second-most proud of, after "Hotel California," also came out of the *Long Run* album. It is a short guitar solo in "Sad Café," a song Don wrote, loosely based on days at the Troubadour club. I wrote a multitrack acoustic solo for it, inspired by the song "Midnight at the Oasis," by Maria Muldaur, which had been a huge hit. It's only about eight bars long, but I was very happy with the way I was able to take that section and create a six-track harmony that worked. I can still listen to that and smile to myself.

Glenn had only brought one song to the album so far, a number called "Teenage Jail," which was by far his worst writing effort and had a crazy, balls-to-the-walls guitar solo at the end of it. My solo was the result of a four-in-the-morning, whacked-out, coked-out session, and to this day, I'm embarrassed to have played it. It just keeps lingering like a bad smell. Glenn fled back to L.A. and called up his old friend Bob Seger to ask if he had anything. Fortunately he had—and between them they came up with "Heartache Tonight."

We raced back to Miami to record it for Glenn to sing, and he was as happy as could be, knowing that he finally had something. In it, he made the prophecy that someone was going to hurt somebody before the night was through.

When it came to recording solo guitar parts in the studio, there was considerable competition. Glenn would take first shot, then me, then Joe, and whichever guy came up with the coolest part won. We each had totally different styles, but somehow they worked together as well as separately. It was a real challenge in terms of personalities, because Joe and I hit it off personally and musically, and we really wanted to write stuff for a two- or three-guitar band. Between the two of us, there was a lot of camaraderie, which really produced some original and unique sounds. When we were cutting "Those Shoes," we recorded live onto those basic tracks and found a place for a guitar solo. The first couple of times nobody played, and then the last time, Joe played, and it was great, so it stayed on the record that way.

There was a lot of trying out new material and ways of playing it for the good of the project. On "The Long Run," I played keyboards for the first time on record. I just started playing in the studio, and it worked. Joe used to play keyboards on some songs too. Everybody did whatever was necessary to make the best record without trying to insist on playing solo or stepping up to the mike. That was the musical dynamic when it was at its best.

When it was at its worst, drugs were usually to blame. Cocaine and alcohol with Quaaludes thrown in was bad medicine, even if it did smooth off the edges. It's amazing we're all still alive. I can't count the number of nights I drove home from the studio with the sun coming up. I'd cruise down Ocean Boulevard, my nose still tingling, heading for a house I shared with Joe in Key Biscayne. I could hardly keep the car on the road for grinding my teeth. I'd have been up all night, I'd reach home by six, fall into bed, then wake up, and have to get back to the studio and start all over.

In the end, I became fed up with driving home, worried that I was going to kill myself. And I was always afraid a Miami cop would stop me and throw me in jail after finding drugs in my pocket. Even on so-called days off, I'd leave the studio at five in the morning, high as a kite, and keep going. Joe and I might play golf at one in the afternoon with a couple of beers, then continue partying. Sure enough, our day off became another marathon. Instead of recovering, we'd rush right back in.

I didn't want to be locked into that life anymore, so I booked myself a little suite in the Coconut Grove Hotel, a few blocks away from the studio. Now when I left, I just had to stagger few blocks. I'd push a button, enter the elevator, fumble with my room key, and crash out. I'd wake up and order room service instead of going downstairs to fumble with pots and pans. Since they had a gym, I could also work out and maintain some semblance of normality. I didn't mean to withdraw from the others. I was just tired of that long drive.

The studio marathon went on. We were down to our bare nerve endings in terms of stress. I think the whole band had been suffering from postpartum depression after *Hotel*, and now we were heavily pregnant again with the next baby, and the strain was showing. To allow us to spend more time with our families and less in Florida, some of the recording was moved to the One Step Up Studio in West Hollywood. It would be fair to say, I think, that this became our least favorite album because it represented such a dark time personally. We were struggling to write, we were struggling with drug and alcohol abuse, and we were struggling with interpersonal relations and egos. The whole album had this dark cloud of dissension around it. It finally divided us into two camps, Don and Glenn versus me and Joe, the guitar players. Timothy was somewhere floating around, the Wanderer, as ever. Finally, we exhausted ourselves, exhausted our patience, and took so many drugs that nobody could see any further solutions except to finish what we had and walk away from it.

The album became known as the Long One at the record company. It wasn't helped by the way we worked, which was actually quite a strange and lengthy process. We'd start with a basic track—intro, verse, second verse, chorus, third verse, chorus, bridge, and out—and set some device to help us keep our tempo together. We'd fill up ten to twelve reels over two or three days, each reel having three to five takes on it, recording that same track over and over, constantly arranging and creating it. Then there'd be an editing session, where we'd put up twenty-four-track tapes and listen to each reel to find out what the best feel was for the drums.

From tape twelve, we might take the first eight bars, from tape three the second eight bars, and from tape five the first bar and a half of the second bridge. Bill would listen with those fantastic ears of his and say, "Oh, good first verse" or "Nice bridge" from one tape, and then shake his head and say, "Well, that's about it." Then on the next tape, he'd listen and say, "Oh, good, great intro, that was a really good intro" or "The drum fill was really great going into the chorus," and so on, until the floor of the control room was literally carpeted with two-inch tape standing on edge. All these little pieces would start coming out of these basic tracks and be edited together until that the drum track sounded really good, even if everything else sounded awful, because we could fix all the other stuff later.

When our master tape went by on a twenty-four-track tape machine it looked like a zebra, there were so many edits. Each one of us would then have to repair our guitar, keyboard, and bass parts. We did so much of this that Bill had to lay those tapes on an edit block and resplice them with a razor blade, because they'd start to fall apart from going around and back and forth so many times. And he didn't want to monopolize two machines, so we had to work on that master only.

Finally, when all the recording was done and ready to mix, Bill—whose new nickname became "Coach" because of his role in the studio and his passion for sports—would sit in the control room and not allow anyone else in for a couple of hours until he'd got a mix that he wanted everyone to hear. They we'd all go in, each carrying a legal pad, and make notes as the track went by, suggesting various adjustments—echo too loud, drum fill too soft, and so on—and Bill would try to make those corrections by hand on his console, feeling what he was mixing. Finally we'd get to the point where we liked mix number five or seven, and we'd all go away and shoot pool or have dinner while Coach got up the next mix. If we finished one mix every day and a half, we were doing really well. We'd take a batch home with us and listen to them again for a few days, in the car or on the stereo, to see if our choice still held up.

Bill was great at holding the reins while letting the horses run at their own pace. He never pushed us or forced us to make creative decisions. He'd sit and let us listen, with his eyes closed. If his head was bouncing, you knew you had a great take, but if he stopped and stared at one of the speakers, you knew he'd heard something he didn't like. He really had a marvelous set of ears, listening for a coherent performance, in which we all meshed perfectly as a band.

"Well, Bill," we'd say at the end, our faces hopeful, "do we have all the pieces yet?"

"I'd like to hear a couple more good bridges," he'd say, and we'd do as he asked, concentrating really hard on playing that particular part well.

Trouble is, you can't go back and record another bridge three or four days later. It won't splice in. The sound is different, the humidity is different that day, people play their instruments a little differently, and so you have to keep going, keep recording until you have all the pieces. Which is where cocaine comes in.

If you listen to Eagles records, there's nothing out of tune, there are no foibles. They are almost inhumanly flawless and, in my opinion, sometimes to a fault. Because of Don's perfectionism and Bill's professionalism, the two of them kept raising the bar for us to leap over. Unfortunately, in the end we took that bar and hit each other over the head with it. And I think that many of our gutsiest, most spontaneous performances ended up needlessly on the control room floor. We tried so hard to be better and better, but in doing so, I think we lost something of the passion. Was this how B.B. King worked?

On September 24, 1979, *The Long Run* was released. It had taken eighteen months, almost a year longer than *Hotel California*, and it nearly killed us. The notes on the back of the album sleeve described it ominously as our last studio album. It debuted at number one, but the critics savaged it as "a considerable disappointment." *Rolling Stone* was ambivalent. Their reviewer described it as "a bitter, writhing, difficult record, full of piss and vinegar and poisoned expectations," but added, "Because it is steeped in fresh, risky material and unflinching self-examination, it's also the Eagles' best work in many, many years."

The magazine ran the review with a critical cover story by a reporter who'd spent two years hanging out with us and who claimed Don had likened himself to God. Don fired off a series of angry letters. Many read them and sensed we'd reached the endgame. We reluctantly agreed to some interviews to publicize the new album, but Don, Glenn, and Irving continued to control all the information released to the press. Only Don and Glenn were allowed to answer direct questions, and they had a series of pat answers ready if anyone asked about strife within the band.

"How's everyone getting along?" someone would ask.

"Oh, we loathe each other, as you can see," Glenn would reply, smiling.

"That's why we just agreed to work together again for the last eighteen months to bring out this new album. Can't stand each other's guts," Don would add, winking.

Steering the conversation away from controversial issues to the new project, they became masters at handling the media. Their quotes in a number of magazine profiles were eerily similar, as if they'd precisely rehearsed the answers. Joe Walsh was allowed to give some interviews, and I did a few with *Guitar* magazine, but we were all discouraged from speaking with the press. The policy thereafter became minimal contact. Fewer interviews, they hoped, would maintain a mystique and spin certain awkward situations.

Instead of resting, as we should have done, we played Japan, Hawaii, the East Coast, and the Southern states, before embarking on another world tour. Every waking moment seemed to be spent eating, sleeping, and dreaming the Eagles.

I took Jesse with me to Japan, hiring local nannies to care for him, just so I could spend some time with my son. He was six years old, and I felt we barely knew each other. Taking him into the toy shops in Tokyo after a ride on the Bullet Train was a dream come true for any father. His little face lit up under his white-blond hair, and I told him to pick out something he wanted. He was so overwhelmed, he couldn't decide what to pick at first but finally settled on trunkloads of Legos. I took him to a sumo wrestling match, courtesy of our very gracious promoter, Mr. Udo, and he met one of the great champions after the match, who, coincidentally, was called Super Jesse Sumo Man. Little Jesse watched this man-mountain slamming into a telegraph pole in training backstage and felt the ground shake beneath his feet. He became a lifelong fan. He almost lost his balance staring up at the huge piles of flesh towering over him. I don't think he ever forgot that.

In Japan, I bought Susan a beautiful silk kimono, hand-embroidered, in heavy material. Don Henley bought twenty, for his collection. During the remainder of the tour the road crew complained bitterly about having to lug them around. They were already transporting his personal mattress and sheets of plywood, to ease his bad back in the various hotel rooms he had to sleep in, and the kimonos represented one packing case too many.

"Heartache Tonight," the first single from the new album, written by Don, Glenn, J.D., and Bob Seger, topped the charts and sold over half a million copies. "The Long Run," the second single, rose to number eight. Our next single, "I Can't Tell You Why," started by Timothy, reached the same level. Interest in us was still at an all-time high.

Speaking of all-time highs, the cocaine abuse went crazy. Everybody in the music business was involved, even upper-echelon executives. One of the presidents of a very large label probably had the biggest cocaine habit I knew of. Coke even had many of the lawyers, doctors, and managers strung out. It was the same with musicians and DJs; it had infested the entire industry. Nobody yet realized the long-term damage that would result from it. We just thought it was great, like pot; we'd have a great time, and there wouldn't be a problem. It was the fun party drug of the seventies, and until you'd lost your house, your car, your family, and your kids and wound up in the hospital or rehab, you didn't realize how dangerous it could be. The movie *Blow*, with Johnny Depp, offers a perfect synopsis of what happened back then.

The constant pace cocaine set didn't do much for our relationships. Being high allows for a false sense of camaraderie, but as soon as the drug wears off, you realize how fake it all is. Sometimes, just sometimes, everybody got along great. We'd drink together, get high, write songs, and jam. It was so fantastic when something good happened, we'd all look at each other in amazement and wonder if it could possibly last.

There were some real highlights in the shows we did around this time, the memory of which I shall feed on forever. Among them were the nights Roy Orbison opened for us for a series of concerts at the Los Angeles Forum, our first shows in our adoptive hometown since 1976. Orbison was amazing. We'd be sitting in our dressing rooms and know exactly where he was in his set when we heard the audience explode because he'd hit the high note in "Crying." You could set your alarm clock by him. Every night, like clockwork, we knew that after that high note, there'd be two more songs and we'd be on. The audience responded really well to him. Some of these kids didn't even know who he was, and yet he got them going every night. He was a shy, quiet man, unbelievably humble. He just stood there dressed in black with his sunglasses on, singing his tail off. I was honored to be on the same stage as him. If there had been any justice in this world, we would have been opening for him.

Another great memory of the L.A. Forum gigs was working with the Blues Brothers—John Belushi and Dan Aykroyd—and Elton John when they came on and jammed with us during one of our encores. Man, that was really something. I think it was one of the best performances we ever gave. It felt incredibly emotional, playing with these guys, backed by a huge orchestra, hearing our music fill the whole place, and all in our "hometown."

Elton John was like the Liberace of rock and roll, with his huge glasses and flamboyant outfits. On the radio, he came across as a completely different person from the man who appeared on stage. He was completely over-the-top but always very friendly and charming—the quintessential polite Englishman. I liked him a lot. Don was, by then, dabbling in gambling, and he and Glenn and Irving took Elton to a casino one night in London after a gig. Elton had a great night but didn't come away with as much as he would have liked to have won. The following day, the guys bought the blackjack table he had been playing on and had it sent over to his house with a tongue-in-cheek note which said, "For the amount you lost last night, you should at least own the table."

During one gig with Elton and his band, I wandered into the men's room and found one of his musicians rolling around on the floor, screaming in pain and holding his nose.

"What's the matter, man?" I asked, rushing to him. Blood was pouring from his nostrils.

"I dunno," he wailed. "Someone just came in and offered me some blow, and I took some, but it stings like crazy. I think it must have been cut with something."

We called the paramedics, and they flushed his sinuses with water before rushing him to hospital. Someone had cut the coke with rat poison and nearly killed him. That event was a big warning to me, never to take any drugs offered by a stranger. You never knew what nutcase was going to wander up to you and say, "Hey man, I love your stuff. Here, have some of this," and maybe have it laced with cyanide or something, just to get their name on network news.

John Belushi became a friend of the band. We reciprocated the Blues Brothers' guest appearance with us in L.A. by playing at their Blues Bar after a gig at the Chicago Stadium. John had a party house in inner-city Chicago, with a pool table, a bar, and a bandstand set up with guitar, drums, and a mike, and we'd just go along and jam with him all night, taking drugs and hanging out. He was everybody's favorite bad boy and such an upbeat, excitable guy, who loved music and would pour himself into it, like Joe Cocker. He was one of the funniest people I ever met, full of energy and brilliance.

I still mourn his untimely death. Of all the wastes of life due to drug abuse in the music business, I think that was the one that hit me hardest. I couldn't get over the fact that all that vital, vibrant energy had been snuffed out in one single, stupid moment. It gave me serious pause for thought.

Another great moment of that tour was playing Wembley Stadium in England. It was a huge art deco place with something like seventy thousand people all standing on the field and in the stadium, with us down at one end. The acoustics were such that the sound carried away from us like in a baseball stadium, when you see the ball fly and hear the crack of it against the bat later than seems possible. We could see these people jumping to our music in tiers around the stadium, but all in sequence a bit like the Mexican Wave, as the music reached them. I'd never seen that happen before. It was awesome. We had a lot of laughs during that show. The place and the people just made us high. We didn't need anything else.

On nights like those, I realized that we kept going and remained together because we all knew this was the best any of us could do musically, financially, and artistically. There was no place else to go. The sad part was that we were so completely burned out, physically and creatively, that the moments of pure joy were rare. The machine kept wanting more, and we simply couldn't deliver. The strain was becoming too much, and the drugs were making us increasingly paranoid. We were a train wreck waiting to happen.

The new decade began with us at the top of the charts. *The Long Run* was certified platinum and topped the record charts for thirteen straight weeks, making it 1979's biggest-selling record. It sold five million copies and helped put *Greatest Hits* and *Hotel California* back into the Top 100. The music we'd provided for the film *Urban Cowboy* that year also kept us in the public eye. The movie, starring John Travolta and Debra Winger, was conceived and produced by Irving and the sound track featured us, Jimmy Buffett, and Dan Fogelberg. By January 1980, though, nonstop touring was getting us all down. After each show, we'd head off to our individual hotel rooms. The Third Encore parties became a means to an end, not an opportunity for us to hang out together and talk about the gig. Only when the stage lights came on were we a unified rock-and-roll band. Irving tried to spin the situation but finally admitted to the *Los Angeles Times* that *The Long Run* might actually have marked the end.

In February 1980, "Heartache Tonight" won a Grammy for Best Rock Vocal Performance by a Duo or a Group. Critics reviewed our shows in Los Angeles that March as the finest since the *Desperado* days. We'd proved we still had the magic. Our record company, sensing the end was near and panicking, demanded a live album. At the end of July, we booked five nights at the three-thousand-seat Santa Monica Civic Auditorium to record it. The tickets sold out within hours. We took our places in that little theater each night like automatons, standing in the shadows on the stage, listening to the familiar well of noise from the crowd, before launching into our set and playing the best of our classics. It was a spotless, brilliant but utterly soulless performance by five exhausted, shattered young men.

A few days later, on July 31, Glenn committed us to playing a benefit gig at the Long Beach Arena for the reelection of liberal California Senator Alan Cranston, a night that would forever become known as "Long Night at Wrong Beach."

Don and Glenn had been into fund-raising for newsworthy political issues for some years, chiefly for the Chumash Indians and for high-profile antinuclear and environmental projects. I didn't mind about the apolitical events, but I didn't see the point of benefit gigs for politicians like Cranston or Governor Jerry Brown, most of whom I regard with the greatest suspicion. Jerry was all right. He was dating Linda Ronstadt at the time; he came over to my house, and he was cool. He even helped me find a new site for the Malibu Little League team when their baseball field was being turned into the Malibu Lagoon Bird Sanctuary, and my kids, among others, had nowhere else to play. I called him up, and he sponsored a bill that set aside Malibu Bluffs Park for the Little League players, which was neat. But I was tired, fed up with being told what to do and when, and I didn't even know who the Cranstons were. (Later, Cranston was severely reprimanded in the largest savings and loan scandal in U.S. history.) I made my views clear, but I knew that if "The Gods" wanted to get into political campaigning, then I wasn't in a position to argue. Still, you never saw John Lennon, Bob Dylan, or Jimi Hendrix getting into bed with a politician.

Glenn knew I wasn't comfortable with a rock-and-roll band doing a show for politicians. His hostility was compounded when Mrs. Cranston walked up to me backstage to say hello just before we went onstage.

"Hello," I replied. "Nice to meet you . . . ," As she walked away, I added, under my breath, "I guess."

Glenn, standing next to me, heard this and viewed my comment as an intentional slap in the face for the Cranstons, but he was wrong. I truly had no idea who they were, nor did I care, for that matter. He found me in the dressing room and started yelling at me for what I'd said. I don't know if it was the alcohol, the other drugs, or the fact that we'd been on tour for so long, but he just blew up. As usual, I sat there strumming my guitar and let him do his thing. Trying to keep the peace, I finally walked out. Just before we stepped onstage for the benefit, I turned to him and said quietly, "You know, Glenn, what you just did back there? You're an asshole for doing that."

He replied, "That's an honor, coming from you."

We walked onstage, and he came over while we were playing "The Best of My Love" and said, "Fuck you. I'm gonna kick your ass when we get off the stage."

Both of us were burned out after our months on the road. Neither of us really wanted to be there that night, and for me it was one gig too many. If only we'd taken a break after the Santa Monica shows, we could have recharged and rested up. Instead, frazzled and fractious, we focused our unhappiness that night on each other. I started drinking Jack Daniel's and was soon drunker than I'd been in a while. As the night progressed, we both grew angrier and began hissing at each other under our breaths.

In the sound booth, the technicians feared the audience might actually hear our outbursts, so they lowered Glenn's microphone until he had to sing. He continued to approach me after every song to rant, rave, curse, and let me know how many songs remained before our fight.

"That's three more, pal," Glenn said. "Get ready."

"No sweat."

Then we started playing "Life in the Fast Lane," and the crowd leaped to its feet.

When we came offstage, waiting to be called back for the first encore, I kept out of Glenn's way. I knew if I went near him, it would only make things worse. He went over to where the other guys were standing and started shouting something like, "That fucking guy! That fucking Felder!" I could hear him on the other side of the stage.

I stayed by myself, trying to calm down and finish the gig. Then I remembered something Joe would do to release his tension. Whenever he was pissed off, he'd go somewhere and relieve his frustration by smashing something. Before returning to the stage for the encores, I told my guitar tech, Jimmy Collins, "Take that shitty Takamine acoustic guitar I play on 'Lyin' Eyes' and put it by the back door. When I get offstage after the encores, I'm gonna break that fucker."

When the gig finished, I walked off the side of the stage opposite to the rest of the band again. Most of them took off in their limos—anything to get away from the atmosphere between Glenn and me. I thought I'd be the last to leave the building. I toweled myself down in my dressing room, gathered my senses, and headed out toward the back door and the final few cars lined up outside. Seeing the Japanese guitar that Jimmy had put out for me, I took a deep breath, picked it up, held it in my hands for a moment, and then smashed it as hard as I could against the side of a concrete column.

My eyes closed, I repeated the exercise again and again, venting all the anger and frustration I felt inside, feeling the strain on the arm I'd broken falling out of Irene Cooter's chinaberry tree and on the shoulder the drunken quarterback dislocated at the Rucker Brothers gig. I thought of Glenn and of Don, of the way they sometimes treated me, and of my increasing sense of helplessness and isolation. I thought of the sheer exhaustion of being on the road and away from my family and what it was doing to my relationship with Susan. I mourned the loss of my fidelity and regretted the numerous sterile sexual encounters that always left me feeling cold and empty.

That guitar splintered into a million pieces. By the time I'd finished, it was kindling on the floor. Wiping my forehead with the back of my hand, I turned and saw Alan Cranston and his wife standing right behind me, their mouths agape. A few feet away stood a stony-faced Glenn. This had had little or nothing to do with the Cranstons, but Glenn thought I did that right in front of them to drive it up his butt. Honest to God, I didn't even see them there.

"Typical of you to break your cheapest fucking guitar," Glenn told me, cursing, when the Cranstons had hurried off to their car in case I started on them.

Afraid of what I might do if I opened my mouth to respond, I jumped into my limo and sped off.

A few minutes later, Glenn did the same, the two of us locked in mutual enmity.

Within a few days, I'd completely cooled down. I was in Hawaii, staying in a rented house with Susan and the kids, having a rare week off together. Glenn had offered me his place down there, but after the Cranston benefit, I decided not to take him up on the offer and rented somewhere else. After just twenty-four hours in Susan's company, the steam had stopped pouring from my ears and I felt calm again. I promised myself I'd try to stay cool the next time I saw Glenn.

The phone rang. It was Bill Szymczyk. He was in the studio, cleaning up and fixing some of the tracks for the new album, *Eagles Live*. I assumed he was calling to see when I could come in and fix my parts.

"What's the schedule for the band?" I asked.

A small silence fell.

Bill advised me. "There is no band at this time," he said. His voice echoed hollowly over the line.

"What do you mean?" I said.

It was 1980, and the Eagles were history. We would never be the same again.

FOURTEEN

The news came like a slap in the face out of nowhere. Although we'd not been getting along for some time, I never thought we'd split. There was too much at stake. The emotional shock was such that I couldn't even think straight for a moment. I could hear my heartbeat pounding in my ears and my legs virtually collapsed under me. My initial reaction was, "My God, what's going to happen now?" This seemed like the end of the only life I'd known. We'd had breakups before, and there was usually some sort of problem between two or all of us, especially by the end of a tour, but this was different. This was serious. Glenn Frey had called time.

He told one reporter later, "I knew the Eagles were over about halfway through the *Long Run* album. I told myself I'd never go through this again. I could give you thirty reasons why, but let me be concise: I started the band, I got sick of it and I quit."

Don admitted, "We probably peaked on *Hotel California*. After that we started growing apart, as collaborators and friends . . . We put everything we had into it at the expense of our health, friendships, and everything else."

I spent several broken nights worrying that I might have been the sole cause of the split, but I learned much later what had gone down in Miami. There was so much outside pressure from the record label, the critics, and the public to produce high-quality work and surpass the previous album every time that Don and Glenn simply couldn't handle it. Don was the gifted writer and the perfectionist; he'd criticize the work Glenn submitted and ask for slight revisions. Glenn finally announced he was quitting to do a solo album.

Irving called us all up and told us we each had to finish editing the live album without Glenn. I guess he of all people had seen it coming for years. Everyone except Glenn flew to Bill Szymczyk's studio in Miami and started fixing guitar parts, background vocals, drum parts, and bass. Then we flew the tapes to L.A., where Glenn and Bill's assistant in another studio fixed his parts, then FedExed the tapes back to Miami.

There we were, a continent of resentment and unhappiness between us, recording on opposite coasts, entirely separate from each other. Glenn wouldn't talk directly to anybody in the band but was yelling and screaming at everyone else. Finally, he fired Irving, hired his own manager, and withdrew completely.

Everybody kept hoping Glenn would reconsider, even me. We thought he'd get the stress out of his system, do a solo album, and be back. We were at the peak of our success—the biggest band in the world. Why quit now? Yes, it had often been shitty, and yes, he and Don and I often rubbed each other the wrong way, but what else was there? Could there be life after the Eagles?

The record label refused to make any announcement to the fans, trying to keep hope alive. They spoke vaguely of solo albums, rest periods, and studio work. Joe Smith believed that two new songs would sell more copies of the proposed album, *Eagles Live*. He offered us $2 million for the new songs, but Glenn still refused to work with the rest of us. *Eagles*

Live, featuring the best from our gigs in Santa Monica, arrived in the stores on November 7, 1980, reached number six on the charts, and sold over a million copies. Our live cover of "Seven Bridges Road," the harmonic a cappella song we used to sing together in the shower room before each gig as a unifying theme, but which—tellingly—we hadn't sung in years, reached number twenty-seven on the singles charts.

On the liner notes, the album carried a picture of an Eagles nest with four eggs in it and a grenade. Someone has pulled the pin on the grenade.

As far as our fans knew, the Eagles simply vanished. The 1980s heralded a rock scene that relied largely on synthesizers and drum machines. After the assassination of John Lennon in December 1980, it felt like the end of an era for all of us. The music business was something we no longer recognized or felt a part of. Blondie was riding high in the charts, along with people like the Police, ABBA, David Bowie, and Michael Jackson. Irving, who realized his best-selling act was no longer going to make him millions, became head of MCA Records, dropping all but five of the company's almost fifty rock acts and thereby rescuing it from bankruptcy. The move made him one of the most powerful men in the music industry yet didn't prevent his retaining indirect control of Front Line Management or his own independent record label, Full Moon. Joe Smith, head of Warner and the last connection between Warner and the Eagles, resigned.

The only headlines the rest of us were making were unwelcome ones. Don Henley threw a party at his L.A. home at which a minor took an overdose of drugs. The paramedics had to be called and the sixteen-year-old girl resuscitated. Don was arrested and charged with possession of marijuana, cocaine, and Quaaludes, as well as contributing to the delinquency of a minor. He claimed he never even knew she was there among all the other groupies and partygoers. He was fined two thousand dollars, placed on probation for two years, and ordered to attend drug counseling. Later that same year, he and his actress girlfriend were involved in a plane crash in Aspen.

Glenn did some film work in Mexico and ended up detained by authorities briefly in Veracruz after a minor car accident. He was so freaked out by the experience that he chartered a private plane to fly him home to

Aspen, Colorado, as soon as he was released. Joe and Tim were out on the road or doing solo work, and I was home, trying to make some sense of my family life.

The year the Eagles broke up turned out to be one of my worst personally, too. For a time, I felt as if my whole world was falling apart.

The day before the *Long Run* tour ended and I was due home, Susan opened a fan letter from among scores that had been delivered to our Malibu house by the management company. Sacks of mail were collected together and held back until our return, then delivered to each member of the band personally. Susan rarely bothered to read the letters and cards adoring fans sent, but for some reason, this time she did. My mother was staying with her, awaiting my return as well, when Susan happened upon a letter from a fan in Texas.

This particular fan was the most sexually adventurous creature I had ever met. During our brief liaison on the road, in a hotel room in Dallas, she had led me through experiences I'd never previously known. In her letter, she expressed her delight at our "wonderful night together," and cataloged some of the things she'd like to do to me if ever I was in Texas again. Poor Susan, who'd always chosen to ignore the rumors and media stories about the excesses of life on the road, found herself sitting in her own living room, her mother-in-law a few feet away, reading a sexually explicit billet-doux from a woman I'd had sex with. This was irrefutable evidence, in black and white, held in her trembling hand.

When I arrived home the following day, expecting my usual warm greeting, I found myself ducking a machete. She wanted to decapitate me. Slowly. To her eternal credit, she did a brilliant job of publicly pretending everything was normal for my mother's sake and that of the children, but when we were alone, she talked to me endlessly about what I'd done and why.

"I can't believe you'd be so stupid! To jeopardize everything we have for *this*." She waved the letter accusingly at me. "Nine years we've been together. Nine years. We have three small children. What were you thinking?"

There was nothing I could say to appease her. I'd been caught red-handed and I knew it. All the years of guilt and angst conspired against me. I'd managed to persuade myself that none of the women mattered, that my infidelities were insignificant compared with the depth of feeling I had for Susan, but the pain I saw in her eyes made me realize how wrong I'd been.

"I honestly never set out to hurt you, but you must have known what was going on," I said lamely. "I was thrown in with Don and Glenn and Joe, with all that alcohol and drugs, you couldn't possibly have expected me not to crack after all these years." Even as I spoke the words, I knew how shallow they sounded.

Whether she'd suspected or not before didn't matter. The letter she held in her hand made our situation temporarily irredeemable. We started therapy, as a couple and separately, and I came to realize just how much distress I'd caused. I also realized how close I was to blowing my marriage. I'd almost lost her before, when we'd separated in the sixties, and my good fortune at finding her again in Boston after Flow had always been such a blessing. I knew then, as I knew now, that she was the only woman I had ever truly loved, and the thought of losing her snatched the breath from my lungs.

It may have been a little late, but I decided there and then that I'd done all I needed to do in terms of exploring sexual experiences with other women. The breakup of the Eagles had made me realize that what really meant the most to me in my life wasn't the band, it was Susan and the kids. I would do everything within my power to keep them.

My heinous crime wasn't a bear I could fully wrestle to the mat and forget, however. Susan might be able to forgive me eventually, but she could never forget. I'd created a fissure in our relationship that would reside there permanently, irreparably. Even though I tried my hardest by apologizing profusely and telling her how much I loved and admired her, and promising never to touch anyone else, the bear was always there, between us. In therapy, I became dogged with guilt, which I found impossible to purge. I'd been wracked with it enough on the road, but this was in a different league. This was true remorse. I begged forgiveness both from

Susan and from a higher being for the sins I'd committed, the damage and suffering I'd caused, not only to my family but to all those women I'd used and abused.

A great many other beasts were awoken by the therapy too, as they so often are. One was the issue of control. Because I was away so much, Susan had understandably assumed control of the house and the kids and the Mexican maids and our three pet dogs. It was she who chose and bought the furniture and the drapes, disciplined the children, and decided where they should go to school and how they should dress. When I came home and tried to impose a different regime, or make a suggestion about something she might like to consider, my input was largely ignored or overlooked. The kids knew that when Dad was home, things were suddenly more ordered, but as soon as I was gone, they could all relax and go back to their normal lives. The effect had been to make me feel less and less involved in family life and more and more on the periphery, which, our therapist explained, had helped push me into the arms of other women.

"Don needs to feel a part of his family and this home," she told Susan. "He needs to feel that the little authority he does have isn't constantly undermined. Until he does, he'll never be able to come to terms with the two very separate parts of his life. Or worse, he'll start to feel more comfortable with the on-the-road persona than he does with the home one, and you may lose him altogether."

The therapist made a lot of sense, although she still made me feel like a complete failure as a husband and father. She also made me realize—too late—that being a rock star wasn't a horrible thing to be. I'd learned to cope with the negatives and savor the positives, like the money and the fame and the ability to play music. There was a thrilling element to my life that allowed me to walk out onto a stage in front of tens of thousands of screaming fans and do my stuff. But when I came home and wanted real intimacy, to counter the increasing isolation I felt on the road, despite or perhaps because of the women I slept with, I was faced instead with control issues and a distancing between Susan and me that only fed my guilt. Often, she made me admit, it was a relief to go back on tour, to a life that was more familiar and easier to deal with.

If I could have turned back the clock and been a better person then, I would have done so. Susan, Jesse, Rebecca, and Cody were my life, and there was, I knew, a very real danger that I might lose them. And for what? To satisfy the carnal beast? To impress my fellow band members and not be regarded by them with suspicion and contempt? I prayed for extra strength to help me through the many trials I was now facing. Was this how I was going to end up?—an embittered, unemployed guitarist, divorced from his wife, a weekend dad, living in some apartment alone somewhere? I prayed not.

Perhaps not surprisingly, within six months of the band splitting up and the start of my problems with Susan, I was hospitalized with chronic diverticulitis, inflammation of the colon, which erupted within me like a burning spear. I'd been trying to deal with the stress of my life in a very self-healing way, but internally my body was eating itself alive. I spent a week in the Santa Monica Hospital on intravenous antibiotics, feeling utterly wretched about myself and the path my life seemed to be taking.

A nurse brought me a telephone one afternoon. "Felder, it's Irving," the voice on the line said.

I was touched at the thought of Irving calling to see how I was. I should have known better.

"Just to let you know," he said, without asking a single question about my well-being. "Joe Walsh is putting together a solo album, and he's recorded one of the songs you wrote for the last album which didn't make it. It was the one called 'You're Really High, Aren't You?' He's gonna redo the lyrics and change it around a bit, and would like your permission to use it on his new album."

"Er, well, Irv, I was kinda keeping that one for the future," I said, at a loss for what to say, my head flopping back onto my pillow with a searing wave of pain.

I felt as though he wasn't asking me, he was telling me, as Joe's manager, that this was how it was going to be. I think I was supposed to be grateful.

• • •

I'd always been careful about spending money. When you come from poverty, you never quite believe your luck will last. In L.A., I saw plenty of other people make mistakes. They'd join bands, have some success, and make lots of money. Ten years later, they'd be subsisting in run-down little condominiums in the Valley because they'd blown it all. I was somewhat cognizant of this danger. I also had a good business manager, who'd invested in some profitable real estate ventures for me, but I was still only in my thirties, and none of my investments had yet left me financially solvent for the rest of my days. With the lucrative income from touring cut off, a future living on royalties alone would obviously have a big impact on my family and me. I had enough to live on, but if I wanted to maintain our lifestyle, I would definitely have to reconsider my options.

I'd bought a big house on a two-acre lot in Bonsall Canyon, Malibu, from Tommy Chong of the comedy duo Cheech and Chong, both of whom became close friends. My immediate neighbors were Jimmy Pankow from the band Chicago on one side and the actor Nick Nolte on the other. Nick used to have such wild parties with Gary Busey and his friends that Jimmy would call me up in the middle of the night and say, "Hey, Felder, turn that music down!" and I'd yell back, "It's not me, it's Nolte."

Jimmy was a great family man, living high on the hog with seven acres filled with thoroughbred horses and Rolls-Royces. He was always inviting me over for barbecues with his friends, most of whom were his fellow band members. I can remember watching them all getting along so well, their wives and kids in tow, and wishing our band had been like that.

Our house was a California-style property designed by the man who built the Disneyland Hotel. It had a living room forty feet square that was like a hotel lobby. Irving had recommended his architect and interior designer to us and Susan met with them and decided what we wanted, which was effectively a whole new house on the back of this living room, so we had to move into rental houses until it was done.

When the band split up and I came home to live in the remodeled house, I just didn't feel comfortable. There was far too much marble and granite for me; it felt more than a little gauche. I'd come from meager means, and my new home seemed opulent and pretentious. I was, quite frankly, embarrassed by it. Worst of all, I felt I had been completely omitted from the planning. Everything seemed very feminine, and there wasn't even a corner for me to have a comfortable recliner to feel at home.

I discussed it with Susan, and we eventually agreed that there was no point in my feeling uncomfortable in my own home, so we sold the house and bought a five-acre piece of land at Paradise Cove, for which I started designing a new house. To supplement my income and stop myself from going mad, I went back to school and acquired the qualifications I needed for a real estate license, to broker my own property transactions. I hoped that by doing that and trying my hand at a few different jobs, such as writing movie scores, or doing some TV work, I could finally get to stay home with my wife and kids after years on the road.

For the first few years of their lives, my kids had grown up with an absentee father. I'd come home and they'd look at me and say, "Oh yeah, you live here, don't you? You sleep with Mom. I remember you." I'd be there for a week or two, then go. I missed school plays, parent evenings, soccer games, and many of the major events in their young lives. OK, I was Santa Claus each time I came home, laden with gifts and toys, my plunders from the big wide world, but it wasn't the same. Our grueling schedule prevented me from being an active participant in their development, despite all the astronomically expensive telephone calls. Poor Susan was effectively a single parent. Now all that was going to change.

I refused, point-blank, to go back on the road—even when friends in the industry offered me a chance to tour with them. I was enjoying time with my kids again. I'd get up at six o'clock in the morning and make strawberry pancakes for breakfast, each one with their initials cooked into the batter. I drove my kids and their friends to school in the car pool. I became the Little League and soccer coach.

Jesse was wild about technology and computers and building things like remote-control cars and gliders, so I encouraged him to follow his passion. Warner Brothers gave us one of the first Atari computers, and he and I played a game called *Lemonade Stand* on it, in which you had to decide how many lemons and how much sugar to buy to make lemonade, depending on the weather predictions for the next few days. Man, he loved that. Later I bought him *Millionaire,* a stock market game in which he built up his own imaginary portfolio. I took him to the New York Stock Exchange to see how it worked firsthand. He even appeared in *People* magazine at America's first computer camp when he was eight years old. With his white-blond hair, he looked like the kid from *The Champ.* I could have called him Cotton.

When he was ten years old, he came to me and asked me to teach him how to play guitar. At first I discouraged him and refused, using reverse psychology to make him want it even more. He'd beg me to teach him a few licks, until finally I'd relent, but only after I made him listen to B.B. King and Eric Clapton and Duane Allman.

"I knew Duane Allman," I'd tell him. "It was he who taught me how to play slide. And I once shook B.B. King's hand."

"Really, Dad?" he'd say, not sure whether to believe me or not. Then he'd go up to his room and practice for hours, cranking it up on his own, but never in public. He was far too shy.

I spoiled all the kids rotten, and they were constantly complaining that I was too affectionate with them in public. I guess I was trying to compensate for the lack of physical affection my parents had shown me. Whereas I'd had very few birthday parties, they had massive, catered events with balloons and clowns and magicians. Christmases involved the biggest tree, with me dressing up as Santa and dishing out gifts like huge scale train sets or rocking horses. It was a million miles from my Christmases in Florida, with two small gifts under the tree for Jerry and me— usually much-needed items of clothing or shoes—and the crafts for Mom and Dad that we'd made at school. Or from my first Christmas in that first-floor apartment in Culver City with Susan and Kilo, where we'd made a star out of tin foil and cut pictures from magazines to decorate our skinny little tree.

I don't think my kids really understood that their father was a rock star. To them I was just Dad. I played guitar and was away a lot. The only thing that made me stand out from the crowd was the way I looked, with my shoulder-length hair, beard, and mustache. One day, when I'd just dropped Rebecca off at school and was walking her to her class, I overheard one of her friends, who'd previously only seen me from the back, cry, "Rebecca! Your mom's got a beard!" Maybe my dad was right. Maybe it was time to shave.

When Don Henley invited me on the road with him for his first solo tour, I turned him down. Not only did I not want to tour again, but the salary he offered was five thousand dollars a week—that of a sideman, not a band member or the lead guitarist of the Eagles. He made the offer through Irving, instead of calling me direct, and I wrote and told him that I wasn't really interested, despite my enormous respect for him as a singer and songwriter. His letter of reply said, "I don't see any reason why we can't write together and remain in touch," and so we did. I'd send him tapes now and then, and he came and sang on a few records for me, but he was writing with Danny Kortchmar and other people he felt were fresh and new. He was enjoying heading in a different direction and that was cool.

Instead of going on the road, I concentrated on the completion of our new home, in between writing and performing some songs for film, including the soundtrack for an animated movie called *Heavy Metal*. I also wrote the title theme song and sound score for an animated Saturday morning CBS series my kids loved called *Galaxy High*. I did another song, called "Wild Life," which became the title track for a Neil Simon movie called *The Slugger's Wife*, and I contributed some music for a film called *Fast Times at Ridgemont High*, written by none other than little Cameron Crowe, the *Rolling Stone* reporter who'd been on the road with us.

I did some session work for people like Stevie Nicks, Bob Seger, Warren Zevon, Boz Scaggs, and the Bee Gees, and I helped my friends Chicago out a couple of times when their guitarist, Donnie Dacus, left them. I worked on an album by Mickey Thomas of Jefferson Starship, which saw me back working with the inimitable Bill Szymczyk, and I helped Joe Walsh with his solo records. I even ended up cohosting a music video program for kids called *Fun TV* or *FTV*. My kids loved it. They were much more impressed with that than anything I'd done with the Eagles.

• • •

The record company waited two years before they officially confirmed that the Eagles had split, and in May 1982, shortly after the announcement, Glenn released his first solo album *No Fun Aloud,* more than half of which was cowritten with Jack Tempchin, his collaborator on one of the band's first hits, "Peaceful Easy Feeling." Glenn swapped his trademark long hair and handlebar moustache for a clean-cut look, and the distinctive Eagles sound for his Detroit rhythm-and-blues roots. *No Fun Aloud* sold around five hundred thousand copies. Don Henley, meanwhile, was in the midst of his nationwide tour when his hit single "Dirty Laundry" climbed to number three and helped his album *I Can't Stand Still* sell around seven hundred thousand copies.

The trouble was that, after years of keeping our names out of the newspapers and our faces off Eagles album covers in favor of the artist Boyd Elder's incredible decorative cattle skulls, no one really knew who Don Henley and Glenn Frey were—or any of us, for that matter. For years, we'd been able to walk around L.A., into restaurants, clubs, and theaters, and melt anonymously into the crowd. It is one of the great bonuses of being an Eagle. No one knows what we looked like. Furthermore, Don and Glenn were now competing in the charts against *the Eagles' Greatest Hits Volume 2,* released by Asylum/Elektra in time for the 1982 Christmas market, cobbled together from *Hotel California* and *The Long Run.* Despite its lack of direct involvement with the band, it far outsold both solo albums. It was a hard act to follow.

When asked if the Eagles would ever reunite, Don famously replied. "Yeah, sure, when hell freezes over."

My mother, who was leading a full and busy life in Gainesville, remarried in 1982, having met her new husband, Oliver Reynolds, through the church. She finally moved out of the house I'd grown up in and into Oliver's concrete-block property with a yard, closer to her sister. The old house remained in the family; my father's younger sister moved in. Once again, I paid for that old house to be completely remodeled and refurbished. My mother rejected my offer of a Hawaiian honeymoon as a wedding present and asked for a small check instead.

She remained as active as ever, although she finally gave up work when she remarried, spending her time taking bus trips with Oliver instead. They traveled quite a bit and enjoyed church outings, until Ollie developed Alzheimer's and my mother became his full-time caregiver. Even then, she wouldn't accept help. Jerry and I paid for someone to come in three days a week to cook, leave food in the refrigerator, and do the heavy cleaning, but she lasted less than two weeks before my mother told her to get out and not come back. "She didn't do things the way I like them," Mom explained.

The same year she and Ollie were married, David Blue, whose career had nosedived in the years since I had stopped playing with him, dropped dead while jogging in New York. He was forty years old. I didn't hear about it until some time later, but the news was shocking. He and I had been contemporaries out on the road together, and now his life was over. I couldn't help thinking about the time we'd spent together, snorting cocaine, smoking pot, and taking Valium, and I wondered if that had anything to do with his sudden demise. The loss only made me think longer and harder about what I was doing with my life and made me work even harder to keep my marriage going.

In November 1982, our fourth child, Leah, was born. With this birth, we felt we had come full circle from that sad time. Our family was complete. We had survived the traumas I had wreaked upon us, and we had a new baby to concentrate on. I'd lie in bed early in the morning, Leah's still, warm weight upon my chest, and pray silently to the Lord to thank him for the blessings I'd been given. What had started as a dreadful beginning to the new decade was suddenly looking brighter. I wondered what the next few years would bring.

With Glenn and Don embarking on solo careers, and Joe and Timothy talking about doing a record each, I decided I might as well give it a try, as long as I didn't have to do any extensive touring. I'd had enough of walking around on eggshells and not saying what I really felt about songs and lyrics. I just wanted to do what I wanted to do and not be a slave to someone else's agenda. As an inducement for the last Eagles album, Elektra/Asylum had offered each of us a record deal, so I decided to take up the offer.

My budget was around $300,000, which wasn't huge, so I converted my guesthouse into a full-blown recording studio, with a drum room, a twenty-four track, and a piano. That way I wouldn't have to be looking over my shoulder all the time or worrying about spiraling studio costs of around $20,000 a week. With time on my side, I'd be able to experiment: If I didn't like something, I could redo it. The only other person in the studio was an engineer I hired to record the music while I played. I had scores of tracks I'd written for the Eagles, which had never been used. Unearthing them, I chose the best, and worked on them, endlessly re-shaping the original sound.

I called the new album *Airborne,* to signify that this Eagle wasn't grounded, and worked on it for over a year. I invited friends like Jimmy Pankow and Lee Loughnane (of Chicago), Dave Mason (of Fleetwood Mac and Traffic), Kenny Loggins, and Timothy B. Schmit to provide backup music and vocals, along with a whole bunch of buddies from the business. I played all the guitars, sang all the lead and most of the backup vocals, and played some synthesizer. We had a lot of fun together in the studio, and I enjoyed every minute of working with such outstanding talent.

Cody, who was about four years old and absolutely fearless, would often come into the studio to sneak up on me. "Hey, buddy," I'd say as I saw his mop of white Felder hair bob up and down past the studio window. "Wanna come in and listen to what Daddy's doin'?" He'd sit on my lap, smiling at me, gap-toothed, listening to the music I was making. It was sheer delight to spend such time with the children. These were simple pleasures I'd been denied for so long.

With the album nearly ready, I was painfully aware of the comparisons that would undoubtedly be drawn with the Eagles. One song was called "Still Alive," a comment on my journey through life with the Eagles and my relationship with Susan. Another song, called "Night Owl," was about the lightless rock-and-roll lifestyle—living in the darkness and going to bed when the sun comes up, a statement on the slithering, intoxicated nights we had allowed to devour us. A song called "Bad Girls," with a couple of great double-guitar parts, was a track I'd originally offered to the Eagles for *The Long Run*. Joe and I had come up with it in one all-night drinking session. It was previously entitled "Wild Turkey." I finished it for this album and wrote a different lyric. My favorite was a number called "Who Tonight?" on the theme of fidelity. It was not unlike that timeless song from Stephen Stills, "Love the One You're With."

The trouble was, I still had serious inhibitions about my voice. I mixed my voice down so low that you had to strain to even hear it above my guitar playing. For years, I'd been browbeaten into believing that my voice was mediocre at best. When it was time for me to step up to the mike for my own album, my self-confidence was a bludgeoned, bleeding thing, and it showed.

I remember Joe Walsh telling me once how hard it was to be a solo artist because you had to do everything yourself, and I suddenly understood what he meant. Even at the lowest moments of the Eagles, we'd always had each other as sounding boards, even if it was just to sound off. Our biggest arguments were over the music and trying to get it right. Now, I felt stuck out on a limb with no one to ask how I was doing. There was no Don or Bill to ask, "Hey, what do you think of this one?" It felt horrible to be so alone.

While I plodded on, doing my own stuff, everything was changing at the label. The likes of the Eagles, Joni Mitchell, Jackson Browne, and Linda Ronstadt were no longer vital to the organization, which had been completely restructured. Asylum had done a 180-degree shift, and its new direction was in black R&B acts. By 1983, Michael Jackson was the undisputed king of the charts with songs like "Billie Jean" from his best-selling album *Thriller.* I eventually delivered *Airborne* to a company that had no interest in it and had even closed its offices in Los Angeles, relocating to New York.

I was just relieved and happy to have finished the album, which had taken all my strength. I turned it in and thought, "If it sells, that's great. If it doesn't sell, it doesn't really matter." Which was just as well.

I had a whole new relaxed attitude to life and so, I think, did the rest of the band. It had been incredibly hard work being an Eagle, and until we stopped, we didn't quite realize how hard it was. Being an Eagle was burdensome—the stress and pressure of writing, recording and touring, the media, and the fan frenzy. When that machine gears up, it has a loud roar. It takes a lot out of you to get up every day, put on your Eagle suit, and have every note or word you write put under a microscope by other band members and the critics. It's oppressive.

Now we were free of all that, and it felt good to be home with our families, writing and recording the music we liked, having a few beers, doing our own stuff, playing with our kids, and being ourselves. The magnitude of what we'd become had torn us apart. It wasn't just Glenn. We'd all been ready to run from the machine.

FIFTEEN

Don Henley was flying high. He released his second solo album, *Building the Perfect Beast,* in 1984 and had his greatest success to date with his single, "The Boys of Summer," an editorial on the failed dreams of the sixties. The video of the single won the MTV award for Best Video of the Year, and within twelve months, he'd also won a Grammy for Best (Male) Rock Vocal Performance. In 1985, he was watching *Late Night with David Letterman* when he saw Glenn interviewed and singing "Desperado." He called him after the show for a chat, the first time they'd spoken in five years. Irving, ever hopeful, heard of their contact and organized a dinner for the three of them that Christmas in Aspen, but no Eagles reunion was forthcoming.

Glenn went on to have some success with the song "The Heat Is On," written by Keith Forsey and Harold Faltermeyer and featured in the film *Beverly Hills Cop,* starring Eddie Murphy. Glenn also starred in an episode of *Miami Vice,* thus fulfilling a lifetime dream of becoming an actor. Further roles followed, including one as a plumber turned commando in a film called *Let's Get Harry,* but a television show he starred in made network history by being canceled after just one episode. Few other acting jobs were forthcoming, and he ended up in television commercials promoting a fitness chain.

I spent a few years working with the Bee Gees' producer, an innovative genius named Albhy Galuten. He and I had first met in Miami during the recording of *Hotel California,* when I'd been asked to play on a couple of their albums. I liked the Gibb brothers immensely. Barry, especially, was the perfect English gentleman. Ever since my days in the Maundy Quintet, I'd been a sucker for all things British, and Barry Gibb reminded me of Graham Nash. Albhy and I set up in business together, developing some technical equipment and working with some great musicians. We had a lot of fun. My nickname for him was "Albhy Seeing Ya!" After a few years' successful collaboration, he went off and did his own thing, concentrating on the technical side, leaving me wondering what to do next.

By 1986, things had changed. Don was still reeling emotionally from the breakup of the Eagles, an event—he later said—that took him eight years to recover from. Joe Walsh was opening for Tina Turner, getting divorced, and struggling with drugs and alcohol. Rehab beckoned. Timothy Schmit was making solo records and working as a session player with people like Richard Marx, Bob Seger, Jimmy Buffett, and Gregg Allman. The world largely forgot Randy Meisner and Bernie Leadon, despite their individual successes and diverse solo projects. Only in Japan, where a *Best of the Eagles* album had been released in 1985 by WEA, were we still riding high in the charts.

I shelved plans for a second solo album and concentrated on my real estate ventures and spending time with my family. I learned how to fly a plane—an interest sparked from years of visiting the cockpits of the planes we toured in and being allowed to take the controls—and got my commercial rating. I did some sea bass fishing in the kelp beds off Malibu with Cheech Marin, Jimmy Pankow, and my good friend Jack Pritchett, the Realtor who'd found us our first house in Malibu. On one trip out into a choppy ocean, a freak wave hit my little seventeen-foot boat and almost capsized us. We somehow escaped with just cuts and bruises, despite being tossed up into the air like something out of *The Perfect Storm.* I remember clinging to the side of the boat, half-drowned and praying for a speedy deliverance.

Afterward, Cheech joked, "Hey, man, I can just see the headlines if we hadn't made it: 'Don Felder of the Eagles, Cheech Marin of Cheech and Chong, Jimmy Pankow of Chicago, all drowned in a tragic boating accident . . . with an unidentified male.'" He had wetsuit jackets made up for each of us with our names embroidered on them. Jack's read UNIDEN-TIFIED.

It wasn't the first time I'd nearly drowned. Besides a couple of surfing accidents that left me with a lifelong back problem and a few gallons of the Pacific in my lungs, Joe and I once took his boat, the *So What?*, to Santa Cruz Island, when a storm blew in. Stupidly, high on blow and Jack Daniel's, with an inexperienced young captain, we left the sanctuary of Smuggler's Cove and headed back out across the ocean, because we were due to leave for a European tour the following morning. The coast guard had strongly advised us against attempting the crossing and followed us in their cutter as the waves pitched and tossed us like corks.

"Here, put this on," Joe told me, handing me a plastic garbage bag and some gaffer tape. He hadn't thought to stow foul-weather gear. So there we stood, wrapped up in black plastic bags, swigging brandy, trying to see through the wall of water that was crashing onto our little boat at regular intervals. We made it by the skin of our teeth, and only when we arrived in port did we notice the coast guard helicopter hovering overhead. "Is that there for our benefit?" we asked the coast guard radio operator gratefully.

"No," he growled. "We took photographs of you for training purposes."

"Oh, yeah?"

"Yeah, we're gonna use you as an example of how stupid some people in boats can be."

The Malibu incident frightened the life out of me, so I bought a bigger boat, a twenty-five-foot Sea Ray, for weekend trips out to Catalina and the islands with the kids for swimming, spearfishing, and snorkeling excursions that I think were probably the happiest days of their lives. Even the Sea Ray wasn't quite up to those rolling Pacific waves, so we upgraded to a forty-two-foot Grand Banks, which we called *Nantucket,* after the place where Susan and I spent our honeymoon.

I busied myself with other stuff too. I became a scuba diver, to master level, and I won the Catalina Island Lobster Contest for catching the biggest lobster on opening day. I learned Spanish from my gap-toothed gardener, inadvertently ending up speaking like the Mexican equivalent of Gabby Hayes, and I spent a lot of time playing golf, for pleasure and for charity, with friends like Peter Cetera.

I built Susan a potter's studio at the back of our house and learned how to throw some half-decent pots and vases myself, after she and Cheech taught me, but mainly, I was bored and depressed. My relationship with Susan at that time didn't help. She'd had a serious health scare soon after Leah was born. She needed surgery on what ended up being diagnosed as a benign nodule on her thyroid. I bought her a beautiful gold-and-diamond necklace to hide the scar on her throat. Unfortunately, the problems with her thyroid affected her behavior for a while, and she lost some of the verve she'd always had. Our therapy sessions became ever more intensive, and it seemed to me that the more time we spent talking to a third party about our problems, the less we actually talked to each other. The thought of what was happening in my marriage and my life dragged me to an all-time low. I gained twenty pounds as I tried to reconcile myself to being a husband, a dad, and a retired rocker. The hundreds of people who'd been part of the Eagles machine, whom I'd thought of as my friends, had evaporated. For a while there, I felt pretty lost—a thirty-seven-year-old has-been.

By comparison to Don's career, mine had come to a grinding halt. Most of all, I missed playing and performing music more than I could ever have imagined, even during the darkest days. There's something so emotionally fulfilling in standing on stage and playing live music to an audience. Nothing else beats it, and without a regular fix, I felt bereft.

Ultimately, the Eagles proved to be the best any of us would ever do. The combination of our various talents and the creative tension that fueled them was a heady mix that none of us would ever match individually. Don came pretty close with his hits and videos but didn't quite reach the same magnitude. Everyone's desire was to work together again, but at the time, it was still impossible. We had gone off in different directions and had limits to how much we'd be willing to tolerate again.

After a year of feeling sorry for myself, our therapist suggested that I go on Prozac. "I think it might just help you get through this rough patch," she advised.

"OK." I smiled. "I've done drugs before. Give me some."

Fortunately, Susan's condition stabilized, and she was eventually able to pick herself up and start all over again. I began to feel much more like the old Fingers Felder, so I flushed my pills down the toilet.

Every few months or so, some spark would be lit about the possibility of an Eagles reunion, and Irving would call up. "Hey, Don, how ya doing? I'm just checking in. Still hoping to get the guys together in the same room sometime. If it comes off, are you in?"

"Book it, Irving," I'd always say.

After months of nothing ever coming of it, though, I decided to try something myself. Tired of fishing, sailing, and renovating houses, I told Irving, "If the Eagles aren't gonna work together again, then let's put something together with those of us who will."

Irving seemed nervous at first. I don't think he was sure where a band consisting of two-fifths of the Eagles would fit in. Timothy jumped at the chance. "I'm in," he said. We both contacted Joe, and he agreed to join us. We didn't have a name or much of an idea what we could do, but we knew we needed a singer, so Walsh suggested an English guy who had a really great soulful rock-and-roll voice—Terry Reid. His greatest claim to fame was that he had almost been the lead singer with Led Zeppelin, turning the job down for a solo career before recommending the unknown Robert Plant to Jimmy Page. He'd worked with Cream, Procol Harum, and the Yardbirds, and he had supported the Rolling Stones, the Hollies, the Faces, and Jefferson Airplane. He knew David Lindley, Graham Nash, and Jackson

Browne and had done some session work for Don Henley. He was a couple of years younger than me, and his pedigree was excellent.

The trouble was that both he and Joe liked to drink, and Timothy and I quickly realized that we couldn't work with either of them. Joe was pretty bad by then. He couldn't even drive himself anywhere or walk the streets alone. He was so incapable of dealing with the real world, due to the paranoia caused by his addiction to alcohol and drugs, that he had to be accompanied everywhere by his personal bodyguard, a supposed former White House Secret Service agent called Smokey.

Matters came to a head at a meeting with Irving, when we were discussing a measly $500,000 record budget, which, by the time we'd paid the studios and cartage and the road crew, amounted to around $40,000 each. Joe had known Irving since they were in college together. They'd been roommates in Illinois. Enraged, he jumped to his feet and leaped at him, screaming, "You're just trying to fuck us over, aren't you!"

Joe was blue in the face from rage. He stormed out of the office in disgust.

Irving was incandescent with anger. "Did you see that fucking lunatic? He's so fucking unstable. There's no way he's ever gonna be in this band."

I was shocked. I'd never seen Joe so angry, not even when he was destroying hotel rooms with chainsaws. The last time I'd seen anyone treat Irving like that was when the mild-mannered Jimmy Pankow lost it with him in a hotel room in Honolulu in the late seventies during the *Long Run* tour.

Realizing after this incident that our new band wouldn't work with either Joe or Terry Reid, Timothy and I scouted around for another singer. We tried a couple, including Paul Carrack, another Englishman, a singer-songwriter who'd been involved with Nick Lowe and the bands Ace, Mike + the Mechanics, and Squeeze. I wanted one other singer who could play and write, and we eventually settled on Paul and another great guy named Max Carl from the bands .38 Special and Big Dance.

Now that we had our lineup, we recorded six or eight songs together, including a great track written by Paul with Jim Capaldi and Peter Vale called "Love Will Keep Us Alive." It was a joy for Timothy and me to work with these guys, compared to some of the experiences of recent years. Based at my little studio in Malibu, we laughed and had a good time and played really well together. We put the songs we'd completed on a demo and took them to Irving, who jumped up and down with excitement.

"Hey, Fingers, these are really good!" he said, with obvious surprise. "I think you might have something here. What's the band called?"

We'd toyed with a couple of names like Big Sky or Big Party, but nothing seemed to fit. We couldn't think of anything that really worked, so we gave ourselves a temporary name. "Malibu Men's Choir," I told Irving. Seeing the expression on his face, I added, "Not really, Irv. We just made that up for a laugh. We'll come up with something else, don't worry."

A week later, a fax came rolling off my machine at home. There was no preparatory phone call, no attempt at a proper explanation, just two sentences from Irving's office: "We will not be entering into a recording contract with the Malibu Men's Choir. We thank you for your input, but the material you submitted wasn't strong enough."

I felt sick to my stomach.

Still hopeful of an Eagles reunion, Irving set up more talks after he'd heard that Don and Glenn had spent a rare evening together at the Carlyle Hotel in New York, drinking Cristal champagne and reminiscing.

In the summer of 1989, Don produced a stunning third album, *The End of the Innocence,* which went on to sell over six million copies and swept the Grammy awards. I sent him a bottle of champagne and a telegram that said, "Congratulations on your broad sweep of the music industry. Attaboy, Guano." His response was both warm and humble. Although I'd sometimes found him too obsessive and critical, he'd always had the capacity to be charming when he wanted to be, and he and I had never really had a problem.

The following year, Irving again broached the subject of what he called a possible "resumption" tour. The reactions from Don and Glenn were finally favorable, and the rest of us agreed. As before, my response was unequivocal: "Book it, Irv."

In November, Irving called to tell me "We're on" and give me details of where I had to be and when. I was more than a little anxious at seeing Glenn again for the first time in ten years, but I figured that if he'd agreed to the reunion, then he must have put our spat at Long Beach behind him. I arrived at a little rehearsal hall in North Hollywood, next to Burbank Airport, called the Third Encore, named in fond memory of our legendary tour parties by the guy who owned it, who'd been on the road with us as a keyboard tech and was soon given the nickname Norton.

Don had hired Danny "Kootch" Kortchmar to produce our new project. Danny was a guitarist and songwriter turned producer, who knew Don from the Troubadour days and who'd also worked with Glenn. Danny had coproduced all of Don's solo albums, and Don wanted him on board now. Glenn's suggestion had been Elliot Scheiner, who'd produced his solo records, but Don didn't rate him as high. Our old friend Bill Szymczyk was semiretired and had been out of the loop for a while, and "The Gods" decided that he wasn't up to the job.

A guitar player Don sometimes worked with named Frank Simes showed up, and Joe was due any moment. We had no idea when Glenn would show his face. Days passed, and there was still no sign of Joe or Glenn, so we puttered about, setting everything up, and we waited. Joe was pretty intoxicated most of the time by then and kept sending excuses. Glenn was supposed to fly in from Aspen any day with two or three songs he'd written, but he never showed. He supposedly sent a message through Irving instead saying that he had his songs already written and would meet us in the studio.

We carried on, rehearsing a couple of numbers Don was going to sing and one great ballad called "People Can Change," which Don wrote for Timothy to sing. We all believed it was aimed at Glenn. "Let's hope people can change," I told Don. "It would be great if that could be the theme of this whole resumption." He nodded and smiled. We played with the tracks and worked out a couple of licks, but still there was no sign of Joe or Glenn. After a few more days of waiting, we booked the A&M Studio at La Cienega and La Brea in Hollywood.

Irving told us that Glenn had said he wouldn't be there the first day and would come later.

OK, we thought. At least we don't have to go through the hair-pulling, writing stage. Don has a couple of things, there's something for Timothy to sing, Glenn has a couple of songs, and we were certain Joe would bring in a song or two. "We're gold, we're good," we told each other, not really believing it. "This will be easy."

We spent the first couple of days in the studio setting up the drums, bass, and guitars so that they didn't buzz or hum and sounded just right. It takes a while to get comfortable in a new studio, and we were still waiting. When Joe hadn't shown up on the second day, we put in a call to his house.

His English roadie answered. "Joe was up really late working on something last night and he can't come in today, but he'll be there tomorrow by two," he said. The next day we were all there at one o'clock, hoping for the best. Two o'clock came and went and there was no Joe. Then three o'clock, four o'clock, five o'clock.

We finally called the roadie, and he said, "Oh yeah, Joe's just getting out of the shower now. He'll be down in an hour." By six o'clock, we called again and were told that Joe was so tired, he'd gone back to sleep. On the fourth day, Joe finally showed up, reeking and carrying a little black shoulder bag clutched to his side, which he took into the bathroom frequently. It was uncertain exactly what the poison of the day was, probably copious amounts of Jack Daniel's or gin combined with cocaine, but his breath could probably have propelled a small aircraft. We were heavily disappointed that he was in such a state of disrepair, but late in the morning, when he was so inebriated that I thought he'd fall off his stool, he plugged in his amp for his "Layla"-type guitar solo on one of the tracks and played one of the meanest licks I'd ever heard.

"OK," we said, looking at each other in surprise. "Joe can still play. Cool. This could really work."

Over the next day or two, we started recording tracks that Don would sing, convincing ourselves that Glenn could come in later and play his guitar or add whatever he felt they needed. He kept putting us off until finally Irving arrived, stone-faced.

"Glenn's not coming to the party," he said, his dismay evident. "He's decided not to do it. It's over."

For a split second I wondered if Glenn had ever really agreed to do this in the first place, or whether Irving had been yanking our chains. Maybe he thought that if he told us Glenn would do it, and we all got together and started, then Glenn would actually agree. Whatever his plan, it wasn't going to work.

We looked at each other and shook our heads in disbelief. Someone said, "Well, if he doesn't want to do it, let's just go ahead without him."

No one really wanted that. Our hearts weren't in it, especially not after my failed attempt with Timothy and Joe. If it wasn't all of us, it wouldn't be the Eagles. Maybe Glenn was right. Maybe he was the leader of the band after all. None of us felt like we should do it without him.

Don summed it up. "Without Glenn on board, it would just be like Don Henley and his backing band."

Glenn threatened to go to the press and say we weren't the Eagles without him. He said he'd even file a lawsuit to stop us from going ahead. He issued a series of increasingly angry statements, enough for us to say, "OK, maybe we really shouldn't do it."

The saddest thing is that we had some great songs. One was by Frank Simes, on which Joe and I had a rocking guitar track. It was an outline for a song, sort of a ZZ Top, straight up, rock-and-roll number. It would have been fun, but we had to shelve the whole project. I guess those songs will be lost forever now. All I have to remember the experience by is a short videotape of those of us who showed up fooling around in the studio, having fun, and hoping for the best. I'd wanted it to record a little bit of music history, the regrouping of a great band. Instead, it became its video epitaph. I filed it away on a shelf and called it "Almost the Eagles."

Being rich and famous is fantastic. You get to live in a fabulous house, drive fancy cars, own boats, take great vacations, and buy yourself or your loved ones whatever you like. Trust me, it's worth all the effort it takes to get there, especially when you happen to be anonymous. Because of my "reclusive" tag, I've never been easily recognized, not like a movie star. I've been out socially with friends whose faces are far better known, and they get stopped on the sidewalk or approached in restaurants and asked for their autographs, while I sit there silently smiling to myself and thanking the Lord that nobody knows who I am.

The minute someone discovers my connection with the Eagles, their attitude changes instantly. From being vaguely polite and interested, they suddenly become my new best friend. Everybody seems to have a daughter or a brother or a cousin who wants to make it in the music business and has a CD they want me to hear. More often than not, I do listen to them, because you never know when the next John Mayer or Beyoncé is going to pop up. I don't mind using my celebrity status to help people along the way, to lend some extra influence to a charity event, or to further somebody else's cause.

But in modern-day America, there is another, more sinister, element to celebrity that has to be considered, even for those of us who are anonymous—personal safety. By just living in a particular area or being in this industry, you can inadvertently lay yourself open to those who begrudge you or feel they own a part of you.

When we were on the road, we were always being asked to sign autographs. Young women would scream at stage doors to take the pen they offered and write your name across their breasts. Hopeful young guitar players would hold up their tattered Stratocasters or their personal copies of *Hotel California* and ask the same. I never minded signing whatever they wanted me to, and I never once knowingly refused an autograph to a genuine fan. More often than not, however, the people at the door were professional autograph hunters, people who made a great deal of money by selling signed memorabilia to Eagles fans. The professionals were usually pretty easy to spot: They carried stacks of LPs instead of just one, or they had four guitars at their feet. They could get a lot of money for an Eagles black-and-white photo with *all* our signatures on it, and thousands for a guitar. Without my name added to the others in ink, the same item was only worth fifty bucks.

We learned how to spot them by asking, "What's your name?" A genuine fan always wants the record, photograph, or T-shirt signed to themselves, and I'd duly write: "To Marcie, with love, Don Felder." Autographs are worth far less when they're signed to a person, and the professionals jump down your throat if you try it. "No, man, don't write anything, just sign your damn name!" After that, they'd get one signature from me and I'd move on to try to find a genuine fan.

To professional autograph hunters, I've been a pain in the ass. For no reason other than where and how I lived, I was often not with the other Eagles when it came to collecting signatures. They might have all the other guys' names on a stack of LPs or guitars, but not mine. When the band split up in 1980, the price for Eagles memorabilia skyrocketed. Likewise, when someone dies, their back catalog suddenly becomes worth so much more. Without all five signatures on their precious cache of goods, their haul was almost worthless.

I was well accustomed to people contacting me through the record company and Irving's office, asking me to sign something for them. If I felt they were true fans, I'd always invite them to send me their LP or whatever and I'd gladly sign it and send it back. I was happy to. If not for our devoted fans, we'd be nothing, and I have always been grateful for their support. When "Almost the Eagles" happened, the venue was meant to be secret, because nobody wanted the press or anyone to know, in case it ended as it did. Word somehow got out, however, and on the second day, there was suddenly a barrage of professional autograph hunters at the door of the Third Encore. It still astounds me how thorough people are at getting information from those who rent rehearsal halls, drive limousines, or deliver cable or beverages to somewhere like that. They knew more than I did—where it was taking place and what time we'd be coming and going. There were dozens of "fans" waiting to pounce. Once again, I tried to find the genuine article among the professionals, although I think most of them went away happy.

When that project sadly ended and I returned to my home and my privacy, I suddenly became unavailable again. Most autograph hunters accepted that and approached me for signatures through the usual channels. One, however, was more determined. I began to receive letters from him at my house in Malibu, begging me to sign all his stuff. He must have run a title search for my name on all the property I owned and driven out to the various addresses until he figured out which one I lived in. A little un-nerving, to say the least.

At first, he was extremely polite: *"Dear Mr. Felder, I'm a huge Eagles fan and I have a massive collection of memorabilia signed by everyone but you. I'd be honored if you'd meet me somewhere to sign it. Thank you."*

I wrote back to him, via Irving's office, telling him, *"Thanks for your letter. I'm sure you understand that I wouldn't feel comfortable arranging a meeting with a complete stranger, especially not after you contacted me directly, but if you want to send me a bunch of your stuff, I'll gladly sign them and send them back."*

His response was angry. *"That wouldn't be acceptable,"* he wrote, tersely. *"There's too much and anyway these things are very precious to me and I'd be afraid I wouldn't get them back. We have to meet, face to face."* In the six or seven exchanges that followed, my same calm response was followed by his angry reply.

Our home in Malibu sat on six acres and was surrounded by a six-foot-high chain-link fence and specially planted prickly privacy hedge. I had two Labradors and a German shepherd named Emma, who'd been trained as a Schutzhund 3 attack/guard dog. I'd acquired her after another incident, a few years earlier, when a complete stranger, wearing odd clothes and with straggly hair, suddenly appeared at the French windows of our house. I don't even know how he got in, but he asked me where a wedding was and placed three .45-caliber bullets in my hands with the words, "These will protect you."

I ran inside, locked the doors, and dialed 911. As I did so, I saw Susan coming up the garden path right behind him.

"Who are you? What are you doing here? Get off my property!" she shrieked, waving her arms at him. The kids were just a few hundred yards away in the pool, when he raced back down the driveway, looking spooked.

I ran out and pulled Susan and the kids inside and told the police to get to my house urgently. We watched from the window as the guy went down to his car, which was inexplicably parked in our drive, and opened the trunk. I honestly thought he was going to get a gun out and come back up to the house to kill us all. I didn't even have a weapon on the property, and all I could think of to do was grab a kitchen knife. As we watched, he stripped off all his clothes and put on a woman's dress. I had visions of him, as in a horror movie, coming up and massacring us all, wearing this dress. Instead, he took some more bullets out of his pocket, threw them around on the ground like he was blessing us with them, got into his car, drove to the gate, and disappeared. The police eventually picked him up in my neighbor's garden. He was from an insane asylum in Camarillo. Somehow he'd escaped his guards and gotten hold of a gun and some ammunition. The officers told us we'd had a very lucky escape. He was arrested while in the process of trying to convince a lady who lived down the street to look at something in the trunk of his car. She said she thought he was going to shove her in the trunk and take off.

That incident really spooked me. Susan and the kids were my chief concern, so I bought a .357 Magnum pistol, and she and I took shooting lessons at a local range. I updated my security and bought Emma. The Labradors, which I'd owned for years, had just thumped their tails in greeting at the lunatic.

By the time I began to receive this stream of letters from the determined autograph hunter, I was pretty happy with my security. That was, until one November day in 1993, when I was out in the yard working on the '57 Chevy pickup truck I'd bought in memory of my dad, into which I was fitting a Corvette engine. I was in old jeans and a sweatshirt, covered in grease from my fingers to my elbows, having a private journey down Memory Lane, back to Gainesville and my father working under the hood of his old Chevy while I passed him some tools. Hey, Dad, I said to myself, are you watching me now? Are you impressed?

I was awoken from my reverie by a rustling in the bushes. "Hey, Don!" I suddenly heard. "Don Felder! Over here!"

Looking up, I could see a man leaning over my fence and six-foot hedge, waving something at me. "Hey, Don, I've got some of those albums I want you to sign. Over here!"

Wondering where on earth the German shepherd was when I needed her, I stared at this guy in total disbelief before striding purposefully into the house. Emma came as soon as I whistled and stood growling at our intruder while I grabbed the phone. I'd heard of not taking no for an answer, but this was extreme. First he'd found out where I lived, and then, when he refused my offer to send his stuff to me, he came to my house to confront me. "Holy shit," I yelled, angrily, throwing down a wrench. "Who the fuck does this guy think he is?" I didn't mind signing anything for him, but after the experience with the psycho, this was too bizarre. I dialed 911 and asked the police to come right away. "There's a man trespassing on my property," I told the sheriff, as I locked all the doors. "I'd like him removed at once."

The police arrived and picked him up. They drove him several blocks away and warned him that if he were ever caught harassing me on my own property again, they'd arrest him. I hoped that would be enough.

A couple of weeks later, just a few days before Christmas, my Realtor friend Jack Pritchett called me up. "Hey, how you doin'?" I asked. "Wanna do some fishing this week?"

"Yeah, maybe," came the distracted reply. "Listen, Don, I've just driven past your house, down the Pacific Coast Highway, and I saw something really strange. I had to stop the car and turn around to make sure I was seeing it right."

"What? Seeing what right?" I asked.

"Well, there's this guy dressed as Santa Claus standing out on the street, holding up a giant placard."

"Yeah, and?"

"The placard says, DON FELDER IS UNFAIR TO HIS FANS. HE WON'T SIGN AUTOGRAPHS."

I'm the strongest advocate of free speech. Heck, I've done benefit gigs advocating such rights, but Psycho Santa—as he will forever be known in our house—was behaving so strangely that I called the police again. The sheriff found him and issued another warning, but he was too far from my house to be arrested for harassment. I felt really bad about calling the cops. I didn't want to see the guy in prison; I just wanted him to accept my offer to sign his stuff and leave me and my family alone.

A couple of weeks after Christmas, I received a videotape in the mail. It was from Psycho Santa. In it, he gave me a guided tour of his bedroom, which was set up as a shrine to the Eagles. It was too weird. His voice close to the mike, narrating where he'd acquired which item and why, he slowly panned around the room, showing me his stash of T-shirts, albums, posters, football jerseys, and guitars, all set up in a very obsessive way. Anyone can be a fan, but this was way beyond the norm. He was almost salivating over the memorabilia he slept with every night, and his breathless narration made my flesh crawl. He was scaring my wife, my kids, and me. I sent the tape to my attorney and had a restraining order issued for him. He'd given me no other choice.

"Please Lord, may we never hear from him again," I said to Susan.

And, for a long time, we didn't.

One night in 1993, I was at home flicking through the TV channels absentmindedly, when I suddenly spotted Don and Glenn onstage, performing at a charity event without Timothy and me. They were playing "Hotel California." I was staggered. No one had approached me or even told me about it. I felt like a spouse betrayed. This was the second time I knew of when other members of the band had played together after the split. Don had done a benefit concert in Massachusetts for the Walden Woods Project, a pet campaign of his to preserve from developers the Massachusetts land that inspired the writer Henry David Thoreau. I had a horrible sinking feeling that events I knew nothing about were happening without me.

I found out later that Glenn and Joe had decided to do this latest gig together as part of their *Party of 2* tour, and Irving, still hopeful, had invited Don to sit in. It was on Glenn's home turf, and as there wasn't the pressure of walking into a studio and facing all of us, he still felt like he was in control. A few other gigs followed, and I'd receive messages from friends all over the States about them.

"Hey, Don," they'd write, "I see the Eagles are doing a gig in Portland, Oregon. Any chance of some tickets?" It would be the first I'd know of any gigs, and when I made inquiries, I'd discover it was just Glenn and Joe playing together.

Performing with the Eagles, October 1979

Me at one of the many Eagles stage performances

Recording vocals for
Heavy Metal

Fishing trip with Jimmy Pankow, Jack Pritchett, Joe Walsh, and Cheech Marin

Airborne album publicity photos

Me on FTV television show, 1986

MIA BEARDE

Hell Freezes Over **publicity photo**

JOHN HALPERN / RETNA

Me writing in the studio in Malibu, 1998

The Eagles (from left): Bernie Leadon, Joe Walsh, Don Henley, Timothy Schmit, Don Felder, Glenn Frey, and Randy Meisner appear together after receiving their awards and being inducted into the Rock & Roll Hall of Fame in New York. The thirteenth annual Rock & Roll Hall of Fame induction dinner also honored Fleetwood Mac, Santana, The Mamas and Papas, Gene Vincent, and Lloyd Price.

With Kathrin Nicholson

Me performing with my daughter Leah Felder at the Rock Cerritos for Katrina benefit concert for American Red Cross and Salvation Army Katrina relief efforts at the Cerritos Center for the Performing Arts in Cerritos

Backstage at the Don Felder & Friends Katrina benefit 2006

Stephen Stills and I play Katrina benefit together, 2006

Felder family group shot (Rebecca, Virginia, Erin, Jesse, Kurt and me; Cody and Leah standing)

Performing with the Eagles, March 30, 1978; Toronto, Canada

HEAVEN and HELL

There was another gig in Central Park, for the Democratic campaign, with Don, Glenn, Timothy, and a backup band, and there were a couple for the Rainforest Foundation. Only once was I was invited to join in, for some antinuclear gig in Long Beach with Timothy and Don and Lindsey Buckingham, of Fleetwood Mac. Glenn was supposed to participate, but never did. Instead, he sent an apologetic video from his hospital bed, where he was recovering from stomach surgery, saying, "Hey, guys, I'd love to be there with you, but as you can see I'm tied up here for a while." I sent him a bouquet of flowers and wished him well, but never heard a word back.

When I asked Irving why I hadn't been asked to any of the other gigs, he told me, "Don't worry about it, Felder. It was hard enough to get those guys to work together. You were omitted so that there wouldn't be that specific friction between you and Glenn that would make him refuse to do it. I thought if we started this way, it would be easier to include you later."

I still felt sick to my stomach. I wondered how much it really was a ploy to get Glenn to play ball, or whether Irving was saying, "Fingers, we can do this without you."

Glenn and I still hadn't spoken since the Alan Cranston incident thirteen years before, although I'd tried half a dozen times to extend olive branches. When Glenn divorced his first wife after just three years of marriage, I sent him a note expressing my sorrow and asking if there was anything I could do. As with the flowers, I never received a reply. It was all very strange, because I couldn't ever recall doing anything to Glenn that warranted his behavior. I never screwed his wife behind his back or stole anything from him. I just became the scapegoat for the breakup of the band and the ongoing "sibling" rivalry between him and Don, because I'd dared to vent some feelings publicly, as Glenn so freely and frequently did, and because I had occasionally asked some searching questions about the way the band was being run.

I can even remember being in a little studio in L.A. with Glenn one night after we'd recorded "Those Shoes" for *The Long Run*, when he told me that what I'd brought to the band would propel it to a whole new level of success.

"Man, what you've added to our sound with *Hotel California* and all the musical changes you've made, is awesome," he said. "I knew when I first heard you play slide that you were perfect for this band, and you really are one of the main reasons the Eagles have risen to this level."

I was staggered. It was so unlike Glenn to give credit to anyone. I will never forget that night, sitting there after everybody else left, snorting some cocaine together while he expressed his sincere appreciation of me and acknowledged what I'd done. How could it have gone so wrong—or was it just the drugs talking?

Later in 1993, Irving Azoff rounded up some of America's biggest country stars in Nashville and issued an album of covers of Eagles songs. It was called *Common Thread: The Songs of the Eagles* and featured stars such as Alan Jackson, Travis Tritt, Trisha Yearwood, Brooks & Dunn, and Clint Black. Irving had resigned from MCA, and had set up Giant Records. Don Henley, one of his first new clients after splitting from David Geffen, again, was intimately involved in the Nashville project, and a portion of the proceeds of the album sales were to go to the Walden Woods Project.

Common Thread was like the remake of a favorite old movie, and it sounded great. After years and years of hearing those songs sung in the same old way, without a single note altered, it was good to hear fresh voices with a new take. I was impressed. The album sold three million copies in its first six months and rose to number one on the country chart and number three on the pop chart. It was even named Album of the Year by the Country Music Association. The first single was "Take It Easy," written by Glenn and Jackson Browne, sung by Travis Tritt.

To promote the single, Travis wanted to come up with something really different, an eye-catching video to be released for Christmas 1993. He suddenly suggested getting the Eagles back together again. When everyone stopped laughing, someone said, "Why not?" The record company asked Don first and then the rest of us, and, amazingly, Glenn agreed.

The original idea of the shoot was that Travis would be singing in a seedy bar in downtown L.A., and we'd be his backup band, shooting pool and hanging around behind him. There were to be a couple of shots of all of us, walking along a road five abreast, arriving and leaving the bar to-gether.

The filming was all very secretive. Streets were blocked off, and everyone was sworn to silence. A funky Spanish-looking bar in North Hol-lywood was selected, and for the first time in thirteen years, we were all going to be in the same room together. There had been a lot of nervous anticipation in the days leading up to it, and when we arrived for the shoot, I felt the way I had on my first day at F. W. Buchholz High School in Gainesville, watching all the other kids arrive in their parents' cars, wear-ing brand new clothes. Fortunately, Joe was there early, and he and I fooled around and he made me laugh, instantly defusing an extremely tense situation.

When Glenn arrived, we said hello politely and then hugged.

"Good to see you, man," I told him.

"Yeah," he said. "It's good to be here."

The atmosphere worsened, though, when everyone arrived except Don. We knew of old that he was always late, but the forty-five minutes he made us wait that day seemed like a hundred and forty-five. Was he com-ing? Or was he gonna piss Glenn off by not showing, as Glenn had in 1990? By the time Don eventually walked through the door, I felt so brit-tle, I could have snapped in two. They said hello and hugged each other and began rehearsing "Desperado" almost right away, a song for which Joe and I weren't required.

In urgent need of some light relief, the two of us did something we used to do in the old days, which was sit at the back, not miked up, and look as if we were singing harmonies, when actually we were singing "Desert Rat Hole," "Avocado," or "El Dorado," anything but "Desper-ado." It had started as a childish way of keeping ourselves entertained and awake during the long periods in an Eagles set when only ballads would be played, but it helped break down the tension of that sizzling day.

Within a few hours, though, we were shooting pool together, jam-ming, and actually having fun. It was like a high school band getting back together for a twenty-year reunion and playing "Louie Louie." There was even a mock-up of us lined up against the wall outside the bar, being arrested by a highway patrolman, which brought back some old memories of a few close calls. It felt good to be back together and making music again. Glenn and I spoke to each other quite cordially and even hugged again at the end.

"We should do this more often," I told him, trying to resume my old diplomatic role in the band as a sort of marriage counsellor between the warring factions.

"Yeah," he nodded. "We should."

The planets were aligning.

The video was a great success and sparked what one leading rock journalist described as "Eaglemania." The ever-resourceful Irving attempted yet another reunion. After the Northridge earthquake destroyed Don's L.A. home and he decided to return to his native Texas, Irving quickly organized another lunch in Aspen, to which Don, Glenn, and Joe were invited. Timothy and I weren't. The numbers being thrown around this time for a resumption tour were too tempting for any of them to refuse.

The Eagles had never originally been about making music for money, but suddenly it became the main focus of interest. Irving called everyone, conducting a litmus test to see how we felt. Word came back that, if the money was right, there might be a possibility. It's amazing how a few zeros on the end of a check can make you forget how much you dislike someone and justify your putting up with them again after all these years.

After more than a decade of silence and inactivity, everyone agreed to try again, to rehabilitate, get back into shape, relearn old skills, and put away our differences. Glenn had first come up with the word "resumption." We weren't reuniting, he insisted, just resuming. We honestly didn't know if we could pull it off, and nobody knew how long it would hold together if we did—six months was the initial estimate—but $300 million can sure put a smile on a person's face. The resumption tour was on.

Irving faxed the media a four-word message to announce the news. It said simply, "Hell has frozen over."

SIXTEEN

Despite such momentous news and the effect it was about to have on my life, my family had become the main focus of my concern, chiefly my second son, Cody, the most free-spirited of all our children. Sweet, sensitive, gorgeous to look at, he had all the confidence of a third child and spent his childhood with scabby knees and scuffed hands. He looked just like I did as a kid, only he was ten times more accident-prone. He became such a regular visitor to the emergency room at the local hospital that they were on first-name terms.

When he was eleven, he was diagnosed with attention deficit disorder (ADD) and after a battery of tests, we were advised to place him on the now-controversial amphetamine Ritalin, then commonly prescribed for ADD kids to help them focus. Having had plenty of personal experience with amphetamines myself, I didn't approve of Cody taking pills at such an early age, but we'd tried everything else, and this was a last resort.

By the time he was in seventh grade, I realized we may have inadvertently given him a lifetime taste for drugs. Some kids at school introduced him to pot and speed. The first time I noticed the telltale glazed look in his eyes my stomach did a flip. Memories of my own unhappy encounters with my father flooded my brain. I was suspended in an agony of indecision. Part of me wanted to yell at him, grab him by the shoulders, shake him, and tell him how stupid he was being. I could almost envision the effectiveness of using my belt.

The other part of me wanted to buckle under, drop to the floor, and cry like a baby. I, of all people, knew what drugs could do, and I had a dreadful sense of foreboding that this was the start of something serious. In all the years I'd been in the music industry, I'd seen dozens of promising young people fall by the wayside. Not just famous rock stars like Jimi Hendrix, Janis Joplin, and Jim Morrison, but personal friends like some of the guys from Flow, and friends like John Belushi, lying cold in his grave. I didn't have a clue what to do.

In my young son, I saw echoes of myself, of Joe Walsh, of all the people I'd known who were addicts, and I felt physically sick. I began driving him to and from school and picking him up from his friends' houses. I tried to talk with him, reason with him, and explain that I wasn't saying this just because I was his dad.

"I know the temptations, son," I told him. "I know what it's like to be persuaded into trying things by your buddies, but you've got to fight it, stand up for yourself, and say no. If this sort of behavior carries on, we're gonna have to take you to see someone, to get some professional help, and you don't want that, do you?"

Cody would stare up at me with those big blue eyes of his and promise never to try anything again. "I'm sorry, Dad," he'd say. "I only tried it once and I didn't like it anyway." His answers stuck in my craw, because they were the same I would have come up with.

Even more poignantly, at the same time I was dealing with young Cody's problems, I had to drive my old buddy Joe Walsh to a clinic in Santa Monica for drug and alcohol rehabilitation, after Don and Glenn decreed that unless he was sober, he'd remain in the fires of hell.

Susan and I and Cody underwent some searing encounter sessions and family therapy. It was an extremely salutary experience. I seemed to be to blame for just about everything that had gone wrong in his life. I was either never there, or when I was, I wasn't paying him enough attention. Maybe he was right. In the hope that Cody might find some release in music, I bought him a guitar. The next time I saw it, the guitar was leaning up against his bed with the words I HATE DAD scratched deeply into its mahogany veneer. Tears pricked the back of my eyes.

I knew I was to blame. I'd failed as a father and as someone with experience of drugs who'd, luckily, never felt the barbs of addiction. I'd been absent for much of his young life, following my dream at the expense of his. The guilt nearly killed me. Cody had always had that wholesome, kid-surfer kind of look, with his blond hair and bright eyes. Now his eyes had lost their sparkle, and he seemed like a different child. It broke our hearts, not least because it felt like we were losing him.

Amazingly, one of the people who helped Cody during this difficult time was Graham Nash's son. He'd gone through similar experiences the previous year but had come out the other side. I'd hardly seen Graham since 1974, when I told him I was joining the Eagles and wasn't going back on the road with him and David Blue, but now he and I were attending parent-support sessions and family therapy meetings together, often at his house, to try to help our children find their way through the labyrinth of their youth.

"Hey, buddy, you were once my big brother, and now your son's doing the same for mine," I told him one night, as we hugged each other warmly and tried not to break down. We leaned on each other a lot during that hellish nightmare, and once again, my respect for him as a person increased tenfold.

I arrived to resume work with the rest of the band in January 1994, at the very beginning of our troubles with Cody, Now there was the added worry of what it would be like to be an Eagle again. Glenn and Don had been up to their old tricks. This time, I was told, there would be no attempt to sit down and try to write great new material together, as we had in the past, for fear of opening up old wounds. Instead of a whole new album, they'd decided independently that we were going to record a live album, along with three songs the pair had written with collaborators, plus a fourth new song. The remaining eleven numbers would be a rehash of old hits like "Hotel California," "Desperado," "Tequila Sunrise," "Take It Easy," and "Life in the Fast Lane," sprinkled with songs like "New York Minute" from Don's solo albums and "In the City," written by Joe Walsh. Elliot Scheiner was to be the producer.

Before, we had tried our hardest to recognize our strengths and limitations, but this album found us tolerating weaknesses, especially in those members who couldn't bring in any worthwhile songs. If we hadn't let them slip something mediocre onto the disc, they wouldn't have anything on the album at all. This was especially true of Glenn's "Girl from Yesterday," written with his old friend and collaborator Jack Tempchin, which had everybody's eyes rolling. Don remarked, when Glenn wasn't in the room, that his song was not his best work and that any country singer from Nashville could sing it better. I agree, the song didn't sound very good, and it went down badly at our later gigs, so we eventually dropped it from our set.

Most irritating, the fourth new song on the album was to be "Love Will Keep Us Alive," the number written by Paul Carrack with Jim Capaldi and Peter Vale for the "Malibu Men's Choir" demo album that he and I put together. That which Irving had so scathingly rejected as "not strong enough" was suddenly deemed worthy of inclusion in the new Eagles LP. It actually became the single with the biggest airplay from the album.

To add to my feeling of being abused, Don, Glenn, and Irving also announced that they'd struck a deal with MTV for a live performance in April, to be aired six months later. As a final insult, "The Gods" told me they'd formed new business entities that gave them a majority position in the new companies, all but muscling me out. Don and Glenn were to be getting a much larger slice of the pie, while Joe, Timothy, and I were to share the leftovers.

I took immediate issue with the deal and told Irving, "Hey, man, this wasn't what the arrangement was with Eagles Limited. What the hell's going on?" Irving told me not to worry and arranged a meeting in his office. Joe and Tim were summoned in and left the building, happy with the arrangement. Then it was my turn. I walked in to see Glenn and Don looking stone-faced. When they explained to me what they were planning, I was initially rendered speechless. When I finally found my voice, I said, "Well, wait a minute guys, that's not what we've done for the last twenty-something years. We always had equal shares before. Now you want double of everything else. What's changed?"

Glenn sighed and formed his fingers into a steeple. "You know, Fingers," he said, as if explaining something to a child, "this band's like a football team. Some players are more noteworthy and more famous, and they can command bigger salaries, like a quarterback. Others are just defensive linebackers who play OK but don't get as much money. Don and I feel we're entitled to more."

Tears of disappointment welled uncontrollably in my eyes. I just couldn't understand the shift in their minds that turned a long-standing equal partnership into something they suddenly felt they owned more of. To my mind, it was self-serving gibberish. I could hardly believe what I was hearing, especially the fact that Glenn, who'd insisted right from the start that there'd be "no sidemen," was the one who was telling me. Quite apart from the sheer unfairness of what he was saying, his analogy just didn't stand up. He was talking about high-rolling sports superstars brought onto a team to pep up their game as part of some multimillion-dollar deal. He and Don hadn't been brought in. If anything, I was the one who'd been brought in to beef things up.

Furthermore, in the fourteen years when we hadn't been on the road together, neither Don nor Glenn had done any more for the Eagles than Joe, Tim, or me. They didn't perform Eagles shows or do Eagles promotions. They didn't sign any more guitars or photos or T-shirts than the rest of us. They concentrated exclusively on their solo careers, which had been independently successful and lucrative. Now they were claiming that because of their own high self-valuation of their worth as performers since their solo success, they were suddenly entitled to much more than the rest of us.

254 • Don Felder

If that were to be the case, which I disputed hotly, then Glenn should have been paid far less than Don. Worst of all, when I tried to voice my concerns and air my grievances about it, I was stonewalled and told to deal exclusively with Irving, their manager, who was my manager too. I was, in effect, negotiating against my own manager, someone I was paying to represent me. But to me, it felt he was representing Don and Glenn against me, and with much more at stake. It seemed to me the conflict of interest was insurmountable.

In Irving's inimitable way, he ran rings round all of us. "This is in the best interests of everybody," he told me. "Don't get so upset. We'll just see how the tour goes, and then we'll renegotiate. Don't worry, we can deal with your concerns for later legs. You know I've always looked out for you and your best interest."

The rehearsal stage for the MTV gig and our planned tour was at Culver Studios in West Los Angeles, not far from where Susan and I and Kilo had spent our first eighteen months in California. I arrived the first day, feeling frightened and intimidated by the delicate situation our negotiations were in, and I didn't know how to behave. If they'd wanted me to feel like a lowly sideman, then it was working. Thanks to their constant chipping away, I'd lost all confidence in my abilities and even in my usual happy-go-lucky ability to smooth things over. Glenn and I had gotten along OK on the Travis Tritt video shoot and had seen each other briefly in Irving's office, but this was different. This was the official start of the resumption tour, and if I screwed up now, I knew all deals would be off. I was walking on eggshells the whole time. I felt I had to say, "Yes sir, no sir, three bags full, sir" to Glenn. I was unable to relax, and it showed, so much so that halfway through the first day, while we were waiting for Don—who continually defied the specific clause inserted into the contracts about never being late—Glenn asked me to step outside with him for a minute so he could speak to me.

"Oh, shit," I thought, the color draining from my face. "What have I done wrong now?"

"Fingers, relax," he said, placing his hand heavily on my shoulder and giving me a half smile. "I want you to know that I don't harbor any ill feelings about what happened at Long Beach, and I really want this to work. I feel great about us getting together at this time, and it's OK, just take it easy, and then we can all relax and have fun."

My nerves were undoubtedly getting the better of me, but I hadn't realized until then how much they were affecting everyone else. I wasn't sure if I could really trust him, but his words lifted my spirits slightly, and I allowed myself to breathe a little more freely, at least for the time being.

I tried my best to keep the atmosphere easy and show that I was a team player. I was always the first to arrive at rehearsals and the last to leave. I'd get there early and check my setup, instruments, and equipment with the road crew. I wanted everything I did to go smoothly. Mine wasn't an easy path to tread. I was still seething inwardly about the deals that had been foisted upon me. A big part of me wanted to walk away from the egos and the greed and be my own man, but like a battered wife, I was afraid to speak my mind and suffer more blows from Don and Glenn, and afraid of the life outside this marriage. I didn't have anyplace else to go.

Joe was facing his own pressures. He was fresh out of rehab and sober for the first time in decades. I couldn't tell if he was nervous about facing the intense scrutiny of "The Gods," or had tremors from withdrawal from alcohol or other drugs, but, man, he was in a bad way. I was scared for him, because a couple of times, especially when he was trying to play some taxing new parts, he just couldn't do it. His hands didn't seem to have the dexterity anymore, and it was excruciating to watch him try.

I started arriving an hour early to rehearse with him before the others arrived. We'd work on guitar parts during the lunch break or after they'd left. I did anything I could to try to help him practice his parts. It was strange, seeing Joe like this. He wasn't the same old jovial José or Rubber Nose.

When I'd driven him to the Exodus rehab center at Marina del Rey, my car windows rolled down because he reeked of alcohol, I hadn't honestly expected him to make it. His marriage had broken up, his life was in tatters, and he couldn't seem to kick the habit. As his buddy, and with

Cody very much on my mind, I'd tried to warn him that the only way he was going to be taken back to the Eagles was if he was clean.

"Joe, I'm gonna say the same to you as I said to Cody," I told him, as he sat slumped dejectedly in the front seat of my car. "Nobody can do this but you, buddy. Unless you take control of the situation right now, today, then you might as well kiss the rest of your life good-bye."

I was intensely proud that Joe had fought his demons and won. I only hoped to God that my son would be as successful. But, man, I really missed the old Joe and his crazy sense of humor—not to mention his playing ability. In the end, we limited him to a few songs until he could find his way. He played very little at first, apart from a bit of slide on "Get Over It" and a flat-footed Nashville solo on "Girl from Yesterday." During the recording process, Glenn and I handled a lot of the guitar parts and let Joe just stand at the back and play what he could. By doing that, we took some of the pressure off, and he relaxed into it. It wouldn't be too long before he was back playing some of the best guitar he'd ever played in his life, but in those first faltering months of his sobriety, it was horrible to watch someone so talented struggling with something that used to flow out of him so smoothly.

When we eventually set up on a soundstage and started playing together as a band, though, we sounded OK. We listened to the music we were making and thought, "Hey, this is gonna work." Just in case it didn't, we had some serious backup. This was the first show I'd ever played with the Eagles when it wasn't just the five of us. All of a sudden, because Don and Glenn wanted to bring their own people in from their solo backup bands, we had a whole orchestra behind us, with violins and the works, plus another drummer, two keyboard players, and a saxophone/horn guy, none of which the Eagles had ever had. Horns? My father might even have approved.

The only shock came when we all opened our mouths to sing. The magic that had come from years of working together, practicing our harmonies and our ooohs and aaahs in the locker rooms, had withered. All of a sudden, we sounded like five different voices without harmony. This was going to need work.

I don't think I ever fully realized the extent of our transition from an equal band to Don and Glenn with a backup group until we were in that rehearsal hall. The stage designer and production crew brought in a mock-up of the stage design that Glenn and Don had come up with, so that we could see what it would look like on the tour. The model was three feet square, with little light trusses and everything, just as it would be, complete with miniatures representing each of us, to show where we would stand, how we'd be lit, and what we would be doing. Timothy, Joe, and I gathered around to look at the stage design for the first time and were impressed. It had everything, right down to tiny mikes and amps. When the models were added, though, I could hardly believe it. The little dummies representing Glenn and Don, "The Gods," were white, while the rest of us were black or dark brown, nondescript players at the rear of the stage that the cameramen and the lighting crew needn't really bother with. It was so ludicrous, I had to laugh out loud.

"Hey, Glenn," I said, still laughing, "how come you and Don are white and everyone else is black?" I'd hoped there would be some silly explanation or that I'd latched onto some private joke they were now both going to share.

Don looked up at me without a trace of humor in his eyes. "You're not black, Fingers," he said. "You're just rusty." Don and Glenn both broke out into laughter.

The MTV gig was to be filmed on a Warner Brothers stage set in front of an invited live audience and carefully selected friendly media, in the style of the popular *Unplugged* concerts. It would be filmed, edited, and broadcast later in the year to coincide with the release of the new album.

When I arrived at the Warner Brothers studio, I was amazed by what I saw. A stage had been built inside the set, with equipment towers, lights, and orchestra behind it. Chairs had been set up for the "intimate" concert, and the whole set was framed by a large, dark wall at the back. Behind this were parked five Winnebago trailers in a crescent shape, like the circling of the wagons, each with its own bedroom, toilet, and lounge. They were all exactly the same size, year, and color, to avoid dissension. Someone had laid a green fake-grass carpet outside each one, with folding tables and chairs. The tables were laden with cold drinks, food, and chips. It was like a giant family picnic for everyone who'd been invited on set to witness this historic event. There were record industry moguls, famous faces, and media stars in abundance. Even the legendary Robert Hilburn of the *Los Angeles Times*, who was considered by many to be the greatest of all music critics, was there, and we happily posed with him for photographs before the show.

Glenn was his usual cheery self. When I arrived for the first sound check the day before the taping, we started right at the beginning of "Hotel California," but he interrupted and told me we needed a special introduction, "—something the fans haven't heard before."

"OK," I replied, "what are you gonna do?"

"Not me," he said. "Come up with something. What we need is a new acoustic introduction to 'Hotel California.'"

"An acoustic version? Would that work?"

"Just do it, Fingers," he said, not interested.

"OK, when do you want it?" I asked, relieved at least to have been given something useful to do.

"Tomorrow afternoon's sound check at three o'clock," he said, half smiling to himself as he walked away.

I felt like I'd been given a test. If I passed, I could stay. If I didn't, I was out. The pressure was immense. I went back to my trailer and sat down with a nylon-string guitar and played around with it. That night at home, I kept working on it. The difficulty is that when you've written a definitive piece of music that you agonized over, it's pretty hard to come up with something different a few years later. I tried to think back to my original concept of that song, sitting out at my beach house creating what Don had dubbed the Mexican Bolero.

"If I was gonna do that acoustically, I wouldn't use a steel-string guitar," I told myself. "I'd use something more Mexican, in the mariachi tradition." I kept playing with it, trying to figure out how Joe and I could do the double stuff and not sound like imbeciles. I drew on my experiences at the Holiday Inn in Harvard Square in Cambridge, playing numbers I barely knew to earn a five-dollar tip. I'd had to play the most unlikely songs on an acoustic guitar back then, so why couldn't I try something similar now?

I finally figured it out, drawing on my free-form experiences with Flow to give me the courage to play around with the sounds. Arriving at the sound check ready to show Don and Glenn what I'd done, I took a deep breath. Glenn said, "I'll play this chord and then this one, and, Fingers, you just go for it." We tried it through once. I had to improvise a lot, but I'd never done that on a gut-string guitar before. I'm not a flamenco artist.

That night, as the cameras rolled, Don said, "Go for it." After just one rehearsal, in front of a crowd of fans who hadn't seen us play in fourteen years and who must have been wondering if we were still relevant in the 1990s, I made up that new introduction for "Hotel" to shock them, and it turned out just fine. Don and Glenn never said a word, but I knew from their silence that they were pleased.

That MTV gig was truly a Hollywood version of a live concert. Everything was make-believe—the stage, the backdrop, the sound, and our happy smiling faces. The audience had been handpicked to show their appreciation. The critics had been schmoozed into believing that we were still valid and viable. After Glenn announced to the hopeful fans, "We didn't break up. We just took a fourteen-year vacation," we played ninety minutes of songs from our most enduring body of work, plus the four new tracks, to a rapturous reception.

The *Hell Freezes Over* tour began on May 27, 1994. I thought ticket prices were set very high. Like me, Timothy and Joe had no say in the pricing. Irving claimed that others before us had set the precedent, and that this was the way to beat the ticket scalpers. Despite the exorbitant cost, the tickets sold within hours, and we played to sellout crowds, while the media went crazy and Eaglemania took off big-time. We suddenly realized what a remarkable phenomenon we'd become in our absence.

Our first show was in Irvine Meadows Amphitheater (which Irving part-owned), south of L.A., near Newport Beach. We were driven out there in a convoy of limos to our hotel. Among our security staff, still working for Joe, was Smokey, who had supposedly been on the White House security staff through four presidents. He still had his Secret Service badge, and he would flip it out whenever we arrived somewhere, so that the local police and security people would goose-step to his marching orders. He was a very nice guy. On the way to the Four Seasons Hotel in Newport Beach on that first, tense evening, I suddenly had a prickling feeling in the back of my neck in the limo. Psycho Santa stole into my thoughts out of nowhere.

"Hey, Smokey, do me a favor," I said. "Phone the hotel and ask if there's a guest booked in under the name of ___." I gave him the guy's name.

Smokey called the front desk and, as he received the reply to his question, he looked at me with an expression on his face that said, "How did you know?"

I explained about the restraining order and what Psycho Santa had been up to. "Now it looks like he might be waiting for me at check-in," I added. "This is too freaky, man, notify security at the hotel, I want him out of the place, and I don't want him at our shows either. If he has a ticket, tear it up. I don't want that lunatic anywhere near me or my family."

If Psycho Santa had just sent me his stuff as I'd asked, none of this would have happened. He could have sent it by courier if he was worried about it being lost or stolen. I'd have *happily* signed everything and sent it back and been done with him. Instead, he was freaking me out, not to mention the rest of the band. Not since John Lennon had been shot dead had I felt so paranoid.

We reached the hotel, checked in, and moved as one to the elevator, flanked by security. The doors opened and there, right in front of me, stood the man I knew as Psycho Santa, about to be thrown out of the hotel by two security guards. Our eyes met briefly, but nothing was said. In my mind, I wanted to say, "You're not going to do this to my life. I'll sign your damn stuff; just send it like everyone else." Instead, I silently stepped aside to let him pass and watched as he was marched out. That was the last time I ever saw him.

I got the band to hire me a security guard after that, from a company called The Purple Gang, out of Detroit. His name was Johnny Sampson, and he became a dear friend. Not only could I sleep easy at night, but having him with me all the time diminished a great deal of the boredom of being on the road. I had a suite, and he'd be right next door, ready to protect me if necessary. It was intensely reassuring. In the end, everyone hired bodyguards. We were getting much more exposure than we had in the seventies, what with DVDs, live simulcasts, MTV, and the sheer size of the shows we were doing. None of us knew what might be waiting around the corner.

Even with Psycho Santa out of the equation, the professional autograph hunters continued to hound me. There'd be droves of people waiting outside venues, gigs, and hotels, with stacks of stuff for me to sign. At first, I thought, "Hey this is cool. I must be really popular. They're calling for me by name. Now I know how Elvis felt." I soon realized that it had nothing to do with my popularity. These weren't genuine fans; they were businessmen, and I was the missing link. Their stuff wasn't worth nearly as much unless they had *my* signature, too.

In Berlin, we were en route to our next gig in a convoy of limousines early one morning, when the driver of our car suddenly stood on the brakes. A driver had overtaken the convoy along a freeway and pulled in front of us before jamming on his own brakes, forcing us to stop. We screeched to a halt, very nearly rear-ending them. Two guys jumped out of the car and ran back toward us.

"Get down! Get down!" Johnny Sampson screamed at me, pushing my head to the floor with one hand while he reached for a weapon with the other. We didn't know what was happening. Was I being kidnapped? Or assassinated? I lay on the floor, terrified, as these two guys ran to the locked car doors and yanked fruitlessly on them.

Looking up, I suddenly recognized them as a couple of professional autograph hunters who'd been waiting outside our hotel for days and had already been shooed away by Johnny after I'd signed one item each for them. Realizing we were leaving town, they'd come up with their daring plan to get to me before it was too late. They each carried, not weapons, but stacks of photos for me to sign, which they waved hopefully through the windows. Johnny, as angry as I was, told the German driver, "Drive! Drive! *Schnell, Schnell!*" To the two guys' dismay, we backed up at speed and took off. They totally freaked me out.

The opening number of each performance on that tour was still "Hotel California." On the first few gigs, we'd tried to sing "Seven Bridges Road" in the shower room again, in a nostalgic attempt to re-create our magical early days, but our voices simply weren't up to the task. The magic was no longer there. We never tried again. Instead, we'd walk straight up onto the stage, take our places in the semidarkness and await our cue. I'd be standing at the front, my Gibson in my hands, waiting to play the opening bars, the rest of the band behind me watching, waiting to launch themselves with me down that dark, desert highway.

Only this time, it was different. Thanks to the input of Don and Glenn working with a stage designer, pyrotechnics and lighting had transformed our set. Instead of us silhouetted against the photo of the Beverly Hills Hotel as of old, we were silhouetted by strobe lights while rolling thunder crashed overhead. It was a dramatic attempt to drag us into the nineties and silence the many critics who'd accused us of being boring in the past. My cue to start the show was taken from a guy in the pits who wore a special glow-in-the-dark glove and a headset. He'd hold up his luminous fingers one by one, counting us in—five, four, three, two, one—and as soon as a big clap of thunder had died away, I'd play the distinctive opening chords, timing them perfectly with a massive flash of lightning. It was all very impressive, and the crowds were instantly energized.

Even after our long absence, or perhaps because of it, the fans went wild. Just as it had always been, as we walked onstage, the place would be lit with candles and lighters, and there'd be this whistling and humming and an overwhelming buzz of expectancy. Waves of energy, excitement, and sheer adoration washed over us from the auditorium and made us temporarily forget the rifts that still tore us apart. The music was what it was all about. Night after night, we played to capacity crowds who only wanted to hear our songs. By the time all the thunder and lightning had finished and we played the first notes of "Hotel" in a dispersing cloud of cordite smoke and blue light, the place would come unglued.

We were on the road that November, doing four gigs a week, when we learned that *Hell Freezes Over* had opened at number one on Billboard's album chart. It ended up being certified six times platinum, with sales of more than six million. Even we had to admit that it was a remarkable achievement in an era of Oasis, R.E.M., and Nirvana. The tour expanded accordingly.

My concern over the sharing of profits had still not, in my opinion, been properly addressed, and every time I spoke to Irving about it, he tried to deflect me. "When are we going to revisit this one seventh/two seventh deal as you promised?" I'd ask him.

"I know, I know," he'd say, busying himself with something else. "Well, Don's happy to talk about it, but Glenn still has some issues. I'll get back to you."

Nothing more was ever said or done until I finally dropped in on Irving in his hotel suite halfway through one leg of the tour. Angry at being blown off with excuses, bitter at the unfairness of the deal, and sick and tired of endlessly waiting for answers, I walked in, bristling, and said, "Hey, Irv, when are we gonna address this?"

Irving sat behind his desk and glared at me through his oversized spectacles. With a deep sigh, he said, in words delivered with slow deliberation, "Don Henley will never give you a dime more than a seventh." He made it clear that he was not able to renegotiate on my behalf. Even though Irving was *my* manager, it felt to me he was Don Henley's man first, and always had been. He'd allied himself to the one he believed was the cash cow, and there was no budging him. Furthermore, he warned me that if I even spoke to "The Gods" about this, especially Glenn, he could explode, and the whole tour might be cancelled.

I was sorely tempted to quit right there, even knowing that I'd almost certainly be sued for breach of contract. I knew I'd get no support from the others, although I felt like I was fighting for their interests too. Timothy was making more money than he'd ever made in his entire life. Though getting stronger every day, Joe was still on shaky ground. He was unable to walk out of his hotel room without holding on to Smokey at his side. The machine was already up and running, and the message from "The Gods" was clear: It was "their way" or "the highway." I had no choice but to swallow my pride and move on.

SEVENTEEN

We toured for more than two and a half years. We quickly topped the earnings charts for U.S. entertainers, generating an estimated income of $75 million in ticket sales alone. We won three notable American Music Awards that year—Favorite Pop Group, Favorite Adult Contemporary Artist, and Favorite Rock Album for *Hell Freezes Over.* We were also nominated for four Grammys, including Best Pop Album. Not bad for a band of wrinkly senior citizens competing against the likes of Oasis and Michael Jackson.

The media control was now all-consuming, and, realizing that many reporters asked the same questions, we developed formulaic answers, knowing exactly what to say, or rather what not to say. For live interviews, reporters were told to submit their questions in advance, making it even simpler. We knew what was coming and could play with it a little to make it look like off-the-cuff improvisation, when it was actually meticulously rehearsed. Sorry: We weren't the Beatles; they were funny.

Some reporters insisted on group interviews, instead of speaking only to Don and Glenn, so we'd all sit around trying to look comfortable with each other until we were asked a "sensitive" question, like how we were getting along or why we were charging more than a hundred dollars per ticket. If the reporter tried to direct such a question to the rest of us, "The Gods" would immediately interrupt or deflect. Joe, Tim, and I would sit there like ventriloquist's dummies, opening and closing our mouths without words of our own to speak.

Now that Don and Glenn were both in long-term relationships, the nature of the tour changed dramatically. Suddenly girlfriends, wives, and children were in tow, along with nannies, personal trainers, Pilates instructors, hairdressers, and tutors, all filling their plush suites. My children were that much older and in school, so if I wanted to spend time with them, I'd have to bring them out for brief visits or fly home to see them, which wasn't always easy. Worst of all, Cody was back in trouble, expelled in his second semester at the San Diego University for poor grades. Susan now had to cope alone with a rebellious teenager who seemed to hate us both.

I came home whenever I could and tried my hardest to make Cody realize the mistakes he was making, but I again found myself echoing my father. "What are you doing with your life, son?" I'd ask him. "Don't you know where all this is heading?" He'd look at me the way I'd looked at Dad, and I knew that I wasn't getting through.

"How can I make him see?" I'd ask Susan, as we both lay awake night after night, worrying about our son. "What can I tell him that's any different from what my father and Jerry tried to tell me?"

"Maybe you can't," Susan said. Her attitude was to let him get through this wild period in the hope that he'd emerge from it eventually, as I had. Not a day went by when I didn't think of my young son or worry desperately for his future.

• • •

Jesse, at nineteen, had rarely, if ever, strayed off the straight and narrow path, but I fought not to make constant comparisons between him and Cody, as my father had done between my brother Jerry and me. Each of my boys was a unique individual, coping with life in his own way.

Jesse was a student at San Diego University, dating a lovely girl named Erin, whom he'd met in his first week at school. He was eager to carve out a career for himself in the financial business although he'd learned how to play saxophone in high school, having added it to his guitar talents. When I heard him on that thing, I wondered if he'd made the right choice. Man, he could play.

The previous summer, I'd asked Fred Walecki at Westwood Music if he could use Jesse's help around his store. Fred had become something of a legend in L.A., yet he was still lending out free instruments to struggling hopefuls, as he had once done for me, Bernie, and so many others. Fred put Jesse to work. He was remodeling the store and employed Jesse as a junior laborer to the builders. I loved the idea of my son helping out in a music store, just like I had at Lipham's in Gainesville.

Knowing that I was going back on the road, Jesse asked if he could come with me in some capacity with the crew. My guitar techs were delighted to have a new rookie as their slave. "Work him as hard as you would anyone else," I told them, "and offer him no privileges." He put in the long hours in tough conditions without complaint, traveling and sleeping on the crew bus.

One day during rehearsals, we were practicing Glenn's song "The Heat Is On" with a saxophonist and a keyboard player, who were trying their best make up a horn section. It sounded a little wimpy.

"Hey, Glenn," I suggested, "since Jesse's gonna be on the road with us anyway, why not let him play sax on that part too? It won't cost you a cent."

Glenn jumped at the chance, and the next day, Jesse arrived with his instrument. He was so nervous, I thought he might pass out. His eyes were huge and his hands so sweaty they left imprints on the sax, but within a few days, he'd learned the parts for five songs in the show and was playing them like a professional.

On the very first show, he walked up behind the guitar section and stood a few feet away from me, playing his saxophone. I still savor that moment. All those years of lessons, of driving him to and from band practice, the times when the hair on my neck stood on end while he learned how to play in tune, and now here he was, my own son playing in the Eagles with me. I was so proud I almost forgot what *I* was supposed to be playing.

His girlfriend, Erin, waited in the wings for him when he came offstage each night and nearly sucked the skin right off his lips. Ah, that first taste of stardom. After a few weeks, Jesse definitely gained a slight swagger. The confidence he gained from being with the Eagles for a while was worth more than any salary he could have earned.

When summer ended, though, and he had to return to college, his golden carriage turned back into a pumpkin. "Dad, I've learned something very important from this," he told me on the last day. "The people with the greatest skills make the most money, and the people with the fewest skills make the least." When he returned to campus that fall, his grades jumped from C's to straight A's. I guess sometimes the best lessons aren't learned in the classroom.

Later in the tour, my daughter Leah came out with us as well. She and Joe Walsh's daughter Lucy had become inseparable. She and Leah looked like sisters, little blonde bookends, and they had a gas on the road together, shopping, surfing in Hawaii, taking helicopter rides over London, or just standing at the side of the stage during shows, watching their dads strut their stuff. Leah loved to have her own hotel room and order room service and be the daughter of someone famous, not just the offspring of some sweaty old guy in jeans and a checked shirt who was home all the time, tinkering with his old Chevy.

I made a personal commitment while we toured that I'd try to do something for a charity in some of the towns we were in, to give something back instead of just taking all the time. My chosen charities usually involved sick children or centers specializing in kids with drug problems. Leah was with Susan and me on the day when we arrived in Toronto, Canada, and were driving from the airport to the Four Seasons Hotel. On our way downtown, we drove by a large building. "Hey," I asked the driver. "What's that?"

"Oh, that's a hospital for terminally ill children," he replied.

Turning to my daughter, I told her, "Tomorrow, Leah, I want you to go to the mall and fill this car with toys. You choose which toys you think the sick kids would like, and you take them to that hospital and give them to them." With her mom, she did just as I said and had one of the most meaningful afternoons of her life.

"That was great, Dad!" she told me when I saw her later that day, her eyes bright. "The kids loved everything we bought them. Can we do it again?"

With her encouragement, we repeated the exercise often, and she became so committed to the idea that she even called a number she saw on a television appeal in her hotel room one night and made a monthly pledge to another kids' charity, which I still pay today. I knew then that she would never again take our good fortune for granted. And I don't think she ever has.

Hell Freezes Over went on to be a very profitable and successful album. But the carrots that had been dangled in front of us turned out to be much less juicy than some of us had been led to believe. Furthermore, when the video and DVD came out, a large percentage of the camera footage was of Don and Glenn. For much of it, you'd think the Eagles were a two-man band. Even for the introduction of "Hotel California," you only see my hands playing it, rarely my face. Joe had more airplay than Timothy or I, presumably because of his own solo status. The black and white mannequins on the miniature stage suddenly made sense. The limelight belonged to "The Gods" and "The Gods" alone.

That feeling was reinforced by the credits on the album. "Hotel California" was mine. It was my chief claim to fame, and I'd written most of the music at my beach house in Malibu. It was my understanding that, when it came to the credits, the person who contributed most to the song was listed first, followed in descending order by those who added something later, like lyrics. Thus, on the original *Hotel* album, the credits read, "Written by Don Felder, Don Henley, and Glenn Frey." Suddenly, on *Hell*

Freezes Over, the credits changed. After "Hotel California," it said, "Written by Don Henley, Glenn Frey, and Don Felder," relegating me to the final position.

Furthermore, not a single song by Bernie Leadon or Randy Meisner appeared on the new album. The classics they'd written and contributed so much to, like "Witchy Woman," "On the Border," "Try and Love Again" and "Take It to the Limit," had been excluded. Neither of those founding members of the Eagles would earn a penny from our latest success. Faced with such pettiness, the antagonism between us increased. Everything started to become an issue, especially Joe and me larking around onstage with cardboard cutouts and some gimmicky tricks, providing much-needed comic relief but unintentionally drawing the camera away from "The Gods."

Don would spend hours agonizing over publicity photographs, trying to decide if he looked too old or too wrinkled, or if his hair was just right. These were images for T-shirts or for photos to be signed and given away, not to be etched in stone in Mount Rushmore. We accepted his fastidiousness and appreciated that it was sometimes a good thing, both a blessing and a curse. The blessing was that he set new standards that we all had to strive to achieve. If you expect greatness of people, they often rise to greatness. The curse was that it all took time and energy.

The issue of how many people were on the payroll reared its ugly head once more. Don and Glenn had lackeys around them all the time—personal assistants, secretaries, press agents, attorneys, accountants, and various hired hands, even when they were in L.A. My new guitar tech was hired out of Nashville, where he returned between tour legs. On the road, the homeboys would share Don's and Glenn's enormous presidential suites. A constant presence at their side, they would escort them down in the elevator when it was time for the limos to take us to the gig. By contrast, I was given a walkie-talkie and was called up by one of the security people when it was my turn to come down.

These might seem trivial and insignificant matters compared to the bigger picture of being back together again and on the road and doing what we did best, but added to the sense of being taken for a ride financially, these individual digs added up, causing a permanent feeling of dissatisfaction and apprehension—like when you're breaking up with someone and everything they do suddenly annoys you.

Sometimes, I admit, I let it eat me up too much inside. It was truly a case of this could be heaven or this could be hell, depending on how I was feeling on any particular day. Mostly, I was genuinely delighted to be on the road, playing music with the band that I loved. I'd close my eyes, let go, and play from my heart, which was what I enjoyed doing the most. When I was up there on the stage, I'd try to radiate that purity out of me and my music in a positive force that counteracted all the bullshit and gave the fans their money's worth for the three hours they had us to themselves. The audience just wanted to be entertained. That's what they had paid an exorbitant amount of money for.

Behind the scenes, I'd try to work with "The Gods" as much as I could, and not let the tensions destroy me. "Just think about the money, Fingers," Don would say, grabbing my arm if ever he saw me getting upset with Glenn.

"The music is what it's all about," Joe would remind me. "That and the fans are all that matters."

If the stress became too much, I'd take a deep breath, hang out with Joe, have some fun, and try to cool off. Now that he was sober, he'd become a computer nerd and radio ham. All the time he'd have previously devoted to drinking, taking drugs, or playing practical jokes he now spent tuning in to fellow hams all over the world. You could always tell which room Joe was in, because out on the balcony some weird contorted antenna would be set up, and you could hear muffled voices with foreign accents through his bedroom door.

Joe and I had already rebonded as friends in the "guitar camp" to which we had been relegated. He was great at shoring me up. While the new divisions between us and the singers' camp eroded support, confidence, and the willingness to be spontaneous musically or speak our minds, Joe and I grew closer and closer. Without him, Don and Glenn would have sucked *all* the fun out of what should have been the best time of our lives.

Susan was always telling me that I'd never be rid of my stomach problems unless I accepted things more, and I knew she was right. I already had serious back pain, originally caused by a surfing accident in Malibu and exacerbated by so much time sitting in cars and planes. It had flared up on the road, requiring Glenn to have a doctor flown out to treat me. I also needed a different vehicle from the others, just to be more comfortable. Every cloud has a silver lining, however. I began to have daily sessions with Don's personal Pilates instructor, a wonderfully spiritual woman named Isa Bohn, who was already on the tour for him. Isa was in her seventies, with the body of a twenty-year-old. She corrected my guitar player's slump and taught me a great deal about being positive and calm and in touch with my inner self.

"You need to relax," she'd tell me in that silky smooth voice of hers, as she adjusted my posture. "There are things you have no control over and which you need to let go. Life is too short to waste it worrying." She was right.

Our road crew on *Hell Freezes Over* was one of the best we ever had. They worked damn hard, tearing down the set at two in the morning before riding a bus for six hours to the next venue. Their schedule was punishing, and they'd sleep where they could before scrambling to set up the stage for the next show. Meanwhile, we were in five-star suites and limos and private planes with all the glitz and glamour you can imagine.

Usually, the crew slept on the bus, but when we stayed in a town for a couple of days, they would be put up in a hotel. Previously, they'd always stayed in the same place as us, which allowed for a sense of camaraderie and shared experience. We could hang out together after a gig, spend time in each other's rooms, get high, or shoot some pool. With *Hell Freezes Over*, that changed. Suddenly, the band was in the Four Seasons and the crew was in the Holiday Inn.

Among our crew was a man named Bill, who handled our wiring and built the synthesizer racks we used. He played good bass and was a great person to have around on the technical side. The crew had just done several shows in a row, finishing one in Vegas and reaching Phoenix in the wee hours of the morning, finally getting to their hotel rooms. Each was given a plastic keycard at reception. Exhausted, Bill went up to his room. He swiped his card in the door, but it wouldn't open. They'd given him the wrong code, so he went to a friend's room and called the front desk, but the night porter didn't answer. Frustrated, he went back to his room and kicked the door in. A hotel security guard was called, saw the damage, and contacted Irving. The next thing we knew, Bill had been fired from the tour. The message was, anyone who caused problems, even as understandable as this, was gone.

Our press agent, Larry Solters, nicknamed Scoop, had been with us for over twenty years. He was a long-time adviser to Irving, almost part of the furniture. In Germany, Glenn was particularly grumpy. He couldn't buy the particular type of Marlboro cigarettes he smoked, Marlboros in a box. He asked Larry to call the States and have his assistant send some cartons via Airborne Express. The messenger arrived with the package the next day, and Larry literally ran them up to Glenn's room. But Glenn tore open the package and saw they were soft packs instead of boxes, and I soon learned Larry had been fired. There was nothing Irving or any of us could say, although Irving did rehire Larry much later on. The exercise of power seemed to me to be getting out of hand. Anyone's head could be on the block for no reason.

I'd seen such behavior many times over the years, and mostly I tolerated it. We'd tell each other: "Let it slide, think about the money," anything to keep the peace and keep the band together. Older and wiser now, though, I found myself increasingly unable to not only witness the abuse but take it myself and keep smiling. There were times when I could barely stand to be in the same room as Glenn. I guess he picked up on it, because soon he let it be known that I was "making him unhappy." As I once told Irving, "Irv, you made that guy too rich too soon."

Trouble was, we were all thrown in together on the road. There were few areas for avoiding each other. To keep explosive confrontation down to a minimum, Irving, who had long ago decided on a policy of divide and conquer, separated us as much as possible. Hotel rooms were chosen on separate floors or several corridors apart. We'd have five separate dressing rooms. Gone were the days of a jovial a cappella vocal rehearsal in the shower room. The fleet of limos went and was replaced by individual vans, where possible, complete with executive armchair seats, air-conditioning, DVDs, cell phones, and blacked-out windows. There'd be enough room in each van for the immediate families, bodyguards, and assistants to travel with each band member.

Even the stretch Boeing 737 plane we chartered had separate compartments. You could step out of your own car, walk onto the plane, go to your own "room," close the door, and wait for a stewardess to bring you refreshments. Rarely would Glenn or Don abandon the comfort zone of their own private compartment to walk into the communal areas and help themselves from the "trough," with the thirty or so support crew. If they did, there was a clear hierarchy; they had to be served first before anyone else could dig in.

Orders would be issued from the private compartments like edicts from the presidential plane. In New Orleans, someone announced, "Don would like the Cajun shrimp from the NOLA Restaurant. Please arrange for it to be brought to the plane before we take off." Or in Texas, he'd ask for a special chili or favorite barbecue dish. The rest of us were expected to go along with all these directions and just be grateful for the leftovers.

We'd manage to avoid each other completely until the moment when we all had to walk onto the stage with a big smile and say, "Hi, we're the Eagles," and pretend that everything was wonderful. It was a lonely, isolating experience and one that made a complete mockery of how we'd started and what the fans thought of us. If they'd known what each one of us was thinking as we banged out our methodically rehearsed version of our hit songs, they'd probably have walked out.

I can only remember a few times during that whole tour when Glenn and I had a laugh. We'd just arrived at a charter airport somewhere like "Pisshole," Idaho. I went into the bathroom and was at the urinal when Glenn came in and stood at the next one. I told a joke, then he told one, and we were having a good time, standing there with our dicks in our hands. When we were both done and went to wash our hands, Glenn turned to me and said, "You know, Fingers, I wish we could be like this all the time. Why can't we just laugh and have fun together?"

I replied, "I don't know, buddy. That was great."

Smiling, we walked out of the bathroom together, but within the hour, that sense of carefree friendship and camaraderie was gone. We fell back into our self-assigned roles, dealing with the egos and the struggle for power and control. I'll never really understand why. The passive-aggressive atmosphere was all encompassing. The message was still clear. "If you rock the boat too much, you might just tip yourself out. Remember Bernie and Randy." What was so sad was that it was completely unnecessary, because there was never any challenge to dominate the Eagles by anyone other than Glenn, Don, and Irving.

The second leg of our box office record–setting tour got underway in Philadelphia in the fall of 1994, but Glenn didn't show for the sound check. He'd not been well for some time, and we suddenly heard that he'd been admitted to the hospital for surgery. That show and several after it had to be canceled, beginning a sixty-day hiatus.

Don called me in my room after I'd heard the news. "What are we gonna do with this guy?" he asked, exasperated.

"Well, I'm trying to help him by visualisation," I said, my eyes closed. "I'm sending Glenn soothing thoughts in a healing white light all around him." I knew from personal experience how painful his condition could be, and I felt genuine sympathy. I sent him a telegram wishing him luck, and he sent me one back saying, "That's the stuff."

Don was less sympathetic. "You're wasting your time," he snapped. "They're treating the wrong end of that asshole."

When Glenn was better, the tour resumed. Irving kept tight control of the financial reins, promoting the concerts, selling the T-shirt concession through his own company, Giant Merchandising, and controlling everything from parking to posters and programs. The considerable income we generated was handed to Irving's on-tour accountant, who then gave it to the Los Angeles–based accountants, who divided it among us.

Irving placed himself firmly between the box office and the accountants, so that all the i's were dotted and all the t's crossed, the books perfectly balanced.

Whenever I asked to see any financial documentation, though, it was always very informal. I never made an appointment with my lawyers or demanded to see papers, as I could have done. Even so I was often made to feel like a nuisance, as if I was nagging needlessly when all I was trying to do was to make sure that we were on a level playing field.

Because of the way I felt, I found myself constantly questioning my own motives. Was I being too greedy, wanting more when I already had so much? Then I remembered the years of grief in which I had more than earned the right to every penny I was being paid. Whether they liked it or not, Don, Glenn, and Irving had originally agreed to an equal partnership. Now they were appointing themselves as primary recipients of the work that everyone had given their lives to for so long. There were uncomfortable echoes of my father's experience at Koppers. He'd worked from his early teens to his death in his midsixties, giving up his nights, weekends, and Sundays, to do his very best for that company. He died of heart failure, and the only thing I remember them giving him was a gold watch. I found their ingratitude staggering. If this was going to be the Eagles' last tour, as I suspected it would be, then I had to protect my own interests and those of my children.

Timothy and Joe knew that anything they said would be ignored, and although they backed me in principle and told me privately to "go for it," they opted for a quiet life and just took what they were given. Not that I was getting anywhere. Irving would call up between each six-week tour leg and say, "Don and Glenn have agreed to do twenty-five more shows on the East Coast, from January to April, and you're gonna make a bundle. Are you in or not?" There were no more band meetings; this seemed like a dictatorship, and mine was the third phone call, after "The Gods" had already agreed. I have read a great deal about abusive relationships, and that's just what I felt like—an abused wife financially and emotionally dependent on my husband, afraid that he'd dump me if I made too much fuss or did something to displease him. I was usually held off with Irving's repeated maxim, "You make the music, Fingers, and I'll take care of the business."

Susan and I were getting along much better, and she remained a great sounding board for all that I was going through with the band. But my wife had developed her own life, and Cody and I were no longer the priorities we'd once been. The kids were growing fast, and, bored at home, she'd set herself up as a jewelry designer under the name Susan Harris, her mother's maiden name.

As we became wealthier and she began to enjoy the pleasures of jewelry shopping, she studied some expensive trinkets and thought, "I could make that." With my emotional and financial support, she took a course at UCLA and the Gemstone Institute of America and became a goldsmith, a course that proved to be an affirmation of her talent and abilities. She set up an office at home and honed her skills until she felt confident enough to offer her goods for sale. I was all for it, and invested heavily in the business to give her enough capital to get started.

"My wife makes jewelry and sells it instead of buying it," I'd tell my friends, proudly. "How bad can that be?"

Now when I was away on tour for months on end, Susan was busy running her own company, making and designing beautiful one-of-a-kind gemstone pieces, and selling them through Neiman Marcus stores. Within a very short time, she became one of Neiman Marcus's largest jewelry vendors and was able to take on full-time staff. My only complaint was that I could never reach Susan when I wanted to talk to her. She was transformed almost overnight from being a housewife, always there when I called, to traveling all over the States to gemstone conventions, living out of hotel rooms like me, and wearing power suits. My little blue-eyed blonde Susan was suddenly Ivana Trump. The transformation was more than a little unsettling.

• • •

Being back on the road brought its usual sexual temptations—tenfold, in fact, because of our new "rock legend" status. Fortunately, everyone was now married with kids, and the baseline had been moved. Don and Glenn had issued various commandments, sent down from the mountains: For this very high-profile tour, there was to be no drink or drugs, so as not to tempt Joe. And there was to be no womanizing, because wives and children were now traveling with us. No more Third Encores. However, sometimes when I'd pass Glenn's room, food service trays of red wine would be evident, or there'd be a telltale pungent aroma in the hallway.

All of us were faced with an ongoing daily opportunity to be unfaithful. The video crew even put together a film called *The Eagles' Greatest Tits*, which showed the astonishing array of breasts revealed nightly for our delectation by women in the audience. There was always some chick, up on her boyfriend's shoulders, dancing and singing along, who was happy to show us her finest assets then and later. Those sort of offers weren't confined to the fans, nor to the groupies who hung around, ever hopeful. They were also forthcoming from the stewardesses, waitresses, bar staff, and various hangers-on who became our camp followers, even at the affluent, high-end level.

I knew what beasts lurked out there with women, and I knew the battles I was going to be facing. I had burdened myself, quite deservedly, with massive amounts of guilt in the eighties for my earlier bad behavior. I wanted to prove, not only to Susan and to the band but also to myself, that I wasn't the same guy anymore. I'd grown through, out, and beyond that stuff. I made a conscious decision to take things along with me that I could use to transcend those temptations. I really tried to find a way to face the same challenges and prove my own merit to myself.

Using a technique I employed when I quit smoking, I told myself, "I've fallen victim to this before, I have tasted all of its delights, I know what it is, and I also know the damage it causes, so I'm not going to taste it again." I read spiritually enlightening books, having discovered that it is really hard for an animal, such as raw sexual desire, to exist in the presence of something high and spiritual. It dwindles and slithers back into the darkness. I used to leave books lying around in my hotel or dressing room, on the plane, or backstage, and whenever I was presented with temptation, I'd pick one up and start reading it. I even handed one at the end of the tour to a young stewardess on our private plane who was particularly persistent and from whom, I'm proud to say, I rejected all advances.

"Read this and have a happy life," I told her with a smile.

Another technique I employed was to practice my guitar playing in the dead time between gigs and sound checks. There'd often be up to twenty hours a day to fill, and I'd make a point of playing six or seven hours every day. Concentrating on my finger work really diverted my attention from what else my hands could have been doing. I also spent a lot of time e-mailing the kids, faxing, making calls—keeping busy. Most of all, for nine glorious months beginning in January 1995, I had O. J. Simpson to thank. His televised trial on CNN gripped the entire nation. It also served as a wonderful device against temptation. One of our tour jokes became: "Sorry, honey, I can't screw you right now. O.J.'s about to take the stand." Employing these various techniques, I managed to keep my hands clean and Susan happy.

There were some unexpected experiences too—like meeting the President of the United States. Don had been a big supporter of Bill Clinton when he was a governor, and he arranged a benefit concert in Beverly Hills for his reelection campaign. Susan, my mother, Jesse, and Rebecca all came with me and met Bill and Hillary, both of whom were extremely charismatic. Barbra Streisand sang, and I met Sharon Stone, which was a personal high. David Geffen was there, now a film mogul through his partnership with Steven Spielberg. I was pleased to see him. In the short time David's company had managed us, before we moved with Irving to Front Line, he'd always been extremely gracious to me. I longed for a return to such integrity.

In gratitude for our election support, when our tour came to Washington, we were invited to the White House to see the Oval Office and have lunch with the First Lady. It was a great honor, and protocol dictated that we should give the Clintons something to express our thanks. The gift "The Gods" selected, however, was not quite what I might have chosen. Glenn had an endorsement deal with Takamine, the Japanese guitar makers, which meant that every year we were given scores of guitars to autograph and give away for promotional auctions or charity events. One of these was now destined for Bill Clinton.

At various times I suggested we try and make a deal with Martin, Fender, or Gibson instead. "We're an all-American band. We're meant to be *the* quintessential all-American band." I thought we shouldn't be handing out cheap Japanese guitars, least of all to the President of the United States. It should be a special, handmade commemorative American Gibson with the Eagles logo inlaid into it.

No matter what I said, the deal remained. Glenn was even featured on their Web site endorsing their products, complete with a photo of him holding one and smiling inanely.

When we arrived at the White House, Irving had a Takamine guitar that we all had signed. As we neared the Oval Office, it was handed to me to present it to the President. Normally, Don and Glenn would have been only too happy to step into the limelight.

I was highly embarrassed by the nature of our gift. I didn't even really know what we were doing there. I wasn't a particular fan of the Clintons, and other than playing a few benefits for him, I'd had nothing to do with supporting them. Now suddenly they wanted me to step up to the plate. "Bill Clinton is given the most elegant paintings and furniture, jewelry, china, and ornaments, which end up in the Smithsonian for posterity, and all we could manage was this?"

I found myself, red-faced and tongue-tied, standing in the Oval Office, in front of JFK's very own desk, having the dishonor of telling Bill Clinton how much the Eagles would like to give him this special signed guitar. I wanted to say, "Hey, Bill, we heard you play saxophone, so we thought you might like to try a guitar instead," but after the Cranston incident, I hardly dared open my mouth.

We did so many benefit gigs, it sometimes seemed like almost all the concerts we did were for free. If it wasn't for some politician or other, it was Glenn's golf charity, Don's Walden Woods Project, or his campaign to preserve the land beneath his Santa Monica home, a project Joe and I dubbed "Save Henley's View." A great deal of money was being taken out of every ticket each night to go to their personal charities, and after a while, I came up with an idea that I thought everyone would jump at.

In my opinion, who better to benefit from the sort of generosity we had been showing people we hardly knew than the people who had worked for us so loyally for so long? We could do one night's gig for the crew and give them a million dollars or so to split between them by way of a thank-you. That sort of money would allow them to take care of themselves in their old age. We could make these guys happy for the rest of their lives.

Instead of helping our boys, we continued to raise millions for the band's various pet causes, which gave us maximum publicity and some undoubted tax advantages, while our hardworking crew continued slogging it.

EIGHTEEN

I **decided to focus on the music,** to make sure we were providing the best possible service to our fans. At least if that was pure, then the crap would be worthwhile. But I wasn't sure it was. We were playing OK. In fact, as the tour continued, I think we improved daily. It was more that we didn't have the backup we needed.

We'd used the engineer who mixed the "house" sounds in the venues for many years, a guy named Richard Erwin. Glenn, deciding that he looked like Larry of the Three Stooges because he was balding on top, nicknamed him Larry. For some reason, Glenn suddenly decided he didn't like Larry anymore and brought in his own guy, someone he'd used on his solo tours, who knew his songs. Don didn't say a word, and the rest of us had no say.

Personally, I didn't care who mixed the music, as long as they could do the job. The new guy came from Gainesville, and we had some fun chatting about our memories of growing up in Florida, of high school, of

Lipham's, and of driving up to Daytona to see bands. His elder brother was a buddy of my brother, Jerry, and we had several mutual friends. Regardless of those connections, though, I wanted to assess whether the new guy was as good as Larry, because I knew he didn't have nearly as much experience. I asked him to make me some DATs (digital audio tapes) of the house mix for every show so I could take them back to my room and listen to them to see how he was doing. To help me decide, I asked some of the other musicians to listen in too. The idea was that if we felt a particular instrument wasn't being turned up enough or was being played too loud, we'd be able to offer the new guy some advice on how to make it sound as it did on the record.

"You might want to turn up the sax solo on "New York Minute," I suggested, as diplomatically as I could, after hearing the first couple of mixes. "It's hard to hear over the drums and vocal." My hope was that when that solo next came along, he'd remember what I said and crank it up. It was not loud enough to even notice that someone was playing. It just wasn't there.

After about three weeks of listening to the house mixes and noticing little, if any, difference, I was at a loss what to do. I got an opinion from Bill Szymczyk, who came to a couple of our shows, and from Elliot Scheiner, who'd produced *Hell Freezes Over*, and they concurred with me every time. But still this house mixer didn't seem to understand what I was telling him.

Finally, I approached Don. "Hey, man," I said, "I've been listening to the house tapes for a month now, and they're not even picking up the trumpet solo. The lead vocal and the drums are really loud, but everything else is sort of at the same level. I've spoken to the mixer, but I don't seem to be getting through. Maybe you should listen to the tapes and see what you think."

This was the same guy who'd kept us in studios for months on end, worrying about a note out of place or a lick too loud. Suddenly, his perfectionism was forgotten when it came to stepping on Glenn's toes.

When Glenn heard what I'd been saying, he came and found me in my dressing room. "Mind your own damn business, Fingers," he told me, his eyes burning. "The house mixer's doing a good job and he stays." And so he did.

For the previous couple of tours, we'd used Joe Vitale as a backup drummer. Joe was a great guy who'd also helped me with my solo album. We sounded great with two drummers. The Allman Brothers always had two, and it really cranked up the volume and the pace. I was all for it, but Don always resented Joe, who was a far better drummer and also a talented keyboard player and flautist. With his connections to Joe Walsh and me, Joe Vitale was very clearly in the guitar camp, which was somehow seen as a threat.

Needless to say, for *Hell Freezes Over,* Joe Vitale wasn't asked to join us. Instead Don hired his own man, a drummer named Scott Crago, who used to be the percussionist in his solo band. When Don stepped off the drum riser and came to the front of the stage to sing "Boys of Summer" or "Dirty Laundry," Scott would step off the percussion riser and take his place at the drums. He was good, and the band really rocked when Scott played drums. It was like someone cranked us up three notches. We were solid. Then Don would go back to the drums and play in his distinctive, behind-the-beat way, and we'd be the good ol' Eagles again. It might not have been the best sound we could achieve as a band, but it was what "The Gods" decreed.

During *Hell Freezes Over,* I ran into an old friend, a guy we always called Bummer Bob because he always had such bad news. Bob was a bass player from Florida I'd known since my teens. He'd moved to New York around the time I went there with Flow, and he used to hang out with us a lot.

"Hey, man, how you doin?" I said, when one of the security guards took me to him after he'd asked for me at the stage door. "Come in."

We chatted about old times and caught up with the news of a few old faces from the past. Pretty soon, we'd run out of things to say. "Well, Bob," I said, getting to my feet. "Good to see you, man. Thanks for dropping by."

We shook hands, but just as he was leaving, he said, "Oh, I suppose you heard about Mike?"

"No," I said, my ears pricking up for news of Flow's leading light. I would never forget the intricate ink drawings Mike worked on so fastidiously in Dover Plains, or the zucchini sandwiches we'd devour together when stoned.

"He's been living in Woodstock for years, man, and he took a massive drug overdose. They didn't find him for ages, and when they did, his brain had been starved of oxygen for too long. He's in a wheelchair now."

I stared at Bob, speechless at the news. Poor Mike. I wondered if I still had a number for his family and could contact them and see if there was anything I could do. Stupidly, all I could think of to say was, "Bummer."

In Nashville, where we played to sellout crowds, another old friend surfaced. An hour before we were due to go on, Bernie Leadon's face appeared at the open door of my dressing room.

"Bernie!" I cried, jumping up delightedly. "Great to see you! I really hoped you'd be in town. Come and sit down. Have a beer." Even after all these years, he still had that ability to light up a room with his grin and to put everyone completely at ease. Man, I missed that smile.

We hadn't spoken for a long, long time, and I caught up on what he'd been doing since leaving the band. He'd moved to Hawaii before relocating to Nashville, where he'd had a busy career as a player, songwriter, session musician, and producer. He'd set up a number of successful projects, including a spoof country/rap/bluegrass band, called Run C&W, and a period working as a staff writer for a music publishing company. He'd played banjo on Bruce Hornsby's Grammy-winning version of "The Valley Road"; he'd coproduced works by Crosby & Nash and by Michelle Shocked; and he'd designed music Web sites. He produced a group called Restless Heart, which had had a bestselling album called *Big Iron Horses*, with Eagles-style hits. That record had preceded *Common Thread*, which, through the Travis Tritt video, brought about the Eagles reunion. Even at this distance, Bernie had inadvertently affected the path of my life.

Since moving to Nashville, marrying, and having a son, he'd pretty much withdrawn from my life, which saddened me greatly, as he'd taught me so much and had been the one who'd persuaded me to come to California in the first place. I guess he'd felt there was no place for anyone connected with Glenn and Don in the new career he'd carved for himself.

"Have you seen Glenn?" I asked, somewhat nervously.

"Yeah, I just bumped into him in the hallway," Bernie beamed. "He was fine."

"And Don?"

"Yup, him too. But it was getting a little crowded out there, which is why I ducked in here." There wasn't a hint of animosity or resentment in his voice.

"How you doin', man?" I asked, slapping him affectionately on the thigh as he took a seat opposite me.

"Great," he said, and I could tell from the sparkle in his eyes that he wasn't lying.

"I'm really pleased, Bernie," I said, genuinely.

Looking across at him, I was suddenly filled with envy. Bernie had escaped the treadmill the Eagles had become. He had stood up for what he believed in and walked away from all the crap to do what he wanted. With Run C&W he'd injected some of his unique humor into the country music scene and was clearly never going to take the industry too seriously again. If there was one thing I'd learned from Bernie—and there was so much— it was that his kind of music originates in a very selfless place. There are no egos in bluegrass, which comes from Sunday revivals down by the river and a shared sense of fun and community spirit.

His final few months with the band had been an agony of recrimination and hostility, but his contribution had been enormous and his humor desperately needed. Still, until I saw him again, sitting across from me, forgiveness and love in his eyes, I hadn't realized quite how much I'd missed it. Wishing we had more time before we went onstage, I'd have given anything just to sit and jam with him, like the old days. Worse, I suddenly felt anxious about how he'd perceive my performance that night. Bernie was one of the most gifted musicians I'd ever met and when he left, I took over his pedal steel and mandolin and B-string bender guitar parts, which he'd never heard me play.

I needn't have worried. Bernie had come along not to judge, but to enjoy. All he wanted was to see a bunch of old friends, hear the show, and reminisce, rekindling his own fond memories of his years with the Eagles. I thought I'd learned all I could from the streak of brilliance that was Bernie Leadon. But that night, he proved he had still more to teach me.

The final leg of the *Hell Freezes Over* tour beckoned that fall, and I prepared to leave again for Europe with a slightly lighter heart. Something had changed, and I think it had as much to do with my own acceptance of the situation I found myself in as with a changing attitude in "The Gods," each of whom had happier things to think about.

In May of 1995, immediately after the winter tour ended, Don had married his girlfriend, a Dallas model named Sharon. His bachelor life finally behind him, he splashed out on a lavish wedding reception at a ranch in Malibu, at which Bruce Springsteen, Tony Bennett, Sting, and Billy Joel sang. Susan and I were invited, along with the rest of the band and people like Sheryl Crow, Jackson Browne (whom Susan had always wanted to thank for stepping in for me when Jesse was born), and even David Crosby, to whom I said a cordial hello. Emeril Lagasse, the television chef, was flown in from New Orleans to provide the catering. The media helicopters flying overhead trying to film the celebrities were kept at bay by helium weather balloons floated up to block their view.

Don built his new wife a mansion in Dallas. He finally resolved his ongoing legal dispute with Geffen Records, which released a greatest hits album of his work that year. Even though it failed to make much of a mark in the charts, Don negotiated a deal with Warner Brothers for another solo album.

Now that Don was married, he seemed to be a happier man—Glenn, too. After his divorce, Glenn had married a dancer named Cindy, whom he met in one of his fitness videos. Both men were discovering for the first time the comfort and security that marriage can provide, something I'd known for years. We all knew that the tour was moving into its final phase and that the feuding would soon be at an end. I'd been forced to accept the deal offered to me, but I was also grateful for the blessing of being allowed to make as much money as I had. Individually, our lives were taking separate paths. Each of us was discovering a new level of maturity.

That October, Susan and I were in Santa Monica, on our way home from another session with our couples therapist. We were getting along pretty well, and our trials with Cody seemed to be almost over. (I should have had more faith in my youngest son. Like me, he grew out of his rebelliousness and began to lead a full and relatively normal life.) The issue of my infidelities from fourteen years ago and beyond had been faced and wrestled to the mat, and now we were just struggling with the fact that we'd been together for twenty-four years and had lost a great deal of the fire.

Driving back from the therapist, we were talking about how I was going to cope with going back on the road, dealing with the band and the whole business of sexual temptation again. "I'm proud of you, Don," Susan told me, "I know how hard you've tried."

Pulling up at an intersection, we were stopped by a speeding blue-light cavalcade of vehicles, complete with police escort. The convoy of limousines and motorcyle outriders was being chased by media vehicles and helicopters swooping low overhead. Switching on the radio, we heard the news that O.J. Simpson had just been acquitted of murder after his extraordinary nine-month trial. For all that time, I'd been following the case from hotel rooms around America, as I struggled with the vicissitudes of the tour and with my own personal demons. Now, flashing past me, a few feet away, O.J. sat, a free man, in the back of his limo. The coincidence seemed uncanny.

Back on the road, the tour rolled on like some vast moneymaking machine that none of us could stop even if we'd wanted to. It had become a monster that needed to be fed. It was big business for everyone. Audio recordings of some of our live shows—"made for posterity," secured in a vault—would appear for sale a week to ten days later as bootleg CDs, for which the band didn't receive a penny. We couldn't really complain. We were making more than any of us had ever made before, and I tried to keep sight of the fact that I was being paid very well to do what I loved, play music.

At least this time I was seeing the countries we were visiting through clear eyes, unaffected by too many drugs or crazy nights. Japan, always one of my favorite places to visit, had never looked more beautiful, and the sushi never tasted so good. Christchurch, New Zealand, had never been wetter. It was a mudfest, just like Woodstock. I have never seen so many people standing out in torrential rain, soaked right through to their undershorts, having a good time, while we onstage were just concentrating on not getting electrocuted as the rain came slanting down.

I knew how lucky I was to be travelling in such exalted luxury, surrounded by such good friends as Joe, Timothy, and the crew. Gigs like the Rose Bowl in Pasadena, where we played to ninety thousand people, the biggest gig we'd ever played in L.A., provided some golden memories. It was a cold night and we had heaters on the stage, but we played one of our best shows of that entire tour. We'd matured in terms of our playing and our singing, and every note was perfect. It was like some of the best gigs we'd played when we were at our musical peak in the seventies.

The night was clear with stars twinkling in the sky above us, and when each song stopped, you could still hear it and the noise of the crowd echoing through the canyons beyond the stadium. Everyone who was anyone in L.A. was there—musicians, rock stars, and management staff. There were celebrities like Michael Douglas, Jack Nicholson, and Sheryl Crow standing on the side of the stage alongside Susan, Jesse and his girlfriend, and the rest of my kids. It was a Who's Who event, with a huge circus tent set up backstage for hospitality.

The last gig the Eagles played together on *Hell Freezes Over* was in Edinburgh, Scotland in August 1996. We'd been around the States twice, as well as to Canada, Japan, Australia, and Europe. None of us really knew if this was going to be the final gig, or whether we'd get another call from Irving in a few months, but Glenn had privately decided that he wouldn't be doing any more. His attitude toward me that night was different from any other time since the seventies. I think he was genuinely happy to have made it through to the end of the tour with us all in one piece. Despite the undercurrents of unhappiness and the old frictions resurfacing, everything had stayed fairly contained. We'd gone out, we'd played music, we'd made a bunch of money, and—most important of all—we'd gotten through it without killing each other.

When the concert ended, at the end of a beautifully warm Scottish night, Glenn and Don actually went around the whole band and hugged everyone.

"Good job," Glenn told me, slapping me on the back. "We made it, buddy."

"Yeah," I said, somewhat dazed and confused. "Yeah, I guess we did."

Family life occupied me once we'd come off the road. Jesse finally decided that he wanted to spend the rest of his life with Erin, his girlfriend of many years, which was the smartest move he ever made. Their wedding took place in 1997, and within a year, they'd provided us with an unexpected delight—our first grandchild, Kurt. I had suddenly gone from being a rock-and-roll star to being a grandpa. Strangely, I didn't mind one little bit. Jesse had become a successful financial advisor, his early passion for the computer games *Lemonade Stand* and *Millionaire* serving him well.

Sadly, while Jesse's marriage took its first tentative steps, mine was faltering badly. After more than two years on the road, the differences between Susan and me had grown. By the time I returned from that grueling tour, my conviction to Susan stronger than ever, the house and my marriage were empty.

With no one home most days but me, I found myself rattling around this large decadent property, wife and kids absent. I began falling back into my bachelor routines of fishing, boating, flying, and dabbling in real estate. My children were in their adolescence or early twenties, with all the highs and lows that can bring. Mostly, they were away or out with their friends, and the only time they wanted me was to give them some money or to pick them up from somewhere.

I bought myself a sixty-eight-foot offshore boat I called *Wings*, took the necessary advanced navigation exams, and did several seasons of marlin fishing down in Cabo San Lucas, Baja, Mexico, with my old fishing buddies or friends, like Joe Walsh, accompanied as ever by his bodyguard, Smokey.

Jesse and Cody would come with me sometimes, and I was never happier than on the flybridge of that beautiful vessel, a cigar firmly planted between my lips, a glass of champagne in my hand, and my two sons beside me. It was a far cry from the little powerboat I used to mess around with up at Lake Alice when I was their age. I knew how fortunate I was to give my children these extraordinary memories and experiences. Life should have been truly sweet.

There was, however, a new distance between Susan and me that had never existed before. I blamed myself for being away so long this last time, and for not paying her enough attention. In my absence, she'd become a workaholic and was as addicted to her jewelry business as Joe had ever been to Jack Daniel's. If I ever persuaded her to take some time out and come with me to Catalina on the boat, she'd bring along her black day planner, full of her accounting, business schedules, and appointments (although never one for me, I noted with dismay), and these huge bags of gems and gold. Instead of hanging out with me, making love and hiking like we used to, she'd sit in Catalina and make jewelry like a woman obsessed. We were like two friends on vacation, one of them working.

We'd hardly ever have supper together. I'd usually make something for myself and any of the kids who happened to be around, then sit there with the dogs salivating and watching me eat. Susan's working hours were long and erratic. Our intimate moments were few and far between. I felt increasingly lonely, living in this big house by myself, sitting there day after day, waiting for my wife to find the time to play golf with me, or have lunch, or even fly to Europe or Hawaii to help me spend the fruits of my labors.

"Oh well," I finally told myself. "You can't possibly complain after all the time you've spent away."

The rest of the band became homebodies too, busy doing nothing. We did one benefit gig for President Clinton's reelection campaign, and with him and Hillary as honored guests, we attended the official opening of the Henry Thoreau Walden Library, part of the Walden Woods Project, into which Don had poured so much of our charitable contributions. Don was a family man in Texas, with three small children and a new wife; Timothy and his wife, Jean, were raising their kids just outside L.A.; and

Joe, still sober, brought out a new album, *Look What I Did! The Joe Walsh Anthology*, and embarked on a solo tour. Glenn played some golf and landed himself a small part in the Tom Cruise film *Jerry Maguire*. He also launched a record label, Mission, with an icon of a mission bell, which failed despite the success of its first release, *One Planet, One Groove*, by my old friend Max Carl. Glenn then set up a studio in L.A., which he called the Dog House. Don did something similar—but even more high-tech, with bedrooms—out at a Spanish-style house in Malibu.

Then one day, Irving called up. "Hi, Fingers, just to let you know, the guys are thinking of going back into the studio again. They're gonna try and record a brand-new album of all new songs, the first in nearly twenty years."

"OK," I said, somewhat warily, wondering if Don and Glenn could actually bear to sit down and try to write together. Painful memories of *The Long Run* in 1979 were still burned into my brain. "Where and when?"

Even though we could afford the finest producers and recording equipment money could buy, and the stature of our next project deserved the very best, the plan was to use Don's and Glenn's new studios, paid for by the band. Mindful of the failure of the "Almost the Eagles" project over the choice of producer, they decided that this time there'd be no producer at all.

The first band meeting in years was called, at Don's rental house over near Brentwood, just the five of us together. It was the first time in over twenty years that we'd assembled like that without an entourage of managers and attorneys. I arrived early, nervous as a kitten. Over tuna fish sandwiches, Don and Glenn decreed that Joe, Tim, and I had to submit any CDs of tracks we'd prepared, and they would pick which ones they liked. We weren't allowed to hear what they had written.

They played us some other songs, demos from Nashville songwriters—not, sadly, from our old friends Jackson, J.D., or Jack Tempchin. Most of them were, at best, mediocre, without the Henley/Frey magic. I said nothing, but I remember thinking, "Hey, we're the Eagles, we should be playing our own stuff," but I knew I wasn't in a position to speak out. One track, called "I Love to Watch a Woman Dance" sounded to me almost exactly like another song by the same writer called "For My Wedding," just with a different set of lyrics. Don was releasing the latter on his next solo album. He suggested that Glenn could sing this version instead for him with an Italian-type mandolin sound, which wasn't at all right for Glenn's R&B voice.

Another song we were going to try was one that Timothy had written at a songwriting seminar in an English castle. Despite the fairytale surroundings, it wasn't that great either. Joe piped up, "Well, I think I might have a couple of licks." He had one pretty solid track started, which he'd recorded at his home studio. It sounded very much like a recognizable "Life's Been Good," Joe Walsh type of song. I had a song I called "Downer Diner," a semispoof on "Sad Café," which featured electric piano and acoustic guitar with an ascending progression slightly reminiscent of "Sad Café." I also had another up-tempo track with Latino rhythms, called "Little Latin Lover," with gut-string guitar. Glenn loved it.

"Hey, this sounds like the party music wafting over from a neighboring yacht," he said. "Jimmy Buffett would kill for this."

Among us, we had five or six other tracks, none of them very good. One sounded like "Sitting on the Dock of the Bay"—black, spiritual, sixties retro, not at all the sound of the Eagles. When we went into the studio, picked up our instruments, and tried to play it, along with the rest of the Nashville songs, we just sounded like a bad demo band.

Furthermore, because we were constantly running between the two studios, there began to be some serious competitive rivalry about whose studio was best and where the bulk of the recording should be done. It got to the point where personalities would spark over the smallest issue.

To me it seemed that Don's continual tardiness was irritating Glenn. At times Don would arrive late and spend time on the phone making personal calls, preferring to work between about two and six o'clock before he went back to his studio in Malibu to work on his solo album until the small hours. Glenn, like the rest of us, preferred to work from ten until six, so we'd have time to spend with our families in the evening and would be fresh the next day. The constant sitting around waiting for Don caused me to be increasingly impatient.

The jockeying for position became ludicrous. At the Dog House, Glenn would sit in the primary producer's chair in his control room; no one else was allowed in it. The same would happen at Don's place, where Glenn would take a subordinate position on a little roller stool, while Don sat in the big chair. Joe and I desperately wanted to sit in the big chairs and swivel around like naughty schoolboys just to see the reaction, but we feared that "The Gods" wouldn't see the funny side.

Behind each other's back, the two of them complained constantly about the other's studio and equipment. To resolve the constant bickering about which studio was best, I had mixes of the same song made from both studios and listened to them at home. There wasn't a dime of difference between them. They both sounded fine.

Irving called me one day to tell me I wasn't making it any easier. He suggested I just leave everything to him.

"Hey, Irv, I was just trying to help," I explained, "and I don't care if we record this album in my fucking garage. I just want those two big kids to get past this pissing contest."

Knowing that critics were waiting to cut us off at the knees, whatever we produced, injected even more pressure and fear into an already volatile situation. There was a highly competitive market out there, and with artists like Madonna and the Spice Girls hogging the charts, there was no magic team this time. After a while, Glenn decided that he couldn't work this way anymore. Just to appease him, we ended up going back into Glenn's studio.

After months of hoping that we could salvage enough songs for a new album, Don finally pulled the plug. He'd almost finished his latest solo record and was increasingly preoccupied. Irving accepted their decision with a sigh. "Let them just get this stuff out of their system and then we'll regroup," he said. I wasn't sure.

The songs we'd worked so hard on were consigned to digital heaven. The album was never completed, even though we'd recorded four or five tracks. All that's left are a few tapes I took home with me to carry on tinkering with, just in case "The Gods" ever decided to try again.

"Maybe we'll put out another greatest hits, or even a box set," Irving told the rest of us, ruefully, "to buy us some time."

For Glenn's fiftieth birthday, he held a huge party in Palm Springs at La Quinta golf resort, a famous hotel that people used to drive across the desert to in their Model T Fords. Tom Hanks and Don Johnson were invited, along with a list of celebrities as long as my arm. "I want you all to come along, and jam some with me on the stage, while the guests finish their banquet," he said. It wasn't an invitation, it was an order. Glenn played his guests an embarrassing video featuring film clips from his brief and not very successful acting career. After the fifth or sixth clip, someone yelled from the back of the room, only half-joking, "You ought to stick to playing music."

We were each assigned tables, and I sat at my designated place up near the front of the stage and turned to the stranger next to me to introduce myself.

"Hi, I'm Don Felder," I said, extending my hand.

The middle-aged man to my right looked at me and laughed. "Hey, Fingers! Don't you know me? It's J.D."

I was stunned. J.D. Souther, our old songwriting companion, the man who should have been the sixth Eagle, funny and warm, used to have this Marlboro-man, craggy-faced look, with a beard. He could have been a character actor with that face. This guy had short-cropped hair, he was wearing a suit, and there wasn't a wrinkle on his skin. I could hardly believe the change.

"Sorry, man," I said, pretending that I'd known it was him all along. "It's just that you look so, so. . . ."

"Different?" he said, with a wink that barely creased his new smooth skin. "I know."

When it came time to do our jam, we got up onstage and actually had a good time playing blues together. The guests certainly seemed to appreciate it. The champagne and the wine were flowing, and several people had more than their fill, including Glenn's prized house mixer, who had to be carried to his hotel room while someone else leaped behind the console and tried to figure it out.

My birthday gift to Glenn was a white-studded Elvis suit, complete with rhinestones, a wig, and sideburns. He was a huge Presley fan and liked to be called Elvis by his homeboys. He even wore a baseball cap with Elvis written on it, and his party invitations had featured a picture of him as Elvis, so it seemed appropriate.

After that party, we did another benefit gig together for the Tiger Woods Foundation. Tiger was there, and we had our photos taken with him, which was a great honor for amateur golfers like Glenn and me. We played five songs, including "Hotel California," "I Can't Tell You Why," and "Rocky Mountain Way" for the Joe Walsh fans. It was a fun gig, and the best thing about it was that we all seemed to be getting along a bit better. We'd grown up, I guess.

The underlying tensions between us would always be there, and the simmering differences about music, money, and personalities, but for the first time since our early days on the road, we seemed to be able to put them aside and be civil to each other. Glenn and I weren't exactly playing golf together, but we'd help each other out for charity gigs and put on a united front when we had to. Was the ice finally melting, I wondered?

On January 12, 1998, we were to be inducted into the Rock and Roll Hall of Fame as the hundredth members, in the thirteenth annual ceremony. Fellow inductees on the same night were to include Fleetwood Mac, Santana, the Mamas and the Papas, and the late Gene Vincent. We'd all become eligible because it was twenty-five years since the Eagles had released their first recordings. We knew it was a tremendous accolade, and we accepted most graciously. The previous year, my old friend Stephen Stills had become the first person to be inducted twice in the same night—as a member of Buffalo Springfield and also with Crosby, Stills & Nash. Stephen had done me the greatest honor by publicly naming me among his top four all-time favorite guitar players. I was in good company.

The others on his list were Eric Clapton, Joe Walsh, and George Terry, a noted Florida session guitarist.

The ceremony was going to be televised from New York, and we were asked if we could play a few songs. There were a great many discussions before the awards ceremony about whether or not Randy Meisner and Bernie Leadon should be included. If ever I was asked, which was rarely, my answer was unequivocal.

"Absolutely," I'd say. "Bernie and Meis are as much responsible for the Eagles' success as any of us. More so than some. They have to be there."

The counterarguments kept coming back that we should just go along as we were—five guys in the band—and that we couldn't all turn up.

Timothy, Joe, and I strongly disagreed, especially those two, who knew their own contribution had come much later. "They are every bit as entitled to be there as we are," they'd tell Don, Glenn, and Irving, "if not more so. They were the ones who helped make the first greatest hits album such a success. They deserve this."

"Why not ask them and see what they say?" I suggested, as diplomatically as I dared.

As I expected, Bernie and Randy were delighted and relieved to be invited and jumped at the chance. Irving saw their presence as a chance to make even more mileage out of the event. "It'll be the first time all seven members of the Eagles have ever been photographed together," he proudly announced. "This'll make prime-time news."

VH1, which was covering the presentation, made clear that it wanted one thing—all seven Eagles playing together.

Two songs were chosen, and Randy and Bernie were to be allowed to join in.

The ceremony took place in the grand ballroom of the Waldorf-Astoria in Manhattan. Excited as I was by the event, I wasn't looking forward to the few hours when the seven of us would have to be in the same room together, under the scrutiny of the world's media. Don brought J.D. because J.D. deserved to be there as much as the rest of us. We all brought our families. Joe turned up wearing a suit with red bricks painted onto it, in stark contrast to our tuxedos.

Bill Szymzcyk was there, deservedly. Of all the people connected with the Eagles over the years, he was by far the most fondly thought of, because of his warm, loving nature and great sense of humor. It was he who'd tried to quietly mediate whenever Bernie got hotheaded, and he encouraged Randy with his singing. He was very good at instilling confidence and trying to calm the waters. He was an integral part of the whole process.

Sadly, despite Bill's soothing presence, the atmosphere was so tense you could have cut it with one of Joe's chain saws. Some even refused to sign autographs during the sound check. Don and Glenn pretty much shunned Randy and Bernie, and Irving ran around between them.

We were the last to be presented with our awards, after Fleetwood Mac and Santana had performed rousing sets. Peter Green was there as an original member of Fleetwood Mac. The last time Susan and I had seen him, he'd slept on our couch in Boston. "Hi, Peter," I said, extending my hand. "I don't suppose you remember me, but we had some fun jamming together back in Boston in the early seventies." He looked at me blankly. It clearly wasn't a time he recalled well.

Our old friend Jimmy Buffett, also dressed in a tux, introduced us with the words, "We truly look like the people our parents warned us about tonight." He went on, "The Eagles are going into the Rock and Roll Hall of Fame as one of the signature bands that began in the seventies, still alive and kicking ass as we head for the new millennium. They've laughed, frolicked, cried, fought, but most of all they have beaten the odds and are as popular today as they were in that incredible summer back in 1972."

We swept onto the stage and everyone did a brilliant job of feigning back-slapping camaraderie, wearing forced smiles for the cameras. Each of us was to be invited to step up to the mike and make a short acceptance speech. Timothy, Joe, and I were allowed a minute each, while Don and Glenn had unlimited time to ramble on as incoherently as they liked. "The Gods" couldn't be hurried. When it came to the television broadcast, our speeches were all edited out anyway, and only theirs included.

Don thanked Irving first and said that without him we wouldn't have been there today. In a rehearsed aside, Glenn quipped, "Well, we might still have been here, but we wouldn't have made so much money."

Don said of Irving, "He may be Satan, but he's our Satan." He went on to thank producers Bill Szymczyk and Glyn Johns, David Geffen, Jackson Browne, J.D. Souther, the road crew, and his entire family. Of us, he said only, "I appreciate all the work these guys behind me have done," and added, "Old buildings, politicians, and whores all become respectable if they stick around long enough."

Timothy spoke briefly but eloquently and thanked Randy for "paving" his way. Bernie expressed his gratitude to John Boylan, Linda Ronstadt's manager, for giving him his big break. Randy, timid as ever, crept up to the mike and said how honored he was, before thanking his parents. Joe received the most applause in his outrageous suit and by opening with his trademark, "How ya doing?" In his brief speech, he largely thanked the road crew.

I'd agonized over what I was going to say, and I delivered it with considerable emotion. I don't think I'd been as nervous since I stood on the stage of the State Theater in Gainesville and played "Walk Don't Run." Clearing my throat, I began, "I'd like to thank Don Henley and Glenn Frey for writing an incredible body of work that propelled this band through twenty-odd years of life. Thank you guys." Staring Susan straight in the eye as she sat at a table with our four children and my mother, I added, "I'd like to thank my wife, Susan, who put up with me for twenty-six years while we did this." Susan, who deserved this award more than me, blew me a kiss.

Glenn brought up the rear and shot from the hip. "There's been a lot of talk tonight about disharmony," he said. "The Eagles were a very laid-back band in a high-stress situation. A lot has been made and a lot has been speculated in the last twenty-seven years about whether or not we get along. We get along fine. We just disagreed a lot. . . . You cannot play music with people for very long if you don't genuinely like them. I guarantee you that over the nine years the Eagles were together in the seventies, over the three years we were together during our reunion, the best of times rank in the ninety-five percent, and the worst of times in the smallest percentile that obviously everybody but the seven of us has dwelled on for the longest time. Get over it!"

We picked up our instruments and managed to get through our set without incident. Randy was told to stand to the extreme left of the stage, next to Timothy, and Bernie to the extreme right next to Joe. There were several feet of space and a million miles of antipathy between them and Glenn. Randy wasn't allowed to play bass live, so he stood there strumming his guitar silently. With the pain of those barbs still smarting, we began with the band's first-ever hit, "Take It Easy," and followed with our most successful, "Hotel California." When it was over, there was a pregnant pause before the audience rose to its feet as one in open appreciation.

The applause faded away, and we walked off into the wings. Within hours, Glenn left and caught a plane out of New York. Everyone else, including a deeply uncomfortable Bernie, went their separate ways in separate limos. Only Randy went to the bar to celebrate with the other bands. It was just like the good old, bad old days.

NINETEEN

My marriage had, by now, become a serious cause for concern. There was this huge void in my life, which I didn't know how to fill. Susan and I had been together, on and off, since I was with Bernie in the Maundy Quintet. I'd run the gauntlet of snakes, alligators, drugs, and women just to be with her. We'd had four wonderful children together, and I'd held her hand through every birth. Now, I don't think I even knew who she was, this high-powered business executive who had no time to even share a meal with me.

My frustration was epitomized by an evening in the summer of 1999, when I managed to track her down on her cell phone after fruitlessly leaving her messages all day. "Hey, honey," I said, "let's go to see a movie and have dinner tonight out at the new Palace Theater in Calabasas. If we get there early enough, we can be home in time for Leah when she comes back from her friend's house, and I'll bring her some takeout from the restaurant."

"Oh, I don't know, Don," Susan began. "I was actually planning to work late tonight."

"Come on, honey," I pleaded. "I haven't seen you all week."

She relented. "OK. I'll meet you there."

The movie started at four thirty, and I arrived at four o'clock, bought two tickets, and waited around for her, but she was over forty minutes late. When she eventually arrived, she sat down with me, a third of the way through the film, and ate her way through half a bucket of popcorn because she'd skipped lunch. When the film was over, I said excitedly, "OK, what do you feel like eating? Italian? Chinese?"

"Oh, Don," she said, wrinkling her nose. "I'm not really hungry. Do you mind if we skip dinner? I think I'd rather go into the bookstore and browse for a while."

With that, she wandered off to Barnes & Noble and left me standing in the mall, staggered by her attitude. Not only had she almost stood me up, but she'd blown off our romantic evening completely. I walked into the bookstore and told her I was going to order some fettucine for Leah from the Italian restaurant. She still had her nose buried in a jewelry book when I returned. "You know, I don't want this to get cold," I told her. "I think I'll just go home."

"OK," she said, without even looking up.

When I got home, I was too upset to eat. I left Leah's meal in the oven and went straight to my office to surf the Web, unhappier than I had been in many years. I heard Susan come home an hour later and go to her studio without even saying hello. I knew she'd eventually come to bed in the early hours, roll over, and go to sleep. Our evening together couldn't have been more sterile and coldly unromantic. There was never a screaming match where we told each other, "I hate your guts." That might have been preferable. This was like a slow, silent death, and I knew that night that my marriage was all but over.

• • •

In 1999, talks began again about us getting together to possibly record some new material. At the end of the year, we were booked to perform three end-of-the-millennium shows, two to be held at the gilded Mandalay Bay Events Center in Las Vegas on December 27 and 28 and one at the Staples Center in L.A. on December 31. It was hoped that we might come up with some new songs, but it was not to be.

Glenn sent us all a fax, setting out his terms and conditions for any possible resumption. He blamed stress and cited the "unique dynamics" of the band as a contributory factor.

"Unfortunately," he wrote, "the Eagles experience is a stressful one for me. Although it's what I call 'positive stress,' it is stress nonetheless. So the big questions for me are: How do I handle my commitment to the December shows and also continue to make some sort of effort to work on a studio album with you guys? I've given this a lot of thought. At this time, here is what I'm willing to do." He then set out five conditions for his returning to work, which included preparing five "Glenn songs" for the album, along with any songs he might coauthor, and agreeing to work on Joe's material. The lines were being drawn.

To me it seemed the problem was that we hadn't played a concert together publicly for more than three years and hadn't socialized much either. The last time we'd seen each other had been the Hall of Fame awards, and that hadn't been the best of atmospheres.

Irving's new plan was to piece together the best of the Millennium concerts—featuring a few never-before-recorded but nonetheless old songs—for a box set to be released in 2000. That way, we'd be getting a new product out to the public, thus keeping us in the open market until we could finally get it together to release a new studio album. He had also done a deal to offer the previously unreleased songs to download for free on the Internet, setting a new precedent in music marketing (although the songs were later withdrawn due to "unforeseen publishing licensing problems").

I had more serious problems to worry about. I'd decided that, once the concerts were over and the New Year had arrived, I'd be telling Susan that I was leaving her.

It's a terrible feeling, knowing you're about to do something irrevocable and heartbreaking to your wife and kids but being unable to prevent it. Marriage counseling wasn't an option—we'd been in therapy for years—and I knew that neither Susan nor I could or would change. It wasn't that I didn't love her anymore. I always would, but her jewelry business was her life now—a life I had helped her create, as an antidote to being the wife of an absentee rock star. I knew that I only had myself to blame for all the pain and suffering I had caused and that I was about to cause more, but I also knew that I couldn't remain in that marriage a moment longer.

The kids were grown. Jesse was married, with a son of his own and another child on the way. Rebecca was caught up in Susan's business. Cody was finally finding his footing. And Leah was so busy with her hectic teenage social life that she barely seemed to notice my existence. I felt confident that, after the initial shock, they'd come to see that I was right. Whenever I asked them, none of them could even remember the last time they saw Susan and me cuddle or kiss. Was I to stay in that lonely, sterile environment forever, just for the sake of propriety?

I faced the Millennium concert rehearsals just after Thanksgiving with a heavy heart. They would, in some ways, be a welcome distraction. When I arrived at Culver Studios, I quickly gathered that there was much that had to be redone and relearned. Hours were spent in discussion with the lighting designer and the monitor crew, and for some time, we were unable to concentrate on the music at all. For us old-time rockers, the move into the twenty-first century, with its high-tech wizardry, was not always easy.

As well as worrying about the technical side of the gigs, we were running back and forth between the studio and the rehearsal hall near Pico and Sepulveda. When we did try to make music, none of us seemed to be playing very well, and there was even more friction than usual between Don and Glenn, who'd completely abandoned any ideas of writing together. Part of the problem was, I think, that they simply ran out of words. With more than fifty Eagles songs under their belts between them, not to mention their individual solo efforts, their vocabulary, like their patience, was running thin. Their broad-sweeping panorama had always been Los Angeles, and there were only so many ways you could describe the people and the desert and the paradoxes of this extraordinary city before drying up.

On December 7, 1999, a couple of weeks before the gigs, Irving set up a press conference in the rehearsal hall so that we could receive official plaques commemorating record sales for *Greatest Hits, 1971–1975*, the album the record company had released almost as a stalling tactic while we finished *Hotel California*.

"You'll just have to stop rehearsing for a few minutes, come out, say hello, play a song and then you can get right back to work," he told us confidently.

We were right up against the wire, time-wise, and could have done without the interruption, but we did as we were told and conducted a quick sound check before the press conference. The five of us wandered out into the rehearsal hall with cups of coffee and our instruments and sat on five stools in a row, playing a few verses of "Tequila Sunrise" to a half-empty room while some stagehands set up chairs in readiness.

A few hours later, when we walked back out onto that stage, we were faced with a barrage of flashbulbs and a flurry of activity. There were many television cameras, about forty still photographers, and maybe fifty international press reporters, their notepads in hand. The numbers of chairs put out was woefully inadequate. There was a live broadcast on CNN's *Showbiz Today* with Jim Moret, and we were also live on the Web. It was the largest press conference we'd ever faced. I think we all realized then how important this award was. It wasn't just Irving blowing smoke up our ass.

Hilary Rosen, chairman and chief executive of the Recording Industry Association of America, had flown in from Washington to present us with the plaque and to declare *Greatest Hits* the biggest-selling album of the twentieth century, with 26 million units sold. It even outsold Michael Jackson's *Thriller*, which was close behind us and which many considered to be the album of the epoch.

Don told the assembled media that as he couldn't remember much about the seventies, it was nice to have the plaque to remind him what he'd been up to. He added, "I think the real award is that we're all alive and well when so many of our colleagues aren't." We all echoed that.

In answer to a question about the effect the Eagles had on people's lives, Glenn replied, "The music you play is the soundtrack of your life. It's your life movie. . . . In the seventies, people did things to the Eagles. They broke up with their girlfriend. They broke up with their boyfriend. They got in a car and drove across America. They went on a fandango. We seemed to be the soundtrack . . . people like having our music in the background of their movie."

I told the reporters, "This is beyond my wildest imagination. It's an amazing award and one none of us really expected. It is a testament to the songwriting of these two guys right here. Those songs stood the test of time."

Asked about ongoing friction between band members, Glenn replied, with one-hundred-percent honesty, "We're putting up a front for you, you know. We're on TV." When the laughter died away, he added, "I think any worthwhile relationship has its peaks and valleys. This band's had some valleys, but we're probably in pretty good shape right now."

Of the Millennium gigs, he added, "I think the nostalgia and the feelings that are associated with a band like the Eagles are going to be amplified to a degree that we've never experienced. To stand in southern California on New Year's Eve and play all these songs, which are so much about California, so many of them written in California, where we lived, I think I'm looking forward to a pretty emotional evening myself. I'm going to cry."

Hilary Rosen assured me privately that Bernie and Randy would each be given a copy of the plaque. In my opinion they should have been there to receive it in person. They were as much responsible for that album as Don, Glenn, or me, and certainly more than Joe or Tim, who were not even on any of the tracks on this album, but "The Gods" would never have allowed it. When we'd received our award and posed for photographs, we picked up our guitars and sat on the stools we'd practiced on earlier and played "Tequila Sunrise." As always, it was a brilliantly convincing performance of unity.

I have to say, that award really blew me away. Don described it, very aptly, as musical Viagra. I'd been completely oblivious to how well that album had actually done. I knew it had sold consistently over the years but didn't realize exactly how well until that moment. Never in my wildest childhood dreams did I expect to surpass my idols Elvis Presley, Bill Haley and His Comets, or B.B. King in record sales. I thought of the time I'd jammed down in Colored Town or stood in that barn watching B.B. play, and I had to pinch myself to believe what we'd achieved.

It seemed amazing to me, at the age of fifty-two, that I could have made my living doing what I'd always wanted to do ever since I swapped my cherry bombs for my first guitar. My marriage had all but survived the rigors of years on the road, even if it was in its death throes now, and I had four fantastic kids, a grandson, and a beautiful home. Whichever way I looked at it, I was rich beyond the dreams of Gainesville and would never have to work again. I think even my father might have been proud.

The Millennium concerts—dubbed by fans the Eaglennium—went ahead, despite a serious dose of the flu that left me barely able to stand. It began a few days before the first show and lasted all the way into January. I was so sick. I had a high fever, was clogged with mucus, and couldn't speak without coughing up fluid from my lungs. There was never any suggestion of canceling. We had a multimillion-dollar performance bond, and New Year's Eve, 1999, was not a gig you could cancel and just reschedule. I knew I had to go on, no matter what.

Jackson Browne opened for us with his usual professional set, featuring his classics such as "Doctor My Eyes," "The Pretender," and "Running on Empty." My old rival David Lindley played with him, and David Crosby joined him onstage for the song "For Everyman."

Then it was our turn. Standing in front of the top half of a giant clock face with Roman numerals, beneath huge stained-glass chandeliers, flanked by a scarlet curtain, we opened with "Hotel California," which the fired-up audience of twelve thousand of our most dedicated fans was well programmed to receive, then continued with the usual playlist: "Victim of Love," "New Kid in Town," and "Wasted Time."

I could hardly stay upright on stage and couldn't see beyond the lights because of my flu delirium. The music we were playing seemed to roar like the sea in my ears. I'd had four different doctors give me different prescriptions. I was dosed up to the eyeballs with injections and pills. Susan and the kids were there to give me support as I lay down on the floor of my dressing room, shivering, between sets. Thankfully, there was a twenty-minute intermission, during which a film, coproduced by Glenn, was shown on giant video screens. It was a montage of music and images of the century, run with a score Glenn wrote with songwriter Jay Oliver, and a series of spoof interviews, with each of us claiming the credit for naming the band and writing "Hotel California," in a misjudged attempt to make us look like humorous best buddies. After the intermission, I staggered back out onto the stage. I tried to keep my voice from breaking during a rendition of "Seven Bridges Road," and then I tried to rock. I was having a really hard time under the hot lights and never received a flicker of sympathy from "The Gods."

In my view, our performances on those interminable three nights weren't great, especially bearing in mind how much people had paid to hear us play. Glenn sang Randy's "Take It to the Limit," but without his uniquely soulful voice, it simply didn't work. Thankfully, the crowd sang along to almost every song, bolstering us through our weakest moments. Our only really good number was a new rhythm-and-blues version of "The Best of My Love," which sizzled. For that song, we were on fire.

To appease those who wanted to hear new or different material, we included some seldom-heard numbers like Tom Waits' "Ol' 55," "Those Shoes," and "Please Come Home for Christmas," saving "Funky New Year" for the fireworks-spitting encore, snippets of which were broadcast live on CNN shortly after midnight on New Year's Eve as the chosen celebration for the West Coast of America. Bang in the middle of "Funky New Year," Don for some reason sang a "Millennium Rap," trying to sound like some New York rap artist and failing badly. "We got back together, we broke up," he said, clicking his fingers in time. "We got back together, we broke up, we broke up, we got back together." Nobody, least of all us, found it terribly amusing, except him.

As the clock struck midnight and Joe played "Auld Lang Syne," I slumped over my guitar with relief. The ordeal was over. I searched for Susan at the side of the stage to give her a kiss, but she was nowhere to be found.

Back home after New Year's Eve, I gradually recovered from the flu and gained my physical and mental strength for what I knew was to come. Susan and I were communicating largely through notes left on the kitchen work surface. I felt starved of affection and horribly lonely in my own home. Finally, one day in late January, I took off to Palm Springs to escape what had become an untenable situation. I'd tried to reach her during the day but eventually left her a note, which said, "Gone to the Palm Springs Film Festival and to play golf."

When she called me at my hotel later that night and asked me why I had just taken off, I blurted out all that I was feeling about my marriage.

"It's over, Susan," I told her, the words sticking in my throat. "I know this probably isn't the kindest way to tell you, but I'm afraid that's the truth. We're not in love anymore. I'm so sorry."

I know I didn't handle it very well and that I should have had the courage to break it to her personally, but I was just so tired of waiting for her to find a window in her busy schedule so I could tell her we were through.

I honestly thought she would have seen this coming, but her response was far from expected. She was absolutely devastated and refused to communicate with me, dealing only with our family therapist. In an atmosphere of bitter recrimination, I moved out onto my boat, and within a week I was served with divorce papers. The kids were shattered. One by one, they came by the boat, and we held each other and cried together.

"I will always love your mother. I just can't live with her anymore," I told them. If I could have taken away any of the hurt, I would have, but it was too late. The sense of cold isolation I felt left me unable to sleep or eat. I felt as if a piece of my heart had been cut out. Thus began a long, sustained period of darkness that crept over every aspect of my life and plunged me to new depths of despair.

Never once did Glenn or Don call me up and offer any support or sympathy over the breakdown of my twenty-nine-year marriage. Not once did they phone to ask, "Hey, man, are you OK?" Glenn had been divorced; he knew what it was like. Joe, Timothy, even Irving called up. Many other people, including some I least expected, offered their support. When you're going through such a shitty time, you come to realize that the ones who step up are your real friends. The rest no longer count.

Work became a welcome distraction. "Let's go into the studio and finish the record from the Millennium gig," Irving told us.

"But we don't even have a record deal yet," I pointed out.

"Don't worry," he assured me, that smile of his ever more unnerving. "The negotiations are well underway. Just go in and do this on a 'good faith' basis, and we'll fine-tune the details later."

The venue was preset: Glenn's Dog House, and Elliot Scheiner as the producer, no questions asked. The recording needed a great deal of post-production work, all of which was done with each member separately and Glenn as an invisible producer, so that he never actually had to work directly with any of the other band members. He'd spent the five months since the gigs deciding which recording of which song to choose from which night. Once he'd made his selection and completed his own vocal and guitar parts, he set dates for each of us to go in separately and fix our own parts.

Don Henley, alias Grandpa, was scheduled to come in last, after everyone else had finished, because every hair on his entire body would have stood straight on end if he had heard the first takes.

Trouble was, we weren't at the Record Plant or Criteria. Glenn was at his home in Hawaii, playing golf or doing some corporate show for big bucks—a lucrative new sideline of his. Don was on tour or busy in Dallas or promoting his new pet project, the Recording Artists' Coalition, professing equality for musicians in the business, campaigning to change what he called the unfair practices of record companies.

Nobody seemed to be talking to anyone else. Joe and Tim were scheduled to come in at separate times from me. Nothing I said seemed to matter. I felt our sound had become glossy, corporate, less human, and in my opinion, downright lousy, if you want to know the truth. Then again, the album's later sales show that millions of people disagreed, so what did I know? They just don't know what they're missing.

Despite Irving's repeated warnings not to make waves, I never stopped asking to see the various documents that would allow me and my attorneys to assess the deals that Don, Glenn, and Irving were making, especially this new one, which could potentially be our most important. Because of my continued interest in the current negotiations, many of the feelings that had been harbored against me in the seventies and eighties resurfaced. I was made to feel isolated and out of the loop once more. For whatever reason, the Triumvirate didn't like me asking too many questions.

Maybe because of my newfound courage from having just dealt with the unhappiness of my marriage, I didn't take Irving's warnings too seriously. Susan and I had a long way to go before we'd be talking again, but the fact that I had faced up to the demise of my marriage and come out the other side lulled me into a false sense of security as to how much I could push a situation. Incident after incident with Don, Glenn, and Irving made me realize that the time was coming when I would have to stand up to "The Gods" as well, and say or do something to stop them treating the rest of us like lowly subordinates. A classic example was that of Timothy Drury and John Corey. Timothy was a multitalented musician who toured with us for years and who'd played on Don's solo tours before that. John, who played keyboards, was much the same and had cowritten some of Don's solo songs.

Timothy had written a short classical segue, a beautiful piece of music that he played on a piano during the intermission of each show every night during the *Hell Freezes Over* tour. John played the string part so that it sounded like an orchestral introduction. When that music started, we knew, on cue, that half of us would walk out from stage left and half from stage right, our gait in perfect time to the music, and set up on five stools placed at the front of the stage. Just as we all sat down, the music would end, and Glenn would say, "Hi, and welcome back to the second half of our show," and we'd launch into an acoustic version of "Tequila Sunrise." It worked like a dream.

When it came to putting together the music for the box set, I heard that Don, Glenn, and Irving decided that they wanted to use that little piece of music that Timothy had written and played live. He was delighted, thinking he'd have a tiny slice of the lucrative writers' and publishers' royalties on an Eagles record, but that wasn't the deal.

Irving told him he just wanted to do a buyout and offered Timothy a couple of thousand dollars.

Timothy was horrified but had told me it was a take-it-or-leave-it deal.

Timothy couldn't believe it. He'd let the Eagles use that piece of music over and over for six years. He'd been pounding around on the road with us for all these years. The music was not included.

Fred Walecki, our old friend from Westwood Music, developed throat cancer that year and had to have his voice box removed. Days after his surgery, which cost six figures and wasn't fully covered by his medical insurance, Bernie Leadon contacted Jackson Browne, Linda Ronstadt, and Glyn Johns—the English producer who'd put the first Eagles albums together and shared Bernie's country rock vision—and the four of them decided to organize a benefit gig. Word hit the streets, and a veteran lineup of California's finest musicians agreed to play the gig that August. Among them were Don Henley, Randy Meisner, Graham Nash, David Lindley, David Crosby, Linda Ronstadt, Chris Hillman, and Ry Cooder. Over two nights at the Santa Monica Civic Auditorium, the friends of Fred Walecki stepped up and played, as Fred sat, with his new electronic voice box, in a seat of honor at the front of the stage.

Randy, Bernie, and Don all played separately. Randy brought his own band and sang "Take It to the Limit" and "Already Gone," Don sang "Desperado" and a couple of his solo hits. Bernie stayed onstage most of the night as a backup musician, but they never all played together. Randy's wife, who wanted a photograph of her husband with Don Henley, approached him with her camera and asked him if he'd mind posing. Without saying a word, Don turned on his heel and walked away.

I was very hurt not to have been invited along. I knew Fred well and would have gladly volunteered my services. I knew most of the people on that stage intimately, and yet no one had thought to pick up the phone. I began to wonder how much my ongoing negotiations with Irving and "The Gods" were affecting every aspect of my life, including my associations with such good friends in the business.

Later that year, I finally moved off the boat and started looking around for someplace of my own to live. I decided to rent a house in L.A. to begin with, until I could find what I wanted to buy. The divorce negotiations were proceeding at a snail's pace, now that Susan's lawyers were involved—even though I'd told her from the start that I was happy for her to have half of everything I owned. I didn't yet know exactly how much I'd be left with or even if I wanted to stay in L.A.

There were times when I wondered where my life was leading. I was homeless, divorcing, and without any sense of self-worth. I hated myself for what I'd done to my family, I resented Irving and "The Gods" for what they were doing to me, and I longed for a return to the happier days of my youth, when the Eagles were just starting out and Susan and I were different people.

"I feel like we're on the brink of something here," I'd said in the Miyako Hotel in San Francisco the night she'd first told me she was pregnant. "Like this could really be the beginning, you know?" Twenty-nine years on, and it felt like everything was ending. The brink I faced now was far less appealing.

During the extremely dispiriting process of being newly single after almost three decades of marriage, while searching for a small rental house on my own, something extraordinary and totally unexpected happened. I met

Kathrin Nicholson who made me feel as if I'd tripped and fallen into heaven. From the moment I set eyes on her, it was like I'd been reunited with someone I'd been madly in love with for hundreds of years. Kathrin was beautiful and, although almost twenty years younger than me, had a wise head on her shoulders. She was like a bright light illuminating the darkest period of my life, a lighthouse on a stormy coast, as steadfast as could be, showing me the way. Believe me, I have clung to that light beam ever since.

After months of trying to find out the details of the deal from Irving, I was finally told. A new company called NEA had been set up to handle the box set, with Don and Glenn as its sole owners.

I was never told what NEA stood for. I assumed it was New Eagles Agreement, although it might well have been Never Expect Anything. Elektra, with distribution through Giant Records, Irving's company, was releasing the box set, called *Selected Works 1972–1999*, in November 2000, in time for the Christmas market. Music from the Millennium gigs would feature on the last of four discs.

When I called Irving and dared to suggest that what he was suggesting might not be fair, the man who'd once said he had more money than God was unequivocal.

"If you don't sign that fucking deal," he screamed at me over the telephone with that terrifying, booming voice of his, "you'll never set foot onstage with these guys again." And I was paying him commissions?

Furious, I screwed all my courage up into a ball and yelled back. "Don't talk to me like that, Irving," I shouted. "Do you ever call up Don and Glenn and scream at them over the phone? If you want to talk to me reasonably about this, then call me back when you've calmed down, but don't fucking scream at me. You're supposed to be my manager too, remember?"

To my amazement, Irving apologized and seemed calmer for a day or two, but within the week, he was back on the phone, swearing and cursing and threatening. Don and Glenn were out of town and permanently unavailable. I hadn't had any contact with either of them since New Year's Eve. When I told Irving I wanted to speak to them, he went into the stratosphere. "Don't you dare call those guys," he shrieked. "They'll freak out if you do, and that'll be the end of it." I didn't know which way to turn.

I knew Irving was playing everybody off against everyone else, as he always did, and that I was probably being portrayed as the one who was unnecessarily delaying matters for the box-set deal, which had to be in the stores by Christmas. I was depicted as "the wrench in the works."

Whatever reservations Timothy and Joe may have had privately, they signed the agreement without question, leaving me completely isolated. I agonized over what to do and spoke to my lawyers about my legal position, but it was obvious I had no real choice.

As one musician who worked with them had once told me prophetically, "We're just pumping gas in Mr. Henley's gas station."

It felt to me like we'd all been on the same farm eating from the same trough, but two pigs had gotten so fat they were crowding everyone else out. If I were to try to force myself into the trough, I'd be run off the farm. I didn't want that to happen. The farm was all I knew. Reluctantly and with bile in my throat, I signed their damn papers. The so-called equal partnership was over.

Christmas 2000 was to be my first on my own, without my family. I didn't have any lights or any ornaments. I'd only just moved off the boat and was living in much reduced circumstances. Kathrin, ever sensitive to my emotional needs and worried for my health since the band had steamrollered me, came up with an idea.

"I know," she said, brightly. "Let's buy a small Christmas tree and invite a few close friends and ask each one to bring an ornament for a festive tree-trimming party. That way, we can start again with our very own decorations." Her suggestion was so genuine and heartfelt, I could have wept.

We invited a bunch of people, including Joe Walsh and Timothy Schmit, to come and help us in our small celebration. I didn't invite Glenn, Don, or Irving, none of whom I'd seen since being forced to sign the new agreement, and not just because of the delicate situation with them, but also because, frankly, I was embarrassed about where and how I was living. Irving's main house is a $25 million mansion in Beverly Hills. Glenn has a similar, $10 million house nearby, and Don's, in Dallas, is even more impressive. I was renting a one-bedroom single-story building off Mulholland Drive, living out of suitcases, my belongings packed in lockers in a downtown storage unit.

I'll admit that, with the way I felt that they were bludgeoning me emotionally and financially, I also didn't feel inclined to invite them into my home at that time. Apart from the unexpected delight of having Kathrin in my life, I was miserable enough about everything without having to put on a fake smile. In any event, neither Joe nor Tim turned up anyway. Their ornaments arrived courtesy of Federal Express.

When Sean, a kid from Irving's office, came around that holiday season with the usual van full of Christmas gifts from the Eagles and Irving's office, the back of his "sled on wheels" was laden with huge baskets of fruit and flowers, toiletries and candy, ostentatiously wrapped in cellophane and ribbons, being sent out to everyone connected with the band.

"Merry Christmas, Mr. Felder," the young assistant told me as I opened the door to my house and prepared to help him carry my gifts inside.

"Merry Christmas, Sean," I said, managing a smile.

As I stood watching, he reached into the back of the van and pulled out two small presents. They were from Timothy and Joe.

"Is that it?" I said, staring at him at disbelief.

"I'm afraid so, Mr. Felder," Sean said, before jumping into the driver's seat and driving off with the rest of his goodies. For the first time in decades, neither Irving nor Don had sent me a thing. I stood there shivering in the driveway as the electric gates slid shut behind him.

My attorney, Barry Tyerman, had penciled a date on his calendar to check back with Irving on the progress of the box-set deal. The date finally arrived in early February, and Barry duly fired off a gentle letter, asking for copies of certain agreements with the record label. A response came back that they were not signed.

Two days later, I went out with Kathrin for the evening to see a play about the Notre Dame football team, at the Ahmanson Theatre, with our friend Gordon Davidson, the theater director. We rode back with Gordon in the car afterward, laughing about how awful the play was.

"It was so bad, it was funny," I joked. Gordon dropped us home, and we walked into the house arm in arm, still laughing about our evening.

It was eleven thirty when I clicked on the answering machine. There was just one message. It was from Irving, left three hours earlier.

"Fingers, call me at home, here's my number, I gotta talk to you." The very fact that he'd called me at all was highly unusual, and there was a tone to his voice I didn't like the sound of.

Sitting on the edge of the bed while Kathrin made some coffee, I dialed his number immediately, even though it was late.

"Irv, it's Don Felder," I said, wondering what was so urgent that he'd give me his home number.

"Hi, Fingers," he said, with a sigh. "I've got some bad news, I'm afraid. The guys have had a meeting, and they've decided to go on without you."

My entire body ran cold as his words lingered in the air, their resonance hitting me in waves. "W-w-what?" I stammered, my mind tripping and tumbling.

"It's nothing to do with your playing, it's nothing to do with you, they just think it's in the best interests of the band if they let you go."

"Oh, my God, Irving," I said, blood rushing to my head. "They can't do this. What do they mean? Why are they doing this? What . . . ?" But the words died on my lips. Tears spurted from my eyes, and I started trembling all over. I felt as if I'd been hit by a truck.

Irving told me to calm down and try to get some sleep, but of course I couldn't. I sat up most of the night with Kathrin, writhing with anxiety. At seven o'clock in the morning, I called Irving back, hoping to catch him before he went to work, but I couldn't get hold of him until about three.

"Yup," he told me. "I've spoken to them, and they're determined to go ahead with this. They're gonna send a letter over to your attorney this afternoon, confirming that you're fired."

I listened in disbelief, still unable to take in what I was hearing. "I just don't understand," I said. "I thought we were meant to be in this together. Forever."

"I know, I know," Irving sighed. "But it just didn't work out that way."

"Irving," I said breathlessly, "I'll do anything, I don't care. Tell them there's been a misunderstanding. I signed their agreements and it's cool. I don't want to be out of the band."

Kathrin sat with me for the next two hours, while I sat by the phone, anxiously waiting for word.

Irving eventually rang back. "Sorry, Fingers," he said. "You're still fired."

"Give me Don's phone number. I wanna speak to Don in person," I told Irving. The numbers I had for him were obsolete. My distress and fear had turned to anger. "I'm fed up with speaking through you. I want to speak to 'The Gods.'"

He didn't give me Don's number. In sheer frustration, I dialed all the numbers I had for Don and left messages with his secretary and his business manager, but he never returned my calls.

In a last exasperated act, I called Glenn's studio, and to my astonishment, he came to the phone. Overwhelmed at hearing his voice, I begged him not to get rid of me. "I'll do anything you say, Roach," I told him. "But don't cut me off like this. The Eagles is all I know."

"I never want to get another fucking letter from Barry Tyerman," he said, gruffly. Hearing the obvious emotion in my voice, he added witheringly, "Try to reach some higher ground on this, Felder." The phone line went dead.

My legs dropped away from under me, and I slumped to the floor. Kathrin helped me into a chair and did all she could to calm me down. The combined emotions of the last year, of all the years of angst I'd gone through with the band, hit me in the chest like a mallet. I couldn't breathe properly and I couldn't speak. I felt physically sick. When I had sufficiently composed myself, the first person I called was Joe.

"What the hell's going on, Joe?" I asked, still distraught.

His attitude was decidedly cool. "Well, I dunno, Fingers," he said lamely, from his home in San Diego. "As far as I can see, those guys have decided that they're gonna do what they're gonna do. There ain't much I can do about it."

I'd never been more in need of my old buddy Joe, but he wasn't there for me anymore. There was no compassion in his voice. There was no offer to "come up and have a beer and we can talk about it." His response was shattering. Joe had always been my friend. We'd spent the most time together of all the band members over the years, hanging out in his room, taking drugs, drinking too much, sawing up hotel rooms, playing on his ham radio. I'd driven him to rehab, for Christ's sake. I'd taken care of his daughter on the road. Now, when push came to shove, he was going with the rest of the band and the money. He wasn't even going to try to fight for me. I felt betrayed.

"Well, thanks, Joe," I told him, angrily. "Right now I feel like blowing my own brains out. If I ever take this nine-millimeter gun out of my mouth, I'll be sure to call ya."

We've not spoken since.

The last conversation I had with any of the Eagles was with Tim, whom I'd also considered a good friend for many years. To my utter dismay, his response was similar to Joe's.

"What's going on, Fingers?" he said, his tone irritable, when his wife, Jean, handed him the phone. "All I know is they sent me some papers, they looked good, and I told my attorney that I'd sign. Why couldn't you just sign the papers like everyone else so we can get on with this? You keep harking back to some deal you made in the seventies, which is history. I don't know why you think you're entitled to more."

"You don't understand," I told him. "I'm not doing this just for me, you know. I'm doing it for you and Joe and Randy, and Bernie, too. My Lord, don't you realize? If Irving was representing us against Don and Glenn, he'd never let us anywhere near these contracts."

Timothy sighed. "You should have just signed the damn papers and sent them back," he said, before hanging up.

My next call was to Susan. After all the years she'd endured of me being an Eagle, I felt she had a right to know. She listened in silence as I told her what had happened and then said something unexpected.

"You know, Don," she told me, "this is probably the best thing that could have happened to you. You've been in that unhealthy, abusive environment for far too long. It's affected your health, and it's indirectly caused the death of our marriage. I'm glad you're out of the whole nightmare. You're a free man. Use that freedom wisely."

My respect and admiration for the mother of my children and the woman I had shared my life with grew enormously. To her eternal credit, her support and sympathy was unequivocal, despite all I'd done to break her heart. I was hurting far too much at the time to realize just how true her words were, but I came to understand afterward that she was right.

The official termination notice sent to my lawyers stated that "the company's board of directors decided that the needs and goals of the company were better served on an ongoing basis" without me. They added that it was "in the best interests of the company" to "terminate" my employment. But there was something else. They wanted my shares in Eagles Ltd. They even sent my business manager a check to buy them back. They had another think coming. On my instruction, he sent it right back.

TWENTY

I dreaded reading the official announcement of my departure from the band in black and white. When I did, in a small newspaper article two weeks later, it was as if someone had taken a baseball bat and hit me in the solar plexus. Up until that moment, my attorney had still been trying to negotiate on my behalf, and I'd held a small, flickering candle of hope that it was all some terrible mistake and that I'd still be able to reach out to Don and Glenn in some way. When I saw the announcement in print, it stuck to the flypaper of my brain. I knew then that hell would never freeze over again.

For months afterward, I was left gasping for breath. I walked around in a daze, wondering what the hell I was supposed to do with my life. My foundations had been shaken, not just with the breakdown of my marriage, but the end of my career. Everything I'd known was gone. For twenty-nine years of my life, I'd been married and for twenty-seven years of my life, I'd been an Eagle. I didn't know anything else. Being an Eagle was my identity. To lose it felt like a bereavement, and I went into mourning for well over a year. I worried that I might collapse under the weight of my grief. Now I knew how Susan felt, I realized with humility, to have had the world ripped out from under her. I suddenly missed everything about being in the band: the hours in the studio, the times on the road, the gigs, the friendships, and the fun. My mind rewound and replayed my times with them, quickly fast-forwarding over all the bad stuff and the long months of hell. If I pressed pause and allowed myself a tiny glimpse, I convinced myself that even those times would be better than this sense of utter desolation and emptiness.

Kathrin was an absolute godsend. I'd wake in the early hours with a panic attack, and she'd comfort me. I'd sit with a cup of coffee, staring into the fireplace late into the night, wallowing in self-pity. Sometimes she'd just sit with me, her hand in mine, soaking up the silence and allowing me to cry. I felt like I was dying inside. There wasn't a single hour of my day when I didn't mourn my loss.

"How could they treat me so badly after all we've been through together?" I'd ask her, my throat closing around my vocal cords. "Don't I deserve better than this?" I felt helpless in the face of their cruelty, their actions cutting through me like a knife.

It took months and months, but very slowly, Kathrin taught me how to accept what had happened and reinvent myself completely. She made me put the whole event into perspective, to see that I was still extraordinarily lucky and to realize that I had to decide what I was going to do and how to rebuild my life.

With her help, I tried to concentrate on the positives. "Count your blessings," as my mother would say, whenever I'd complain as a child about not being able to afford a new bike or a new pair of shoes. I came to see that although being an Eagle hadn't been the easiest of roads, it had enabled me to have innumerable moments of pure exhilaration and unadulterated joy. I'd started as the new kid in town, with long blond hair, a beard and mustache, in a brown leather jacket, driving a battered old Volvo, looking for some session work. Thanks to Bernie's generous introductions, I was a guitar player who got lucky and wound up in a band that, for thirty years, remained in the fast lane of rock's superhighway. After years of the kind of life most guitar players would give their favorite Les Paul for, I had weathered the most savage of storms and come through unscathed—well, maybe a little battered and graying at the edges—but I'd somehow survived to tell the tale.

Whatever else I'd achieved, I know I helped make some great music, arguably some of the most enduring of the twentieth century. It was widely agreed that my guitar playing had been a cornerstone of the Eagles' success. My defining moments had been standing on the stage in the spotlight playing the first few chords of the best song I ever wrote. Between us, we'd made the music that a whole generation had grown up with. They'd laughed and loved and lived and cried to our songs. Some of our older listeners might not be able to remember what they did yesterday, but they can still remember every word of "Hotel California." We still have an estimated 100 million fans worldwide.

But, my Lord, I paid my dues for the privilege. I spent years on the road away from my family, missing my wife and kids; I suffered stress-related health problems and spent sleepless, drug-fed nights wondering if it was all worth it. I endured untold emotional abuse from people who should have been my best friends. We'd been through so much. We'd laughed and loved and lived and cried to the same songs as our audience, but the bottom line is, we never really got along. I realize that now. From the first day I walked into the Record Plant studio, that band was breaking up. Everyone was at each other's throat, emotionally and artistically. We just never clicked the way some bands did. A self-destruct mechanism was constantly ticking away. Beneath a rigid code of silence that hid our fractured, contentious side from the public and allowed our mythical peaceful, easy image to continue, our dream of stardom and togetherness slowly morphed into a Hotel California–style nightmare. Terrified of speaking out in case I made things worse, my years of acquiescence meant that I could check out but I could never leave.

I can remember looking at other bands, like Chicago or U2, and envying their unqualified camaraderie. Those bands were like brothers. They not only got along well with each other onstage and in the studio, they socialized together, went on vacation with each other, and babysat each other's kids. Where was the love like that in the Eagles? It never existed. We might as well have been a group of session musicians who'd never met and didn't give a damn about anything but the music, putting our heads together to create a sound and then going our respective ways. To some of us, money came before friendship at every turn. The minute we came off tour, no one called each other or went over to another's house to say, "Hey, wasn't that great?"

There we were, blessed with this amazing success that should have brought us to our knees with gratitude and humility, hailed as the greatest band America had ever produced, but instead of reveling in every moment of it, sharing the joy of this charmed existence with each other and our families, we were too busy tearing each other apart. As Timothy sang in his haunting song "I Can't Tell You Why," we made it harder than it had to be. Our American Dream was systematically destroyed by egos and perfectionism and greed. We worried away at each other like the tip of a tongue on a sore tooth.

Then, after years of loyal service, of putting up with all the crap, "The Gods" told me my services were no longer required. That really hurt. Although we'd never clicked socially, after all those years of being thrown together in the most bizarre and extreme of circumstances, these guys were closer than family. Hell, they *were* my family.

I know now that they had to get rid of me because I was asking too many awkward business questions and was about to expose them for what they were. I guess they've been busy with the shredders ever since. Well, all right. So be it. In a way, it came as a horrible relief. I was damned if I was going to just walk away from the legacy I'd helped to create, though. After years of being browbeaten into submission, I was finally going to stand up for what I believed.

Three people own Eagles Ltd.—Don Henley, Glenn Frey, and Don Felder. We own the rights to the name *the Eagles*, including the right to use that name on record or on tour and the right to license it for use on merchandise. There was a major difference between my so-called departure and that of Bernie and Randy. I never quit, and I never surrendered or offered up my shares of stock. According to our corporate agreement, which is still valid, someone had to leave of his own volition for that to happen. They couldn't just boot me out of the company, then try to buy my shares back at whatever price they deemed fair. Their offer was both arrogant and misguided. It also made me realize what I had to do.

In February 2001 I filed a lawsuit against Eagles Ltd. in the California Superior Court, Los Angeles. I had two choices, to tuck my tail between my legs and walk away, or to fight back. For way too long, I'd walked away. Now Don, Glenn, and Irving had given me no choice. My attorneys assured me that I had a very strong case of wrongful termination and breach of contract. Judging from past experience, Don and Irving—no strangers to litigation—would fight at first but then settle.

My final suit alleged involuntary dissolution of Eagles Ltd., breach of implied-in-fact employment contract, wrongful termination, violation of public policy, breach of fiduciary responsibility, and breach of written contract, and sought full accounting and declaratory relief. The wording of the suit claimed that Glenn and Don treated me as a "hired hand" for most of my time with the band, and used threats to intimidate me.

By the time my lawyers had finished, I was effectively demanding a complete accounting of every single business transaction by Eagles Ltd. since 1974, including record royalties and revenue from touring and merchandising, in accordance with the contract I signed in 2000, which gave me direct, free, and independent rights to examine the books. Further, I sought all outstanding monies owed to me, a fair market price for my shares in Eagles-related companies, plus attorney's fees and court costs. In a second, later lawsuit I named Eagles Ltd., and Don and Glenn's new companies, NEA, Eagles Touring Co., Eagles Merchandising, Eagles Recording Co., and other companies, as defendants. I also demanded a declaration confirming I could retain my share of Eagles Ltd., since I didn't quit and I didn't voluntarily walk away from it.

That lawsuit stated: "Despite each being a one-third owner of Eagles Ltd., Henley and Frey have consistently treated Felder as a subordinate, with complete disregard for his rights. . . . They have consistently voted as a block on business decisions and implemented these decisions, whether or not Felder objected. . . . [T]hey have repeatedly abused their authority and acted unfairly toward Felder and former band members Meisner and Leadon. This conduct has, almost without exception, been coupled with constant threats that if Felder did not agree with Henley and Frey, Felder would be thrown out of the band. . . . As the final straw . . . (they) terminated his employment with Eagles Ltd. by way of an invalid and sham board of directors meeting. . . . After years of taking advantage of Felder, Henley and Frey now seek to cause Eagles Ltd. to terminate him in order to force Felder out of the band and to deprive him of his financial interest and rights in Eagles Ltd."

Don and Glenn's attorneys countered: "The action of terminating Felder's relationship with the band was taken because it was in the best interest of the Eagles. The Eagles had every legal right to do so, and any claim by Felder to the contrary is completely without any merit. We don't feel it's appropriate to litigate the case in the press. The case will be determined in court, and we're confident that the position of the Eagles will be fully vindicated."

In March 2001, a month after my departure, the Recording Industry Association of America officially announced the Eagles as the third-best-selling band in the U.S. after the Beatles and Led Zeppelin. Elektra rated our sales as in excess of 83 million units.

During formal depositions for my pending court case in early 2002, I sat alone giving testimony opposite Irving—who winked at me across the table shortly before being asked to leave the room as he wasn't a party in the lawsuit. It was an intimidating experience for anyone. Strangely enough, I enjoyed every minute. It was as if my whole life had groomed me for that moment. Every answer I gave felt strong and proud and true. Staring Glenn in the eye, I described what it was like to be bullied and battered and abused. To every tough question, I had an answer. My long silence was finally over, and having found my voice, I wanted to shout from the rooftops.

From the day I first went to court, Don and Glenn deprived me of my rightful share of profits generated by the Eagles. The irony is that Don is still a spokesman for artists' rights, and on recent tours, some of the money raised went to the Recording Artists' Coalition. The trial date was set for September 2006, and a settlement was finally reached.

Emerging from the darkest period of my life and recovering my senses enough to focus on my future, I realized that my life stretched unfinished before me. I began work on a new solo project, the keyword of which was *fun*. Never again would I allow myself to be a pawn in somebody else's mind game. When it's done, I expect it to be full of screaming, guitar-driven tracks, melding the two generations and representing the passing of the baton from the senior to the junior players.

The Eagles went back into the studio, resurrecting Bill Szymczyk to produce their first new studio album together since 1979, and the first without me. Six years on, there was still no album. "There's not a lot of socializing going on," Don tellingly admitted to one magazine. In another interview he said, "Things don't really change that much, you know. People don't change that much . . . they just become more who they really are." Just as in the old days, to buy some time, they embarked on some short tours instead, playing all the old classics. They never replaced me, just hired a sideman to play all my guitar parts.

For three decades, the moneymaking enigma that the Eagles became has been able to keep our worldwide legion of fans in the dark about our inner workings. They've maintained a relentlessly positive image, almost as crucial to the band's success as its music. I was there every step of the way. In ending my silence and giving the first brutally honest account of what it was really like to be in one of the greatest but perhaps one of the most contentious rock bands of all time, I am not seeking revenge. Only to redress the balance for me, Bernie and Randy.

I've learned a great many things, not least that friends and family come before money. You have to stand up for what you believe in, and for too long, I didn't. That is my only regret. Some might say that only the lawyers emerge winners from such protracted lawsuits as ours. Maybe. But the time had come for wrongs to be righted, and I was determined to fight for justice for the sake of my kids, who sacrificed a great deal by having a dad in the Eagles.

I know I've had incredible good fortune. I joined a band that was blessed with phenomenal success. Despite everything, I'll always cherish what we achieved and remember with great fondness the good times we shared. The lust for money and power ultimately destroyed us. Egos got in the way of the music. It happens in many businesses, not just this one, but rarely has it happened in the arts in such a spectacularly disastrous or contentious way.

Looking at Randy and Bernie, I know we're better off for being away from the band. Each of us has found himself in the freedom of life beyond the Eagles. Randy has remarried and divides his time between Palm Springs and L.A. He's had modest success with his three solo albums and has formed a hard-hitting rock-and-roll band called World Classic Rockers, featuring musicians from Steppenwolf, Toto, and Van Halen, which has a lot of fun touring the clubs and corporate gigs of America.

Bernie, who contributed so much to the Eagles and wrote their first Top 10 hit, "Witchy Woman," is happily settled in Franklin, Tennessee, near Nashville, where he lives with his son. After years of being a performer, session man, songwriter, and producer, working with the greats, he became a "ballplayer turned manager" and is vice president of A&R Pioneer Music Group. We have remained in touch over the years, on the phone and by e-mail, and shall always be friends.

To this day, if any of the band members asked me to play with them, I would. I'd even step up and play alongside Glenn. I suspect Randy and Bernie would too. After all these years, those guys still feel like family to me. And like family members you don't always get along with all the time, the physical connection is there, underpinning everything. Blood is thicker than water, they say. We shed enough blood, sweat, and tears in the three decades we spent together, and our ties are strong. Despite the inevitable sadness of the litigation against my former band members, we have a unique history together that's even stronger than the bitterness, the re-criminations, and the addictive compulsion to make a dollar.

The future for me has never looked brighter. I'm fit, in good health, and have the love of a good woman. My children are thriving. Leah is about to embark on a career as a singer, thanks to Patrick Swayze's mother, Patsy, who runs a singing school, and the legendary vocal coach Joel Ewing, who set aside his usual rule against teaching children when he heard her voice. Cody is a brilliant percussionist, working as a writer and producer in Boston, having attended the Berklee College of Music, a few blocks from where Susan and I used to live. He still has his rebellious streak and prefers bands like Rage Against the Machine to the Eagles, but he is doing just fine. Rebecca, who has always been such a sweet-natured girl, has taken over the running of Susan's jewelry design business. Jesse, my eldest son, now has two kids and runs his own successful financial management company in Oregon.

My divorce from Susan finally came through in early 2002 after months of litigation and negotiation, which we eventually resolved through mediation. We sold the house, the plane, and all the rest of my property, and I gave her half of everything I owned, plus her business, without contest. I tried in every way I could to make that part of the process as painless as possible. My attitude was to lose a few dollars but save a few tears. She still gets fifty percent of all my income from the Eagles and has received half of what I was awarded by the eventual settlement. My Lord, she's entitled to it. As a bonus, I threw in *Wings.* She'd always loved that boat, even more than I did. I gave it to her with the message, "May you have sunny skies and calm waters."

We'd been together through all the tough years and only broke up right at the end. Our marriage lasted roughly the same amount of time as my union with the Eagles. We stayed together all that time not only because we truly loved each other and had four young kids but also because our parents never divorced. Susan suffered minute by minute and day by day at my side, and she was as much a part of the Eagles as I was. She knew what went on, and yet she forgave me. I guess in the end we just spent so much time apart that we couldn't hack it together anymore.

"We had four beautiful children together," she told me during the immediate aftermath of the divorce. "We're gonna see each other at weddings and births and funerals. For the sake of the kids, it would be great if we can at least get along. The sooner we can arrive at that place together, the happier everyone will be." We eventually accepted that, and we're fine. She's had a couple of new relationships since, and I wish her every happiness.

When I'm not enjoying my new life with Kathrin, I spend my spare time having lunch or playing golf with friends like Randy Meisner, living a very low-key life in L.A. I travel to Europe as much as possible. I enjoy the time I have with my grandchildren and look forward to having more. I don't live my days in the gossip columns, and I still don't squander money. I can walk down Sunset Boulevard and most of the time not be recognized. I have a good life.

Most of all, I'm looking forward to getting back out on the road and playing music again, promoting the new album and working on other, similar projects in the coming years. There are other singer/songwriters besides Don Henley and Glenn Frey. All I ever wanted to do, and what I came to California for, was to make music. Music is in my blood. My father first fostered it in the days when I used to plug my guitar into the television set and make up the soundtrack for *Mighty Mouse* cartoons, and with his encouragement, I've never lost the passion. I'm not exactly sure which direction I'm going to point the compass on the bow of my boat after this, but it will undoubtedly involve music. It's not as if I have a choice.

Although I didn't realize it at the time, my last performance with the Eagles was on December 31, 1999, at the Staples Center in Los Angeles as part of the Millennium celebrations. It truly was the eve of a new dawn.

I didn't give my finest performance. We'd all played a lot better at various times over the past three decades. Despite my ill health and the divisions that were tearing us apart, we put on a show that seemed to satisfy those who'd paid so much money to hear us play. Glenn was right. Bringing our unique mix of country, bluegrass, rock and roll, rhythm and blues, soul, Dixieland, and folk to the band from all parts of America, we somehow came up with the cinematic soundtrack to a generation. Sonic wallpaper, someone once called it. More than that, the music we'd played had been the soundtrack of our own lives. Every song we'd worked so slavishly over had its own secret story. Every guitar riff, drum track, and vocal had been agonized over. We all had our own favorites, songs that struck a chord with us as well as the fans. For me, "Hotel California" represents the pinnacle of my musical career.

As I stood on that stage beneath those crystal chandeliers and heard the roar of the crowd as I played the opening bars of the song I'd made my own, I knew that, whatever else happened in my life, this was as good as it gets. In my fevered brain, I closed my eyes and swayed in time to the chords I'd written that golden day in Malibu. For a moment, I was back in my childhood bedroom, standing alone under a single red lightbulb, playing for all I was worth. Or on the stage of the State Theater, my shirt sticking to my back with fear, as I hammered out a Ventures classic. Mine had been a remarkable journey. All of ours had. Here we were, the most successful American band of the century, televised to the world, for thousands of people who, like us, wondered what the new millennium would bring.

Behind me, the hands of the giant clock moved inexorably toward midnight. My fingers straining under the pressure of the complicated chords, I belted out the music I loved and allowed my mind to drift momentarily beyond all the petty bickering and the jealousy and the rivalry which had, in its own way, I knew, helped to make us great. It was a blessing and a curse, the price we had to pay for our genius. For now, I wanted to forget all that, to soar away on that dark desert highway. Against all odds, we'd made it. At the start of the twenty-first century, we were still together and still in California, taking it to the limit, one last time.

In March 2007, my mother passed away. She was ninety-one years old, and on her way home from church on a beautiful Florida morning. I went home to Gainesville to help Jerry bury her. The entire family flew in for the service and we had a wonderful get-together, recounting her life in photographs and sharing stories of our childhood. Walking around in my past filled me with a childish sense of wonder. I went to the palm meadows where Leonard Gideon and I used to play forts, and I found the swamp pond where I was nearly bitten by a water moccasin. I searched in vain for Irene Cooter's chinaberry tree, which must have been cut down long before. I took some photographs of the house I grew up in. It's still standing, a testament to my father's remarkable building skills. I couldn't believe how small it was. Two bedrooms with a bathroom in between, and two rooms downstairs. The jalousie windows have long since been replaced.

A battered Dodge was parked in the driveway instead of Dad's old Chevy. Some other young family lives in it now, and I wondered, as I watched their kids playing noisily in the backyard that my mother had us grade so painstakingly, if they had air-conditioning for the sweltering summer nights, or something better than the kerosene heater in the winter.

I like to think I made my peace with my father before he died. I might not have become a lawyer like my brother Jerry, but being in one of the most successful rock groups in the world proved to him, I hope, that I'd done something valid with my life after all. He might never have acknowledged it with me, but he knew from my mom and Jerry how well I had done. The older I get, the more I appreciate just how much of an influence Dad was, from the first time he plugged me into his Voice of Music machine or bought me the gold Fender Musicmaker from the daughter of a guy at the plant. I know now how much we really meant to one another, even if we never got around to telling each other. I have come to realize that, despite all the fighting we did for all those years, it was never really wasted time.

Turning to leave and heading back to the brand-new car I'd rented to drive out to our old house, I caught sight of my own reflection in the glass of the driver's window. Staring back at me was a smiling, tanned, middle-aged man in sunglasses, standing in the dappled sunlight in front of a small and unremarkable building. I wasn't much younger than my father was when he died, and yet I was glowing with good health, having avoided a life of hard labor fixing machinery at the local plant.

My hand went instinctively to my hair. It wasn't as short as he might have wanted it to be, but it was cotton-white, well groomed, and a few inches above the collar line. I think Dad would have been pleased.

INDEX

"After the Thrill Is Gone," 133
Airborne, 226–28
Alexander, David, 171
Allman, Duane, 38, 39, 48, 49, 57–58, 76–77, 112, 123, 169, 222
Allman, Gregg, 38, 39, 48, 49, 57–58, 76, 123, 230
Almost Famous, 123
"Already Gone," 112, 115, 118, 313
Anaheim Stadium, 141
Anderson, Jon, 86
Asylum/Elektra, 106, 131, 159, 173, 192, 224, 226, 227, 326
Asylum Records, 82, 95, 106
Atkins, Chet, 26, 79, 98
Aykroyd, Dan, 206
Azoff, Irving, 95, 96, 107, 118, 119–20, 123, 126, 127, 138, 141, 143, 153, 154, 156, 157, 161–62, 159, 166, 167, 180, 186–87, 189–93, 197, 204, 206, 208, 214, 215, 219, 220, 223, 234, 252, 305, 310–17

Eagles reunion and, 229, 233, 235, 236, 238, 244, 245, 246, 248, 252–54, 260, 263–64, 273, 275–77, 280, 292, 294, 295
Felder's firing and, 317–18
Felder's lawsuit and, 325, 326
at Hall of Fame induction, 297, 298, 299

"Bad Girls," 227
Band, the, 61–62
Barnett, Mike, 53, 57, 59, 61, 64, 69, 76, 284–85
Bayshore Recording Studio, 192
Beach Boys, 86, 87
Beatles, 36, 38, 47, 48, 70, 86, 326
Bee Gees, 179, 199, 223, 230
Belushi, John, 206, 207, 250
Berry, Chuck, 40, 184
"Best of My Love, The," 106, 117, 118–19, 147, 184, 210, 308
Beverly Hills Cop, 229

Black, Ed, 91
Blue, David, 95–101, 103–7, 113, 116, 117, 225
Blues Brothers, 206, 207
Bohn, Isa, 272
Booty, Jan, 54, 55, 57, 59
Boylan, John, 80, 299
"Boys of Summer, The," 229, 284
Bramlett, Delaney and Bonnie, 78–79
Breslauer, Gerry, 120, 138, 190
Brigman, Grandpa, 8
Brown, Charles, 193
Brown, Jerry, 192, 209
Browne, Jackson, 81, 82, 91, 96, 97, 127, 141, 227, 233–34, 246, 287, 299, 307, 312
Buckingham, Lindsey, 245
Buffalo Springfield, 57, 81, 296
Buffett, Jimmy, 123, 181, 192, 208, 230, 298
Building the Perfect Beast, 229
Busey, Gary, 220
Butterfield, Paul, 58
Byrds, 36, 59

Calagna, John, 57, 60
California Jam, 125, 141
Canned Heat, 105
Capaldi, Jim, 234, 252
Carl, Max, 234, 292
Carrack, Paul, 234, 252
Carter, Ron, 56
Castaneda, Carlos, 82, 162
Cavaliere, Felix, 59
Cetera, Peter, 232
charities and benefits, 209, 268–69, 280–81, 291, 296, 312–13
Charles, Ray, 116
Chicago, 194, 220, 223, 226
Chipley, Lee, 25
Chong, Tommy, 220
Clapton, Eric, 76, 78, 85, 116, 173, 179, 222, 297
Clark, Gene, 59
Clarke, Allan, 47
Clinton, Bill and Hillary, 279–80, 291
Cohen, Leonard, 95
Collins, Jimmy, 161, 211
Coltrane, John, 60
Common Thread: The Songs of the Eagles, 246, 285
Continentals, 24–25, 57, 180
Cooper, Alice, 105

Cooter, Irene, 7, 332
Corey, John, 311–12
Cornish, Gene, 59, 69
Corvettes, 59
Crago, Scott, 284
Cranston, Alan, 209–10, 211, 212, 245
Criteria Studios, 170, 173, 179
Crosby, David, 101, 104, 287, 312
Crosby, Stills, Nash & Young, 77, 86, 91, 95
Crosby, Stills & Nash, 64–66, 170, 296
Crosby & Nash, 101, 102, 103, 113–14, 180, 285
Crowe, Cameron, 122–23, 223
Cyrkle, 48, 57

Dacus, Donnie, 223
Danelli, Dino, 59
Davidson, Gordon, 317
Davis, Miles, 56–57, 60, 170
Davis, Patti, 134, 139, 151
Delaney & Bonnie, 78–79
Derek and the Dominoes, 76
Desperado, 95–96, 106, 118
"Desperado," 147, 229, 313
Dillard, Doug, 59
"Dirty Laundry," 224, 284
"Disco Strangler, The," 198, 199
Dog House, 292, 294, 310
drinking, 162–63, 179, 200, 201, 234, 278
drugs, 38, 49, 54, 59, 61, 68, 76, 87, 100, 136, 143, 166, 179, 197, 200, 201, 234, 250, 251, 278
cocaine, 100, 104, 117, 124–25, 134–35, 136, 160, 163, 166–67, 175, 179, 184, 200, 203, 205, 207, 215, 246
heroin, 144
marijuana, 37–38, 53, 54, 63, 117, 125, 144, 215
peyote, 162
Quaaludes, 148, 149–50, 177, 200, 215
Drury, Timothy, 311–12
Dunn, Sam, 5
Dylan, Bob, 95, 98

Eagles:
breakup of, 212, 213–16, 217, 219, 220, 224, 228, 230, 240, 245
Felder fired by, 317–20, 321–22, 324–25, 326
Felder joins, 113–14

formation of, 81–82, 116, 213
Hall of Fame induction of, 296–300, 303
Leadon quits, 152–53, 154, 175–76, 188, 275
Meisner quits, 187–88, 189–90, 275
Millennium concerts of, 303, 304–9, 310, 314, 330–31
resumption of, 224, 229, 233, 235–38, 246–48, 251–64, 265–77, 282–90
Schmit joins, 189–90
Walsh joins, 153–54
Eagles, 82, 118
Eagles—Their Greatest Hits 1971–1975, 159–60, 176, 208, 305–7
Eagles' Greatest Hits Volume 2, 224
Eagles Limited, 119–20, 190, 263–64, 324
Felder's lawsuit against, 325–28
Eagles Live, 212, 214–15
Elder, Boyd, 224
Elektra/Asylum, 106, 131, 159, 173, 192, 224, 226, 227, 326
End of the Innocence, The, 235
Erwin, Richard, 282
Evers, Rick, 141

Faltermeyer, Harold, 229
Fast Times at Ridgemont High, 223
Feiten, Buzzy, 58
Felder, Charles "Nolan" (father), 4–6, 8–16, 17–20, 22, 23, 26, 30, 31, 33, 37, 38, 40–41, 44–46, 50, 51, 52, 55, 66, 71, 73–75, 78, 112, 128–31, 138, 139, 158, 222, 242, 250, 266, 267, 276, 330, 332
Felder, Cody (son), 194–95, 219, 226, 249–51, 256, 266, 267, 277, 288, 291, 304, 329
Felder, Don:
autograph seekers and, 239–41, 242–44, 260–62
birth of, 6
boating of, 230–32, 290–91
childhood of, 2, 3–16, 17–22, 142, 222
Eagles' firing of, 317–20, 321–22, 324–25, 326
Eagles Ltd. and, 119–20, 190, 252–54, 263–64, 324
first band of, 24–25
first public performances of, 21–22, 23–24
guitars of, 19, 20, 27–28, 39–40, 59, 88, 211

infidelity of, 216–19, 278, 288
intruder incident and, 241–42
joins Eagles, 113–14
Kathrin and, 314, 315–16, 317, 318, 319, 322, 330
lawsuit of, 325–28
marital problems and divorce of, 290, 291, 301–2, 303–4, 309–10, 311, 313, 320, 321, 329–30
moves to Boston, 68–70
moves to California, 87–93
polio of, 2, 7–8, 17
real estate ventures of, 221, 230
solo projects of, 226–28, 230, 327
as teenager, 22–33, 34–50
in therapy, 217–18, 232, 251, 288, 304
wedding of, 73–75
Felder, Doris Brigman (mother), 4–6, 8–16, 22, 33, 45, 46, 51, 52, 66, 72, 73–75, 129, 130, 158–59, 216, 222, 279
death of, 331
remarriage of, 224–25
Felder, Grandpa, 5, 6, 8, 9
Felder, Jerry (brother), 6, 9, 11–15, 19–20, 30, 37, 38, 44, 45, 52, 54–55, 71–75, 120, 129, 130, 131, 141–42, 163, 222, 225, 266, 267, 331, 332
Felder, Jesse (son), 127, 128, 129, 130, 131, 136, 137, 138, 142, 149, 150, 158, 168, 183, 194, 204–5, 219, 221–22, 267, 279, 287, 291, 304, 329
guitar playing of, 222
marriage of, 290
saxophone playing of, 267–68
Felder, Jesse "Buck" (uncle), 13–14, 127
Felder, Kurt (grandson), 290
Felder, Leah (daughter), 225, 268–69, 301–2, 304, 329
Felder, Marnie (sister-in-law), 44, 141–42, 159
Felder, Rebecca (daughter), 158, 168, 183, 194, 219, 223, 279, 304, 329
Felder, Susan Pickersgill (wife), 43, 47–48, 49, 51–52, 54, 67–68, 70–76, 79, 83–86, 96, 100, 101–3, 104–5, 112–13, 115, 116, 118, 121, 122, 128, 136–38, 142, 149, 150, 157–58, 163, 168–69, 178, 183, 184, 195–96, 205, 211, 212, 218–22, 227, 232, 241, 242, 244, 251, 266, 268, 272, 277, 279, 287, 288, 299
Felder's firing and, 320

Felder, Susan Pickersgill (wife)
  (*continued*)
  jewelry business of, 277–78, 291,
    301–2, 304, 329
  marital problems and divorce of, 290,
    291, 301–2, 303–4, 309–10, 311,
    313, 320, 321, 329–30
  marries Don, 73–75
  moves to California, 87–93
  pregnancies of, 102–3, 104–5, 106,
    112, 113, 118, 121, 122, 126–27,
    149, 158, 194
  thyroid problems of, 232, 233
Fernandez, Richie, 86, 144–45, 183
Fleetwood Mac, 70, 85, 164–65, 226,
  296, 298
Flow, 53–54, 55, 57–63, 66, 67, 68–69,
  70, 76, 79, 120, 170, 250, 259
Flow, 61
Flying Burrito Brothers, 36, 72, 76, 77,
  80
Fogelberg, Dan, 95, 107, 123, 190, 208
Forsey, Keith, 229
Frey, Glenn, 80, 81, 83–86, 91, 92, 95,
  99, 106–8, 110–19, 122, 123,
  132–35, 139, 141, 143, 146, 147,
  150–54, 156, 160, 161, 164, 164,
  165–67, 170, 173–74, 177, 178, 180,
  183–88, 189, 191–96, 198–201, 204,
  205–6, 215–16, 228, 244–46, 250,
  292–94, 303, 304, 306, 308, 310–12,
  316, 328, 330
  in Eagles breakup, 213, 214
  in Eagles formation, 81–82, 213
  Eagles Ltd. and, 119–20, 190, 252–54,
    263–64, 324
  in Eagles resumption, 235–38,
    246–48, 251–59, 262, 264, 266,
    269–71, 273–78, 282–84, 286, 289,
    290
  Felder's fight with, 209–12, 245,
    255
  Felder's firing and, 318–19, 321
  Felder's lawsuit and, 325–27
  fiftieth birthday party of, 295–96
  fund-raising and, 209, 280–81
  at Hall of Fame induction, 297, 298,
    299, 300
  "Hotel California" and, 171, 172, 173,
    182
  "Life in the Fast Lane" and, 175
  marriage of, 287
  Selected Works and, 314–15

  solo career of, 214, 224, 225, 229–30,
    253–54
  studio of, 292, 294, 310
  Takamine guitars and, 280
  victimization by, 196–98
  "Victim of Love" and, 174
Front Line Management, 107, 215
Full Moon, 215
"Funky New Year," 194, 308
Fun TV, 223
Furay, Richie, 81

Galaxy High, 223
Galuten, Albhy, 230
Gaye, Marvin, 121
Geer, Will, 137
Geffen, David, 81, 82, 94–95, 96, 98,
  106–7, 159, 279, 287, 299
Geffen-Roberts Management, 97, 99,
  100–101
Getz, Stan, 58
Gibb, Barry, 230
Gibbs, Kenny, 22, 24, 25
Gideon, Leonard, 6, 7, 331
Goldberg, Danny, 178
"Good Day in Hell," 112
Green, Peter, 70–71, 298
groupies, 146–50, 164, 278–79
Guitar, 204
Guthrie, Arlo, 67

Hancock, Herbie, 56
"Heartache Tonight," 196, 199, 205,
  208
Hearts Flowers, 59
"Heat Is On, The," 229, 267
Heavy Metal, 223
Hell Freezes Over, 259–63, 265–66,
  269–77, 278, 282–90, 311
Helms, Levon, 85
Hendrix, Jimi, 68, 76, 85, 109, 250
Henley, Don, 80, 81, 83, 85, 86, 99, 106,
  107, 110–12, 114–17, 119, 122,
  132–33, 135, 139–41, 144, 147, 150,
  152–54, 156, 160, 161, 164, 164–66,
  167, 170, 173–74, 176–81, 183–87,
  189, 191–93, 195–99, 201, 203–6,
  209, 211, 244–46, 250, 280, 291–94,
  304, 306–13, 316
  arrest of, 215
  Clinton and, 279
  in Eagles breakup, 214, 230
  in Eagles formation, 81–82

Eagles Ltd. and, 119–20, 190, 252–54, 263–64, 324
in Eagles resumption, 235–38, 247, 248, 251–57, 259, 262, 264, 266, 269–71, 274–78, 282–84, 286, 290
Felder's firing and, 318, 321
Felder's lawsuit and, 325–27
fund-raising and, 209, 280–81
at Hall of Fame induction, 297, 298, 299
health problems of, 183
"Hotel California" and, 171, 172, 173, 178, 182
letter writing of, 178–79
"Life in the Fast Lane" and, 175
marriage of, 287
Selected Works and, 314–15
solo career of, 223, 224, 225, 229, 232, 233, 234, 235, 236, 253–54
studio of, 292, 293, 294
women and, 164–65
Hilburn, Robert, 258
Hillis, Paul, 52–53, 54, 55, 170
Hillman, Chris, 36, 59, 77, 312
Hollies, 47, 65, 101, 233
Hotel California, 2, 173, 175, 180–81, 189, 191, 193, 201, 203, 208, 214, 224, 230, 245–46, 269–70, 305, 307–8
"Hotel California," 2, 169–73, 178, 180, 181, 182, 184, 186, 192, 197, 244, 258–59, 262, 263, 308, 323, 331
writing credits for, 269–70
Hough, Wayne "Boomer," 36, 47
Howe, Steve, 86
Hubley, Season, 54, 65
Hunt, Helen, 175

I Can't Stand Still, 224
"I Can't Tell You Why," 193, 205, 324
"In the City," 198
"I Wish You Peace," 134, 135, 139

Jackson, Jage, 175
Jackson, Michael, 215, 227, 305
Jacobson, Joel, 138
James Gang, 154
John, Elton, 206
Johns, Glyn, 82, 106, 107, 119, 299, 312
Jones, Quincy, 58, 61
Joplin, Janis, 68, 250
"Journey of the Sorcerer," 135, 139

Kennedy, John F., 32–33, 68
Kerouac, Jack, 89
King, B. B., 2, 31–32, 35, 47, 56, 70, 106, 116, 133, 203, 222, 307
King, Carole, 105, 141
Kiss, 140
Kortchmar, Danny "Kootch," 223, 236

Laboriel, Abraham "Abe," 71
"Last Resort, The," 180
Laughon, Tom, 36, 41, 42, 46
Leadon, Bernie, 33, 34–36, 38, 39, 41, 43, 46–51, 54, 57, 59–60, 68, 72, 73, 75, 76, 80, 87, 89–92, 94–99, 105, 106, 107, 126, 134–35, 141, 143, 152, 230, 285–87, 306, 312, 313, 322, 326, 327, 328
in Eagles, 82–83, 84–85, 86, 101, 106, 107, 110, 111, 114–20, 123, 124, 132–35, 139, 150–52, 270
in Eagles formation, 81–82
Eagles Ltd. and, 120
at Hall of Fame induction, 297, 298, 299, 300
quits Eagles, 152–53, 154, 175–76, 188, 275
Leadon, Tom, 36
Led Zeppelin, 113, 123, 146, 233, 326
Lee, Judy, 43, 47, 48, 49, 83
Lee, Terry, 91, 92
Leo, Andy, 57, 60, 69, 76
Let's Get Harry, 230
"Life in the Fast Lane," 175, 180, 192, 210
Lindley, David, 96, 97, 98, 103, 233, 312
Lipham Music, 27–28, 39–40, 52, 267
Little Rock Connie, 148
Loggins, Kenny, 226
Long, Tom, 52
Longbranch Pennywhistle, 81, 91
Long Run, The, 199, 201–4, 208, 213, 216, 224, 227
"Long Run, The," 198, 200, 205
Los Angeles Times, 180, 208, 258
Loughnane, Lee, 226
Luade, Marina and Jacquie, 93
"Lyin' Eyes," 133, 139, 140, 173, 211

MCA Records, 215
MacGraw, Ali, 137
McQueen, Steve, 137
McVeigh, Sue, 41
Maestro, Joe, 25

Mahal, Taj, 105
Malibu Men's Choir, 235, 252
Manassas, 77
Marin, Cheech, 220, 230, 231, 232
Mason, Dave, 226
Maundy Quintet, 36–37, 38, 40, 45–49,
  52, 53, 170, 182, 230
Meisner, Jennifer, 187
Meisner, Randy "Meis," 80–81, 83, 84,
  99, 107, 111, 114–16, 126, 132, 139,
  141, 149, 152, 153, 155, 161,
  165–67, 170, 172–73, 175–77, 179,
  180, 183–87, 230, 270, 306, 308,
  312, 313, 326, 327, 328, 330
  in Eagles formation, 81–82
  Eagles Ltd. and, 120
  at Hall of Fame induction, 297, 298,
    299, 300
  quits Eagles, 187–88, 189–90, 275
Messina, Jim, 81
Miami Vice, 230
Mitchell, Joni, 91, 95, 96, 97, 98, 99, 100,
  101, 227
Monk, Thelonius, 60
Moon, Keith, 137, 138
Mothers of Invention, 105
MTV, 252, 254, 257–59
Mudcrutch, 36

Nash, Graham, 47, 65, 95, 101, 103–7,
  113–14, 116, 117, 230, 233, 251,
  312
NEA, 314, 325
Nelson, Ricky, 81, 116, 175
Newcomb, Chuck, 53, 62, 63, 69
"New Kid in Town," 111, 180, 308
Nicholson, Kathrin, 314, 315–16, 317,
  318, 322, 330
Nicks, Stevie, 164–65, 223
"Night Owl," 227
Nixon, Tommy, 196
No Fun Aloud, 224
Nolte, Nick, 220

Oliver, Jay, 308
One of These Nights, 132, 133, 139–40,
  147, 148
"One of These Nights," 132, 172, 184
One Step Up Studio, 201
On the Border, 106, 116, 118, 121, 131,
  133, 147
Orbison, Roy, 206
"Outlaw Man," 96

Pankow, Jimmy, 194, 220, 226, 230, 231,
  234
Paradise Island, 142–43
Parsons, Gram, 72
"Peaceful Easy Feeling," 82, 110,
  224
"People Can Change," 236
Perkins, Al, 77
Petty, Tom, 28, 29, 36, 183
Pickersgill, Bill, 48, 51–52, 74
Pickersgill, Mary, 43
Pickersgill, Susan, *see* Felder, Susan
  Pickersgill
"Please Come Home for Christmas,"
  193–94, 308
Poco, 81, 189–90
Poor, 81
Presley, Elvis, 18, 19, 170, 187, 307
"Pretty Maids All in a Row," 180
Pringle, Sharon, 8, 22, 27
Pritchett, Jack, 230, 243
Psycho Santa, 243–44, 260–61

Ray, Mel, 55
Recording Artists' Coalition, 311, 327
Record Plant, 108, 109, 114–15, 117–18,
  131, 136, 139, 170, 173
Reid, Terry, 233–34
Reinhardt, Django, 55
REO Speedwagon, 107
Reynolds, Oliver, 224, 229
Richards, Keith, 143, 144–45
Roberts, Elliot, 94, 95, 96, 101, 114
Rock and Roll Hall of Fame, 296–300,
  303
Rogers, Kenny, 81
Rolling Stone, 115, 122–23, 140–41, 155,
  191–92, 203–4
Rolling Stones, 143–44, 146, 233
Rollins, Sonny, 55
Ronstadt, Linda, 59, 72, 80, 81, 97, 105,
  141, 209, 227, 312
Rosen, Hilary, 305, 306
Roxy Theater, 99
Rucker Brothers, 28, 29, 41
Run C&W, 285, 286

"Sad Café," 199, 293
Sampson, Johnny, 261–62
Sanborn, David, 194, 196
Santa Monica Civic Auditorium, 208–9,
  215
Santana, Carlos, 67

Scaggs, Boz, 107, 190, 223
Scheiner, Elliot, 236, 252, 283, 310
Schmit, Timothy B., 81, 192–93, 201,
    205, 216, 225, 226, 230, 233, 234,
    236, 237, 238, 244, 245, 248,
    252–53, 257, 259, 264, 266, 269,
    276, 291–93, 306, 310, 311, 316,
    324
  Felder's firing and, 319–20
  at Hall of Fame induction, 297, 298,
    299, 300
  joins Eagles, 189–90
  Selected Works and, 315
Scottsville Squirrel Barkers, 36, 80
Scurran, Barry, 24, 41, 45–46, 52
Seger, Bob, 81, 116, 198, 199, 205, 223,
    230
Selected Works 1972–1999, 314–15, 316
"Seven Bridges Road," 124, 181, 215,
    262, 308
Shiloh, 81
Shorter, Wayne, 56
Simes, Frank, 236, 238
Simon, Paul, 48
Simpson, O. J., 279, 288
Slugger's Wife, The, 223
Smith, Joe, 159, 192, 193, 214, 215
Solters, Larry "Scoop," 166, 273
Soul Survivors, 81
Souther, John David (J. D.), 81, 91, 106,
    111, 116, 165, 174, 198, 205, 295,
    297, 299
Spanky and Our Gang, 105
Spell, Jim, 5
Spirit, 105
Stannell, Stan, 24–25
Starr, Ringo, 76
Steely Dan, 107, 172
"Still Alive," 226–27
Stills, Stephen, 25–26, 57, 65, 66, 76, 77,
    97, 101, 103–4, 179–80, 227, 296
Stone Canyon Band, 81, 175
Szymczyk, Bill, 106, 109–10, 112, 115,
    117, 119, 134, 170, 172, 176, 178,
    180, 192, 202–3, 212, 214, 223, 236,
    283, 298, 299, 327

"Take it Easy," 82–83, 123, 124, 186, 246
"Take It to the Limit," 139, 185, 270,
    308, 313
Taylor, Creed, 58, 60, 68–69, 120
Taylor, James, 81
"Teenage Jail," 199

Tempchin, Jack, 82, 224, 252
"Tequila Sunrise," 106, 305, 307, 312
Third Encore (3E) parties, 147–49, 164,
    165, 208, 236, 278
Thomas, Mickey, 223
Thomas, Rufus, 38
"Those Shoes," 198–99, 200, 308
Time, 141
Tommy Roe and the Romans, 38
"Too Many Hands," 139–40
Traffic, 226
Tritt, Travis, 246, 254, 285
Troubador, 81, 99, 128, 199, 236
"Try and Love Again," 180, 270
Turner, Tina, 143–44, 230
Tyerman, Barry, 316–17, 318

Urban Cowboy, 208

Vale, Peter, 234, 252
Van Gelder, Rudy, 60
Velvet Underground, 109
"Victim of Love," 174, 180, 308
"Visions," 132
Vitale, Joe, 183, 284

Wakeman, Rick, 86
Walecki, Fred, 97, 267, 312–13
Walsh, Joe, 95, 106, 107, 110, 153–57,
    160, 161, 163, 165, 166, 169–71,
    173, 175–77, 179–82, 183–85, 187,
    198, 200, 201, 204, 210–11, 216,
    227, 230, 231, 233, 234, 236, 237,
    238, 244, 248, 250, 252, 253,
    255–57, 259, 264, 166, 269–71, 276,
    278, 284, 292, 293, 303, 306, 310,
    311, 316
  Eagles joined by, 153–54
  Felder's firing and, 319
  at Hall of Fame induction, 297, 298,
    299, 300
  Selected Works and, 315
  solo album of, 219, 223, 225
Walsh, Lucy, 268
Warner Communications, 106, 159, 215
Warnes, Jennifer, 95
"Wasted Time," 180, 308
Wax, Steve, 185
Wembley Stadium, 207–8
Wenner, Jann, 191, 192
West, Adam, 158
Westwood Music, 97, 267
Who, 146

"Who Tonight?", 227
"Wild Life, 223
Williams, Andy, 191
Williams, Jeff, 25, 180
Williams, Tony, 56
Winter, John, 53, 57, 59, 62, 63, 69, 76
"Witchy Woman," 82, 83, 85, 147, 270, 328
Woods, Tiger, 296
Woodstock, 64–65, 68, 101
Woodstock, 109

Yakus, Shelly, 71
Yes, 85, 86
"You Never Cry Like a Lover," 106
Young, Neil, 81, 99, 105
Young, Steve, 124
Young Rascals, 53–54, 57, 58, 59, 60, 61
"You're Really High, Aren't You?," 198, 219

Zappa, Frank, 109
Zevon, Warren, 223